Author's Message:

NOBUYUKI ANZAI
安西信行
PRESENTS

I'm a pathetic
excuse for a human
being.

MÄR
Vol. 12
Story and Art by Nobuyuki Anzai

English Adaptation/Gerard Jones
Translation/Kaori Inoue
Touch-up Art & Lettering/James Gaubatz
Design/Izumi Evers
Editor/Andy Nakatani

Editor in Chief, Books/Alvin Lu
Editor in Chief, Magazines/Marc Weidenbaum
VP of Publishing Licensing/Rika Inouye
VP of Sales/Gonzalo Ferreyra
Sr. VP of Marketing/Liza Coppola
Publisher/Hyoe Narita

The rights of the author(s) of the work(s) in this publication to
be so identified have been asserted in accordance with the
Copyright, Designs and Patents Act 1988. A CIP catalogue
record for this book is available from the British Library.

Printed in the U.S.A.

Published by VIZ Media, LLC
P.O. Box 77010
San Francisco, CA 94107

10 9 8 7 6 5 4 3
First printing, March 2007
Third printing, February 2008

www.viz.com
store.viz.com

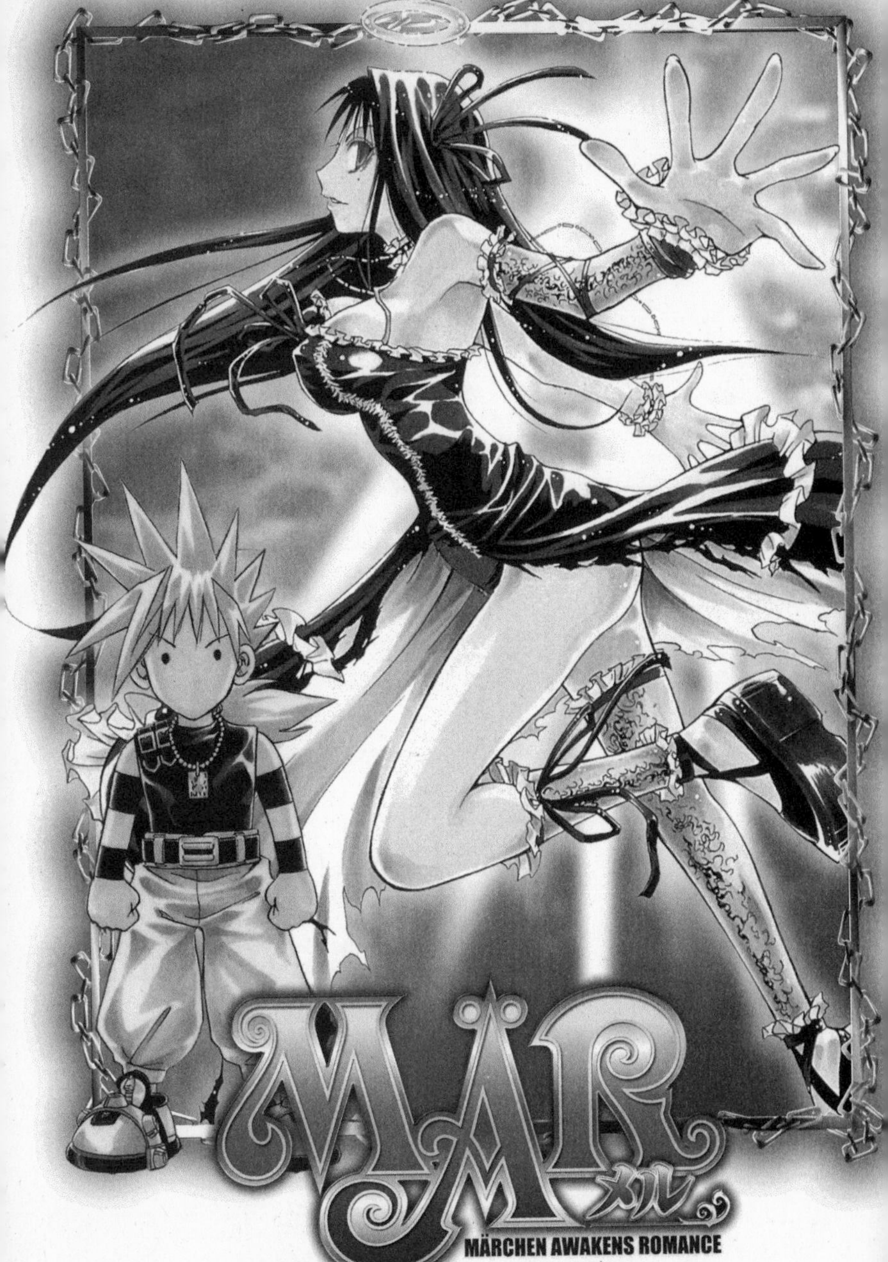
MÄR
メル
MÄRCHEN AWAKENS ROMANCE

Vol. 12

Nobuyuki Anzai

Characters

Alan

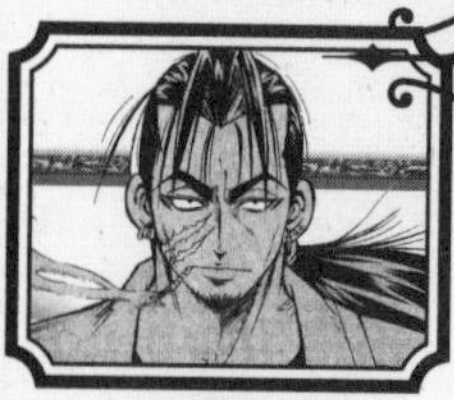

A warrior who played a major role in the war six years ago. For a while a curse trapped him in the form of Edward.

Edward

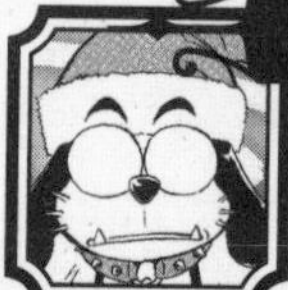

The dog who devotedly serves Princess Snow.

Snow

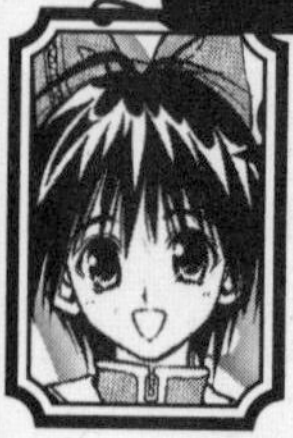

Princess of the Kingdom of Lestava. Participating in the War Games after her castle was taken by the Chess Pieces.

Nanashi

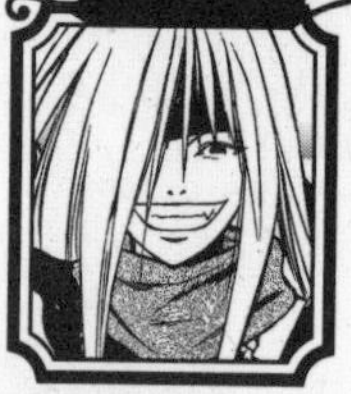

Leader of the Thieves Guild, Luberia. Detests the Chess Pieces who killed his comrades.

Alviss

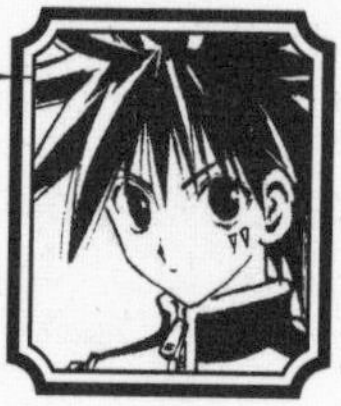

He is the one who brought Ginta to Mär Heaven using the Dimensional ÄRM called the "GateKeeper Clown."

Ginta Toramizu

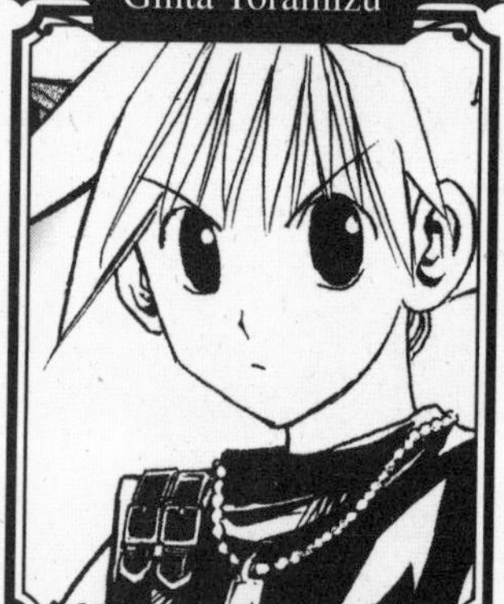

A second-year middle school student who dreamed about the world of fairy tales. Now, in order to save that world, he must fight the Chess Pieces.

Babbo

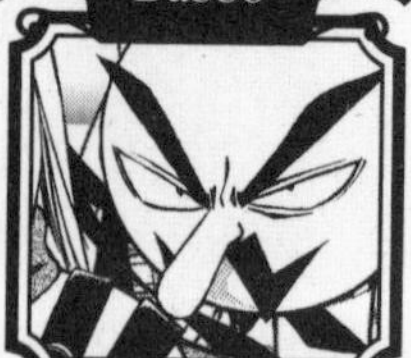

A rare talking ÄRM, who by synchronizing with Ginta is able to change shape—now up to version five.

Jack

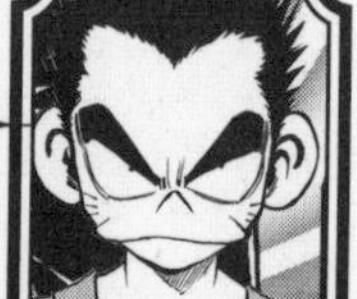

A farmboy who has left his mother and his crops to join Ginta in battle.

Previous Volume

Ginta jumps through a "door" that suddenly appears in his classroom, and finds himself in the magical world of his dreams. Now, at the "request" of the Chess Pieces, the War Games have begun—and Ginta and his eight friends, calling themselves Team Mär, must battle the Chess warriors. They ride a five-battle winning streak into the sixth battle at the Mushroom Fields. Luck turns against them in the first match and Alan loses, but Alviss and Dorothy pull off victories in the second and third matches…

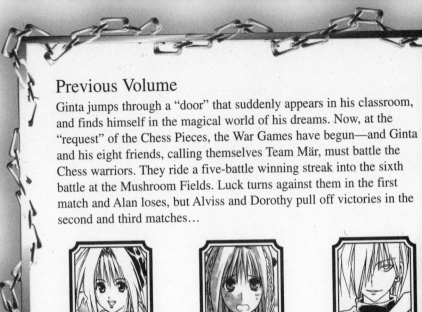

Dorothy

A witch from Caldia, Kingdom of Magic. She has accepted the painful duty of killing the Queen of the Chess—her own sister.

Rolan

A Knight of the Chess who received the Zombie Tattoo from Phantom. Beat Alviss in the third battle.

Phantom

A Chess Knight. The most powerful in the group and the leader of its combat force.

Diana

Queen of the Chess, Dorothy's older sister and Snow's stepmother.

Ian

A mere Rook among the Chess. When he misbehaved, his lover Gido was subjected to a terrible transformation.

Pano

A Rook. She's been in love with Jack since the third battle, where she was shown an illusory, and absurdly handsome image of him.

CONTENTS

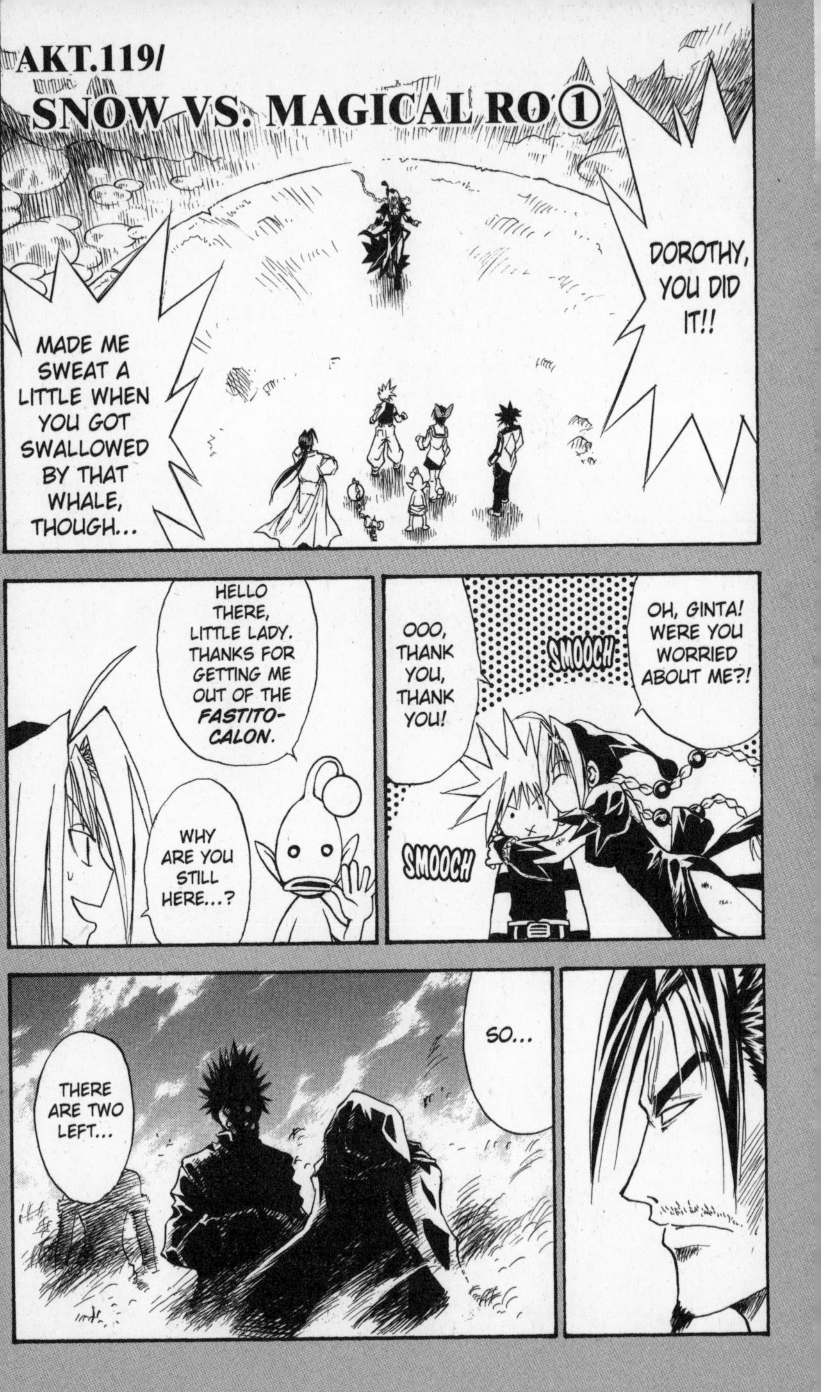
AKT.119/
SNOW VS. MAGICAL RO①
DOROTHY, YOU DID IT!!
MADE ME SWEAT A LITTLE WHEN YOU GOT SWALLOWED BY THAT WHALE, THOUGH...
OH, GINTA! WERE YOU WORRIED ABOUT ME?!
SMOOCH
OOO, THANK YOU, THANK YOU!
SMOOCH
HELLO THERE, LITTLE LADY. THANKS FOR GETTING ME OUT OF THE *FASTITO-CALON*.
WHY ARE YOU STILL HERE...?
SO...
THERE ARE TWO LEFT...

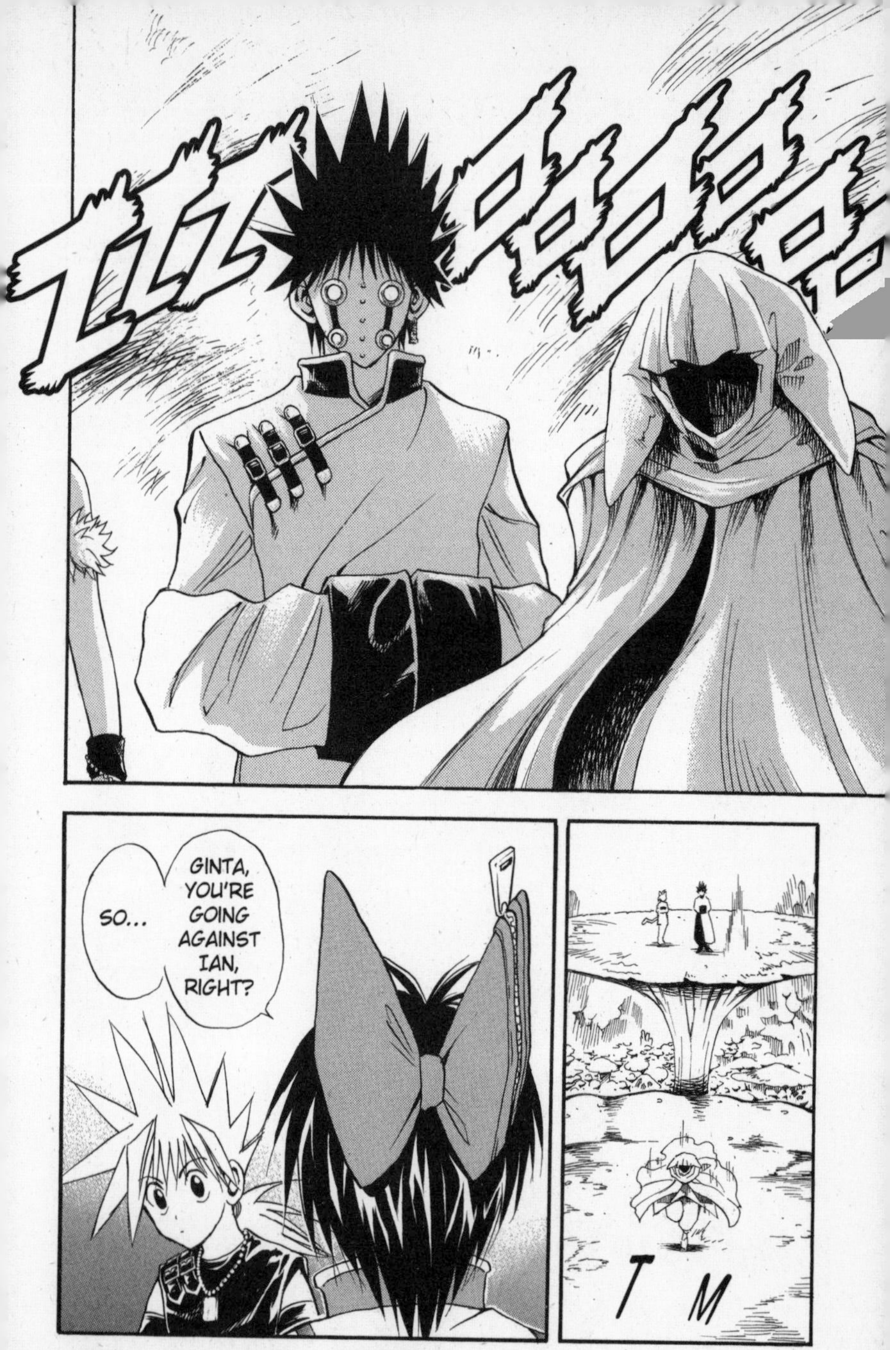
GINTA, YOU'RE GOING AGAINST IAN, RIGHT?
SO...

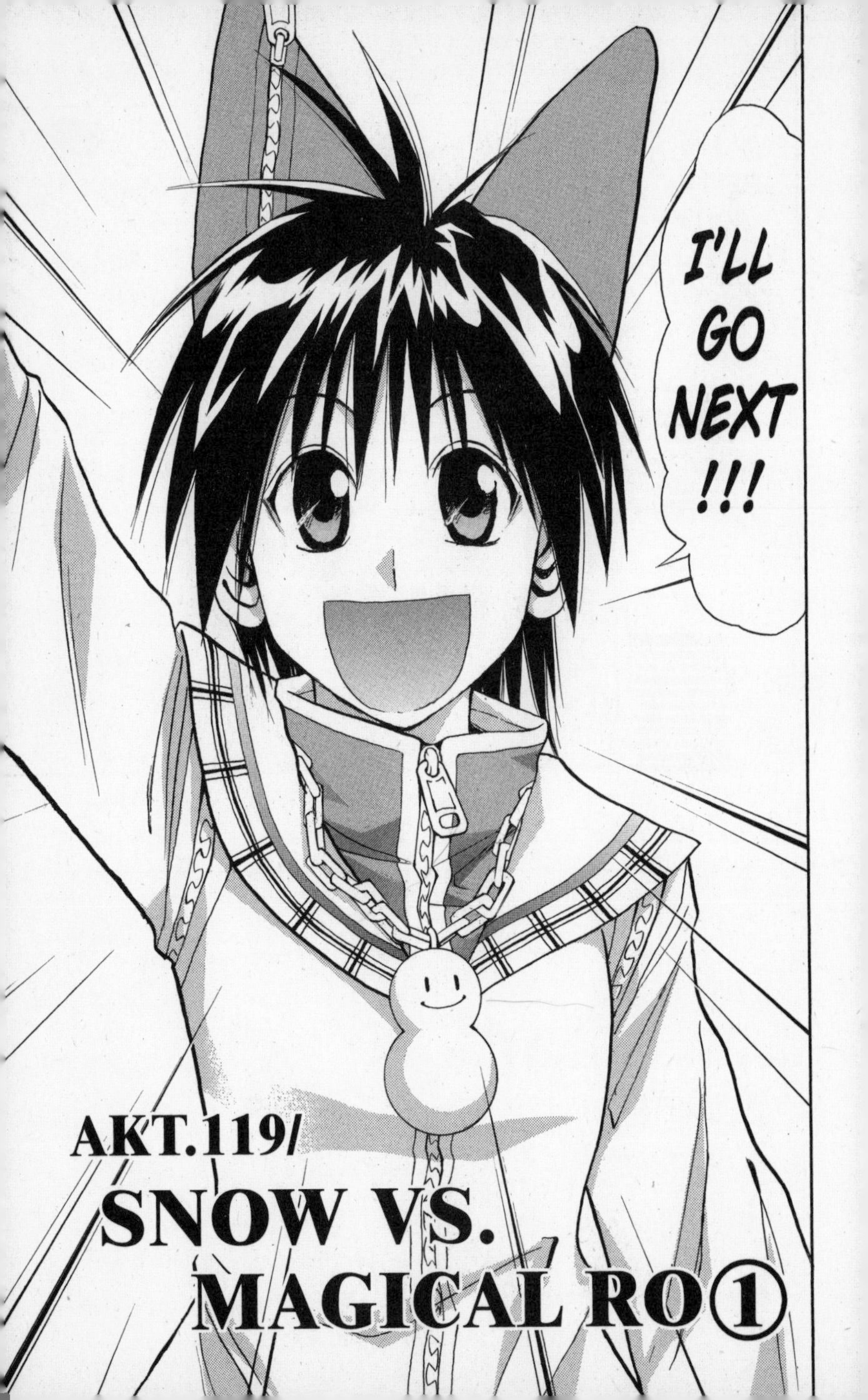
I'LL GO NEXT!!!
AKT.119/
SNOW VS. MAGICAL RO①

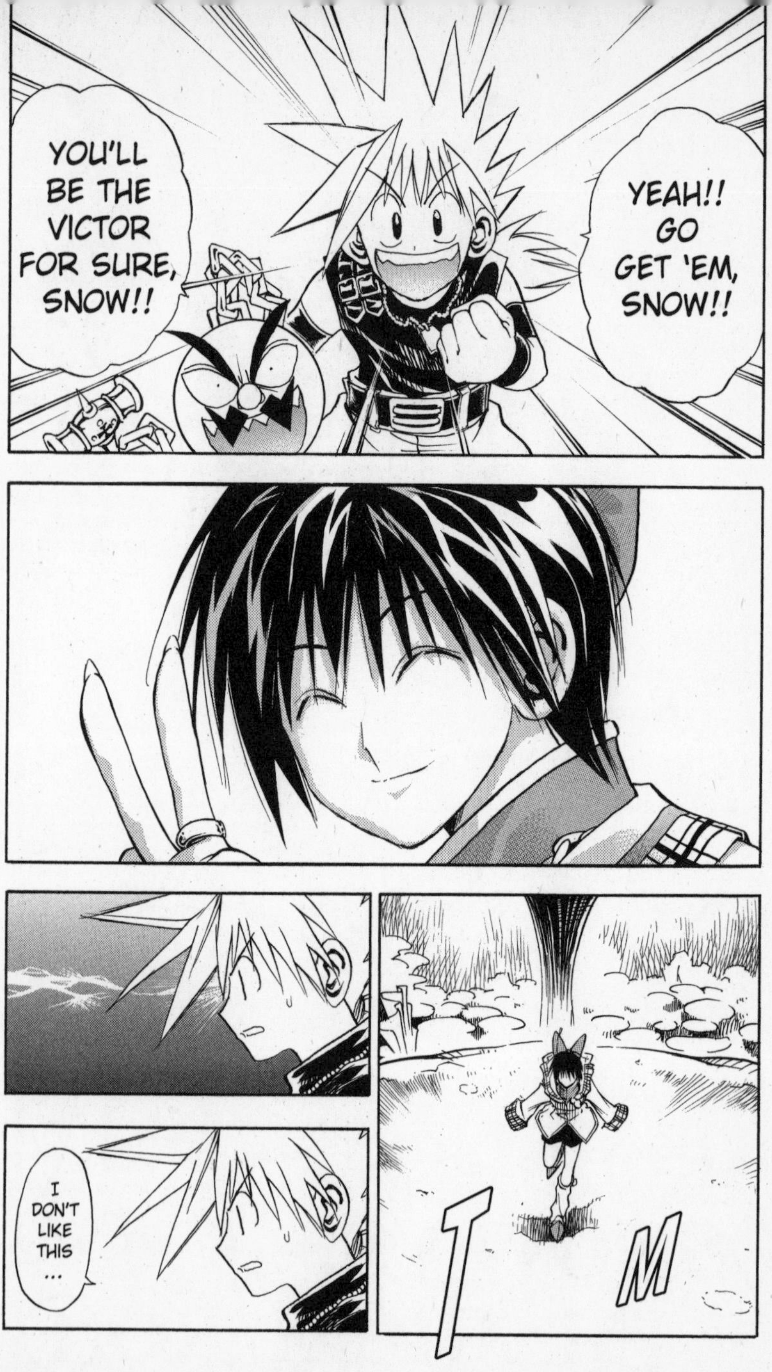
YEAH!! GO GET 'EM, SNOW!!
YOU'LL BE THE VICTOR FOR SURE, SNOW!!
T M
I DON'T LIKE THIS ...

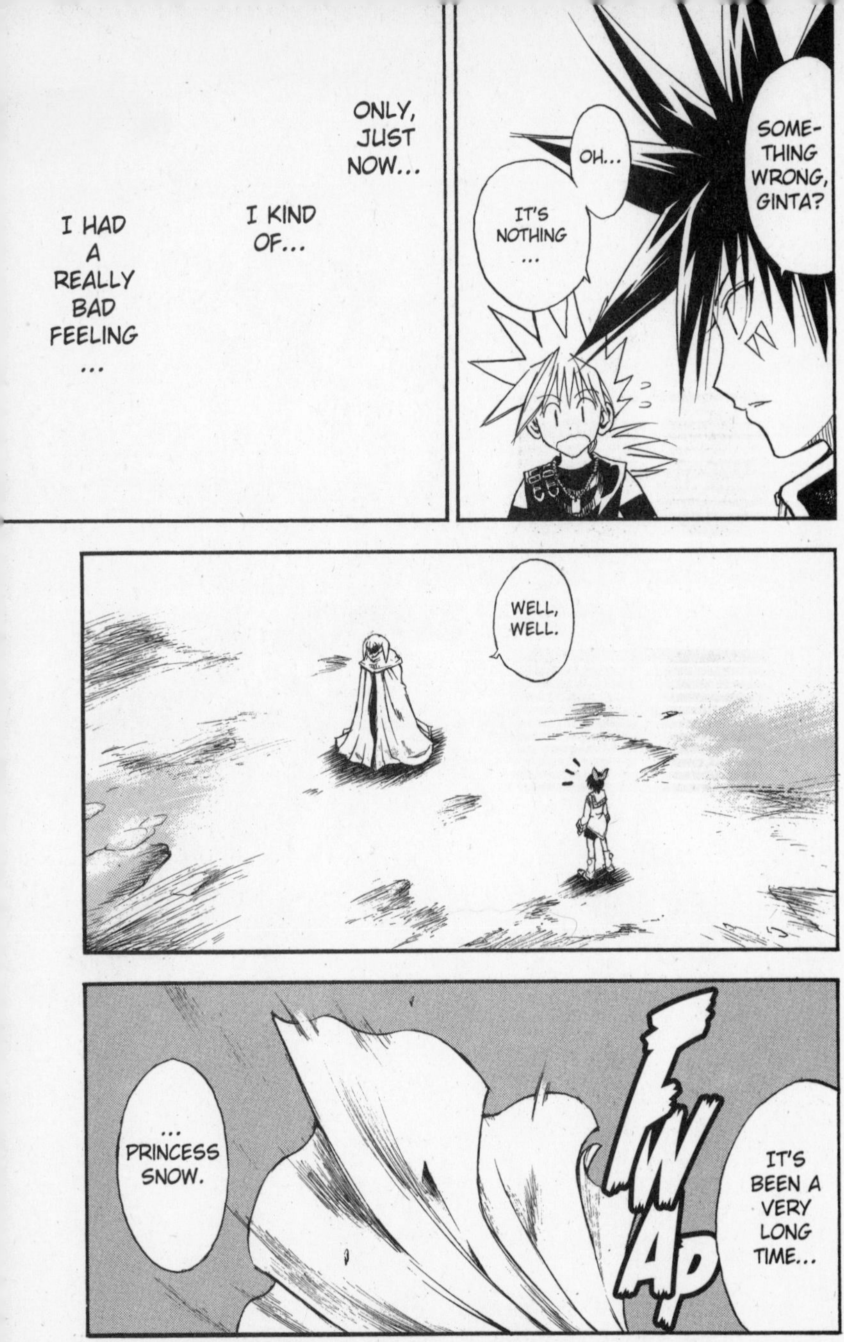
SOMETHING WRONG, GINTA?
OH...
IT'S NOTHING ...
ONLY, JUST NOW...
I KIND OF...
I HAD A REALLY BAD FEELING ...
WELL, WELL.
IT'S BEEN A VERY LONG TIME...
FWAP
... PRINCESS SNOW.

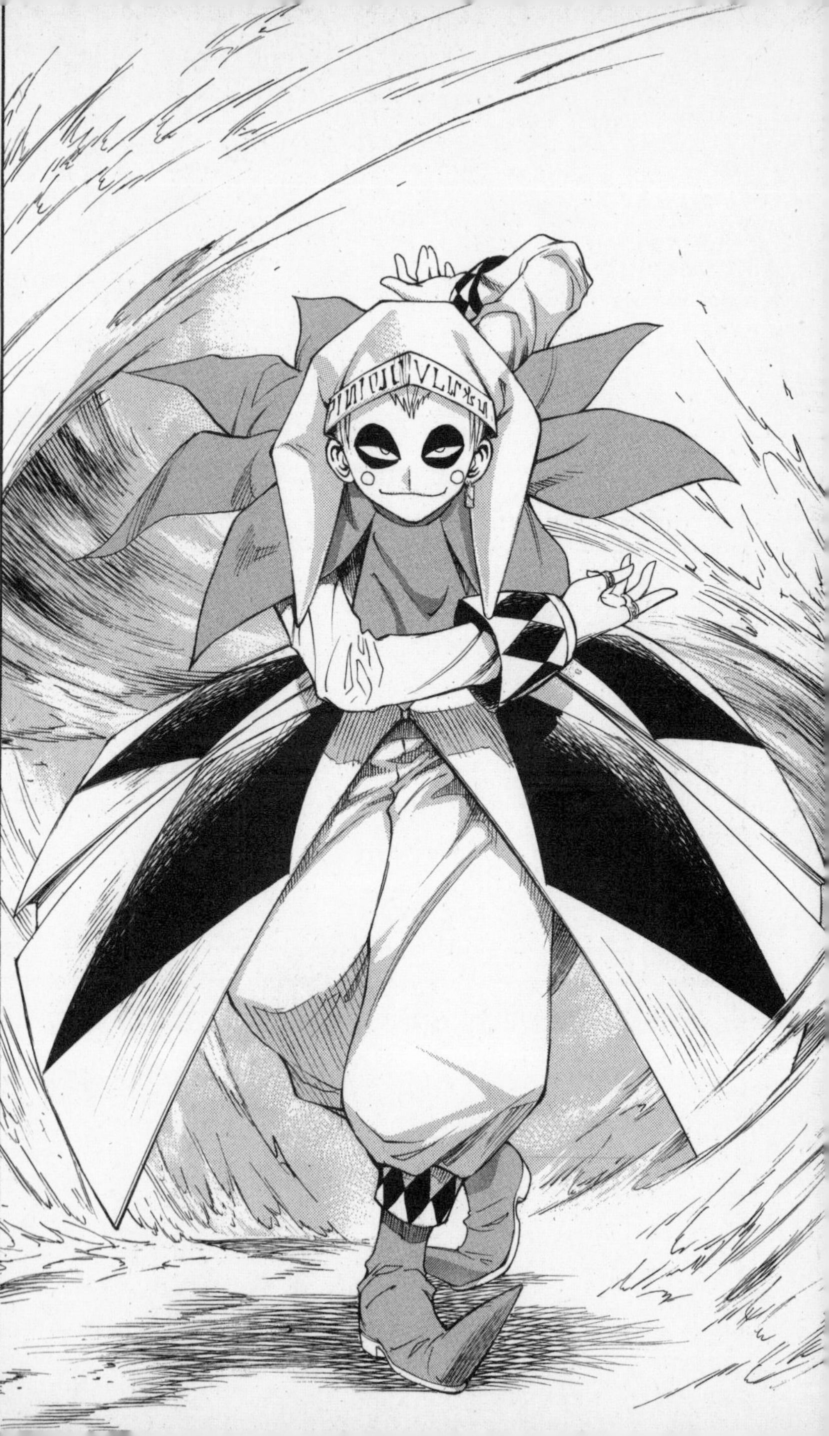

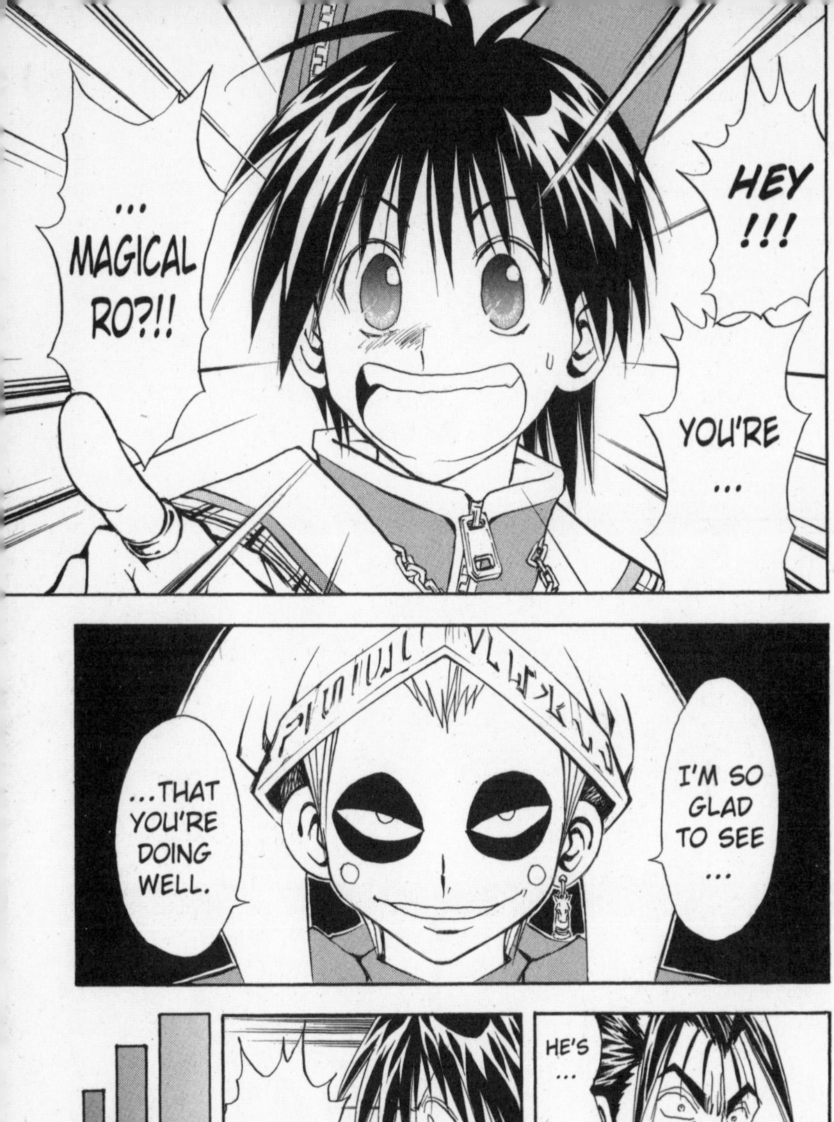
HEY !!!
YOU'RE ...
... MAGICAL RO?!!
I'M SO GLAD TO SEE ...
...THAT YOU'RE DOING WELL.
HE'S ...
HE'S ...
A CHESS PIECE?! BUT WHY?!!

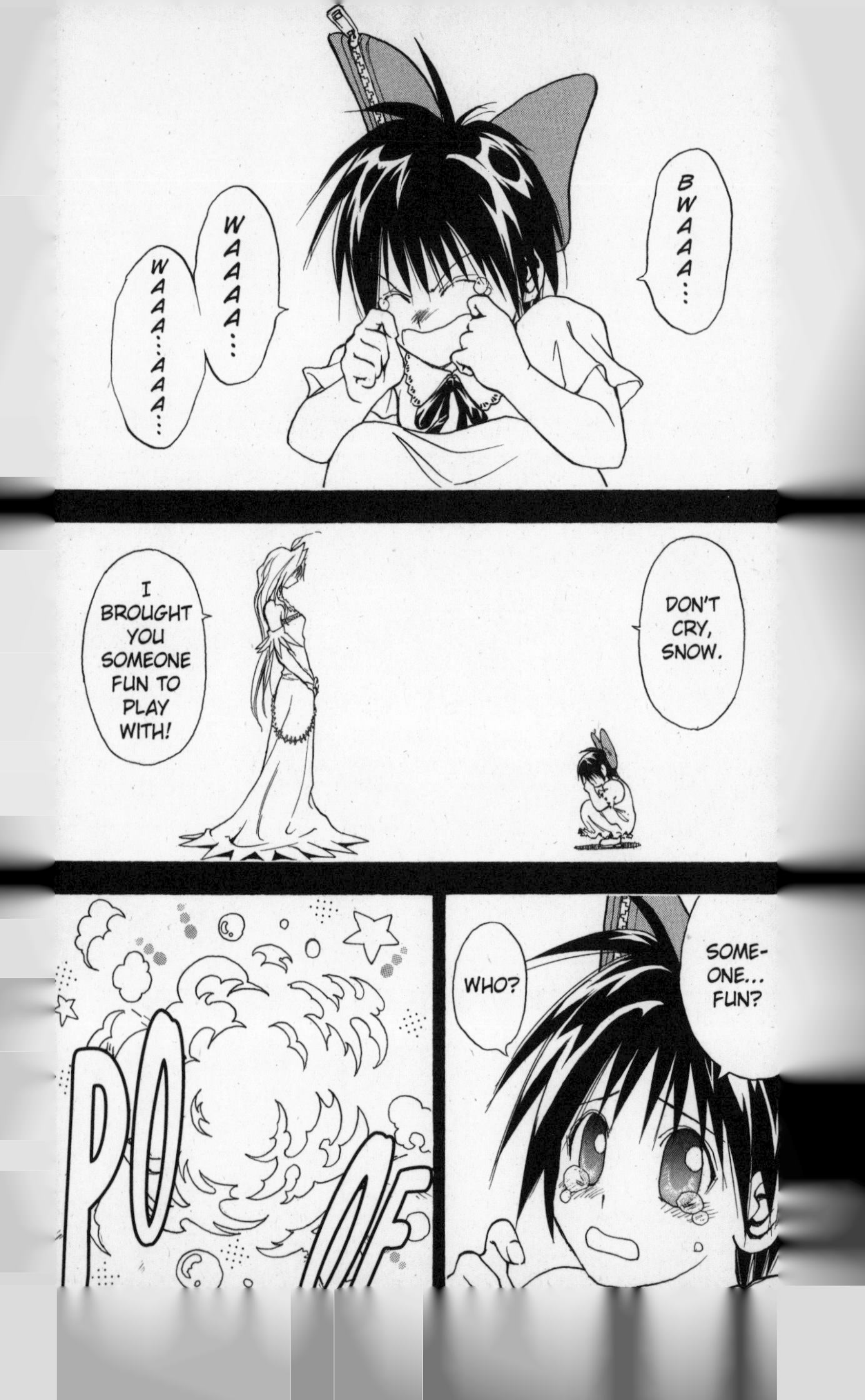
BWAAAA...
WAAAAA...
WAAAA...AAAA...
DON'T CRY, SNOW.
I BROUGHT YOU SOMEONE FUN TO PLAY WITH!
SOME-ONE... FUN?
WHO?
POOF

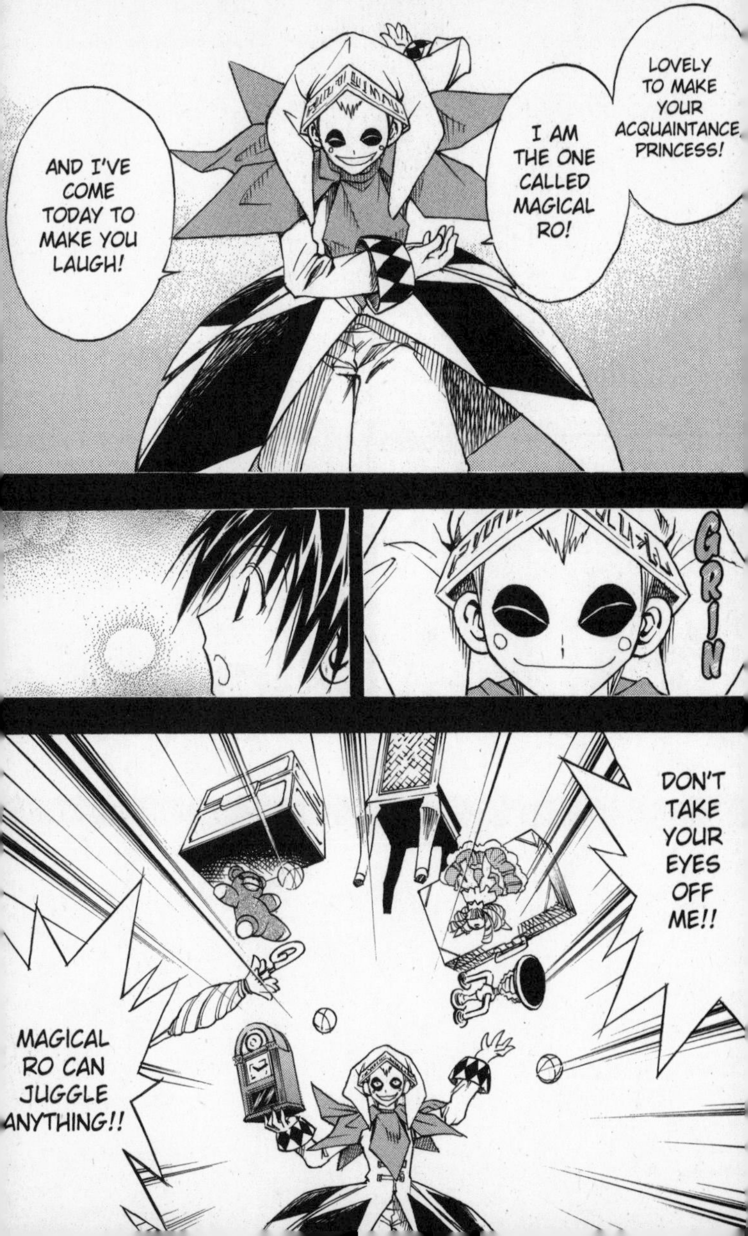
LOVELY TO MAKE YOUR ACQUAINTANCE, PRINCESS!
I AM THE ONE CALLED MAGICAL RO!
AND I'VE COME TODAY TO MAKE YOU LAUGH!
GRIN
DON'T TAKE YOUR EYES OFF ME!!
MAGICAL RO CAN JUGGLE ANYTHING!!

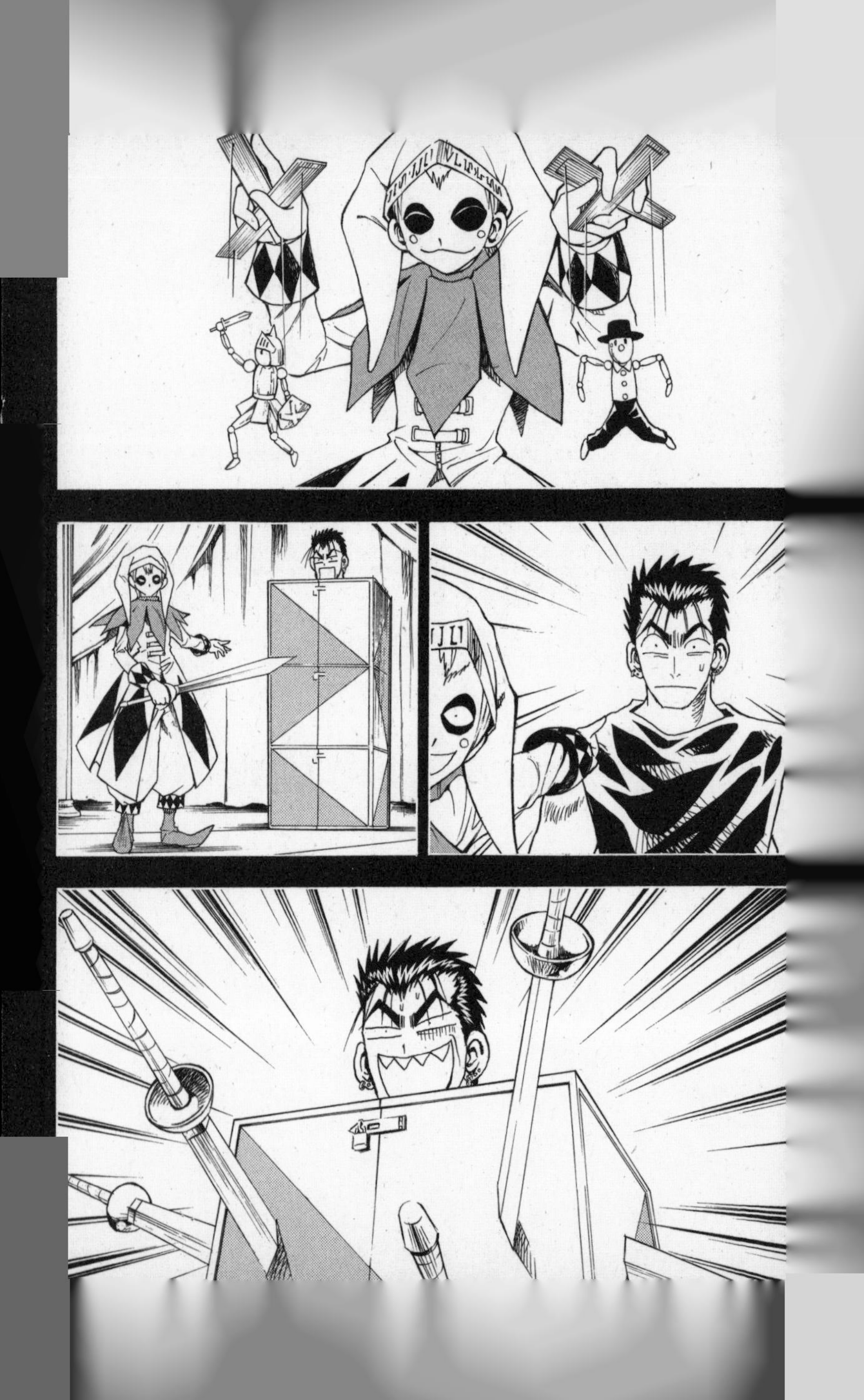

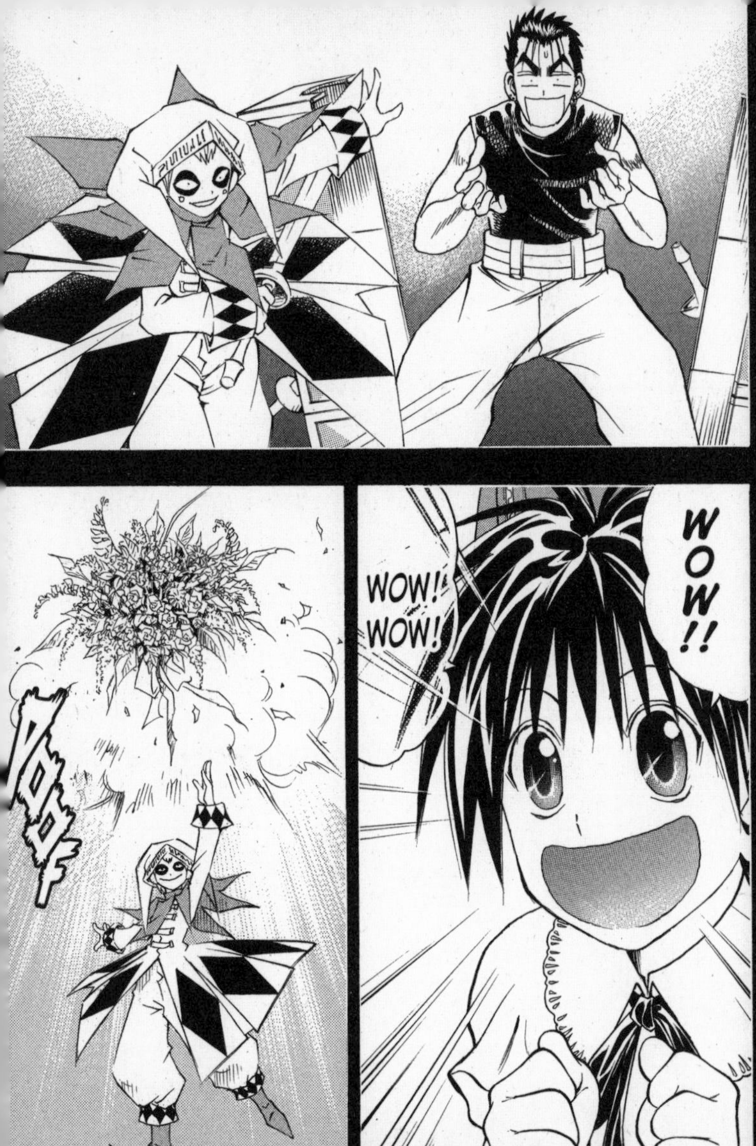
WOW!!
WOW! WOW!
POOF

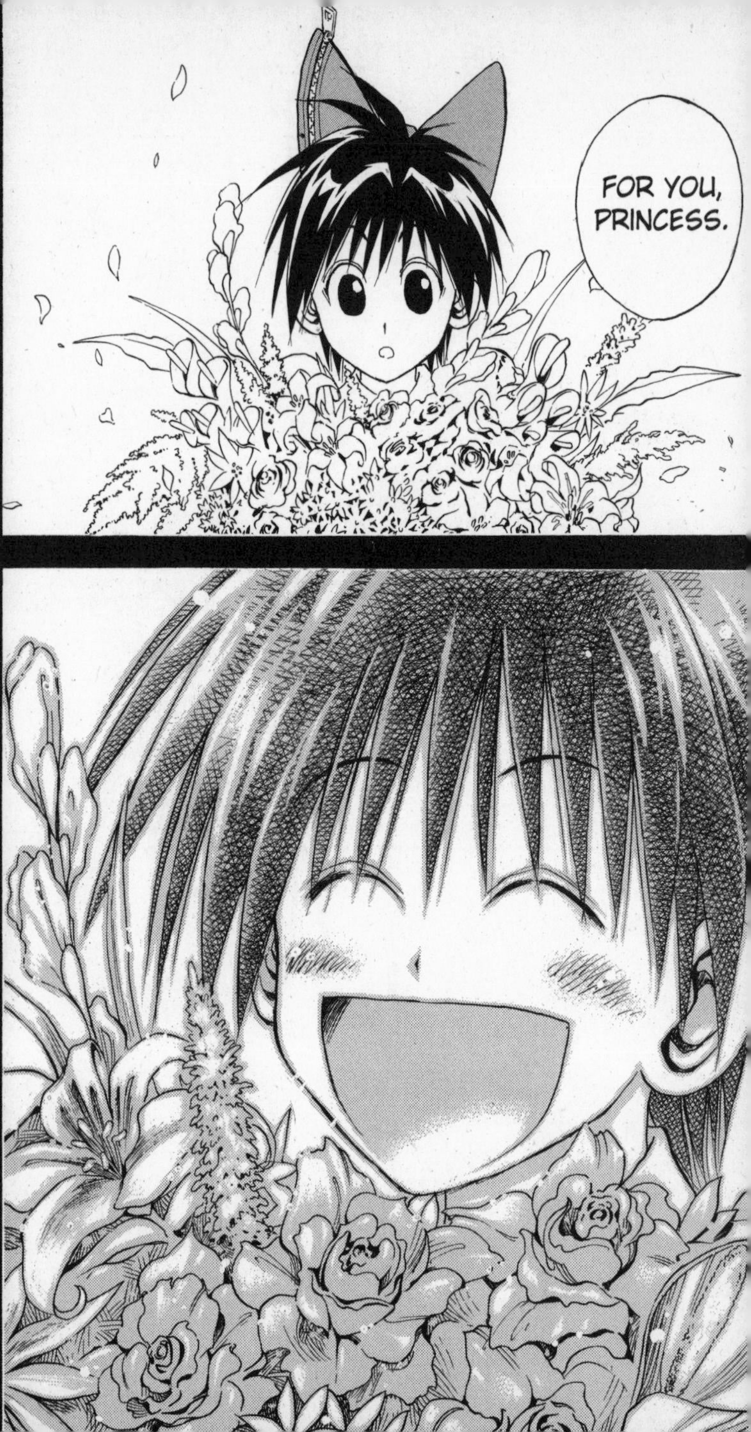
FOR YOU, PRINCESS.

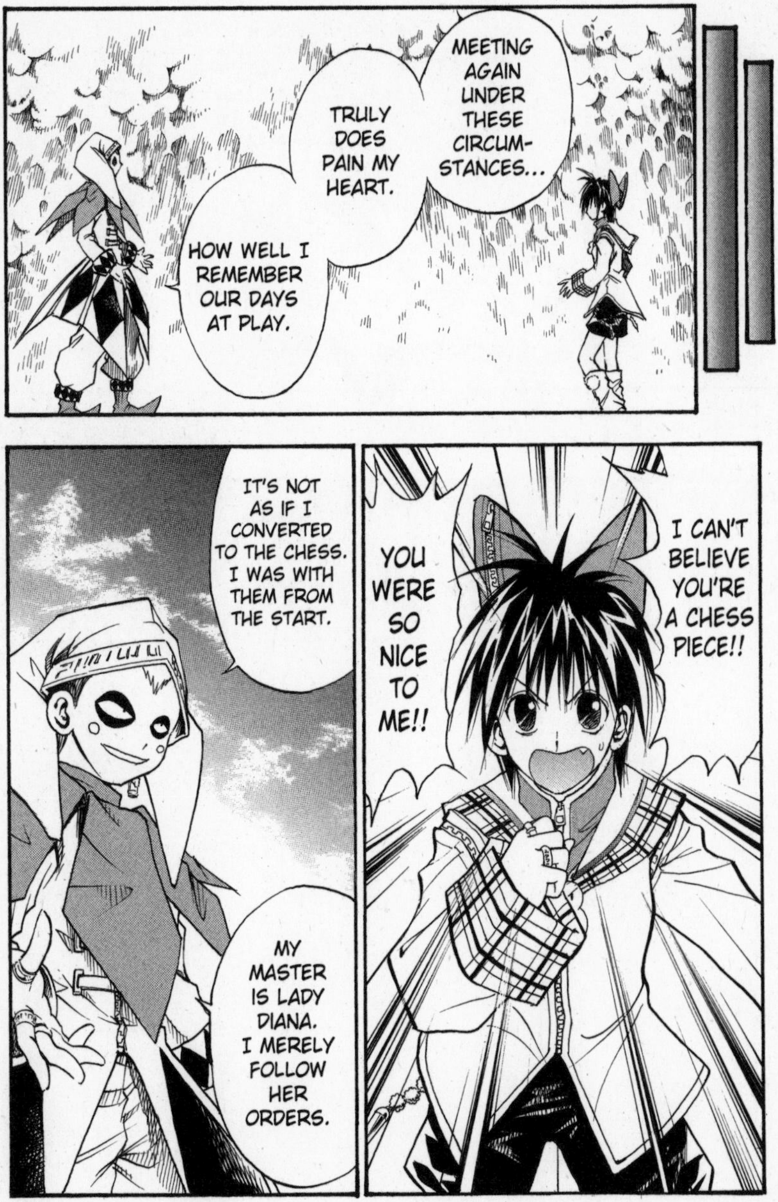
MEETING AGAIN UNDER THESE CIRCUM-STANCES...
TRULY DOES PAIN MY HEART.
HOW WELL I REMEMBER OUR DAYS AT PLAY.
I CAN'T BELIEVE YOU'RE A CHESS PIECE!!
YOU WERE SO NICE TO ME!!
IT'S NOT AS IF I CONVERTED TO THE CHESS. I WAS WITH THEM FROM THE START.
MY MASTER IS LADY DIANA. I MERELY FOLLOW HER ORDERS.

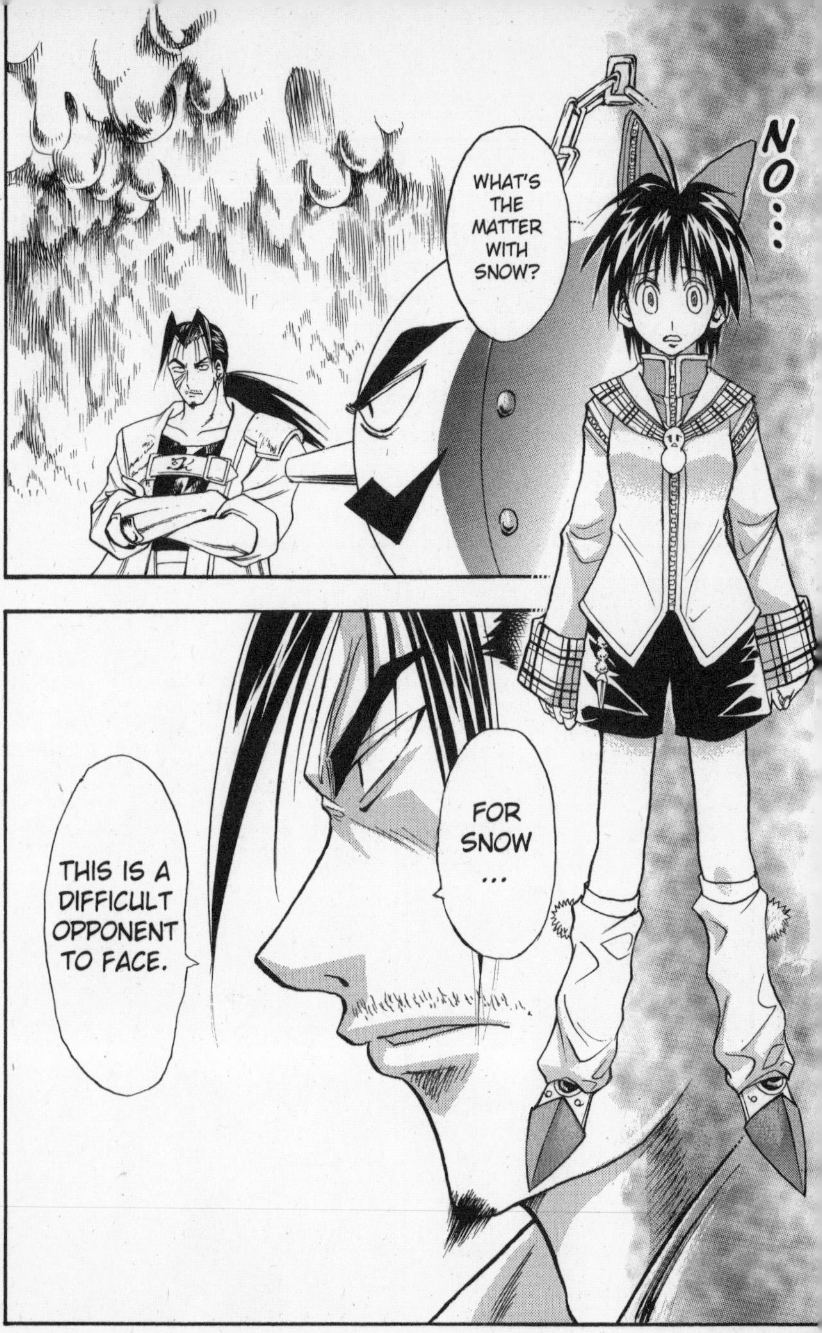
NO...
WHAT'S THE MATTER WITH SNOW?
FOR SNOW...
THIS IS A DIFFICULT OPPONENT TO FACE.

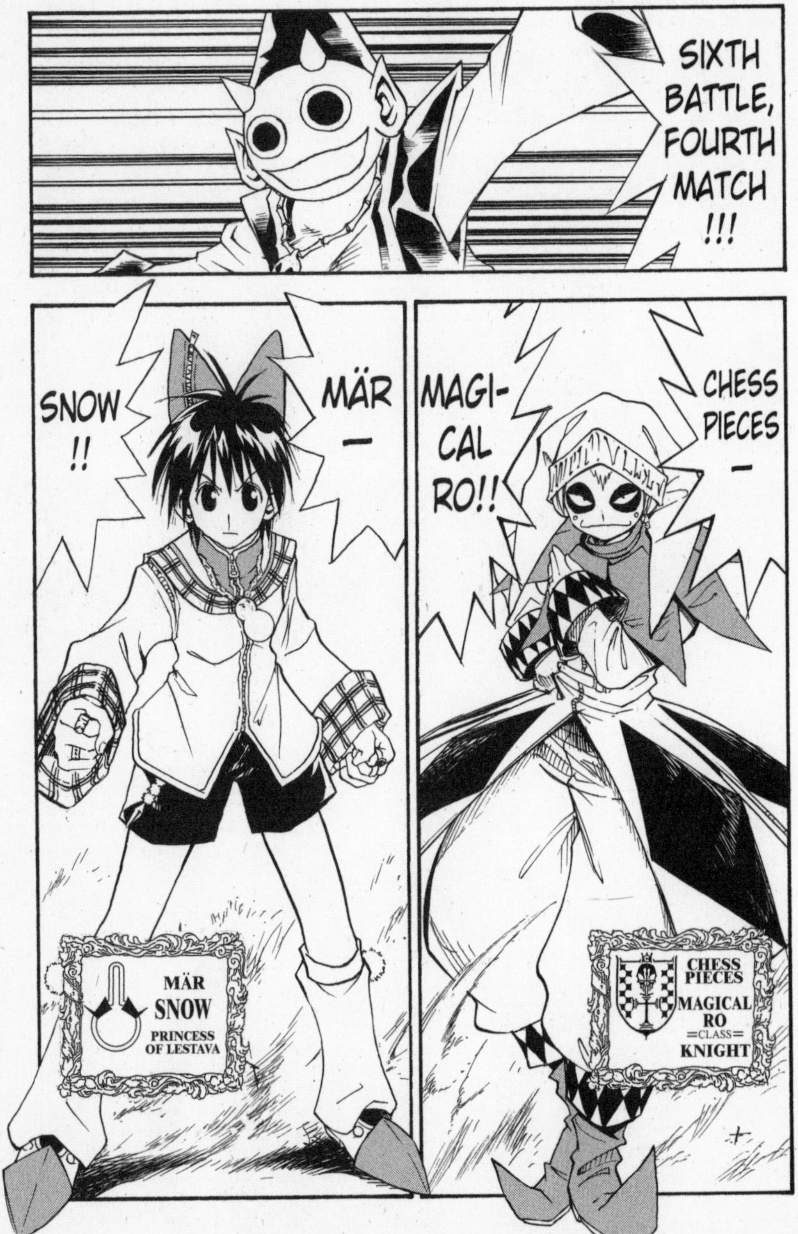
SIXTH BATTLE, FOURTH MATCH !!!
CHESS PIECES —
MAGI-CAL RO!!
CHESS PIECES
MAGICAL RO
=CLASS=
KNIGHT
MÄR —
SNOW !!
MÄR
SNOW
PRINCESS OF LESTAVA

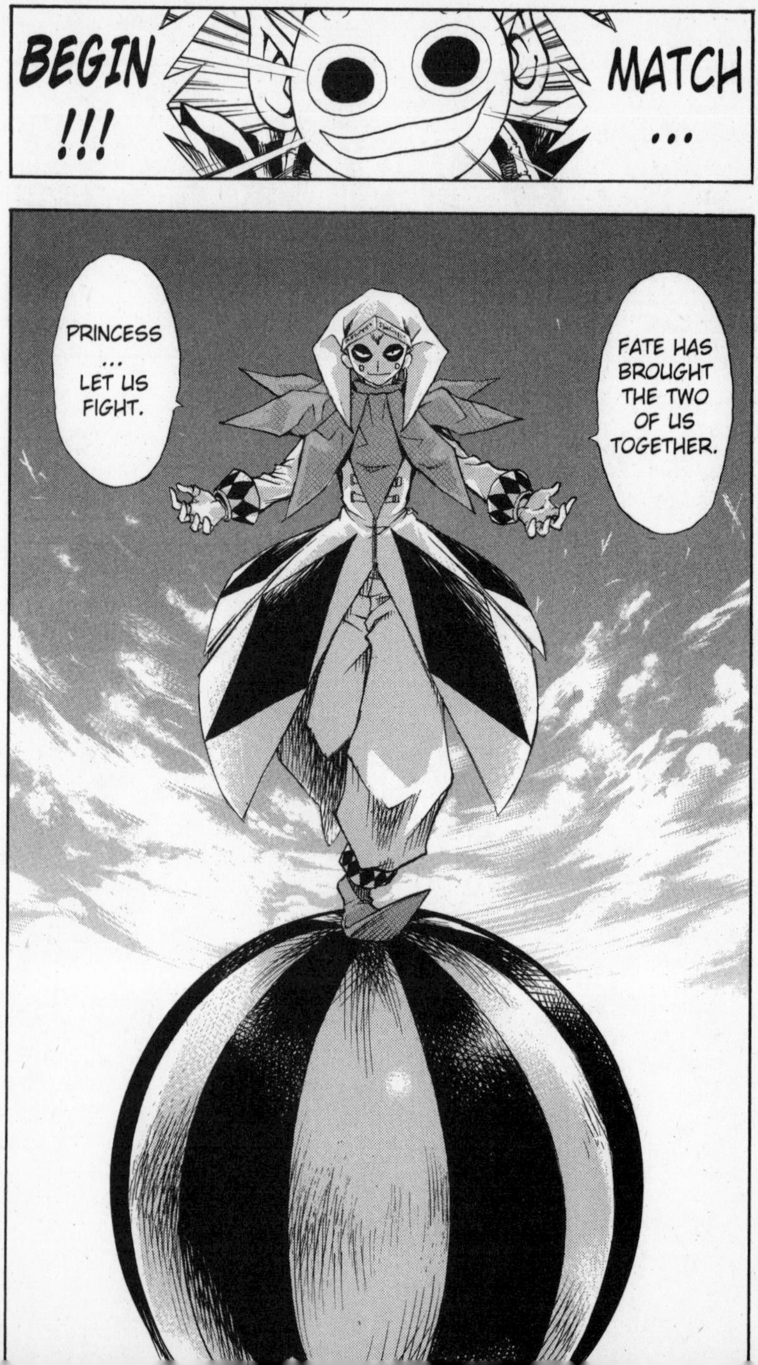
MATCH ...
BEGIN !!!
FATE HAS BROUGHT THE TWO OF US TOGETHER.
PRINCESS ... LET US FIGHT.

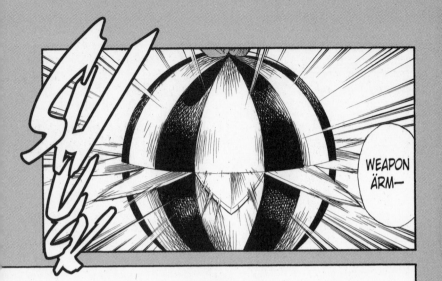

WEAPON
ÄRM—

BLADE
BALL!

AKT.120/
SNOW VS. MAGICAL RO②

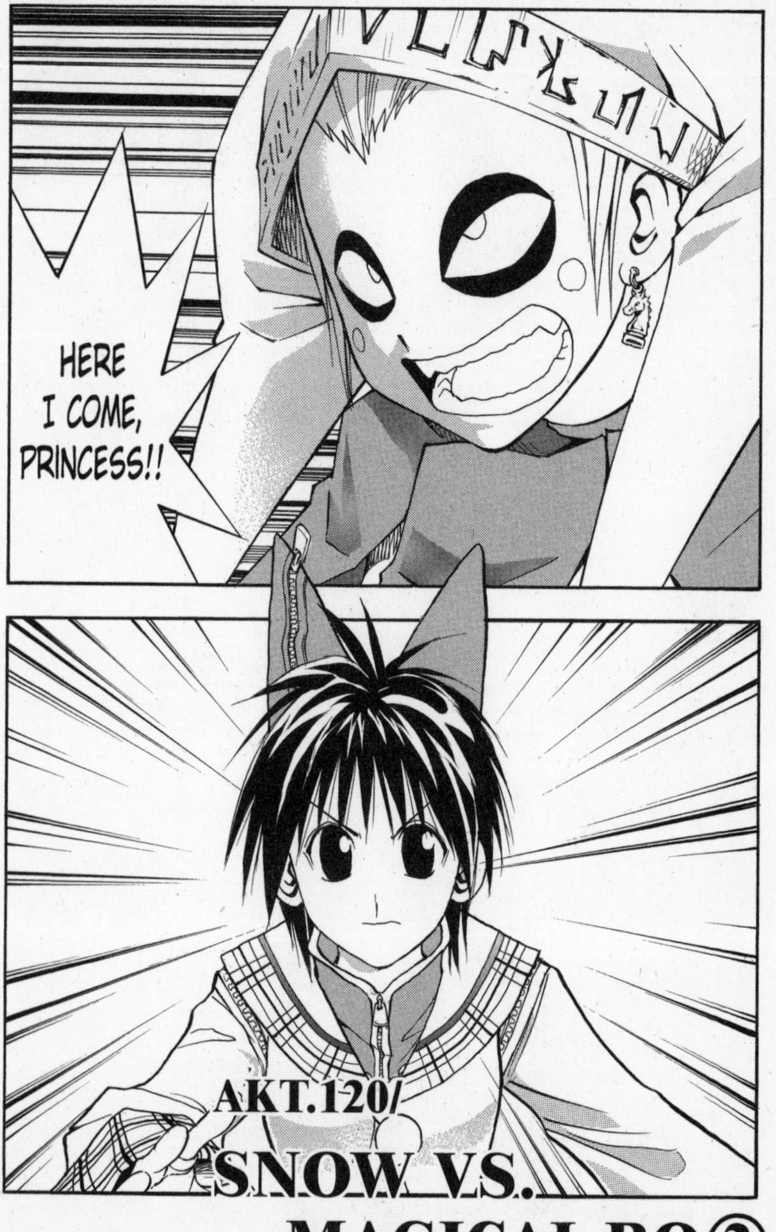
HERE I COME, PRINCESS!!

AKT.120/ SNOW V.S. MAGICAL RO②

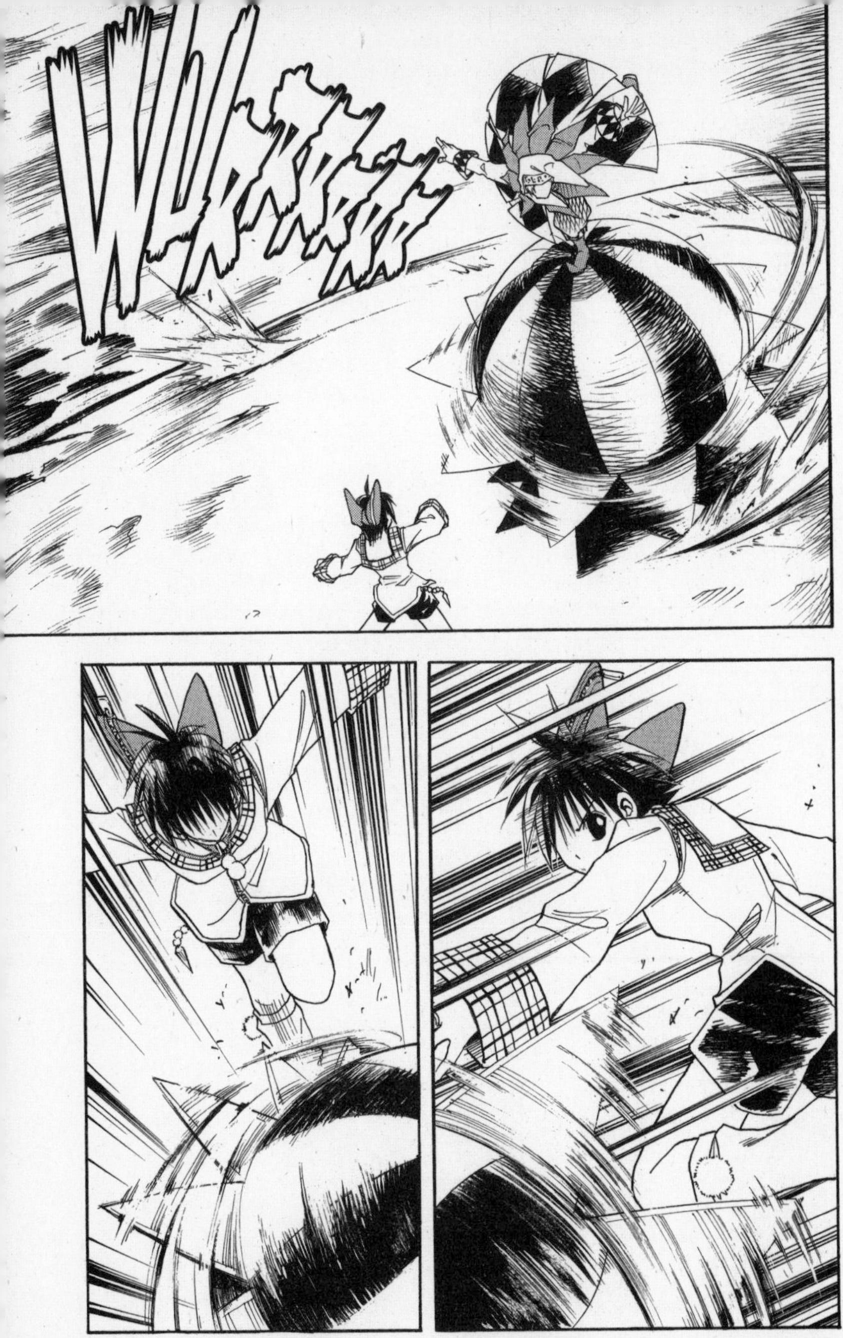

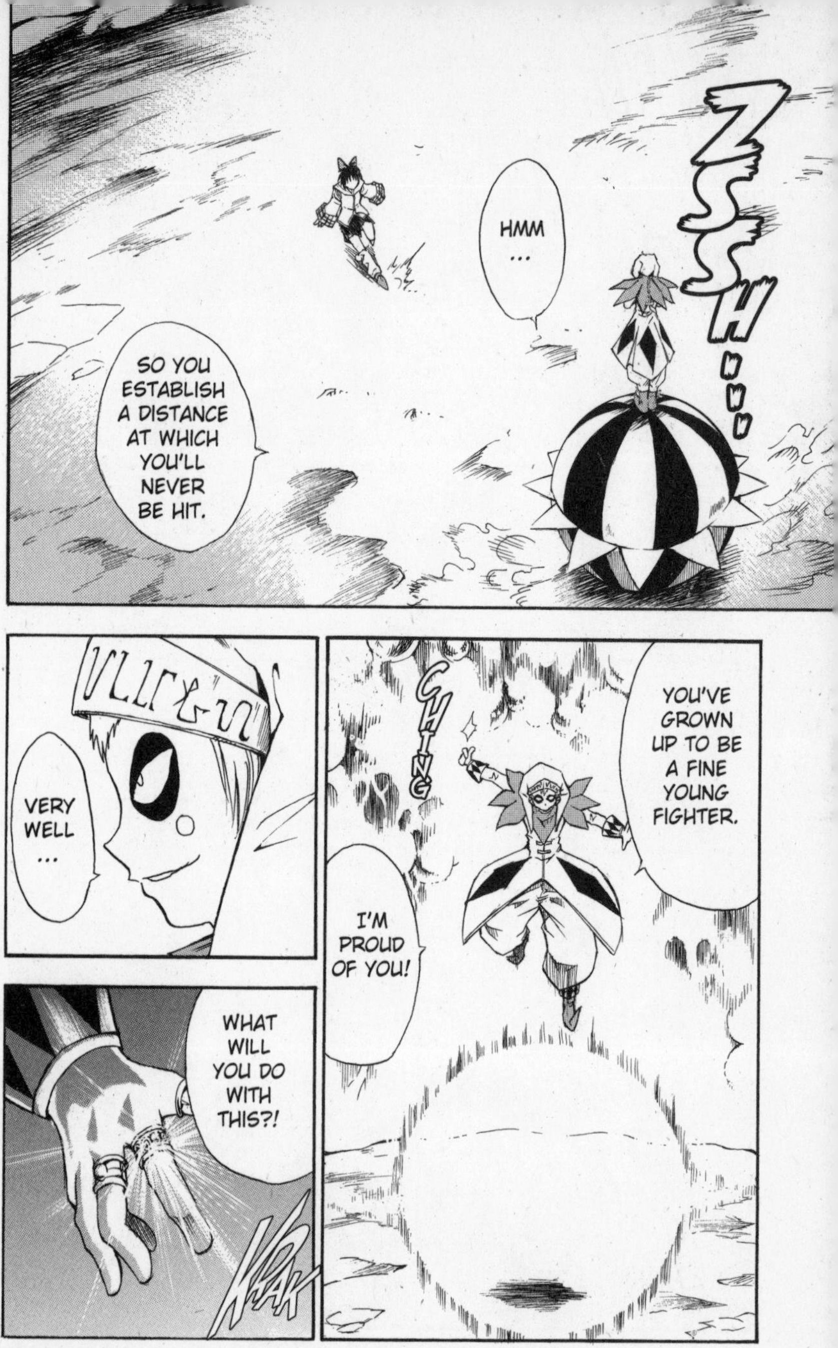
ZSSHUUU
HMM ...
SO YOU ESTABLISH A DISTANCE AT WHICH YOU'LL NEVER BE HIT.
YOU'VE GROWN UP TO BE A FINE YOUNG FIGHTER.
CHING
I'M PROUD OF YOU!
VERY WELL ...
WHAT WILL YOU DO WITH THIS?!
KRAK

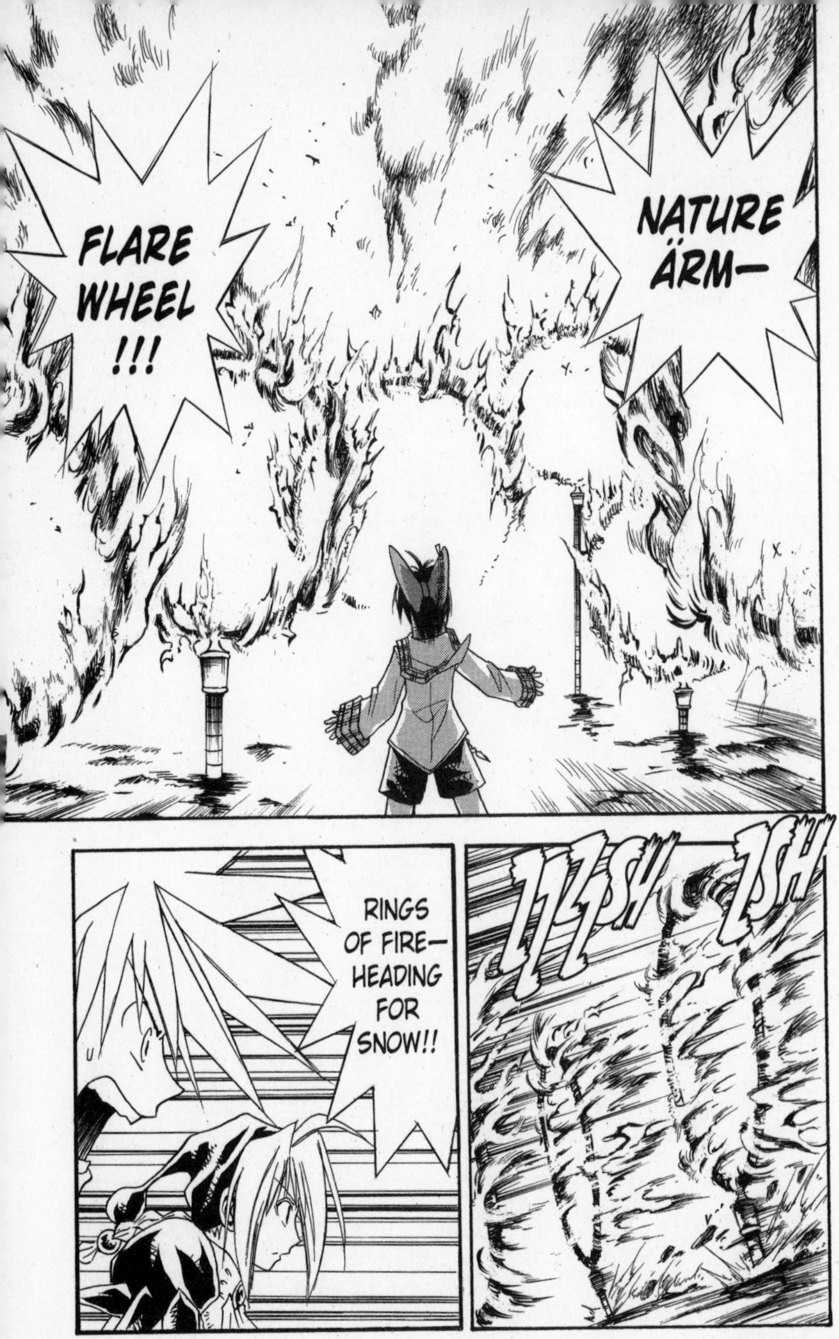
NATURE ÄRM—
FLARE WHEEL !!!
ZZZSH
ZSH
RINGS OF FIRE— HEADING FOR SNOW!!

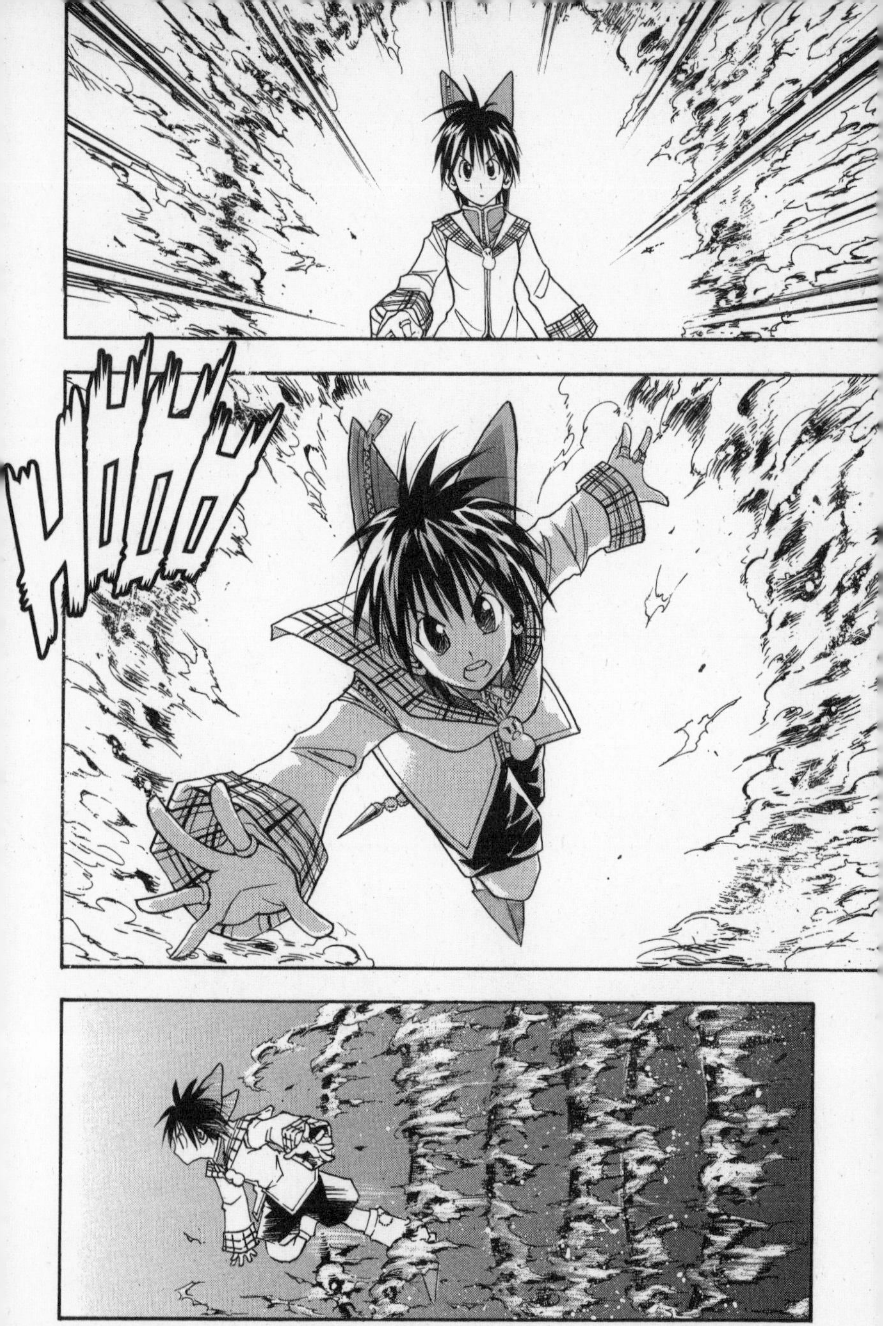
HAAAH

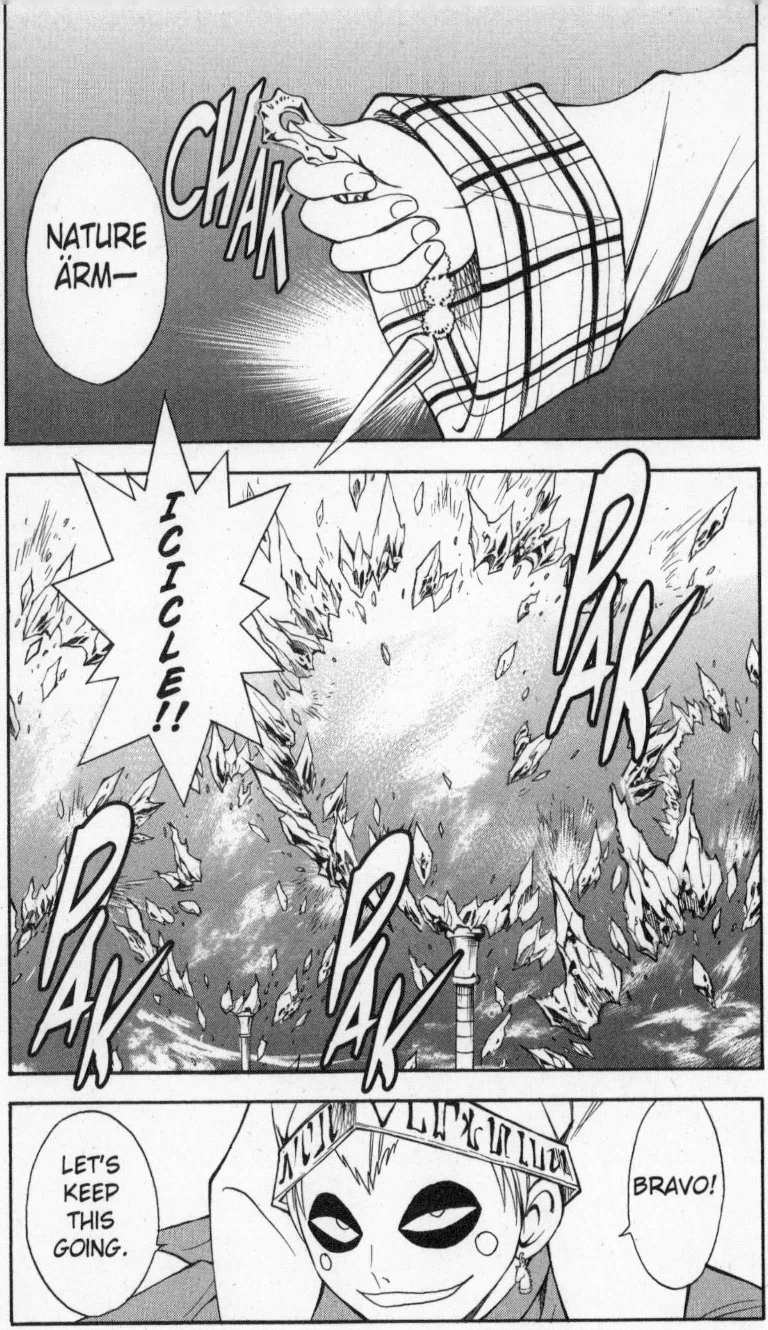
CHAK
NATURE ÄRM—
PAK
ICICLE!!
PAK
PAK
BRAVO!
LET'S KEEP THIS GOING.

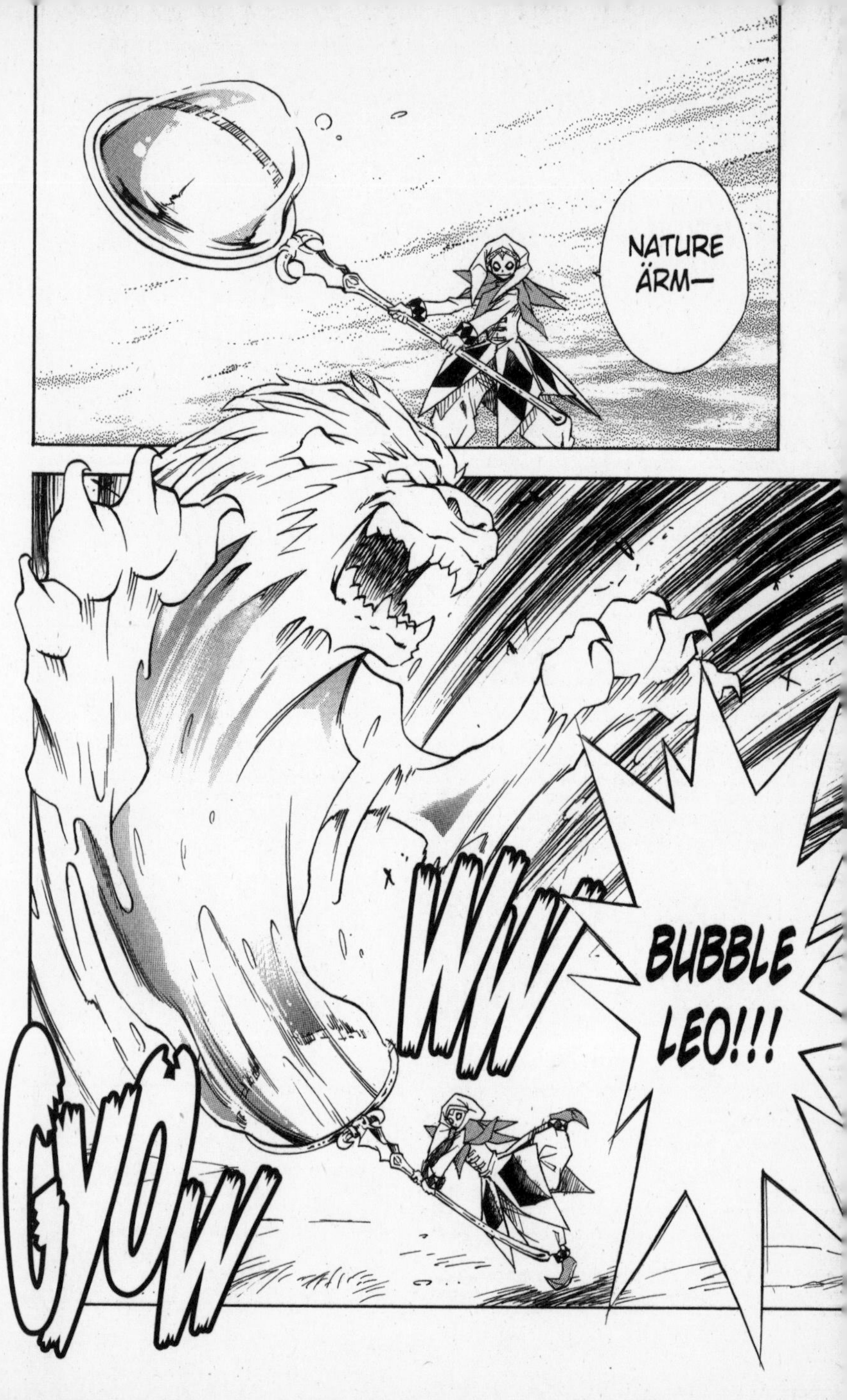
NATURE ÄRM—
BUBBLE LEO!!!
WW
GYOW

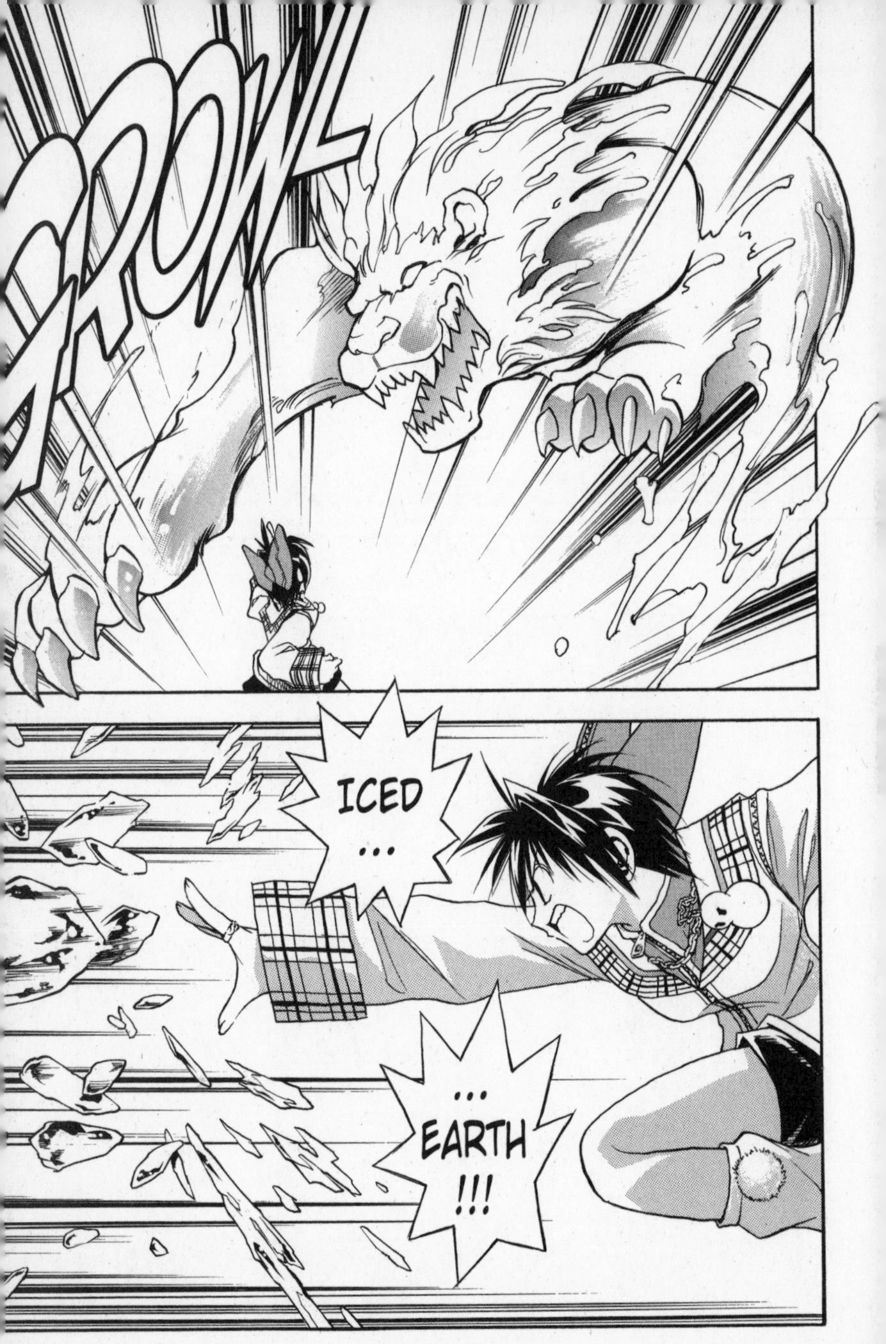

SPOOM
ICED ...
... EARTH !!!

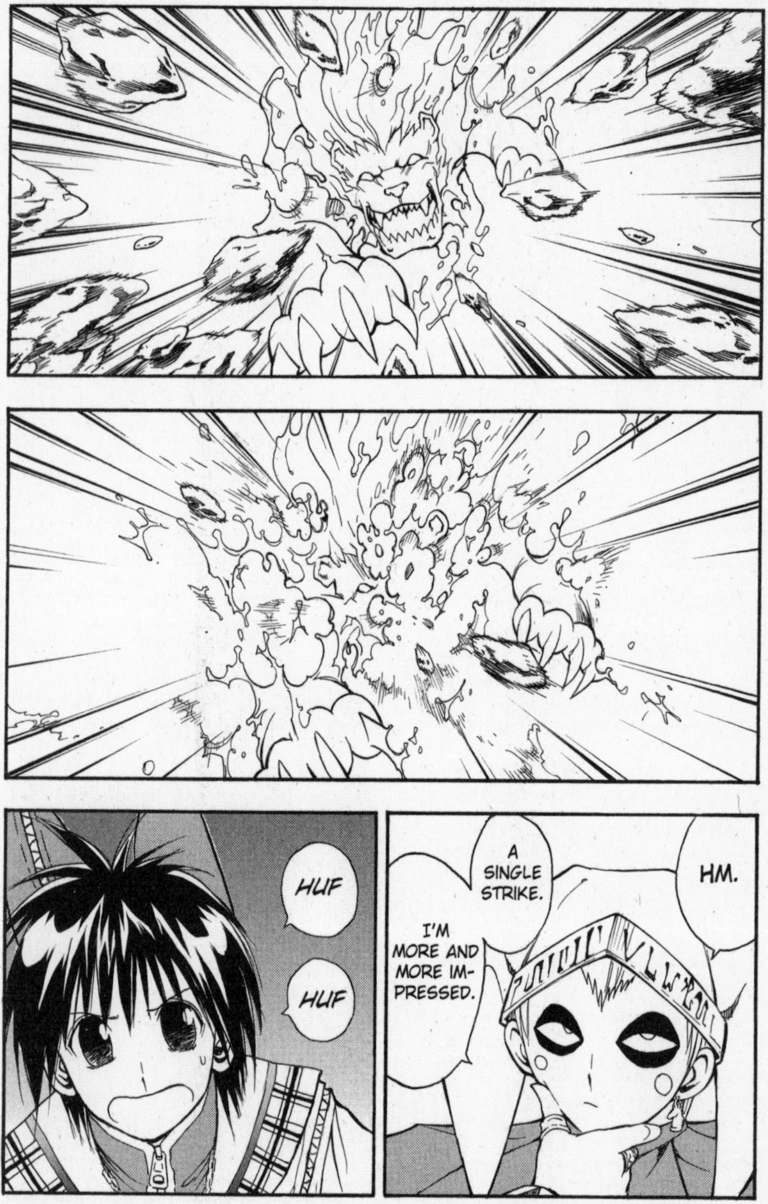
HM.
A SINGLE STRIKE.
I'M MORE AND MORE IM-PRESSED.
HUF
HUF

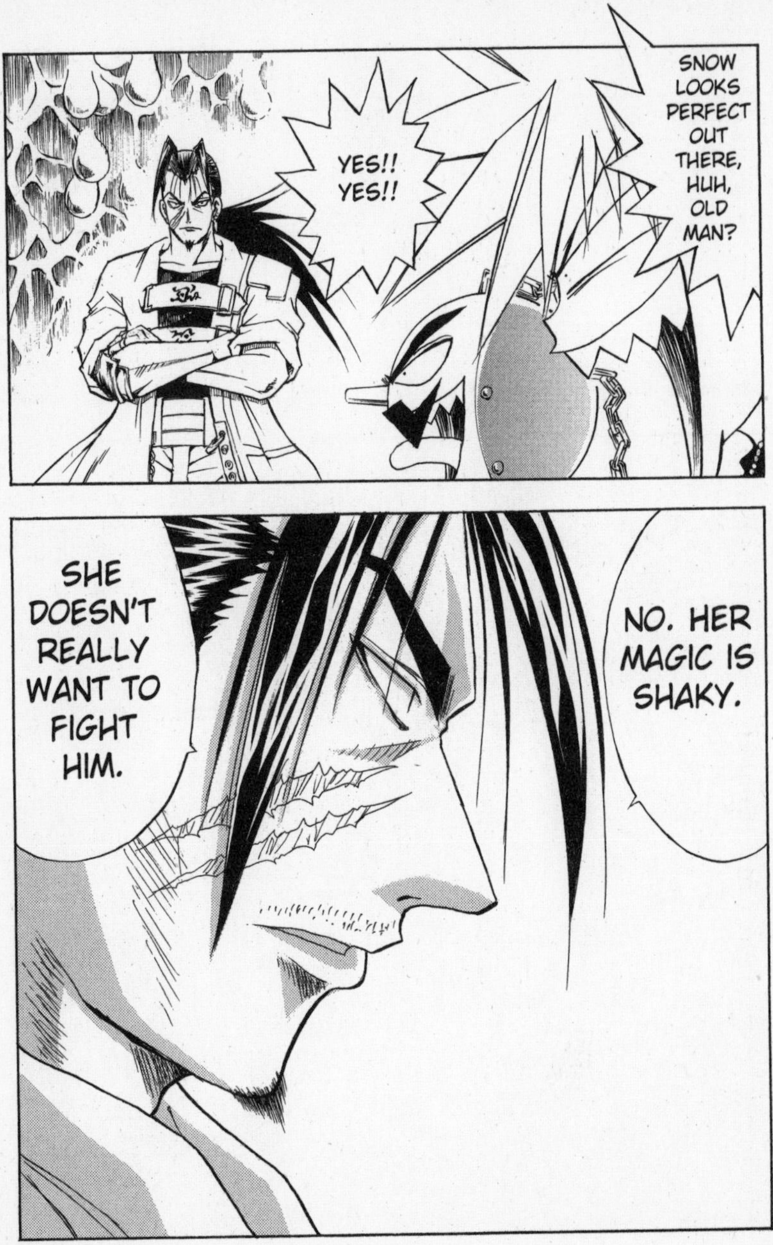
SNOW LOOKS PERFECT OUT THERE, HUH, OLD MAN?
YES!! YES!!
NO. HER MAGIC IS SHAKY.
SHE DOESN'T REALLY WANT TO FIGHT HIM.

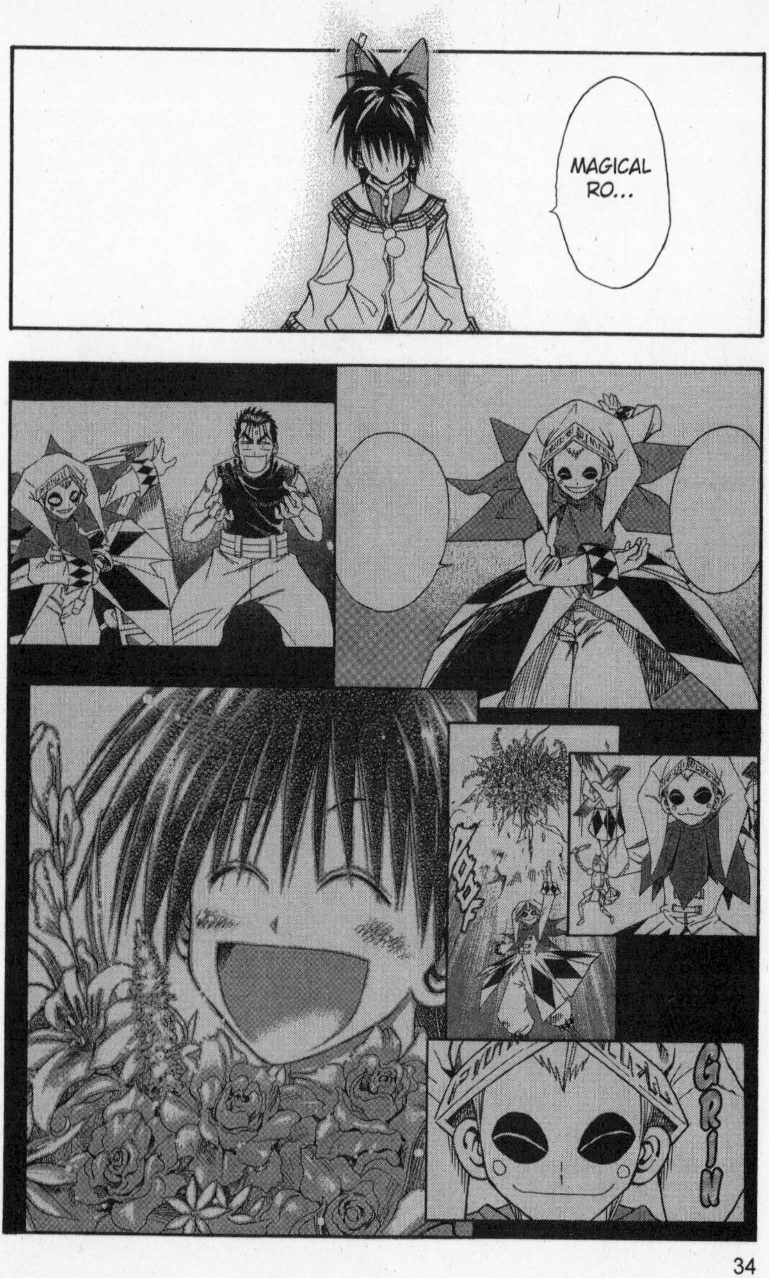
MAGICAL RO...
POOF
GRIN

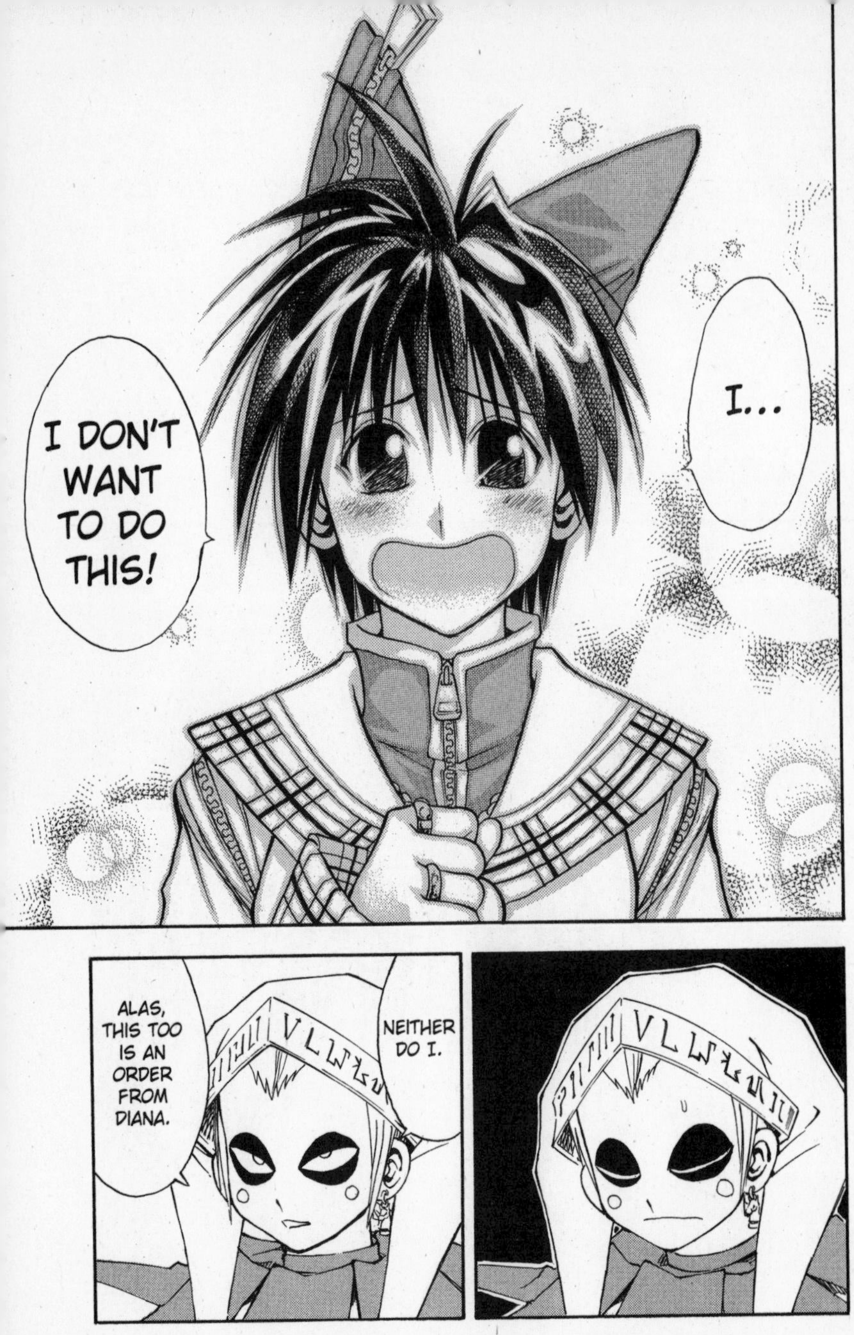
I...
I DON'T WANT TO DO THIS!
NEITHER DO I.
ALAS, THIS TOO IS AN ORDER FROM DIANA.

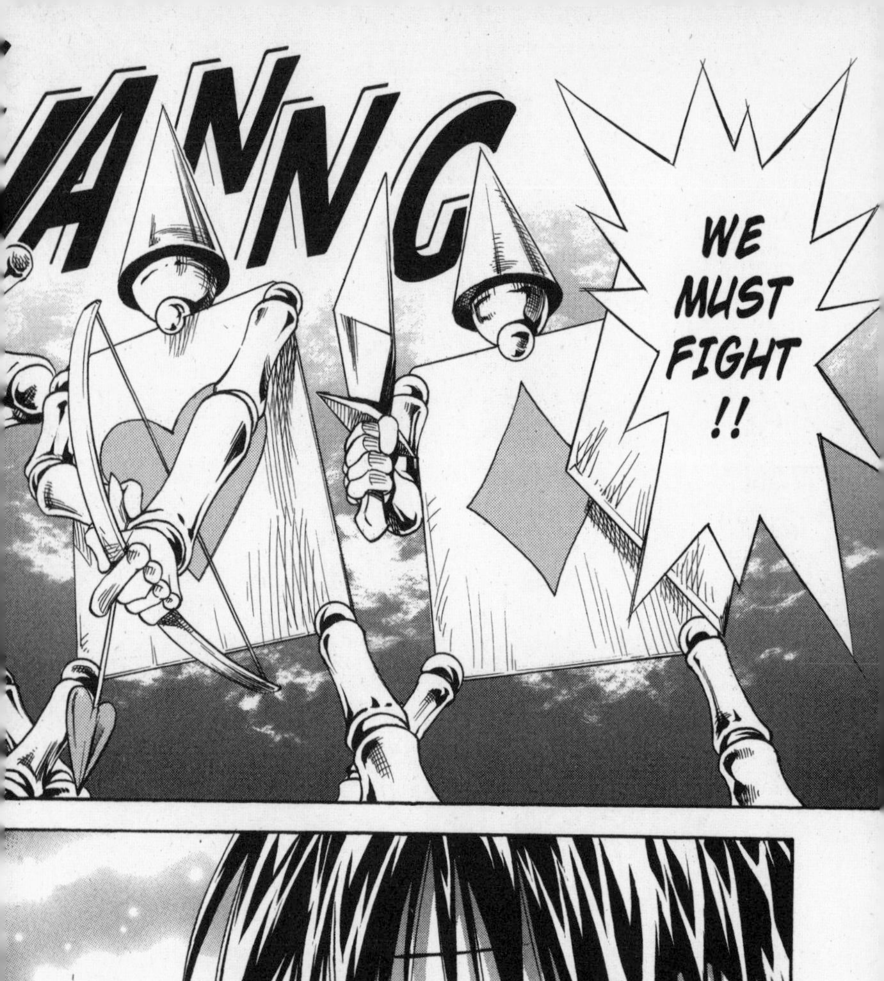
ANNG
WE MUST FIGHT !!
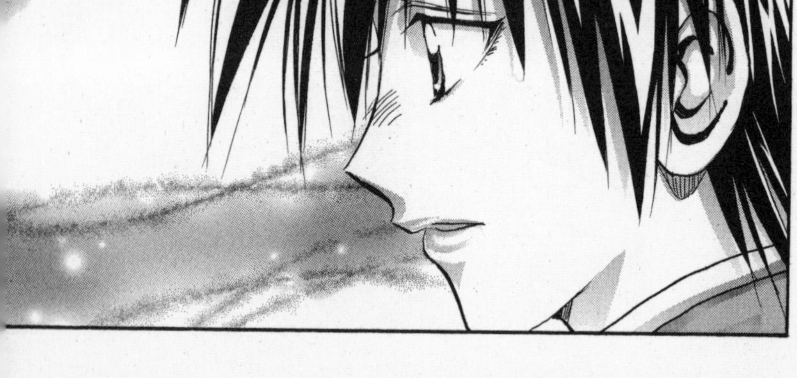

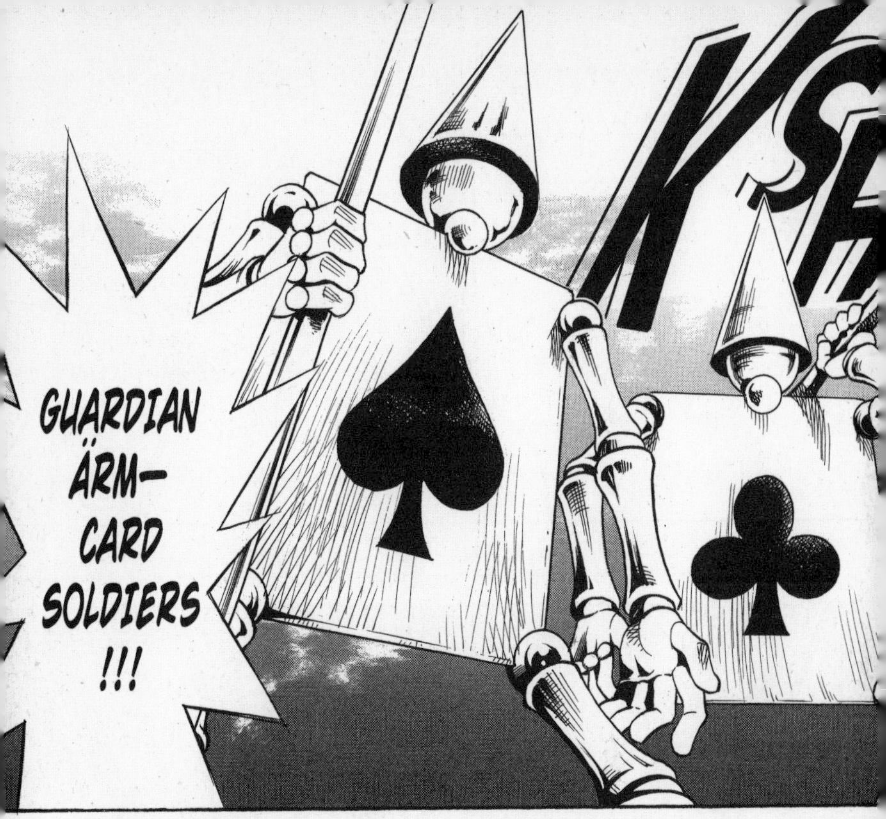
GUARDIAN ÄRM-CARD SOLDIERS !!!

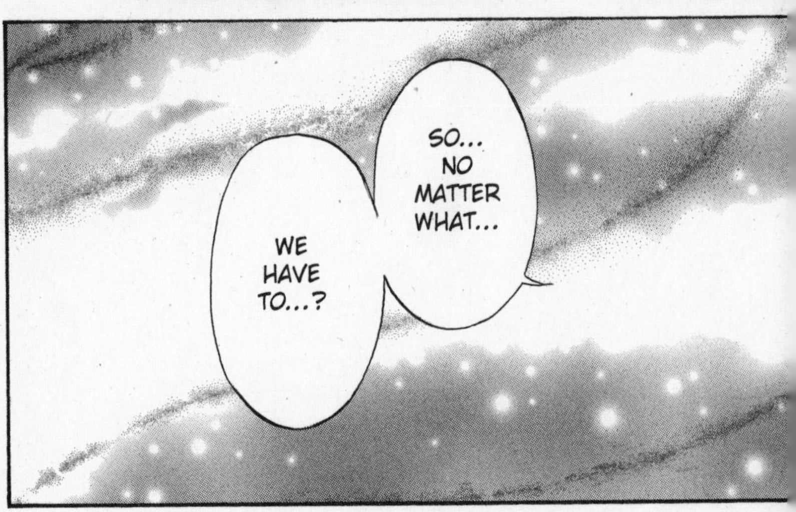
SO... NO MATTER WHAT...
WE HAVE TO...?

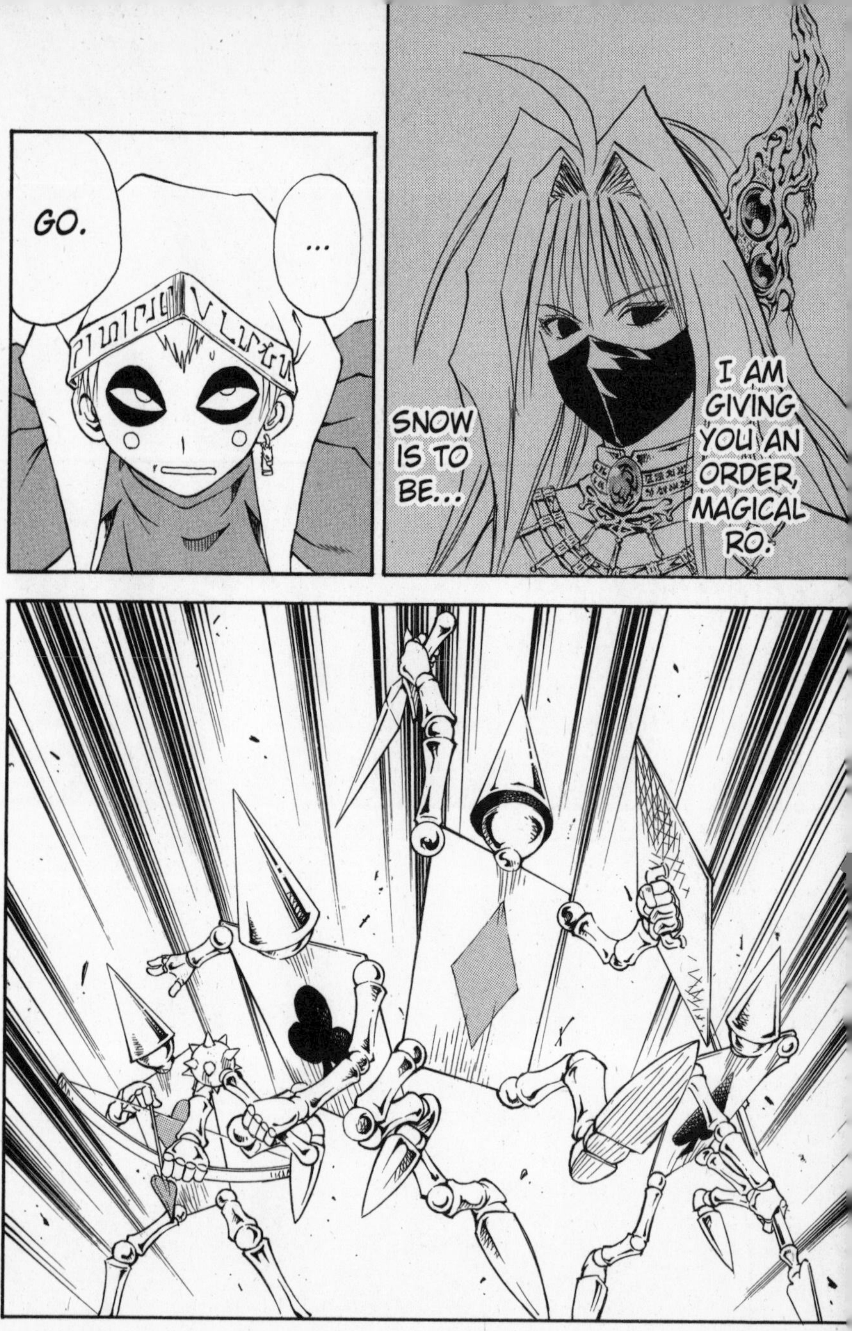
I AM GIVING YOU AN ORDER, MAGICAL RO.
SNOW IS TO BE...
...
GO.

AKT.121/ SNOW VS. MAGICAL RO③

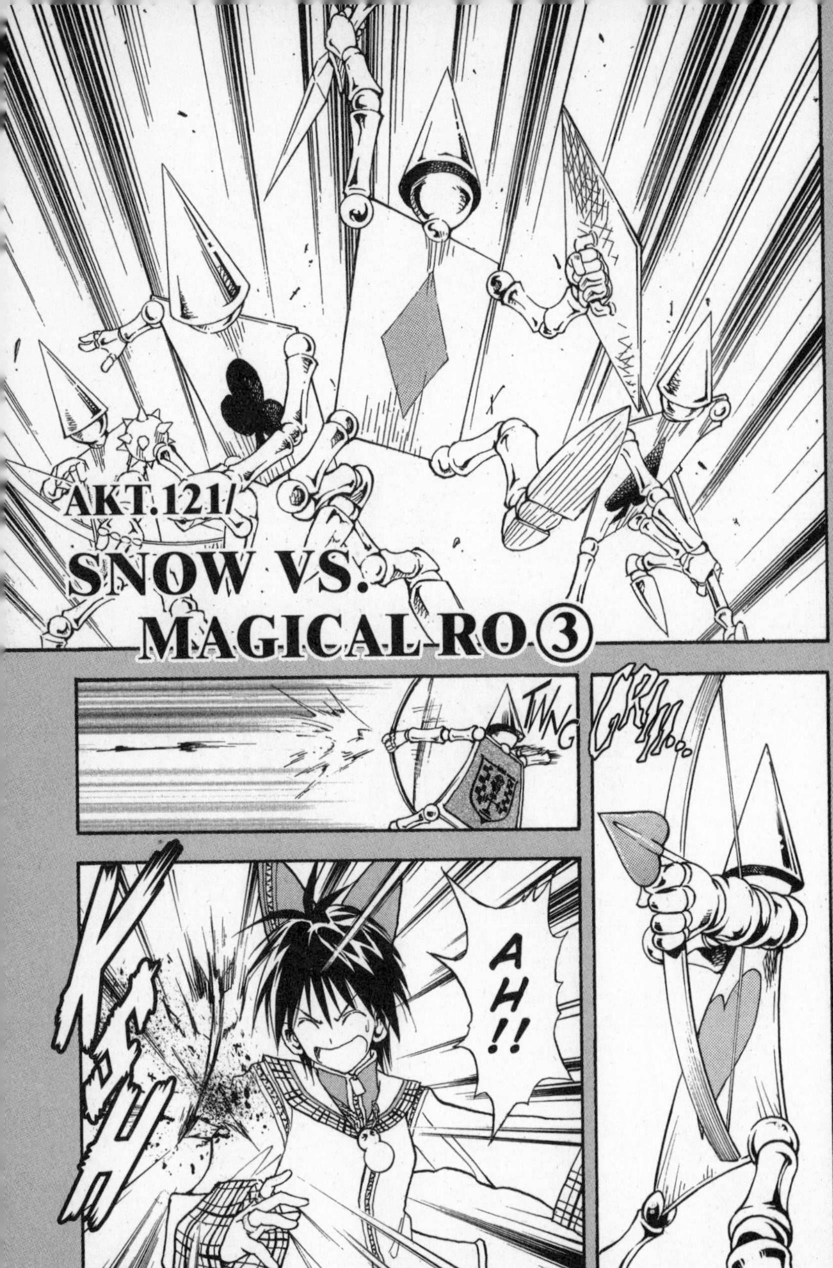
GRIII...
TWNG
AH!!
KSHH

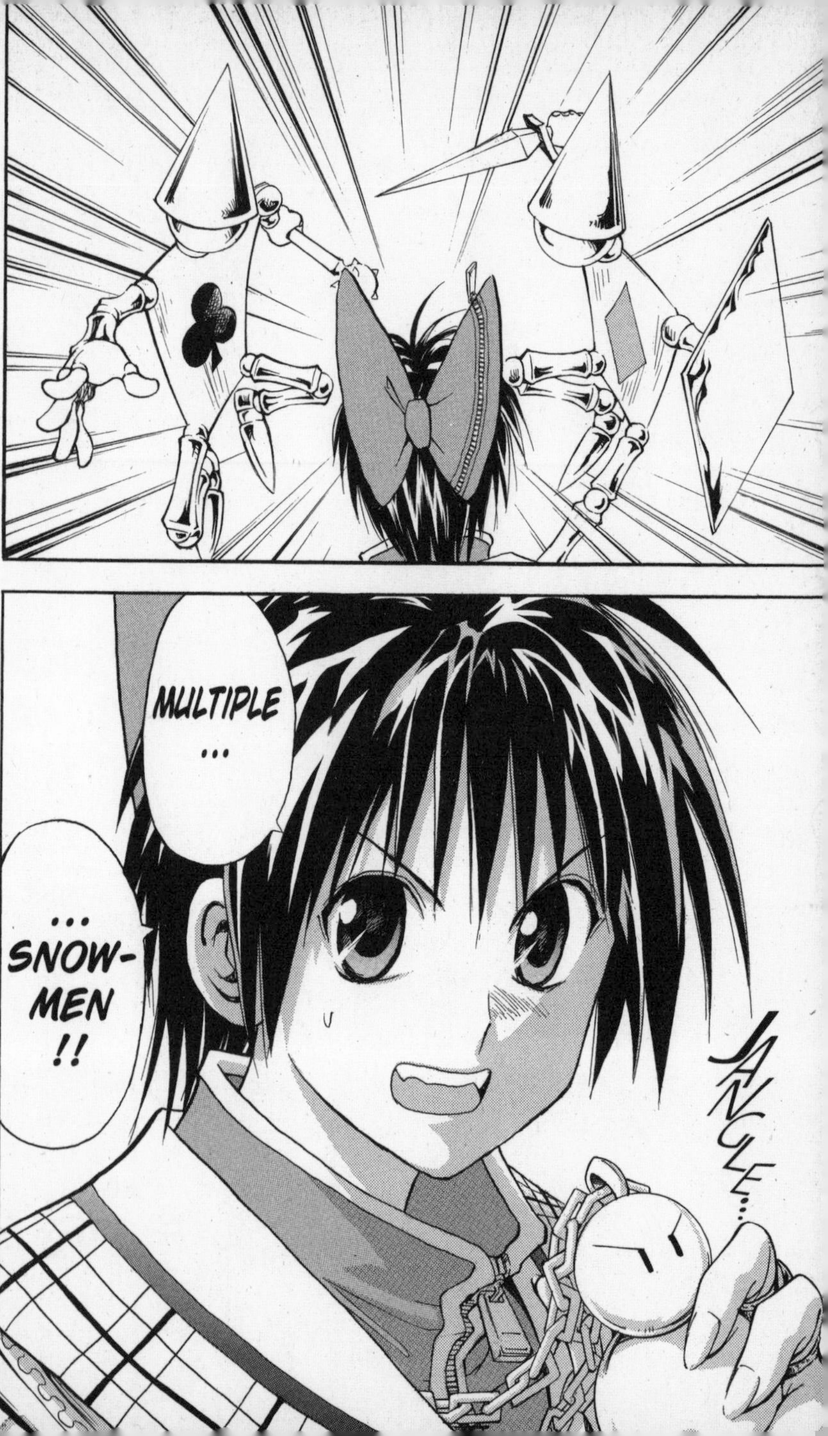
MULTIPLE ...
... SNOW-MEN !!
JANGLE...

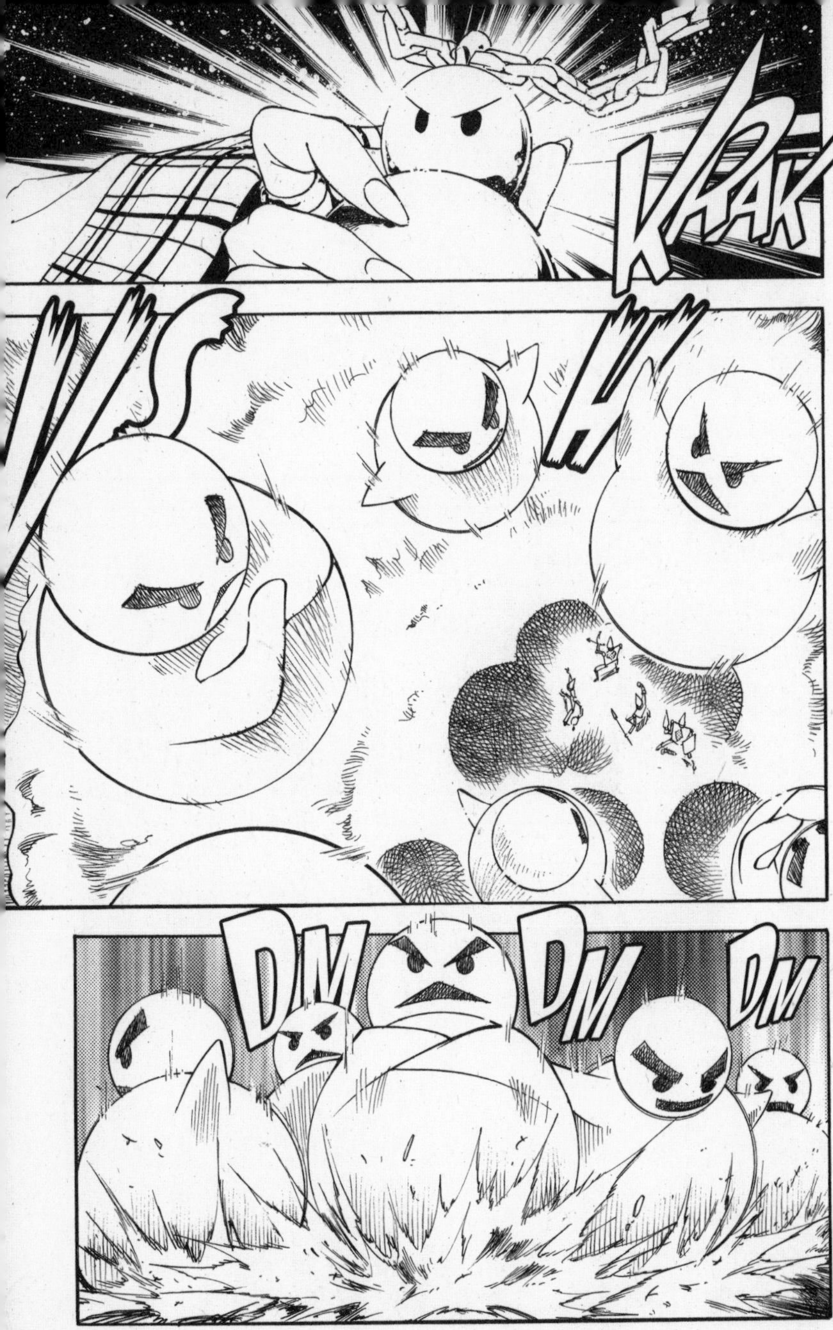
KRAK
DM DM DM

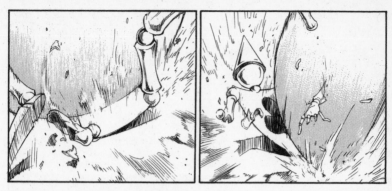

COPY CAT MEDALLION !!!

NOW !!!

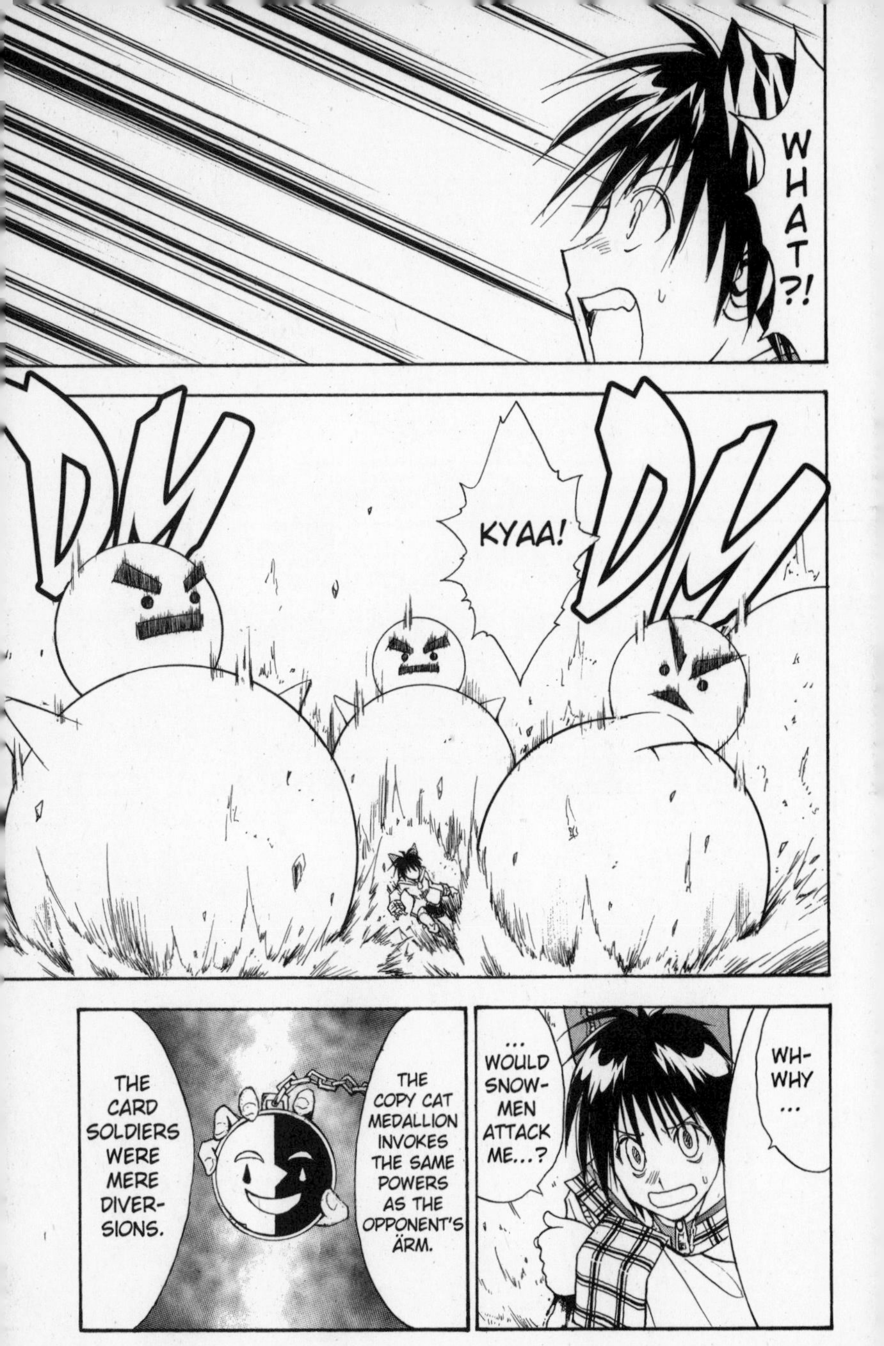
WHAT?!
DM
DM
KYAA!
WH- WHY...
...WOULD SNOW-MEN ATTACK ME...?
THE COPY CAT MEDALLION INVOKES THE SAME POWERS AS THE OPPONENT'S ÄRM.
THE CARD SOLDIERS WERE MERE DIVER-SIONS.

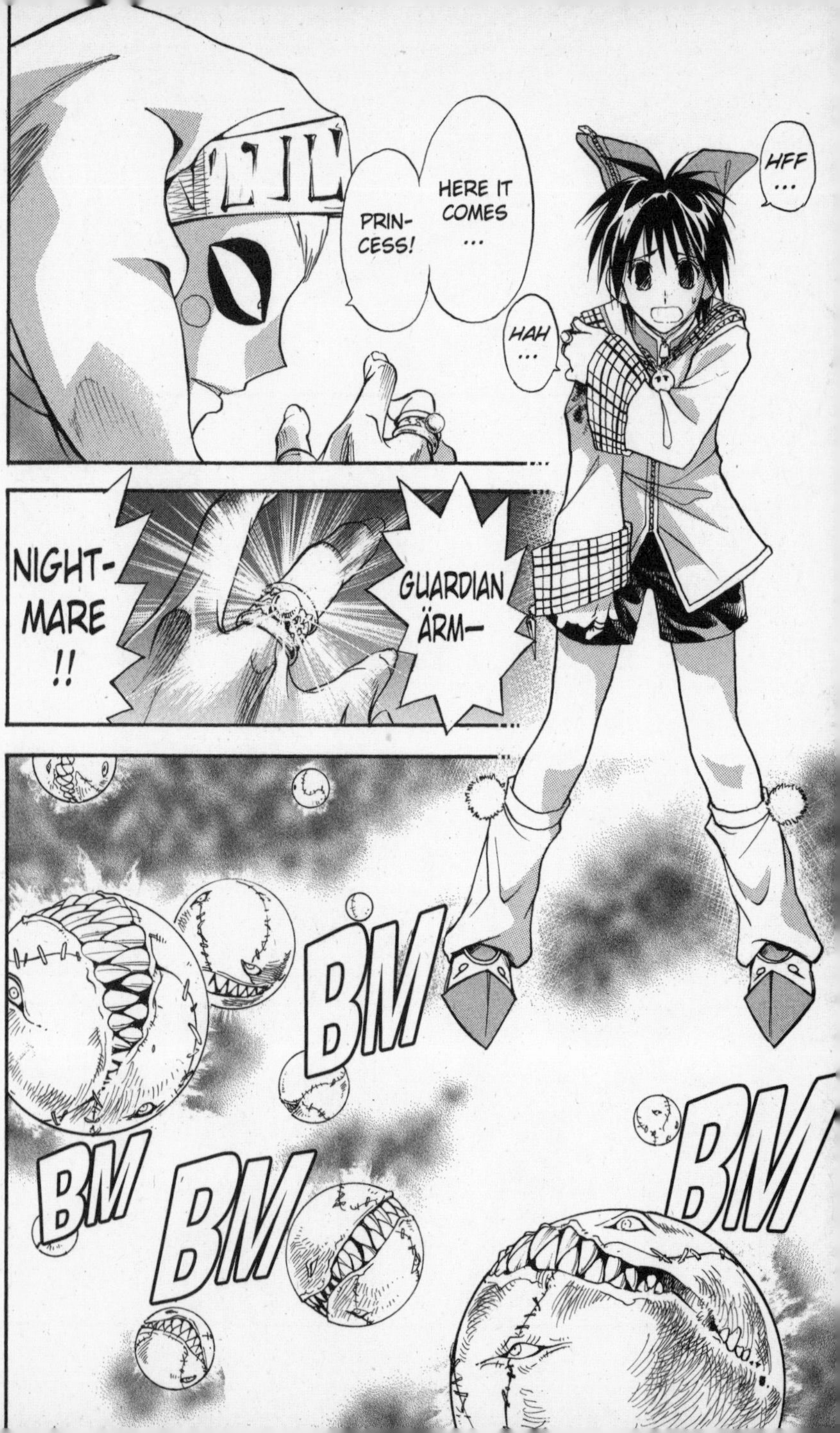
HFF ...
HAH ...
HERE IT COMES ...
PRIN-CESS!
GUARDIAN ÄRM-
NIGHT-MARE !!
BM
BM
BM
BM

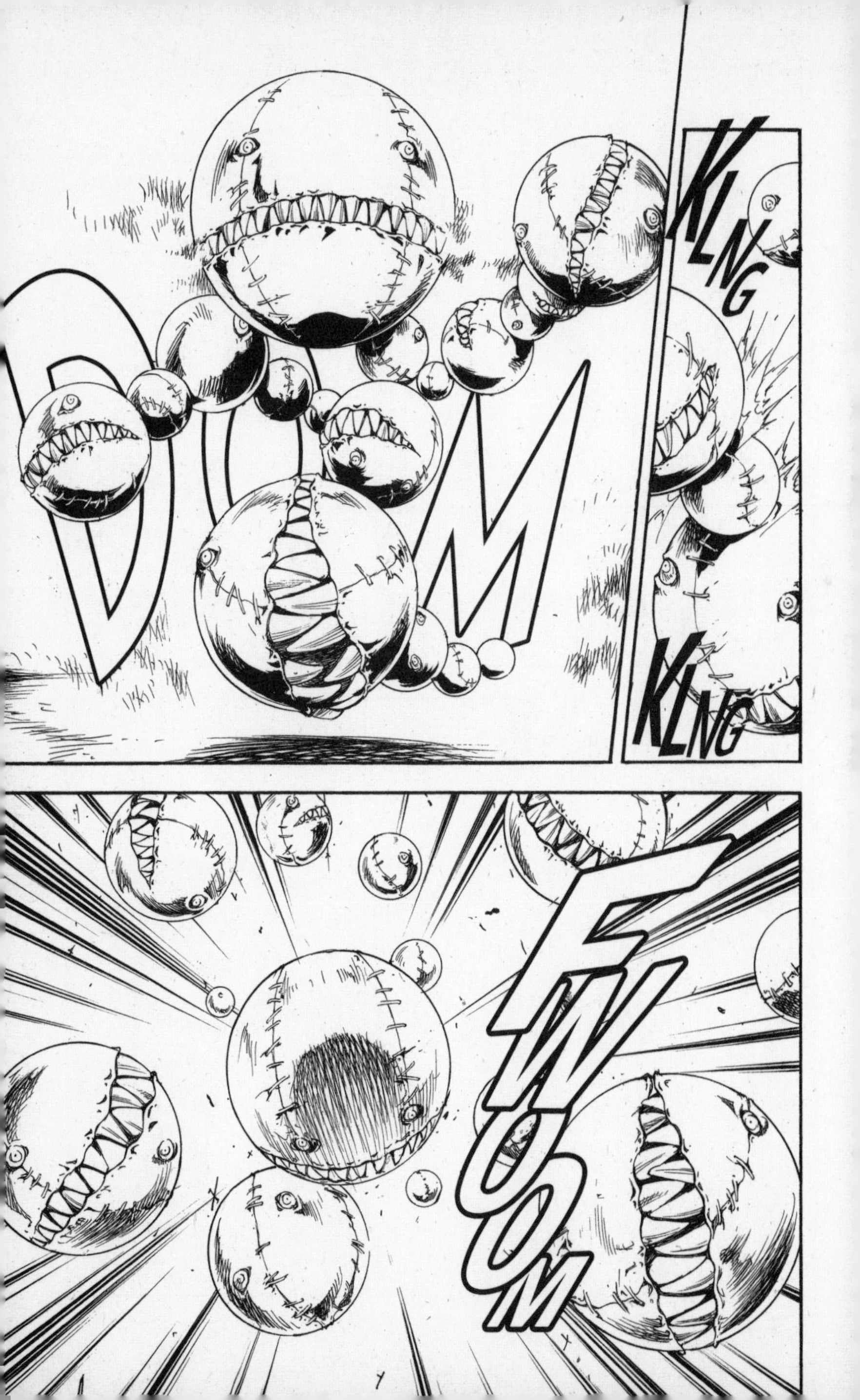
KLNG
KLNG
DOM
FWOOM

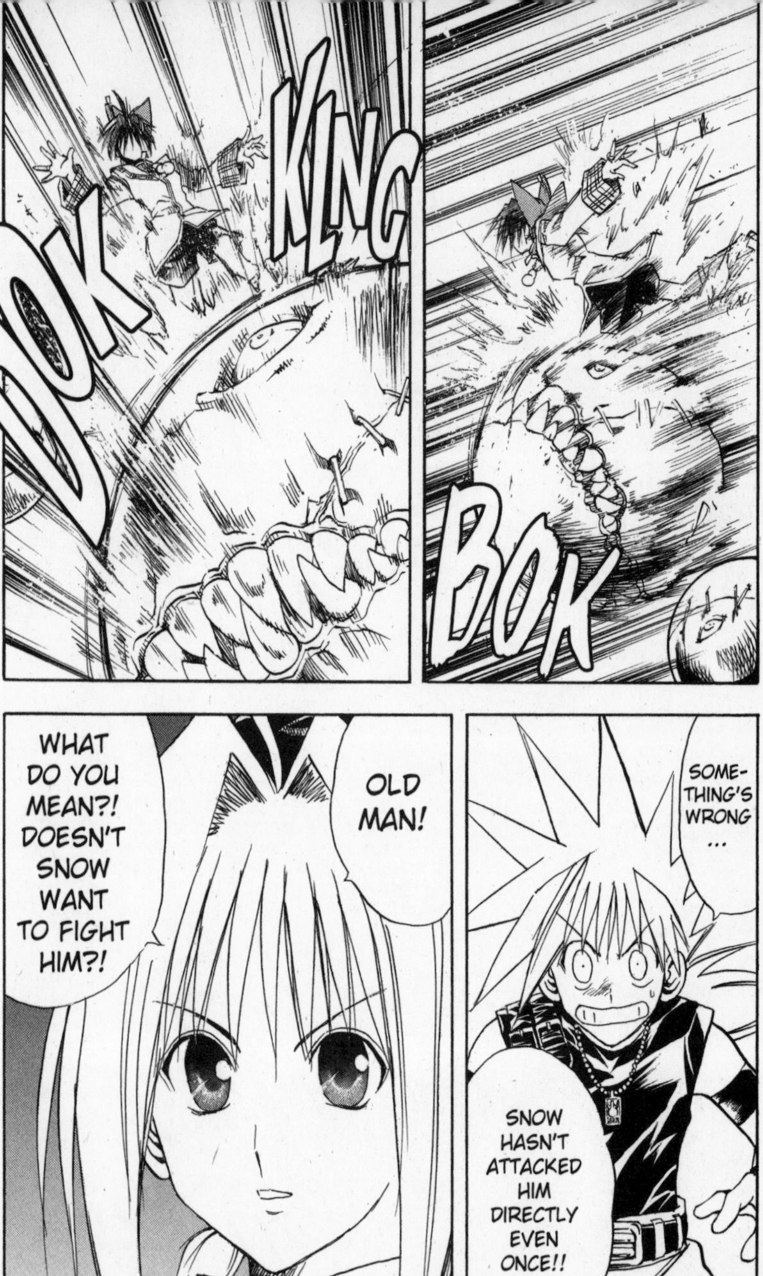
BOK
KLNG
DOK
SOME-THING'S WRONG...
SNOW HASN'T ATTACKED HIM DIRECTLY EVEN ONCE!!
OLD MAN!
WHAT DO YOU MEAN?! DOESN'T SNOW WANT TO FIGHT HIM?!

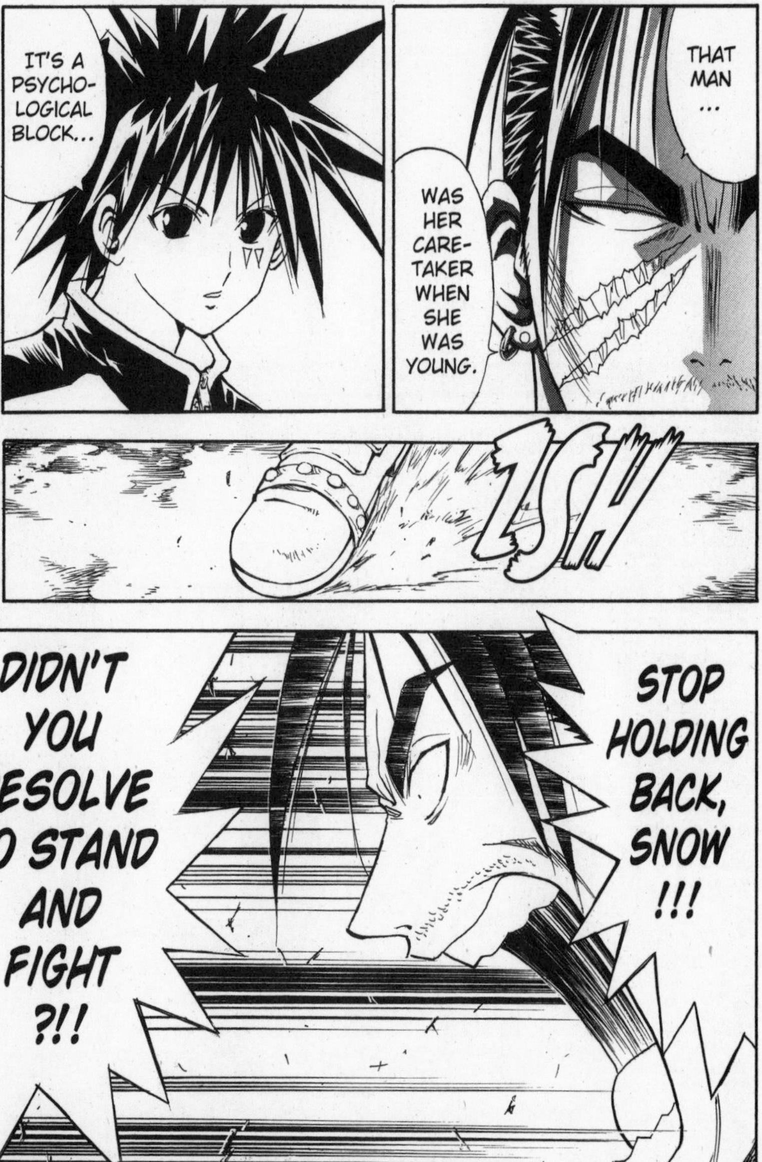
THAT MAN ...
WAS HER CARE-TAKER WHEN SHE WAS YOUNG.
IT'S A PSYCHO-LOGICAL BLOCK...
ZSH
STOP HOLDING BACK, SNOW !!!
DIDN'T YOU RESOLVE TO STAND AND FIGHT ?!!

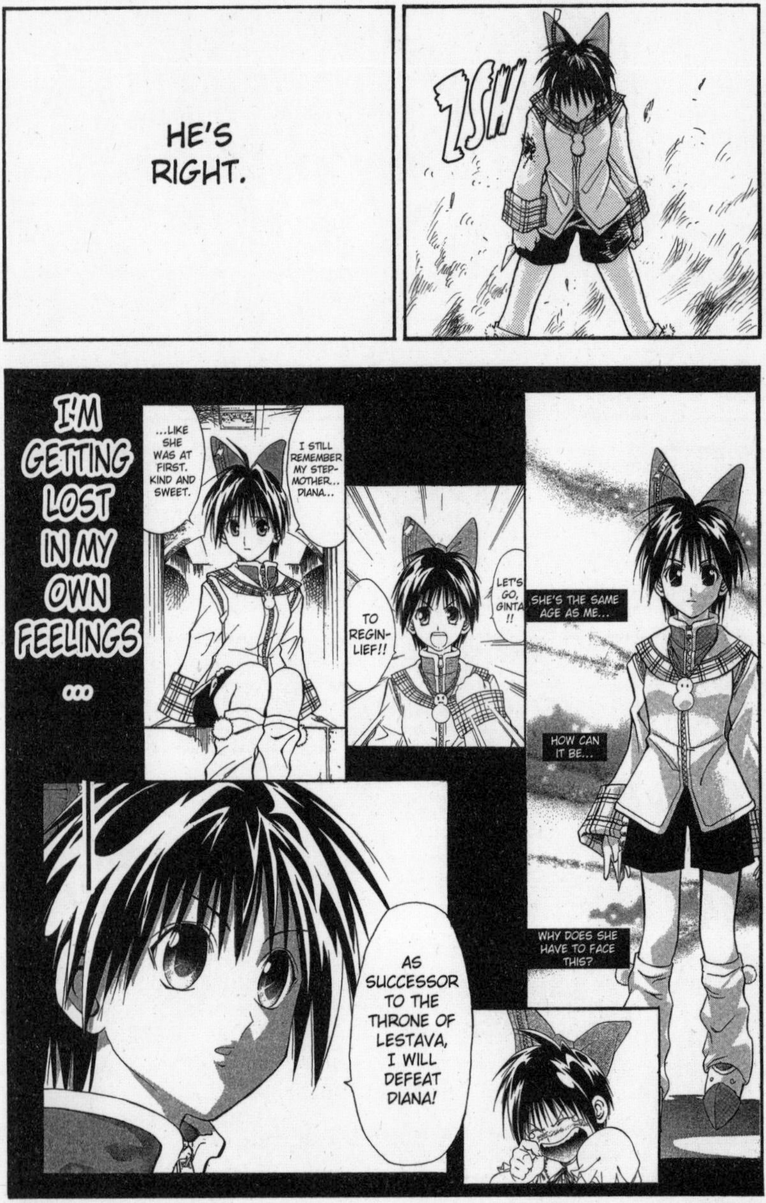
ZSH
HE'S RIGHT.
SHE'S THE SAME AGE AS ME...
HOW CAN IT BE...
WHY DOES SHE HAVE TO FACE THIS?
LET'S GO, GINTA!!
TO REGIN-LIEF!!
I STILL REMEMBER MY STEP-MOTHER... DIANA...
...LIKE SHE WAS AT FIRST. KIND AND SWEET.
I'M GETTING LOST IN MY OWN FEELINGS...
AS SUCCESSOR TO THE THRONE OF LESTAVA, I WILL DEFEAT DIANA!

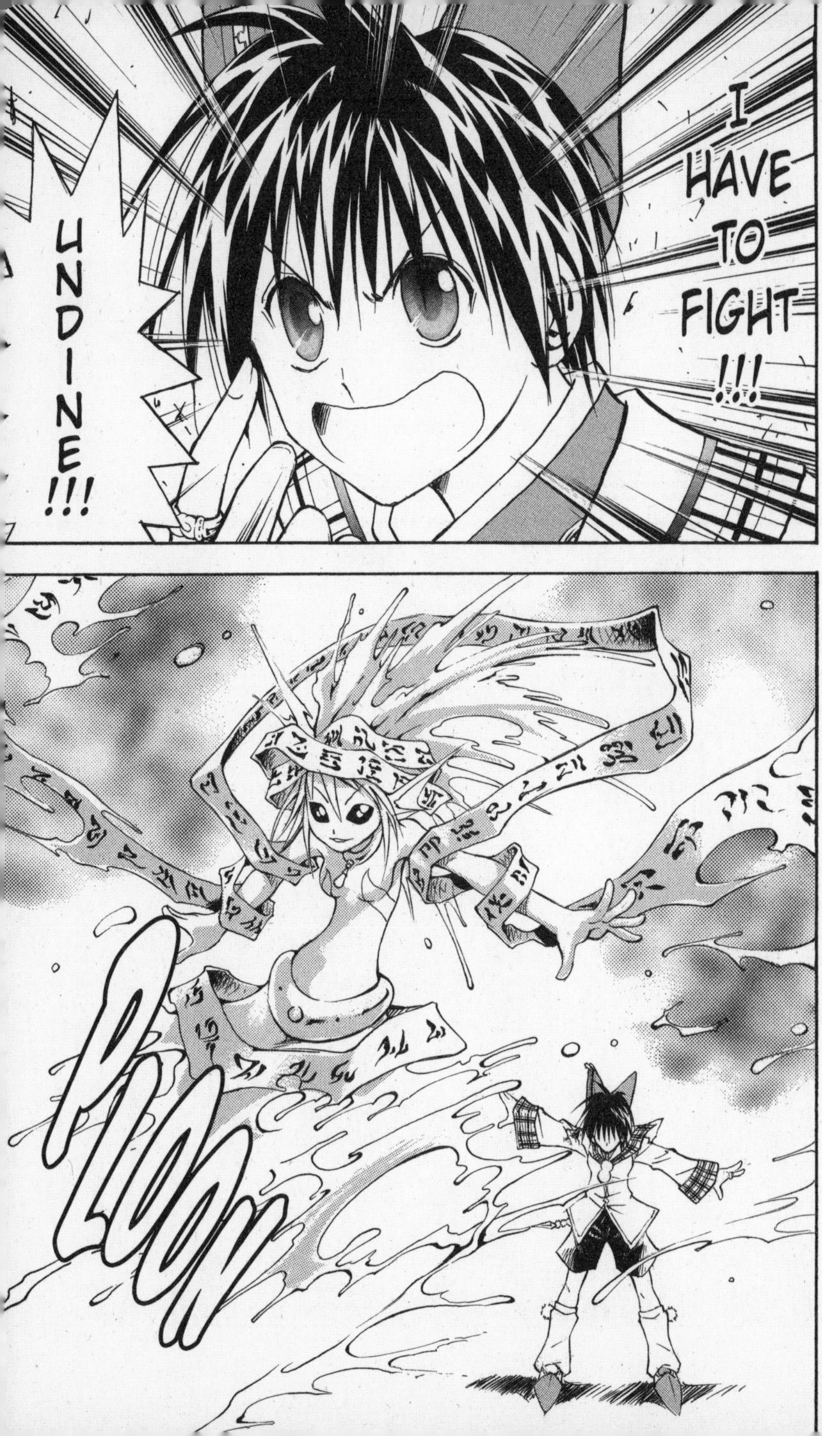
I HAVE TO FIGHT!!!
UNDINE!!!
PLOOM

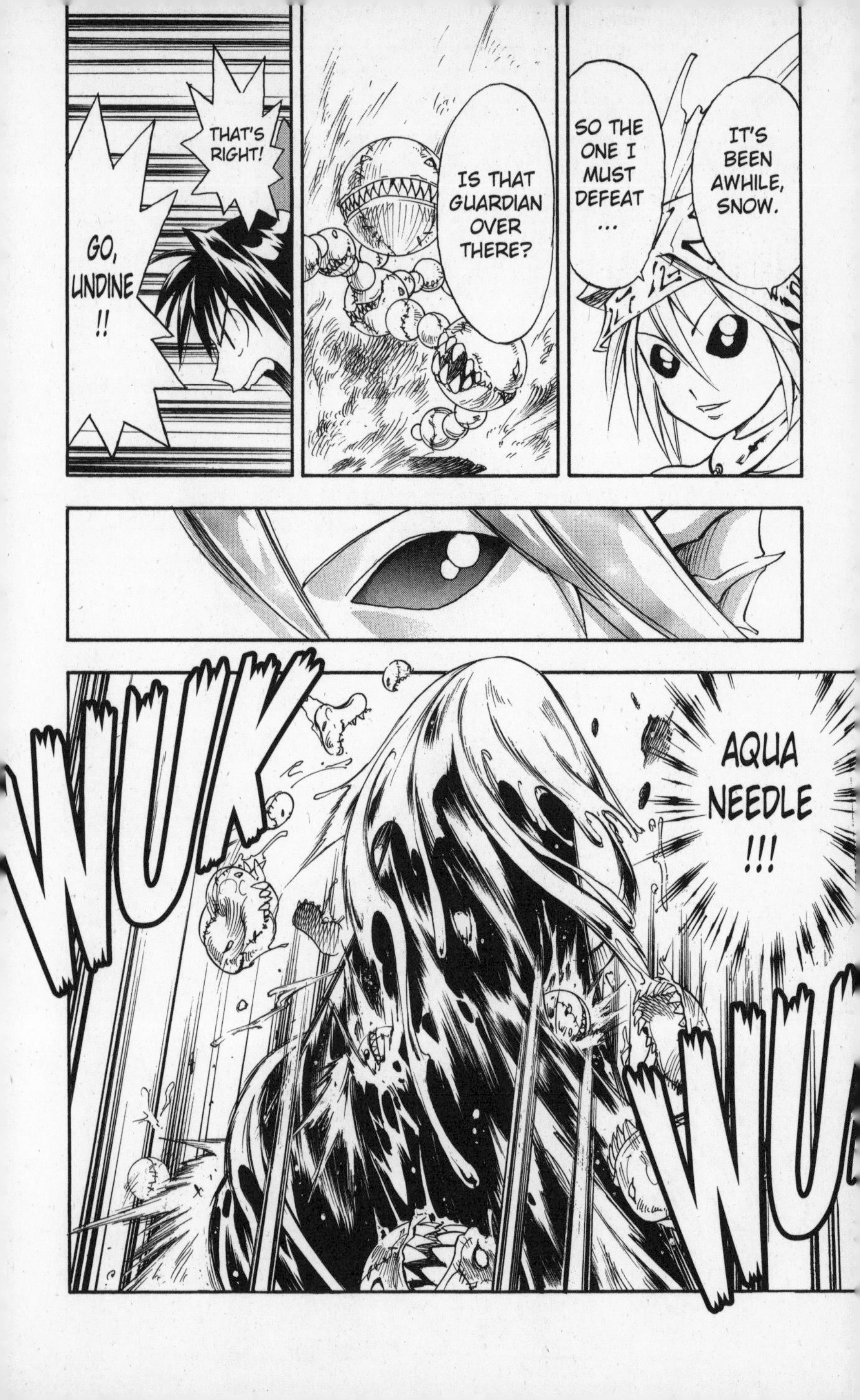
IT'S BEEN AWHILE, SNOW.
SO THE ONE I MUST DEFEAT ...
IS THAT GUARDIAN OVER THERE?
THAT'S RIGHT!
GO, UNDINE !!
AQUA NEEDLE !!!
WUK
WU

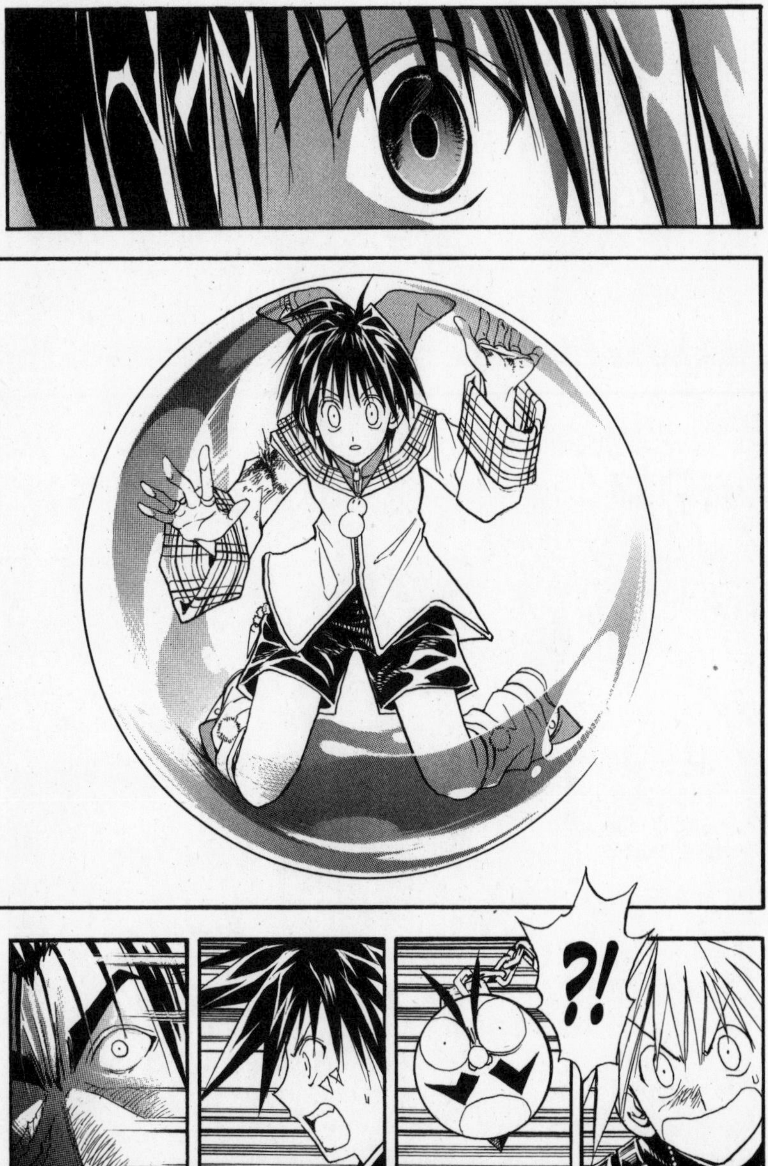
?!

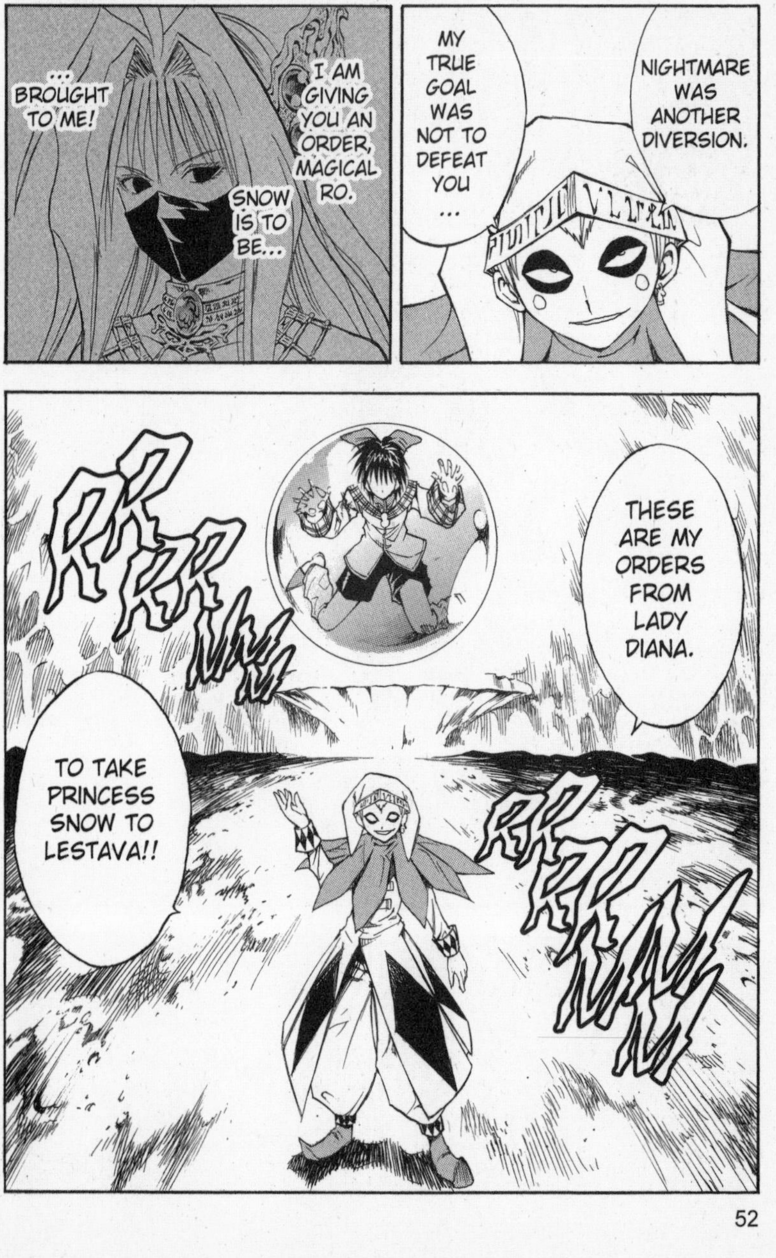
NIGHTMARE WAS ANOTHER DIVERSION.
MY TRUE GOAL WAS NOT TO DEFEAT YOU ...
I AM GIVING YOU AN ORDER, MAGICAL RO.
SNOW IS TO BE...
... BROUGHT TO ME!
THESE ARE MY ORDERS FROM LADY DIANA.
RRRRMM
TO TAKE PRINCESS SNOW TO LESTAVA!!
RRRRMM

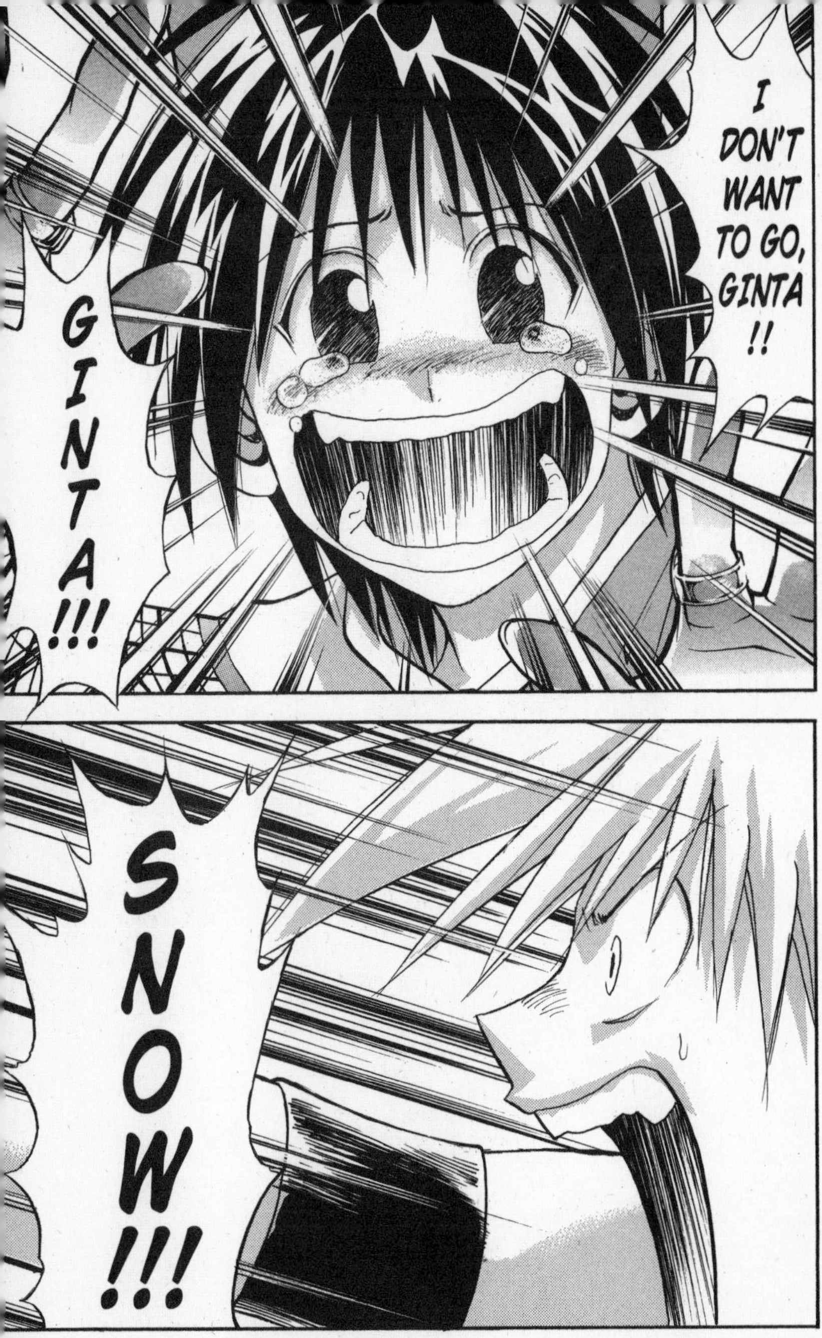
I DON'T WANT TO GO, GINTA!!
GINTA!!!
SNOW!!!

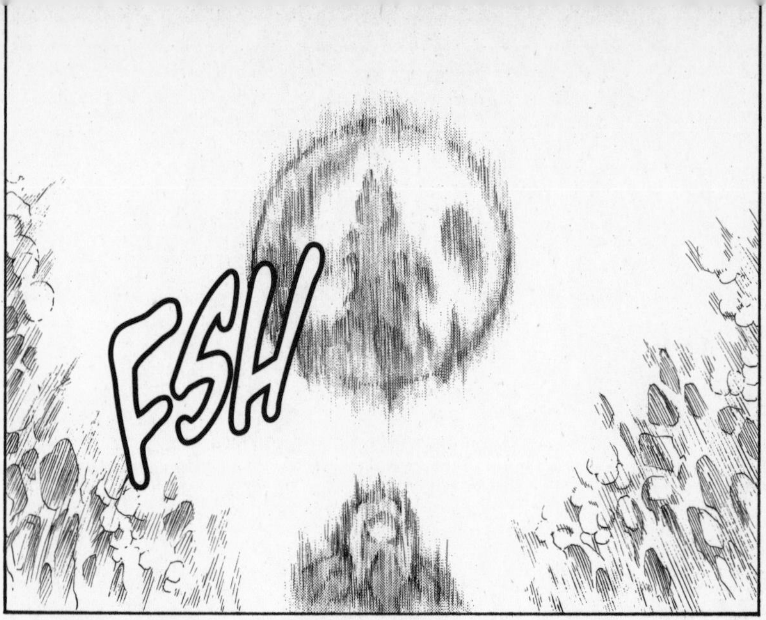
FSH

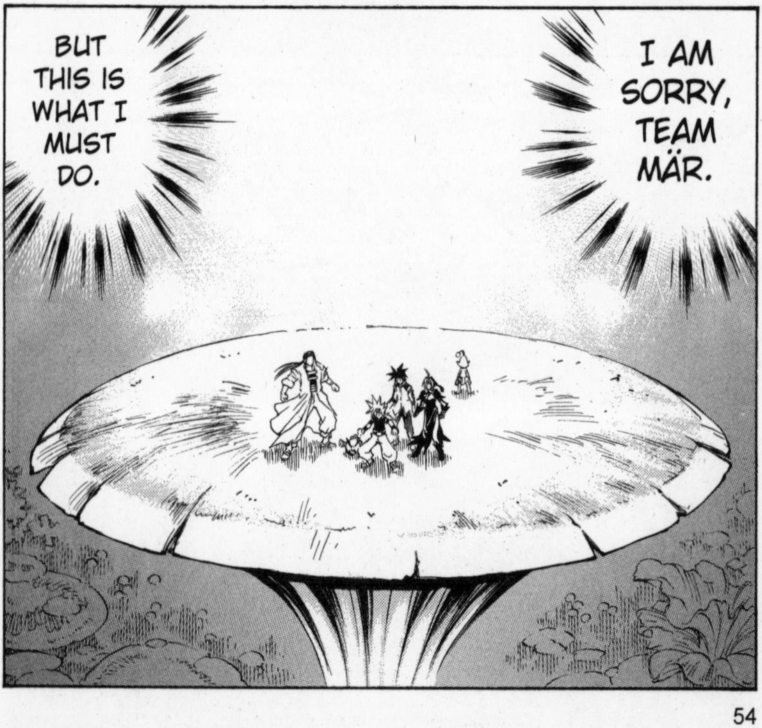
I AM SORRY, TEAM MÄR.
BUT THIS IS WHAT I MUST DO.

AKT. 122/ GINTA VS. IAN ①

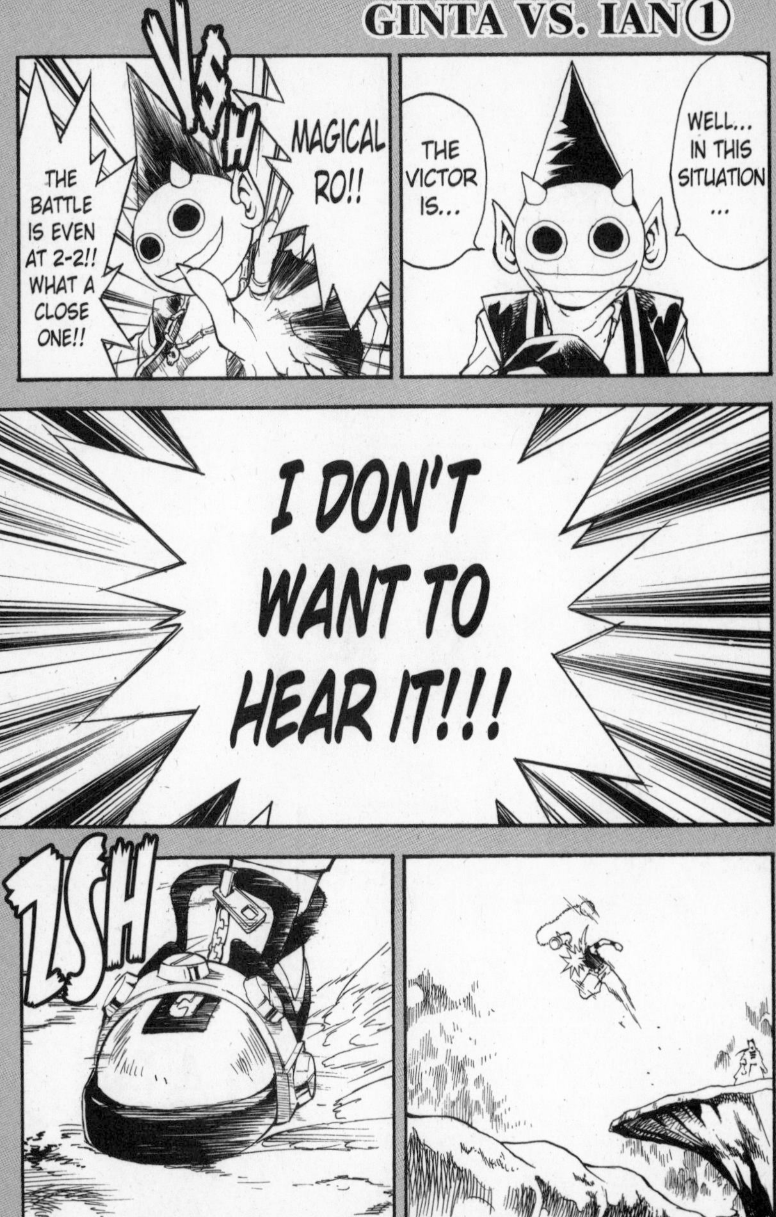
WELL... IN THIS SITUATION ...
THE VICTOR IS...
VSH
MAGICAL RO!!
THE BATTLE IS EVEN AT 2-2!! WHAT A CLOSE ONE!!
I DON'T WANT TO HEAR IT!!!
ZSH

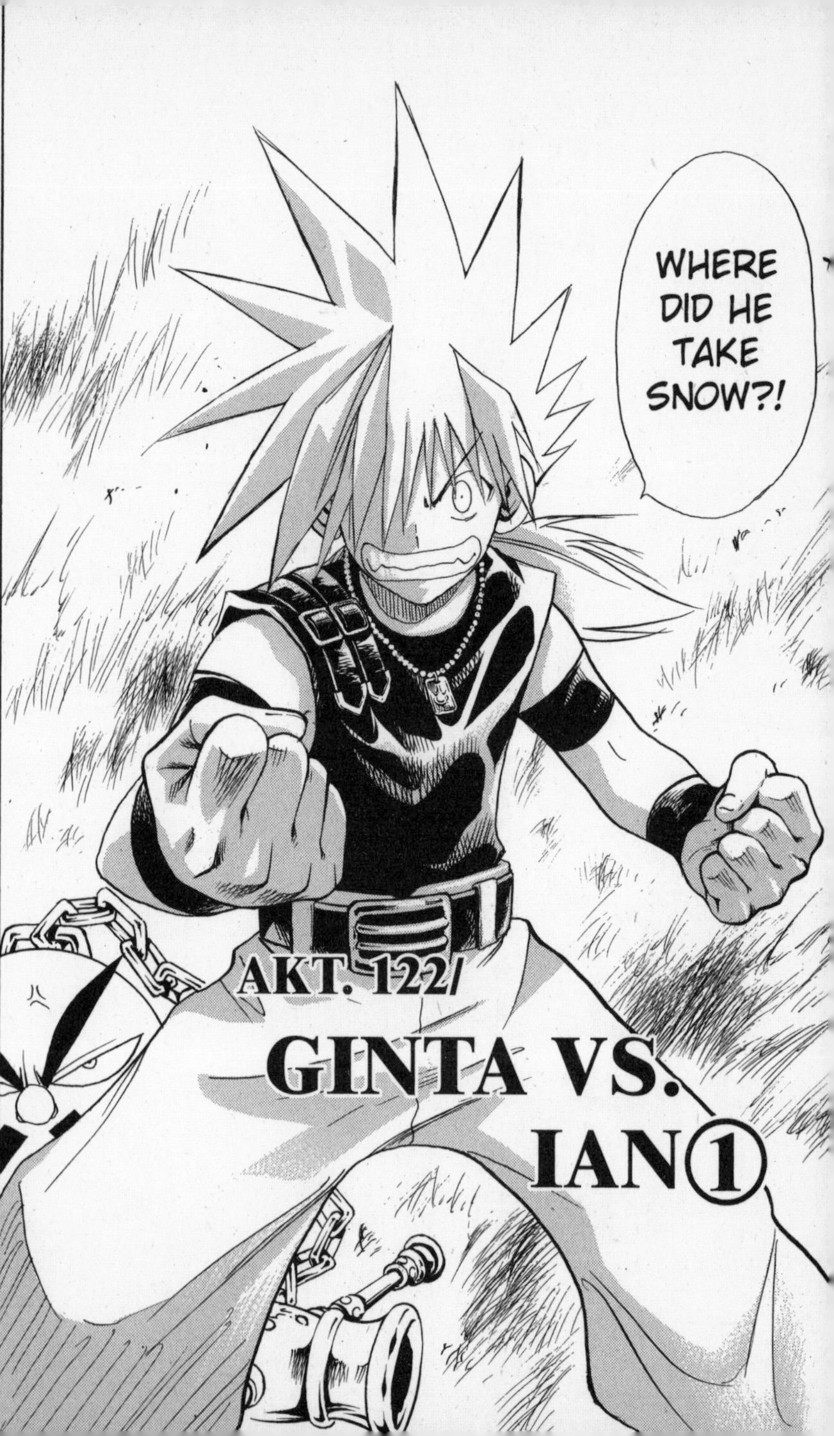
WHERE DID HE TAKE SNOW?!
AKT. 122/
GINTA VS. IAN①

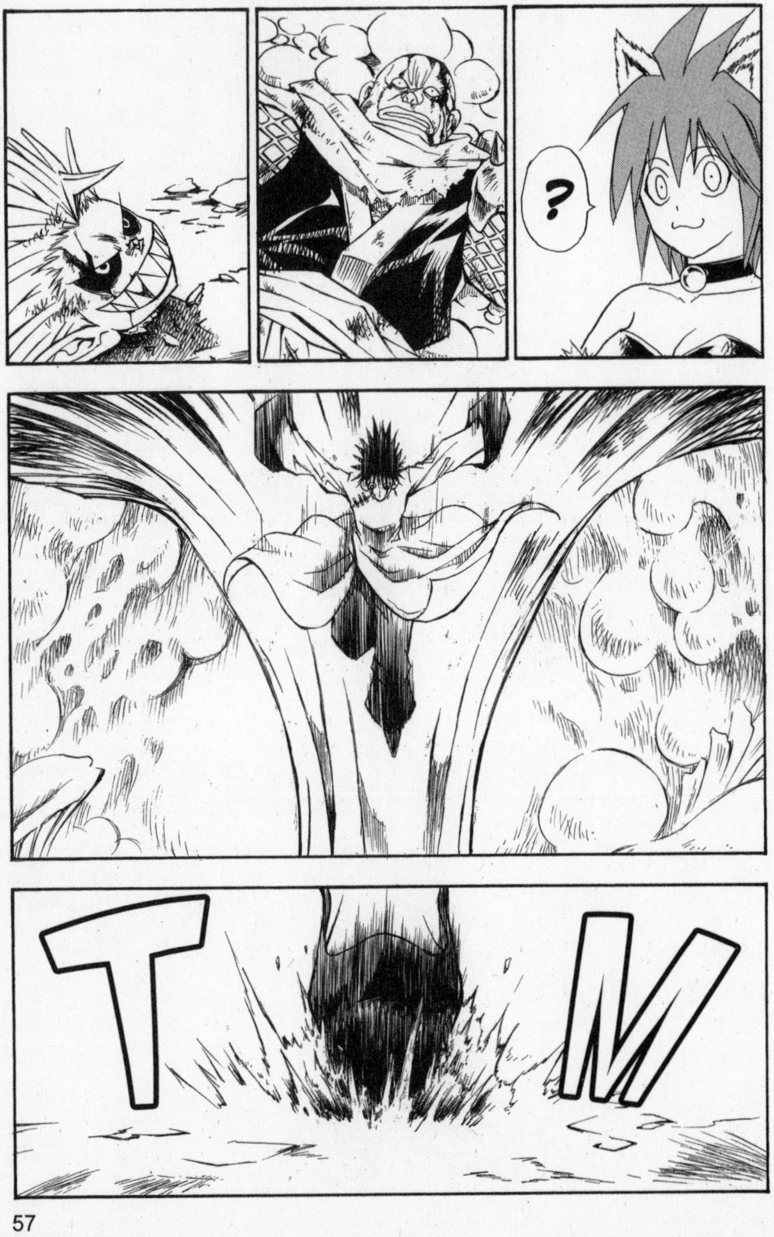
?
T M

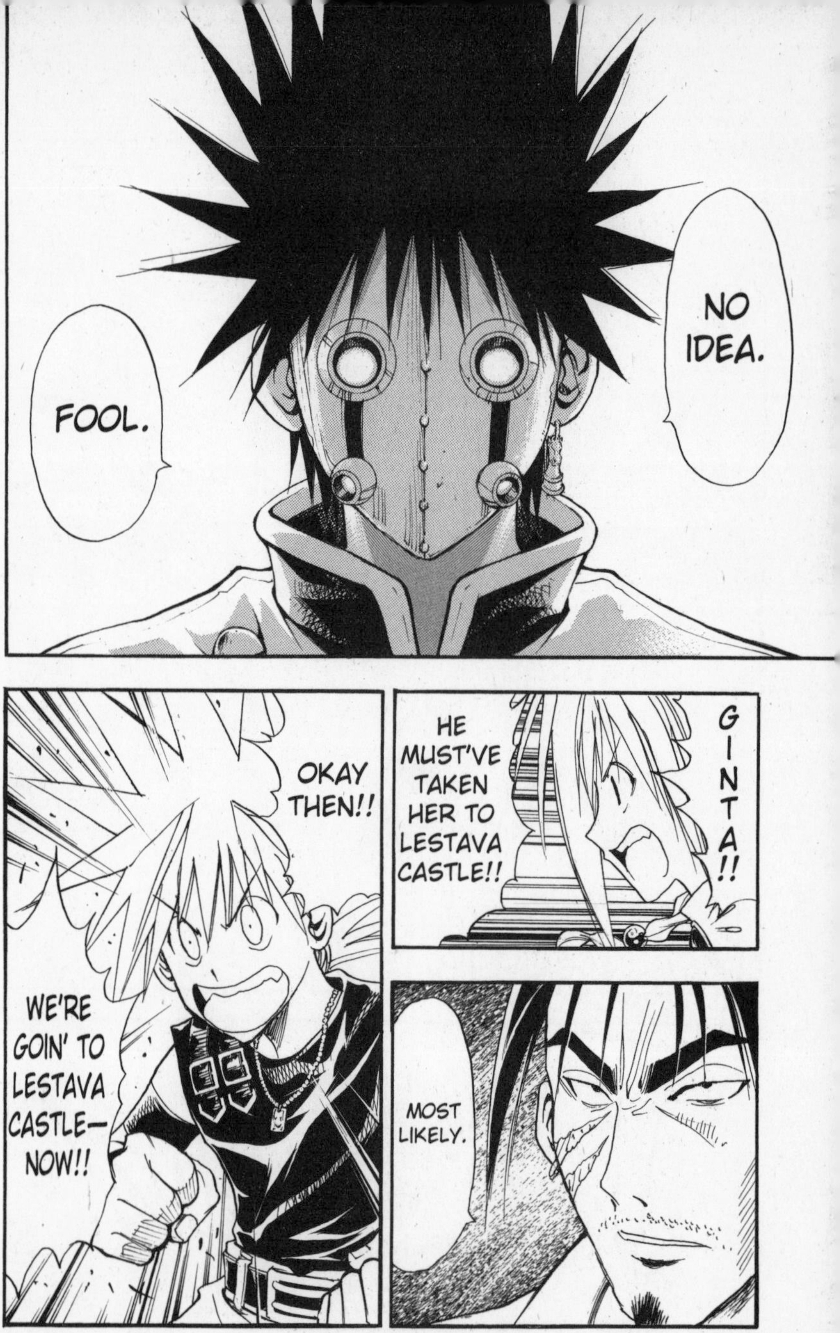
NO IDEA.
FOOL.
GINTA!!
HE MUST'VE TAKEN HER TO LESTAVA CASTLE!!
MOST LIKELY.
OKAY THEN!!
WE'RE GOIN' TO LESTAVA CASTLE—NOW!!

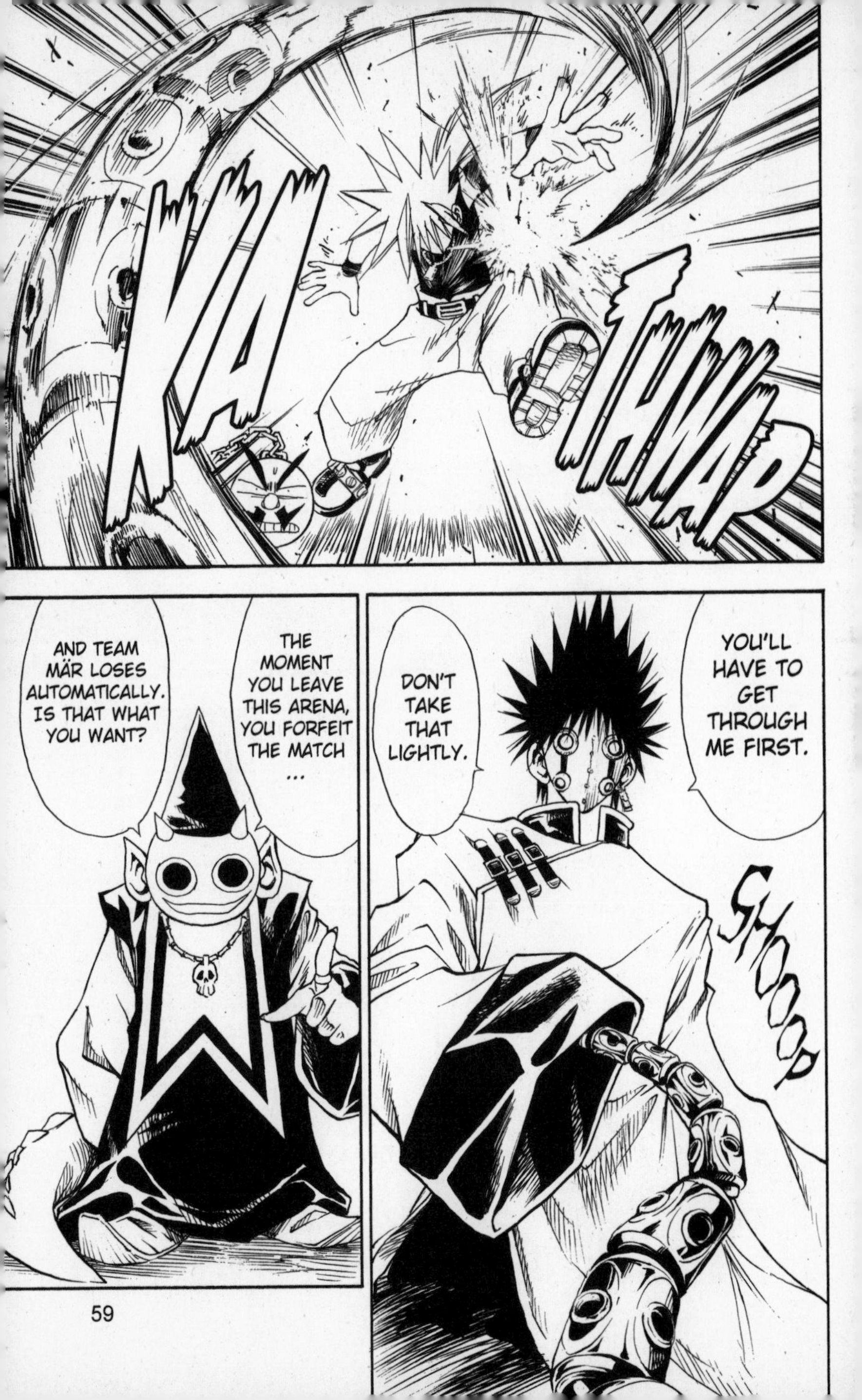
KA
THWAP
YOU'LL HAVE TO GET THROUGH ME FIRST.
DON'T TAKE THAT LIGHTLY.
SHOOOP
THE MOMENT YOU LEAVE THIS ARENA, YOU FORFEIT THE MATCH ...
AND TEAM MÄR LOSES AUTOMATICALLY. IS THAT WHAT YOU WANT?

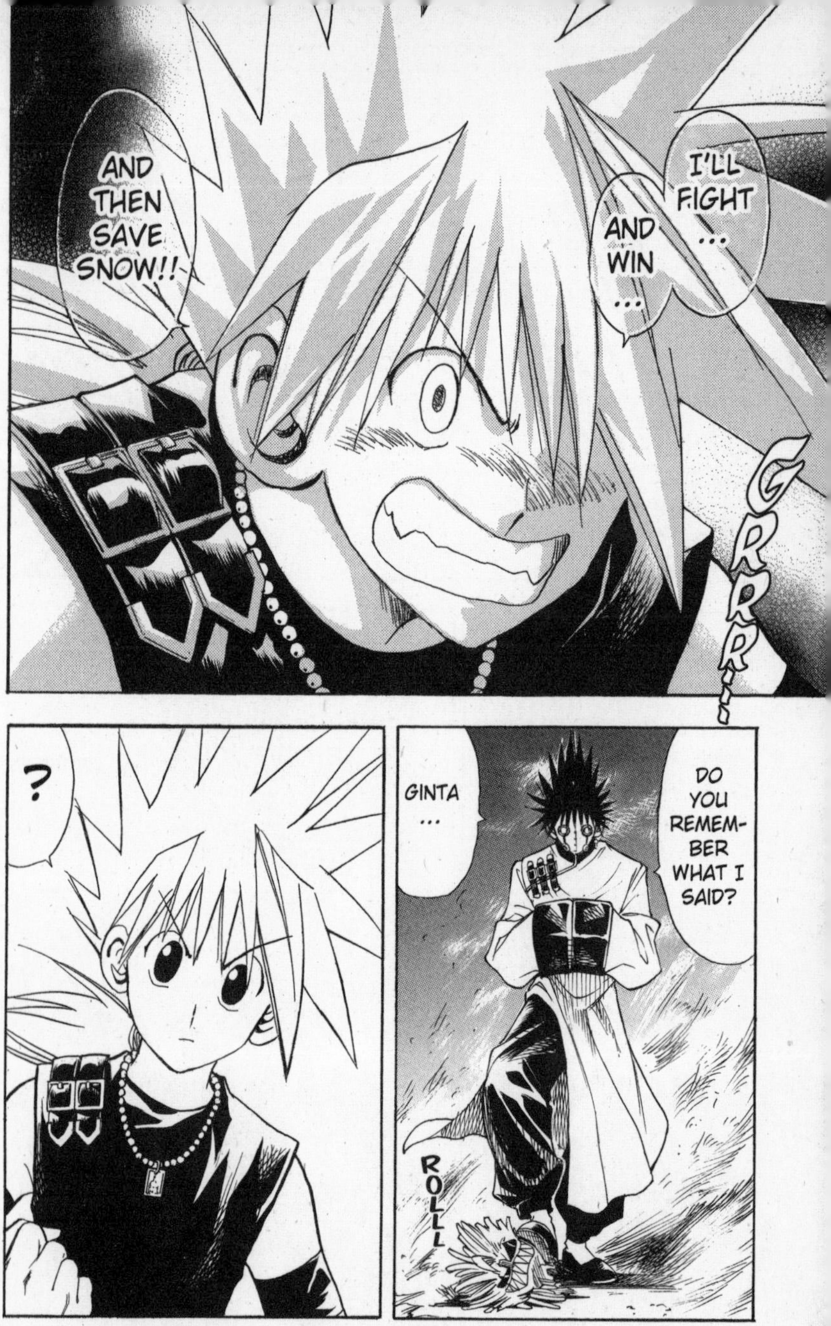
I'LL FIGHT...
AND WIN...
AND THEN SAVE SNOW!!
GRRR...
DO YOU REMEMBER WHAT I SAID?
GINTA...
ROLLL
?

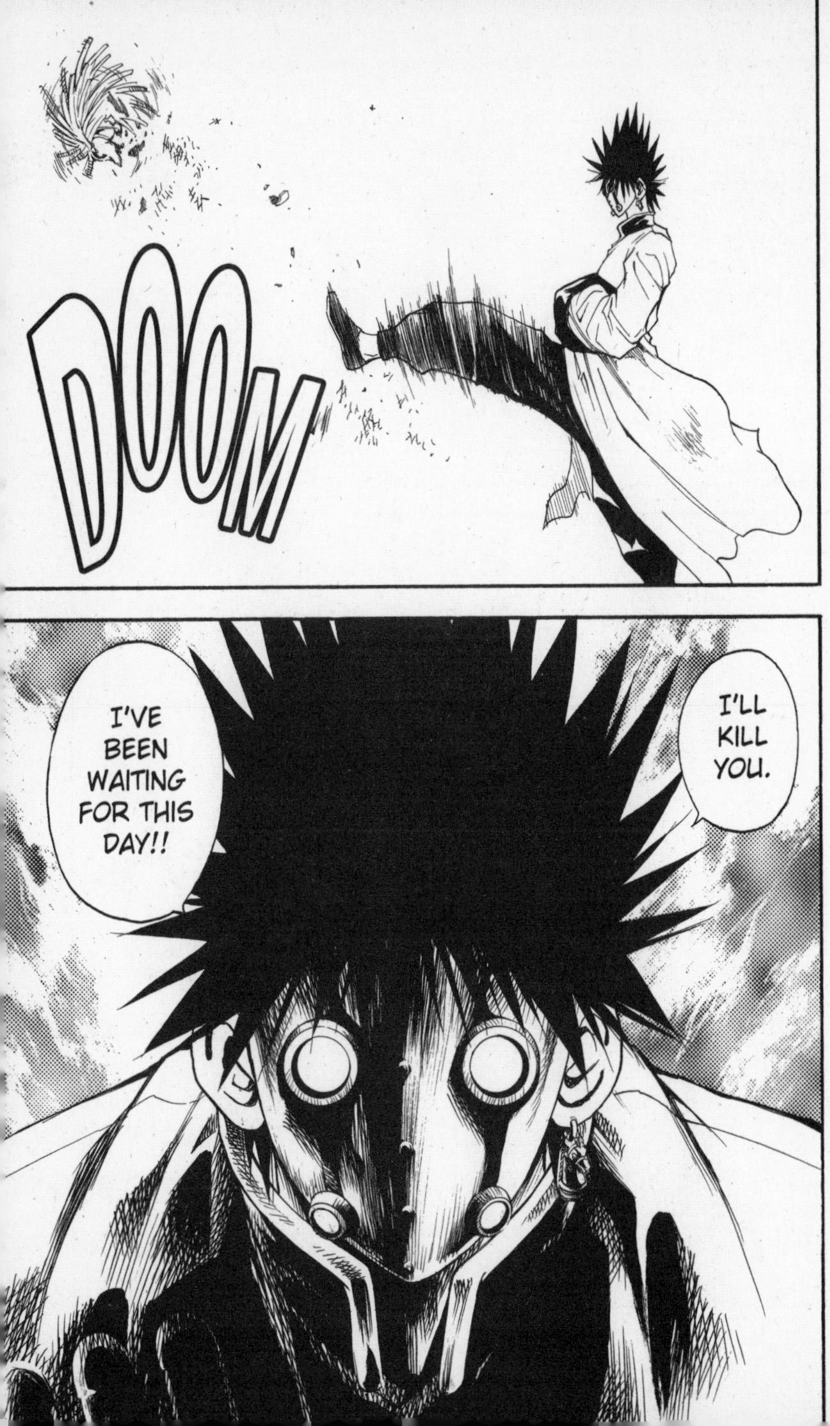
DOOM
I'LL KILL YOU.
I'VE BEEN WAITING FOR THIS DAY!!

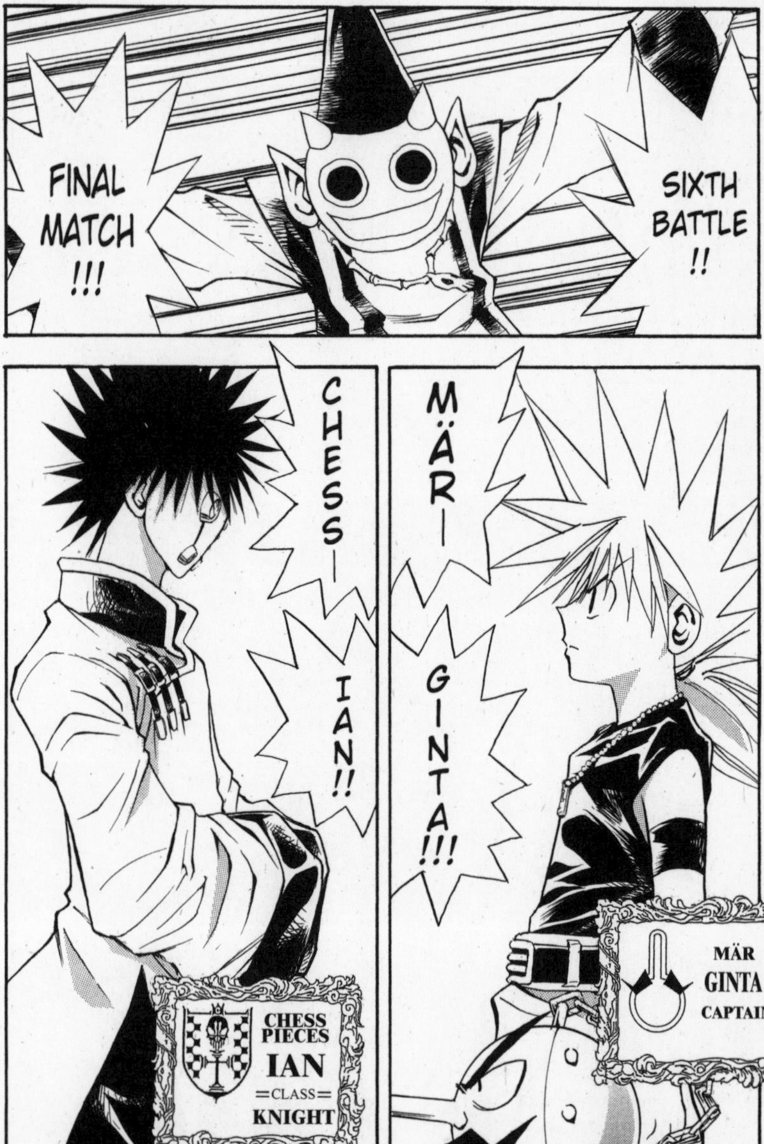
SIXTH BATTLE !!
FINAL MATCH !!!
MÄR— GINTA!!!
MÄR
GINTA
CAPTAIN
CHESS— IAN!!
CHESS PIECES
IAN
=CLASS=
KNIGHT

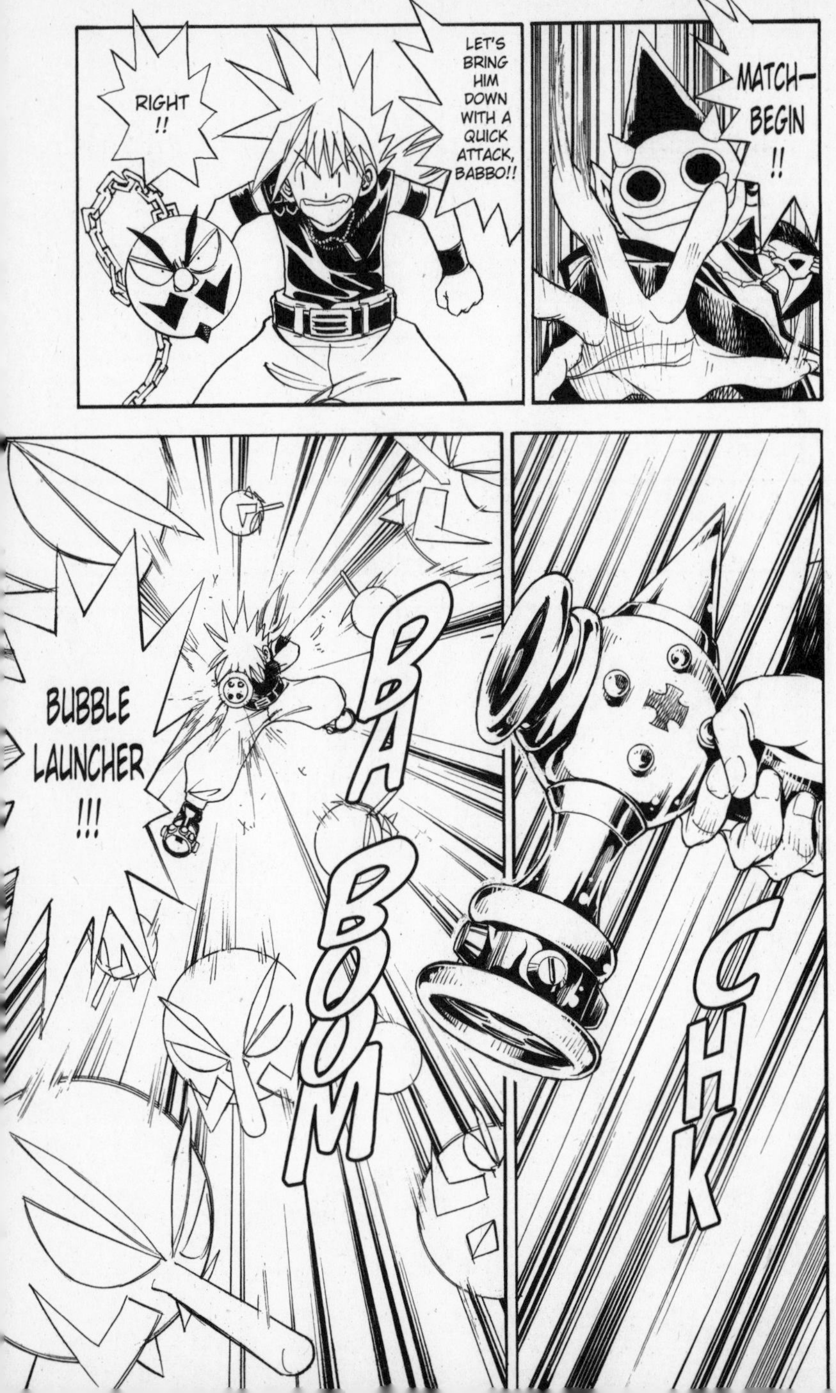
MATCH— BEGIN !!
LET'S BRING HIM DOWN WITH A QUICK ATTACK, BABBO!!
RIGHT !!
CHK
BUBBLE LAUNCHER !!!
BA BOOM

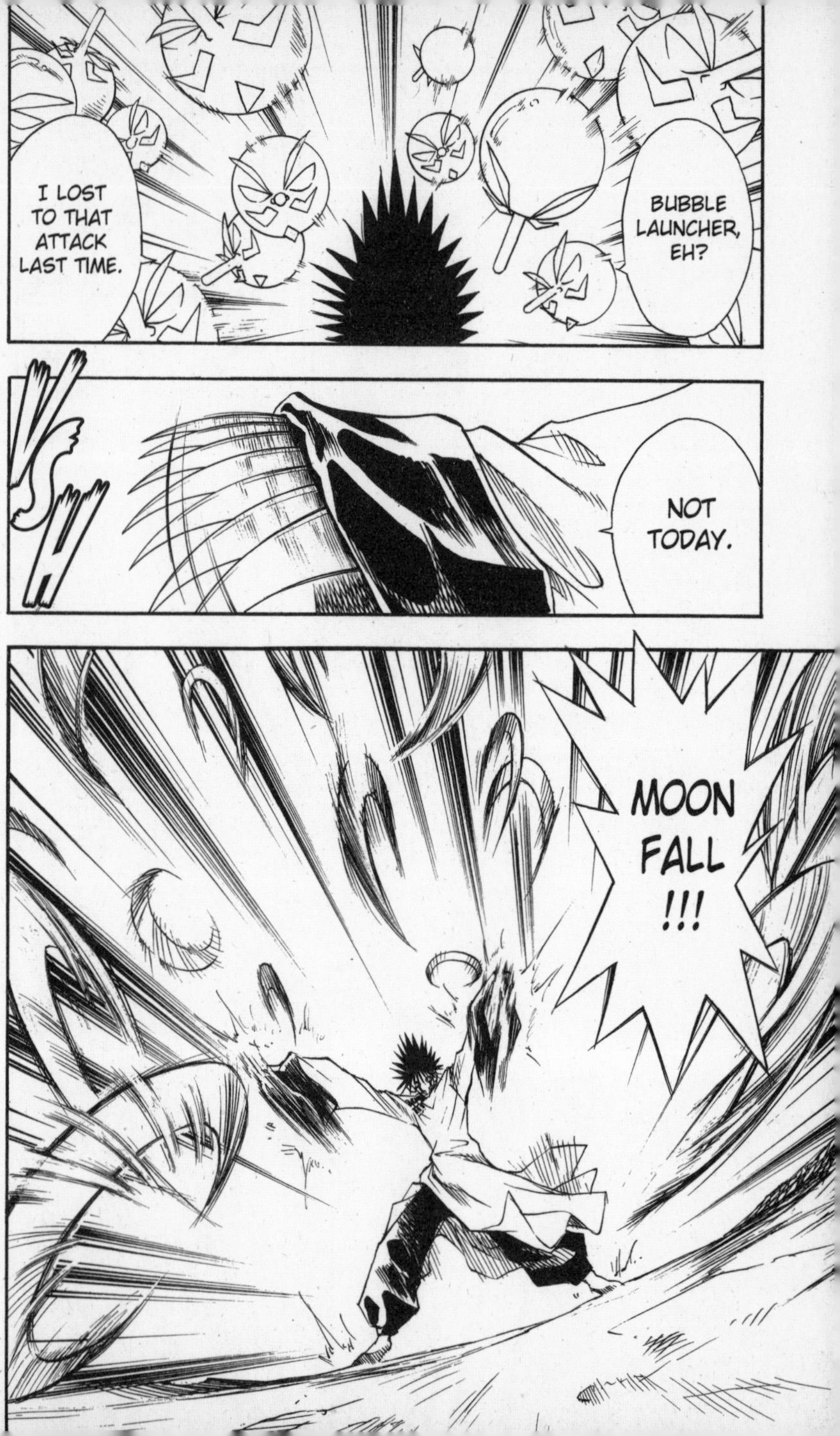
BUBBLE LAUNCHER, EH?
I LOST TO THAT ATTACK LAST TIME.
NOT TODAY.
MOON FALL !!!

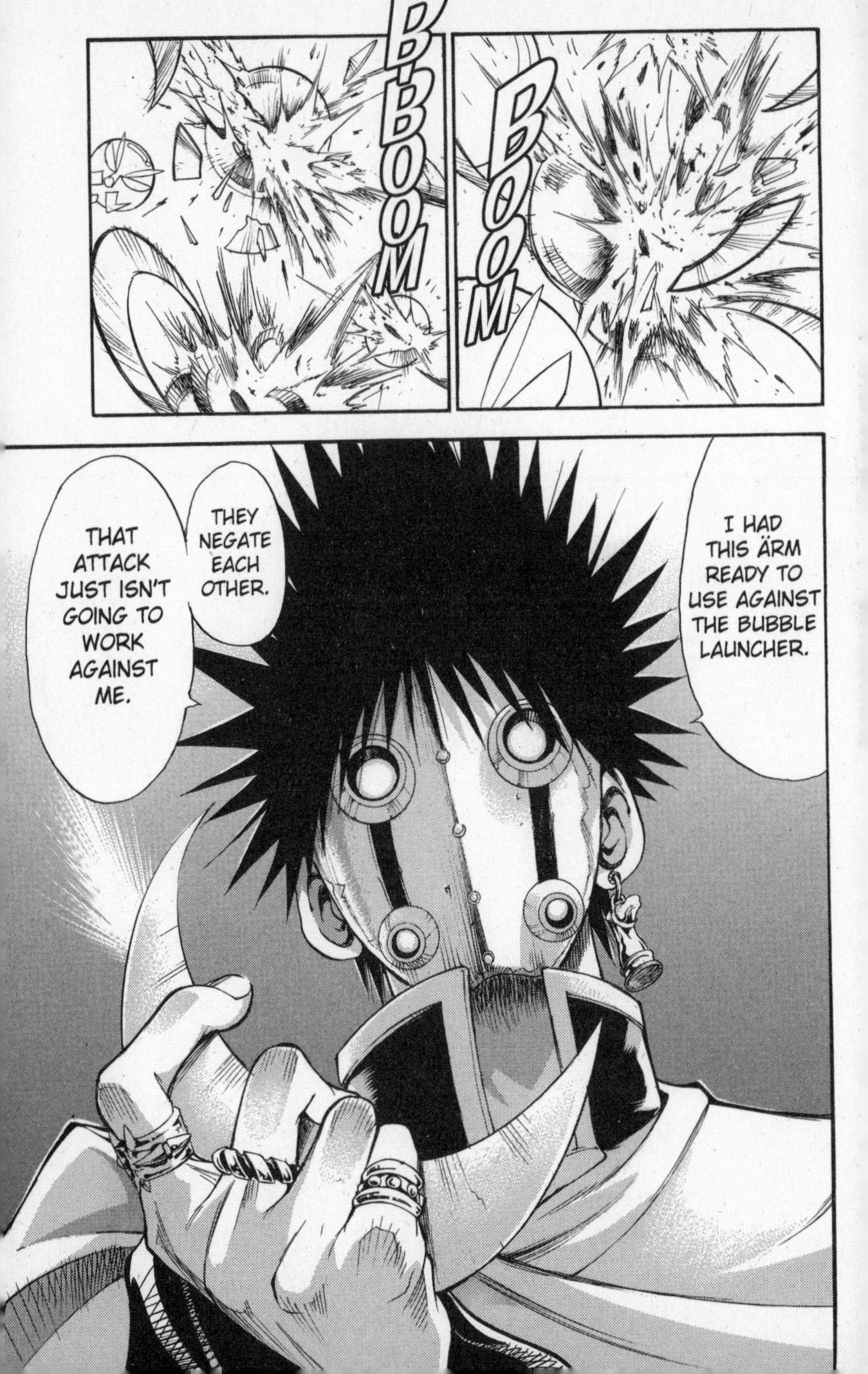

BOOM
BOOM
B-BOOM
I HAD THIS ÄRM READY TO USE AGAINST THE BUBBLE LAUNCHER.
THEY NEGATE EACH OTHER.
THAT ATTACK JUST ISN'T GOING TO WORK AGAINST ME.

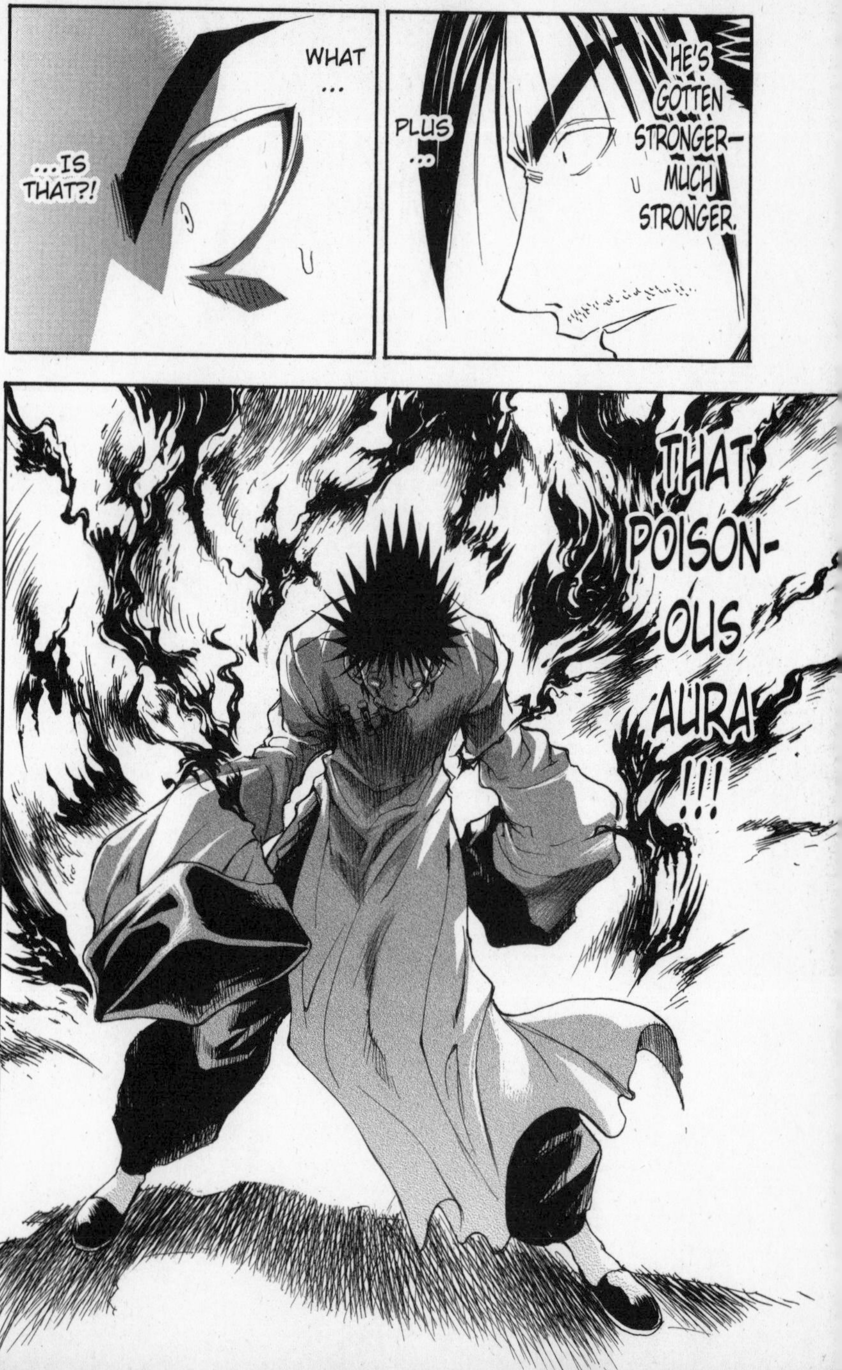
HE'S GOTTEN STRONGER—MUCH STRONGER.
PLUS...
WHAT...
...IS THAT?!
THAT POISON-OUS AURA!!!

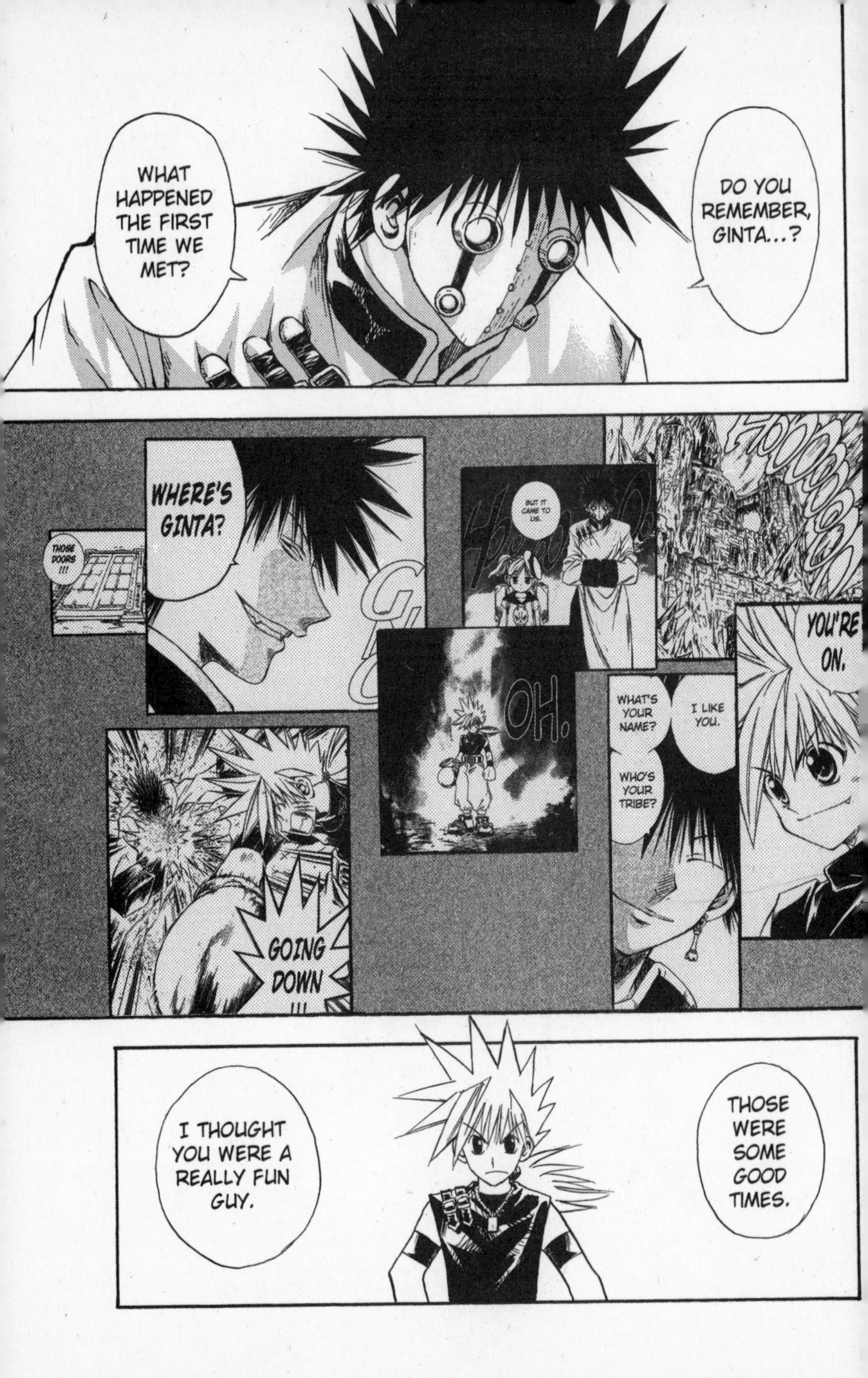
DO YOU REMEMBER, GINTA...?
WHAT HAPPENED THE FIRST TIME WE MET?
YOU'RE ON.
BUT IT CAME TO US.
WHERE'S GINTA?
THOSE DOORS !!!
I LIKE YOU.
WHAT'S YOUR NAME?
WHO'S YOUR TRIBE?
OH.
GOING DOWN !!!
THOSE WERE SOME GOOD TIMES.
I THOUGHT YOU WERE A REALLY FUN GUY.

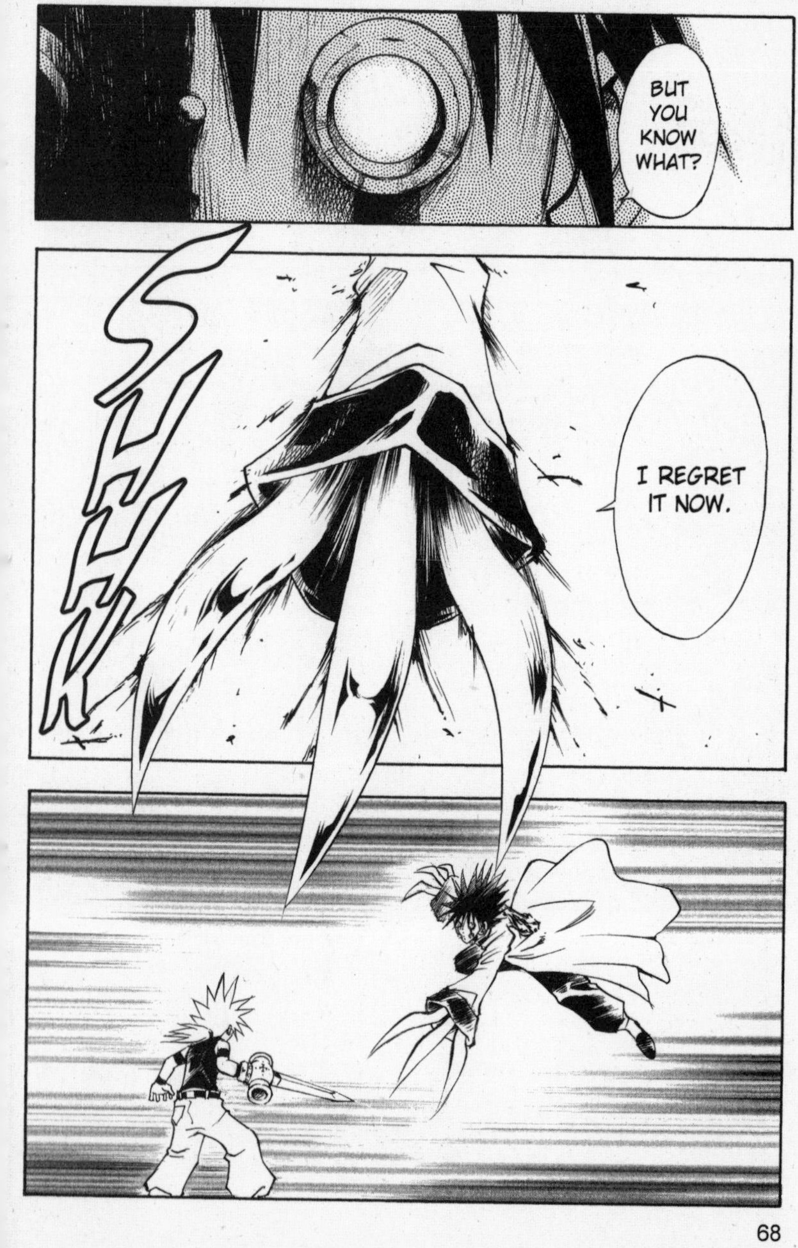
BUT YOU KNOW WHAT?
I REGRET IT NOW.

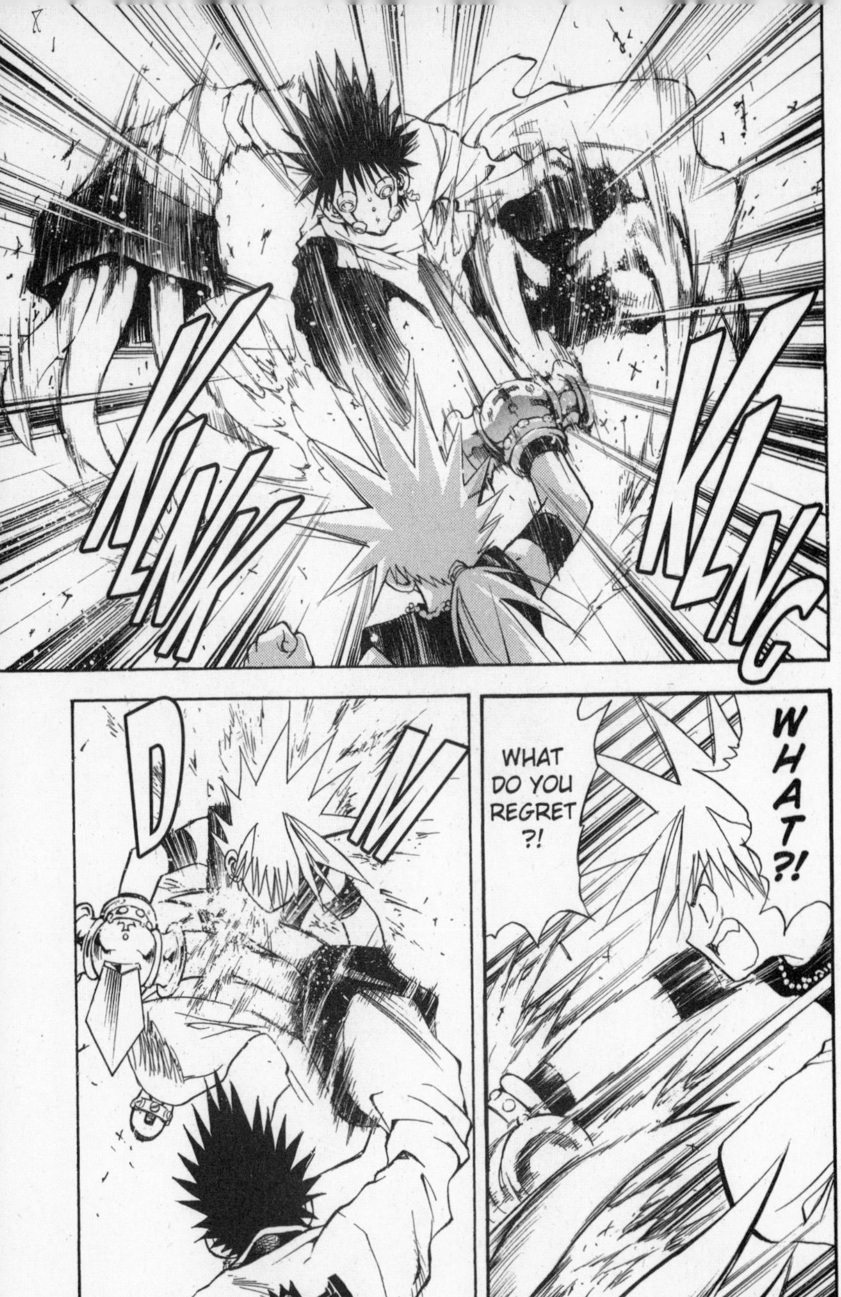
KLNG
KLNK
WHAT?!
WHAT DO YOU REGRET ?!
D
M

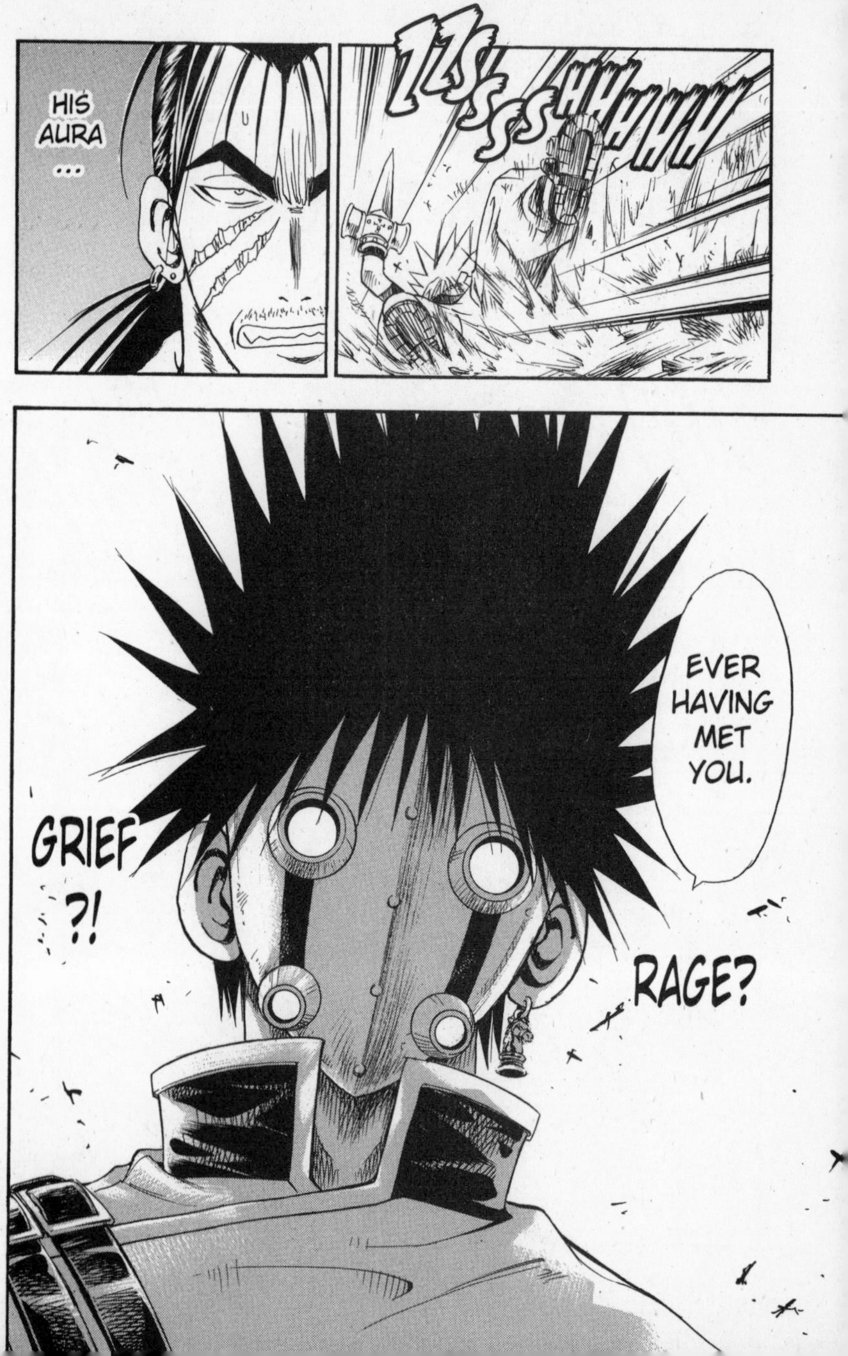
ZZSSSSHHHHHH
HIS AURA ...
EVER HAVING MET YOU.
RAGE?
GRIEF ?!

AKT. 123/ GINTA VS. IAN ②

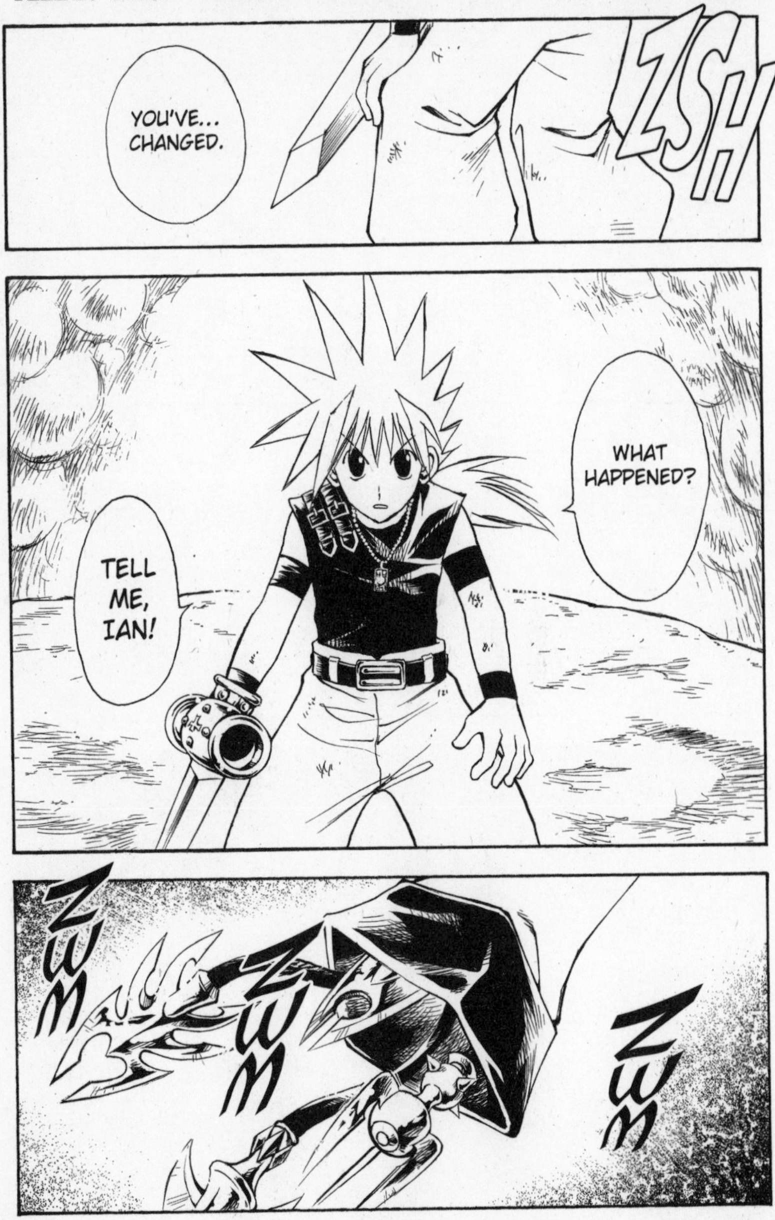
ZSH
YOU'VE... CHANGED.
WHAT HAPPENED?
TELL ME, IAN!

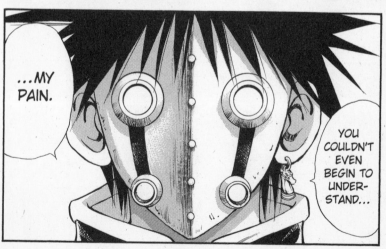

...MY PAIN.

YOU COULDN'T EVEN BEGIN TO UNDER-STAND...

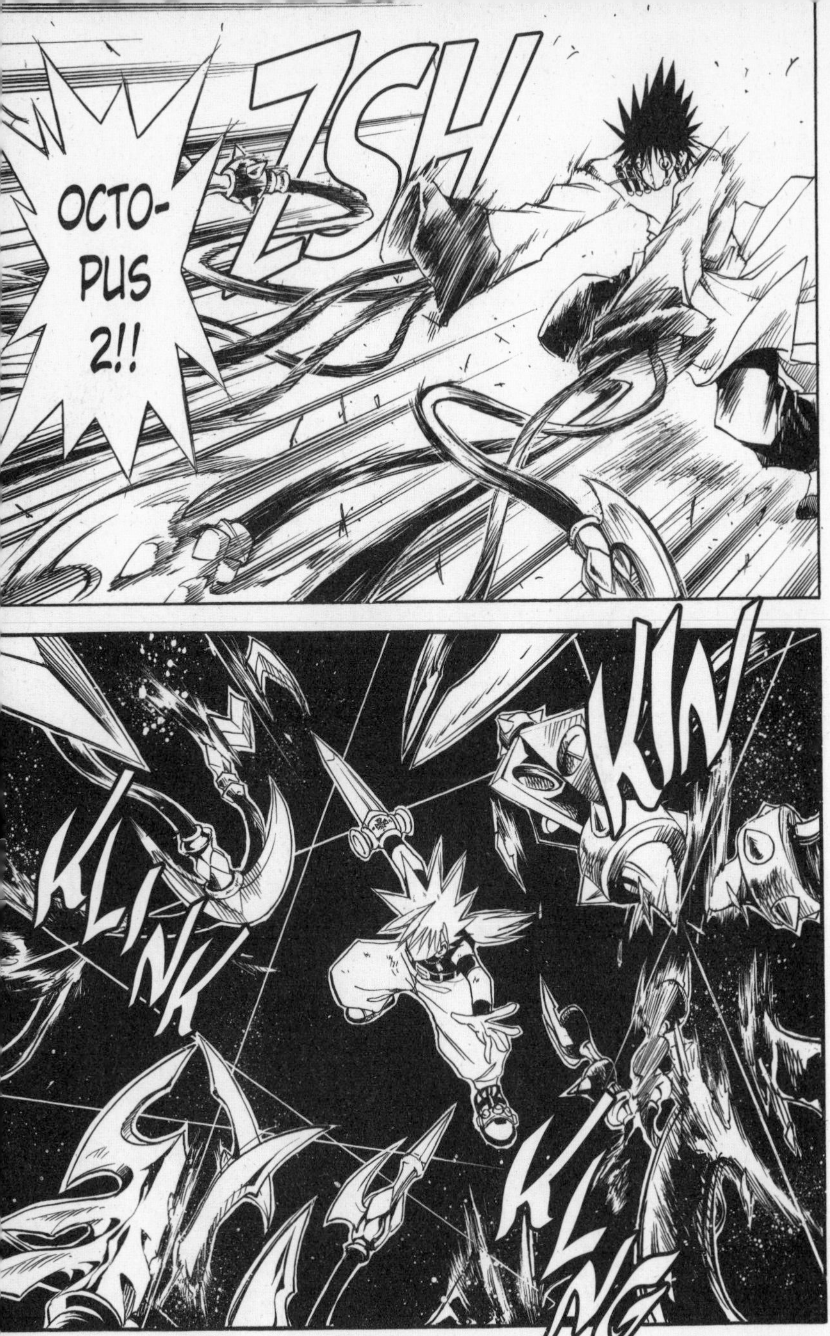
ZSH
OCTO-PUS 2!!
KIN
KLINK
KLANG

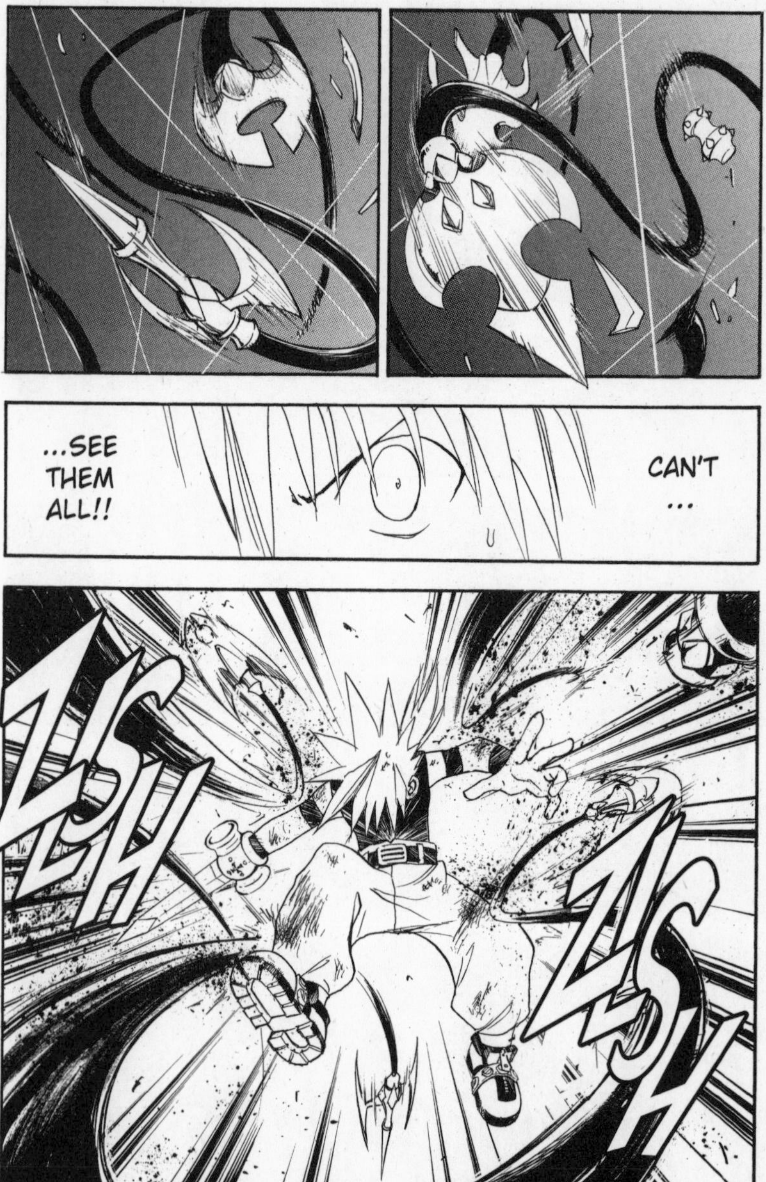
CAN'T
...
...SEE
THEM
ALL!!

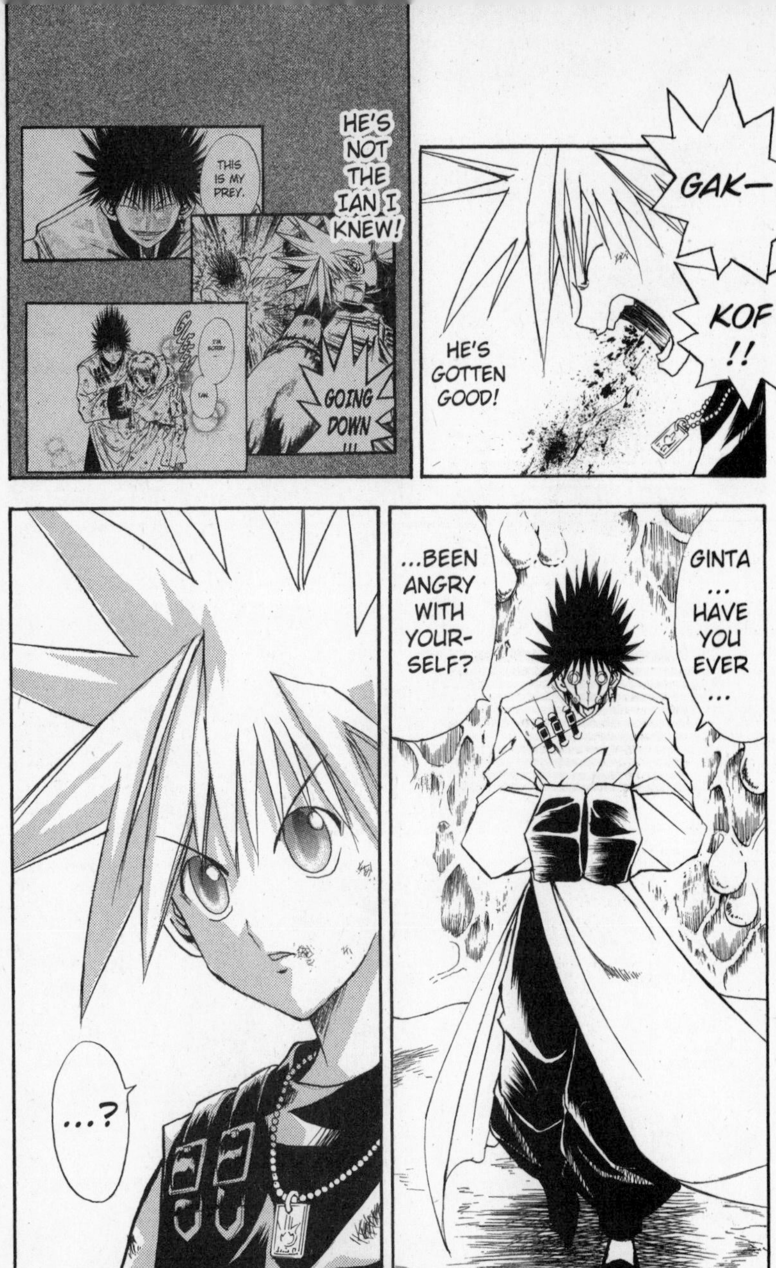
GAK—
KOF!!
HE'S GOTTEN GOOD!
HE'S NOT THE IAN I KNEW!
THIS IS MY PREY.
GOING DOWN!!!
I'M SORRY
IAN.
GINTA... HAVE YOU EVER...
...BEEN ANGRY WITH YOUR-SELF?
...?

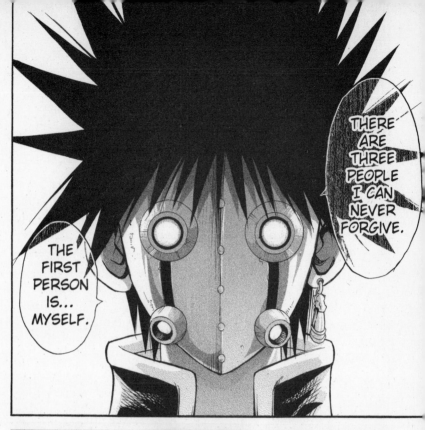

THERE ARE THREE PEOPLE I CAN NEVER FORGIVE.

THE FIRST PERSON IS... MYSELF.

WHERE'S GINTA?

THAT DAY... THE START OF THE SECOND MÄR HEAVEN WAR...

DOG-BOY!

I DISOBEYED PHANTOM'S ORDERS AND WENT TO SEE YOU.

BECAUSE OF THAT, GIDO WAS...

GIDO? THAT PAWN?

WHAT HAPPENED TO HER?

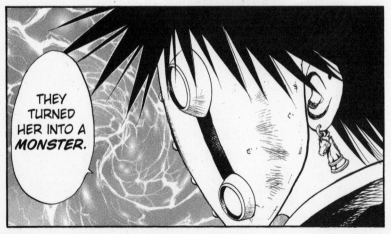

THEY TURNED HER INTO A *MONSTER*.

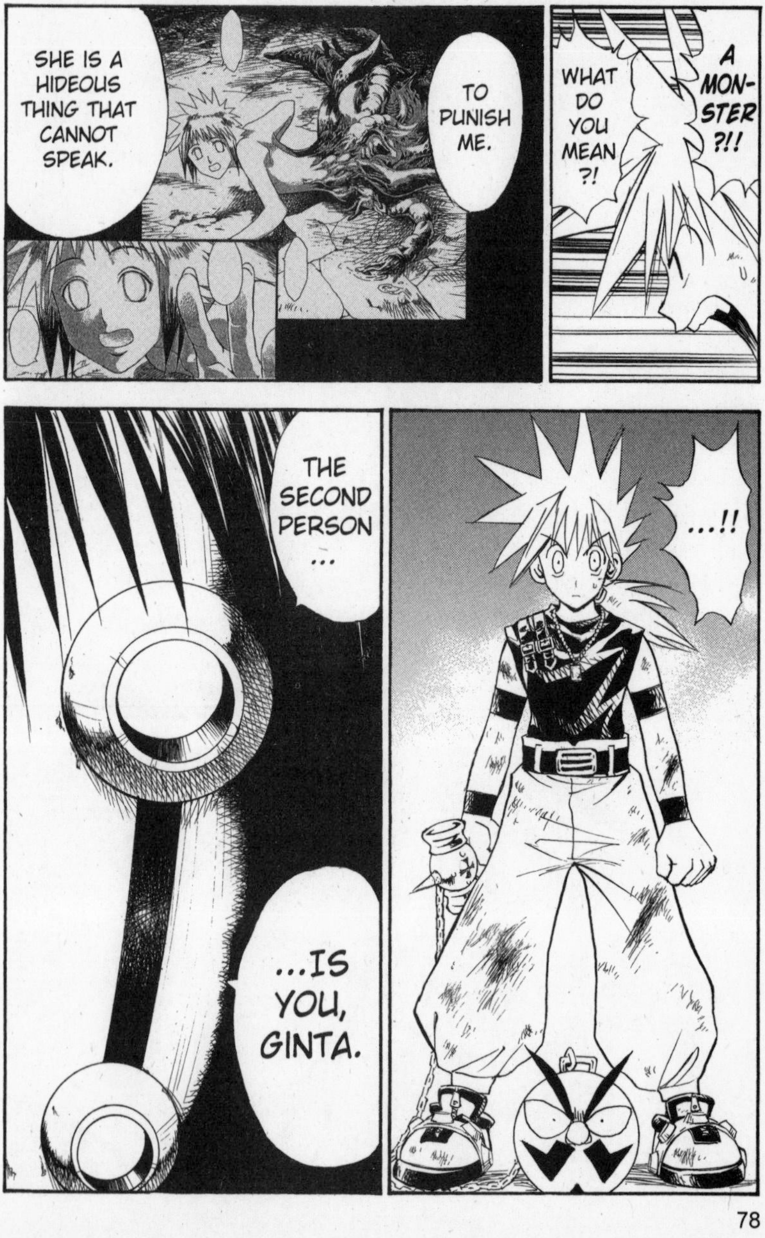
A MONSTER?!!
WHAT DO YOU MEAN?!
TO PUNISH ME.
SHE IS A HIDEOUS THING THAT CANNOT SPEAK.
...!!
THE SECOND PERSON ...
...IS YOU, GINTA.

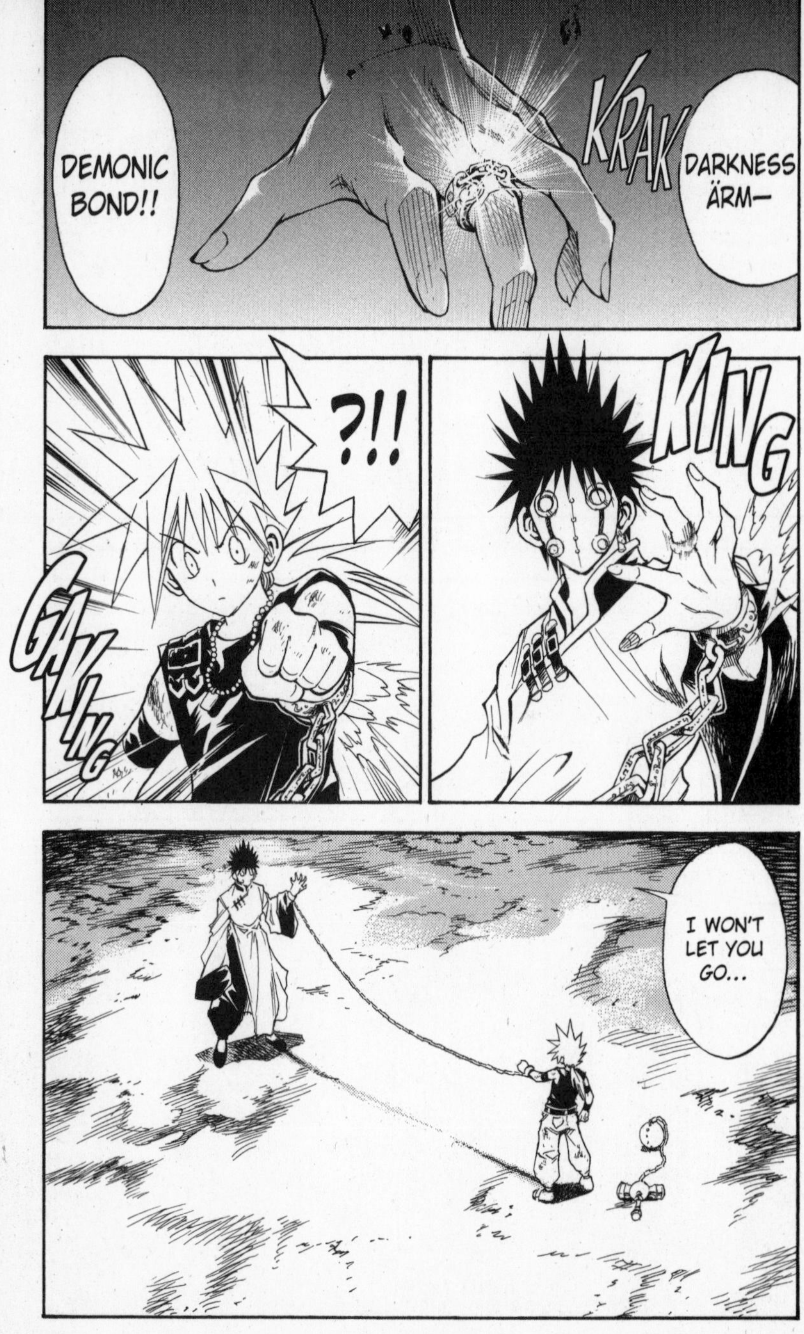
DARKNESS ÄRM—
KRAK
DEMONIC BOND!!
KING
?!!
GAKING
I WON'T LET YOU GO...

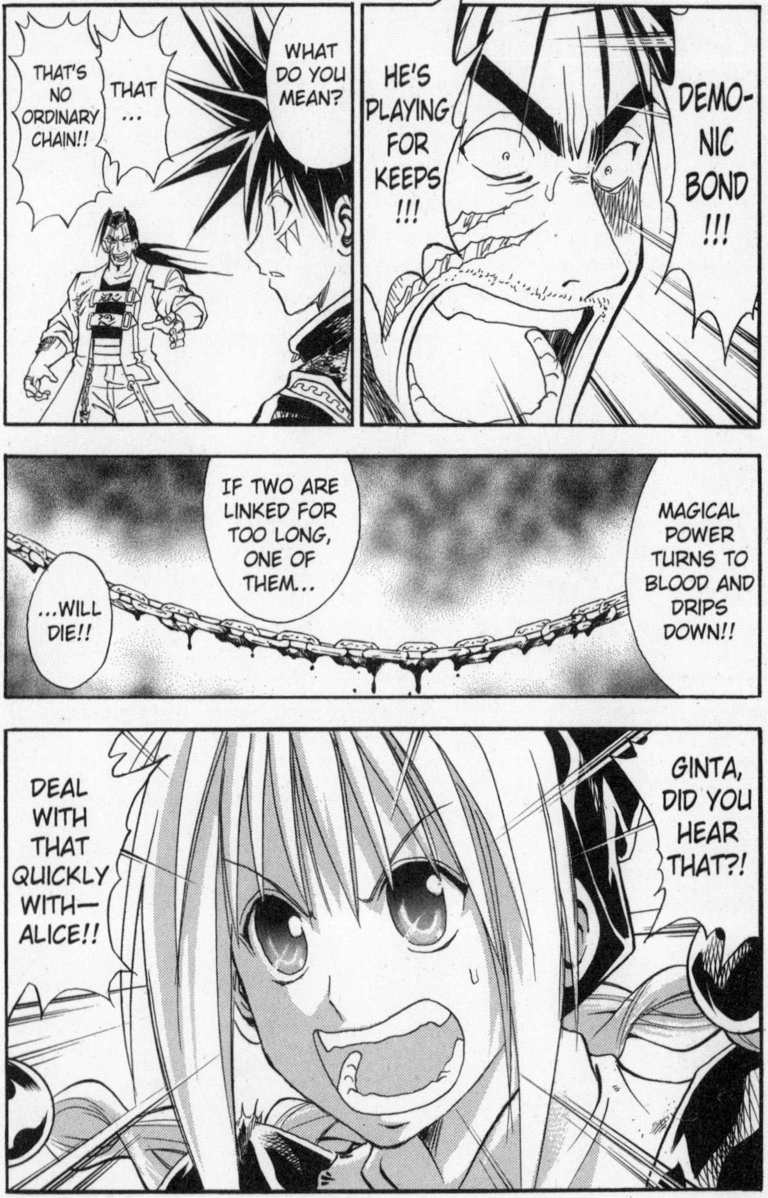
DEMO-NIC BOND!!!
HE'S PLAYING FOR KEEPS!!!
WHAT DO YOU MEAN?
THAT...
THAT'S NO ORDINARY CHAIN!!
MAGICAL POWER TURNS TO BLOOD AND DRIPS DOWN!!
IF TWO ARE LINKED FOR TOO LONG, ONE OF THEM...
...WILL DIE!!
GINTA, DID YOU HEAR THAT?!
DEAL WITH THAT QUICKLY WITH— ALICE!!

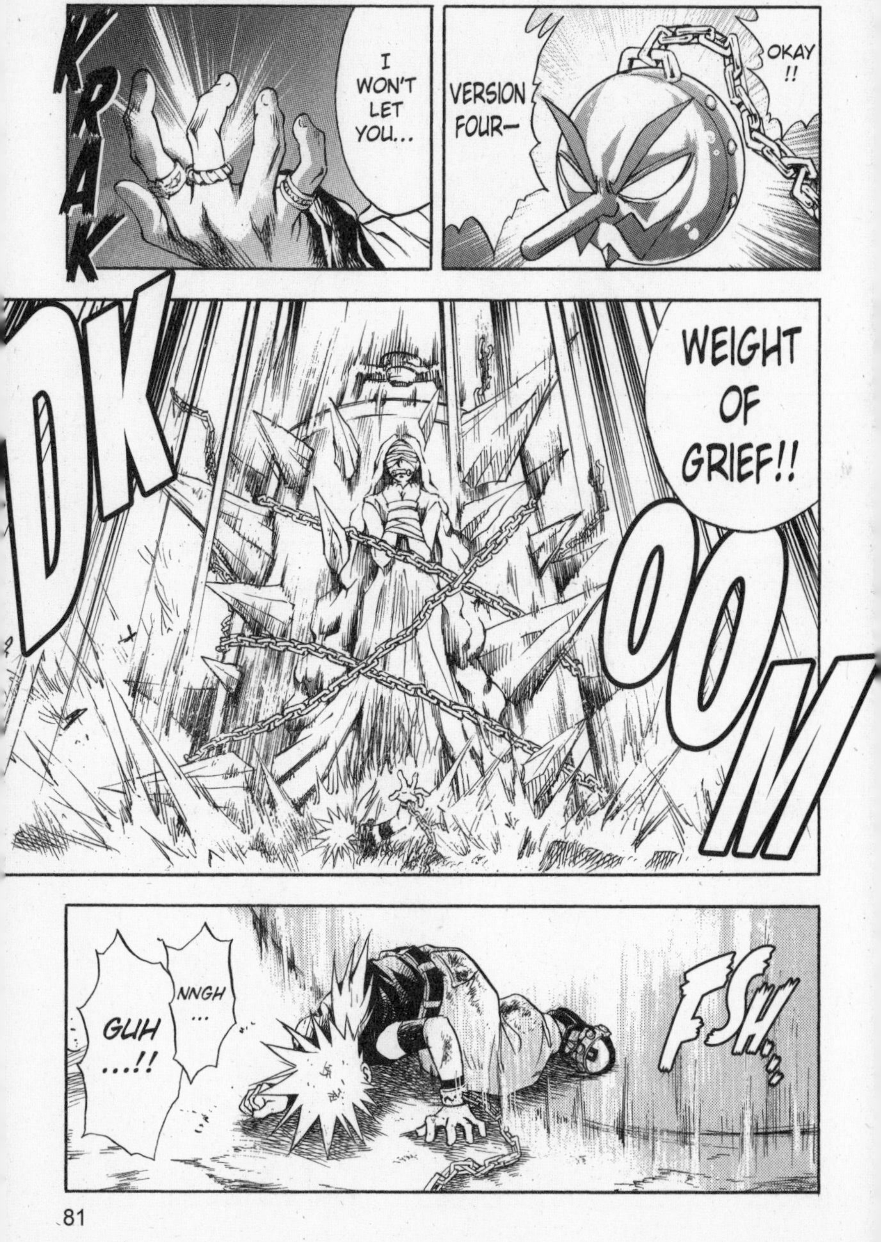
OKAY !!
VERSION FOUR—
I WON'T LET YOU...
KRAK
WEIGHT OF GRIEF!!
DK
OOM
FSH...
NNGH ...
GUH ...!!

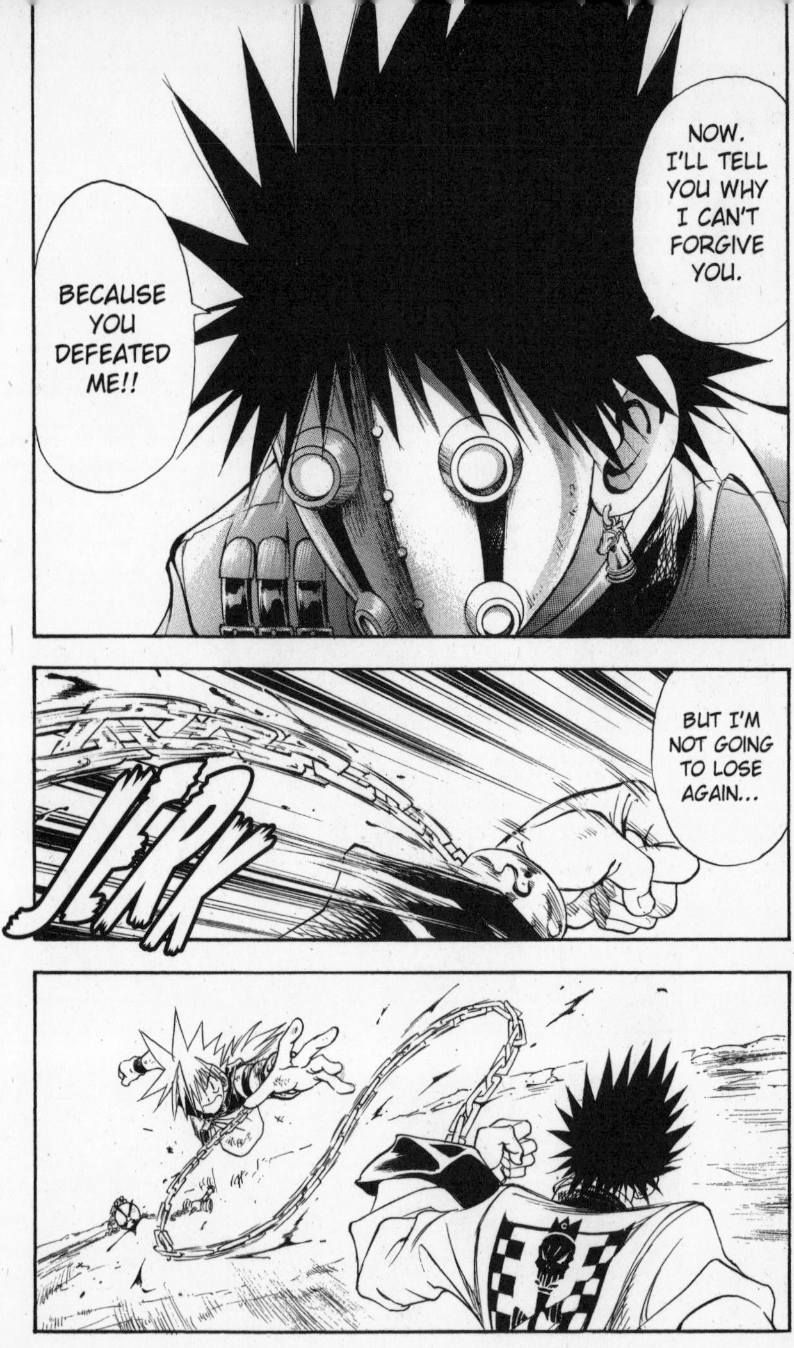
NOW. I'LL TELL YOU WHY I CAN'T FORGIVE YOU.
BECAUSE YOU DEFEATED ME!!
BUT I'M NOT GOING TO LOSE AGAIN...

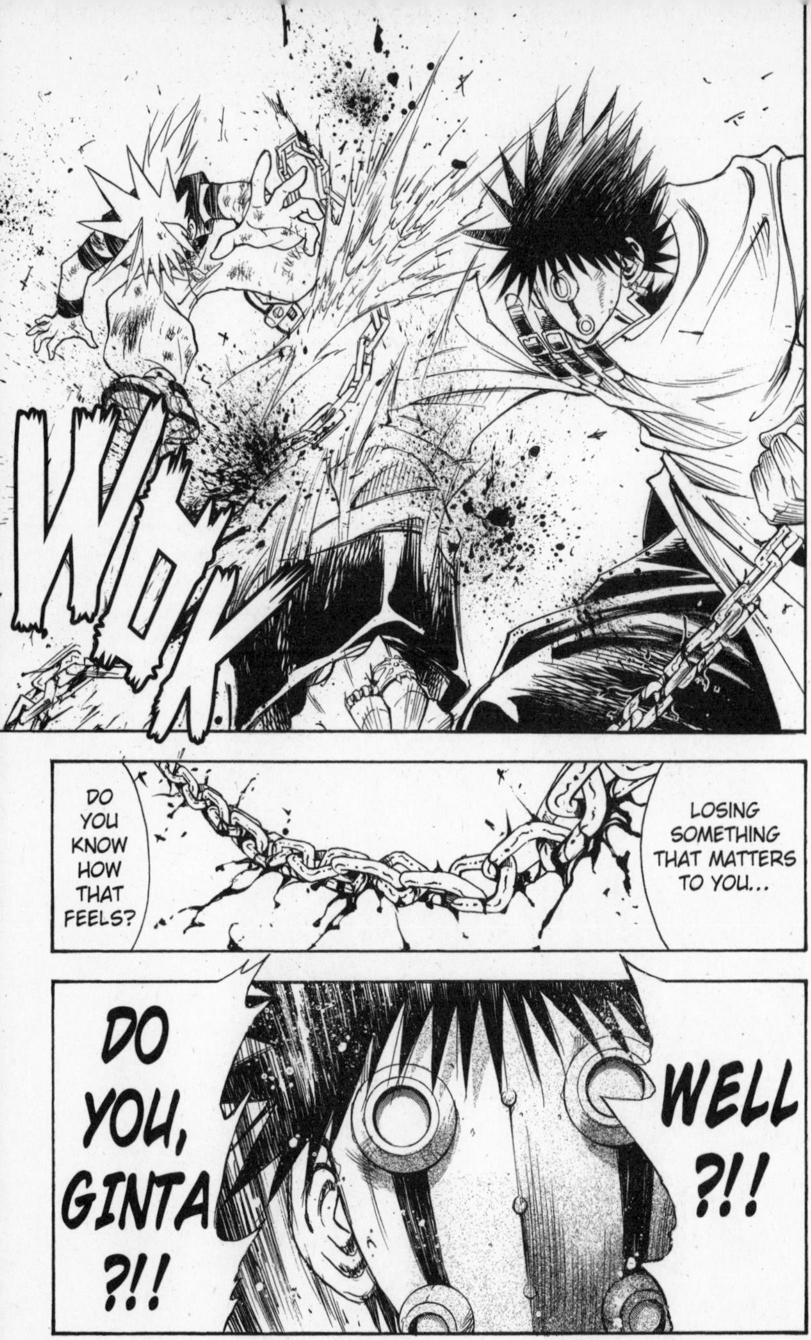
WHAK
LOSING SOMETHING THAT MATTERS TO YOU...
DO YOU KNOW HOW THAT FEELS?
WELL ?!!
DO YOU, GINTA ?!!

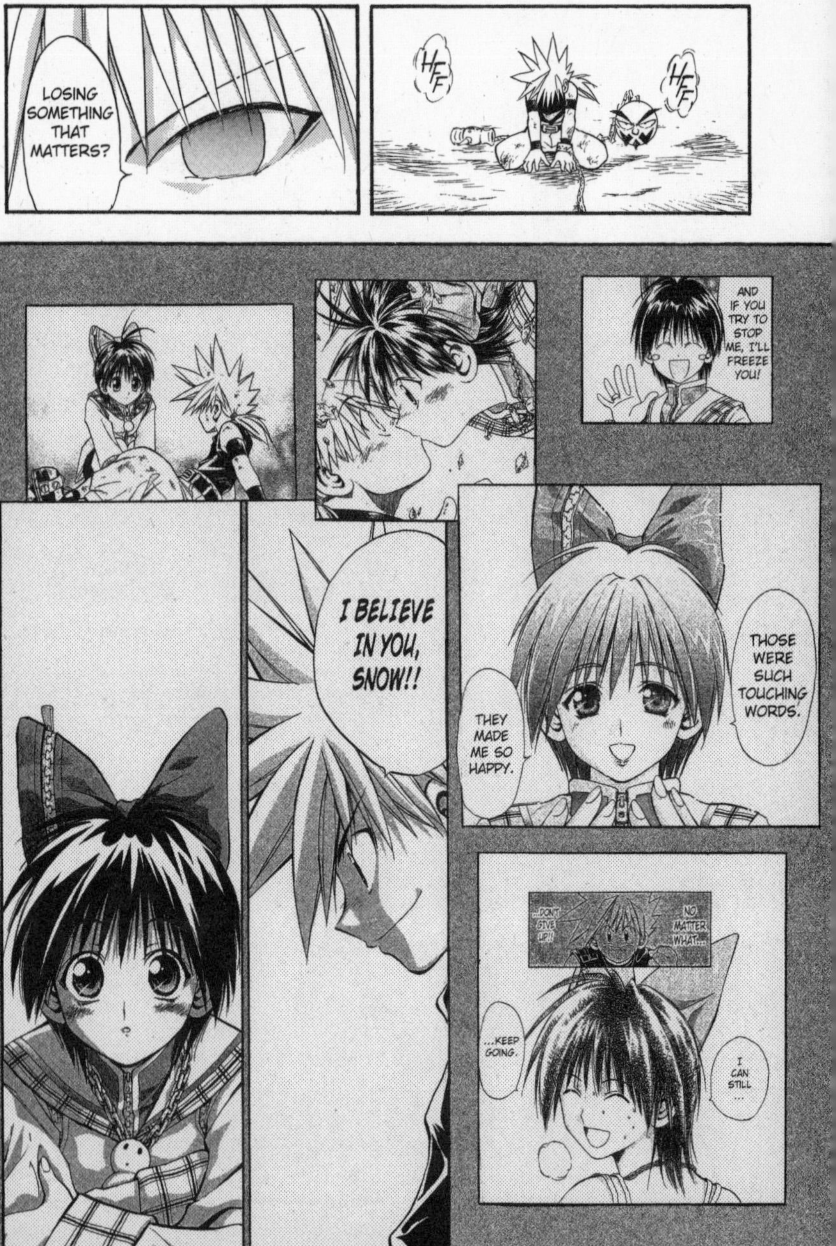
HFF
HFF
LOSING SOMETHING THAT MATTERS?
AND IF YOU TRY TO STOP ME, I'LL FREEZE YOU!
THOSE WERE SUCH TOUCHING WORDS.
THEY MADE ME SO HAPPY.
NO MATTER WHAT...
...DON'T GIVE UP!!
I CAN STILL...
...KEEP GOING.
I BELIEVE IN YOU, SNOW!!

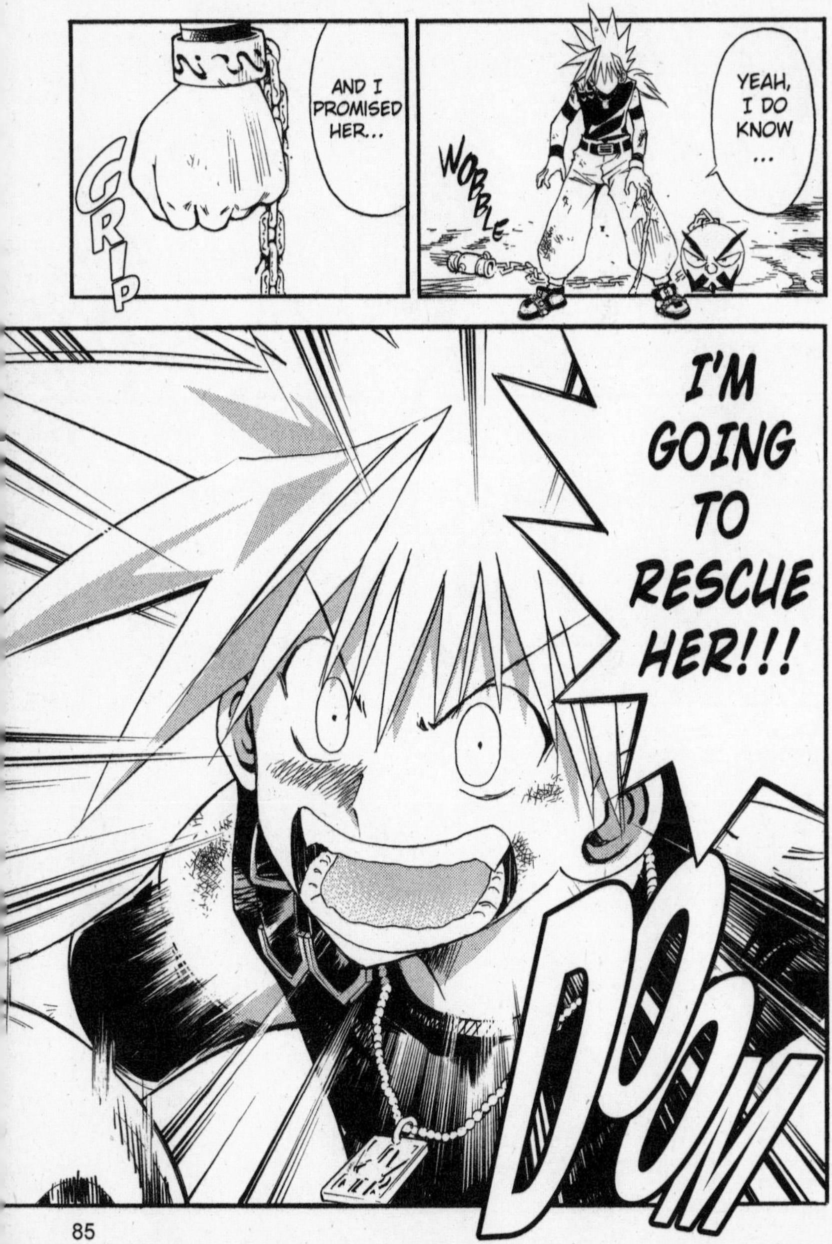
YEAH, I DO KNOW ...
WOBBLE
AND I PROMISED HER...
GRIP
I'M GOING TO RESCUE HER!!!

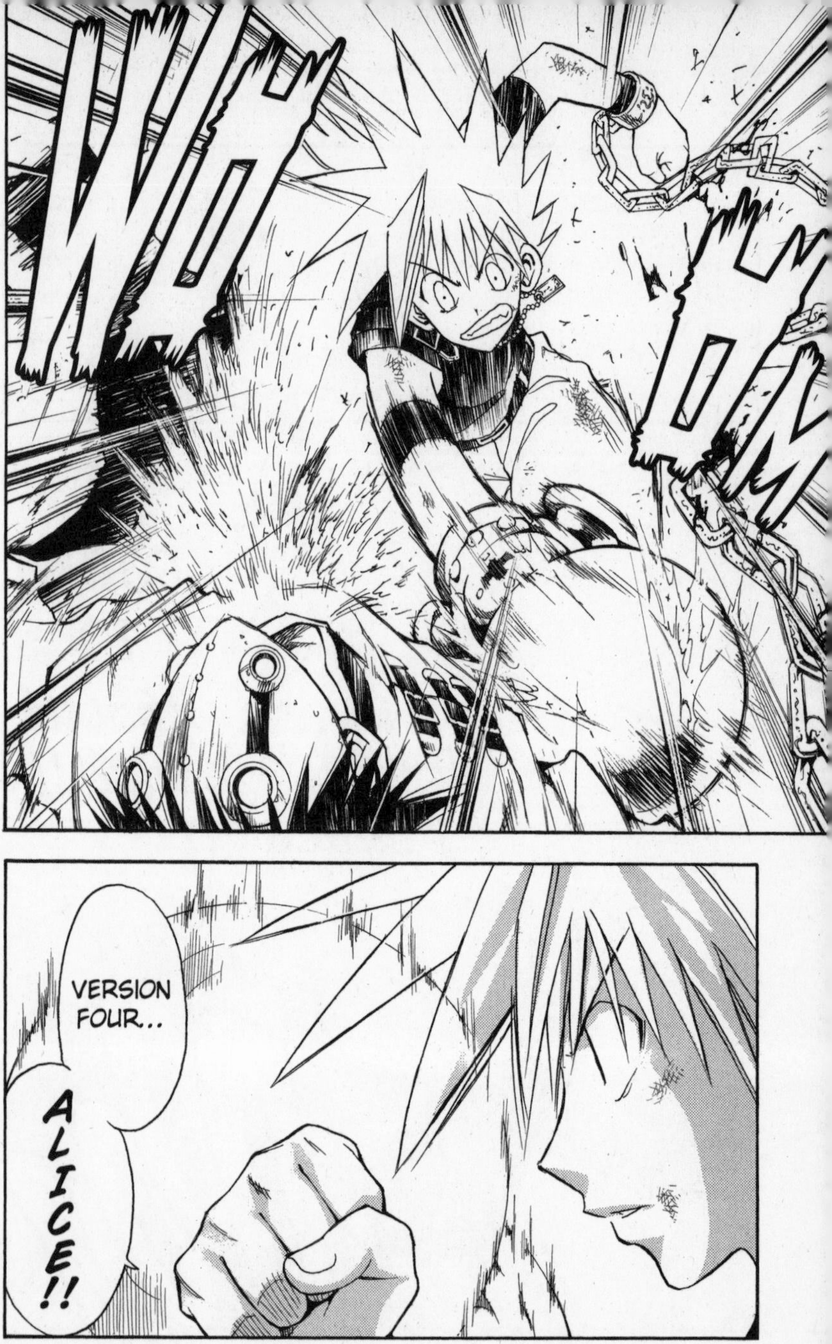
VERSION FOUR...
ALICE!!

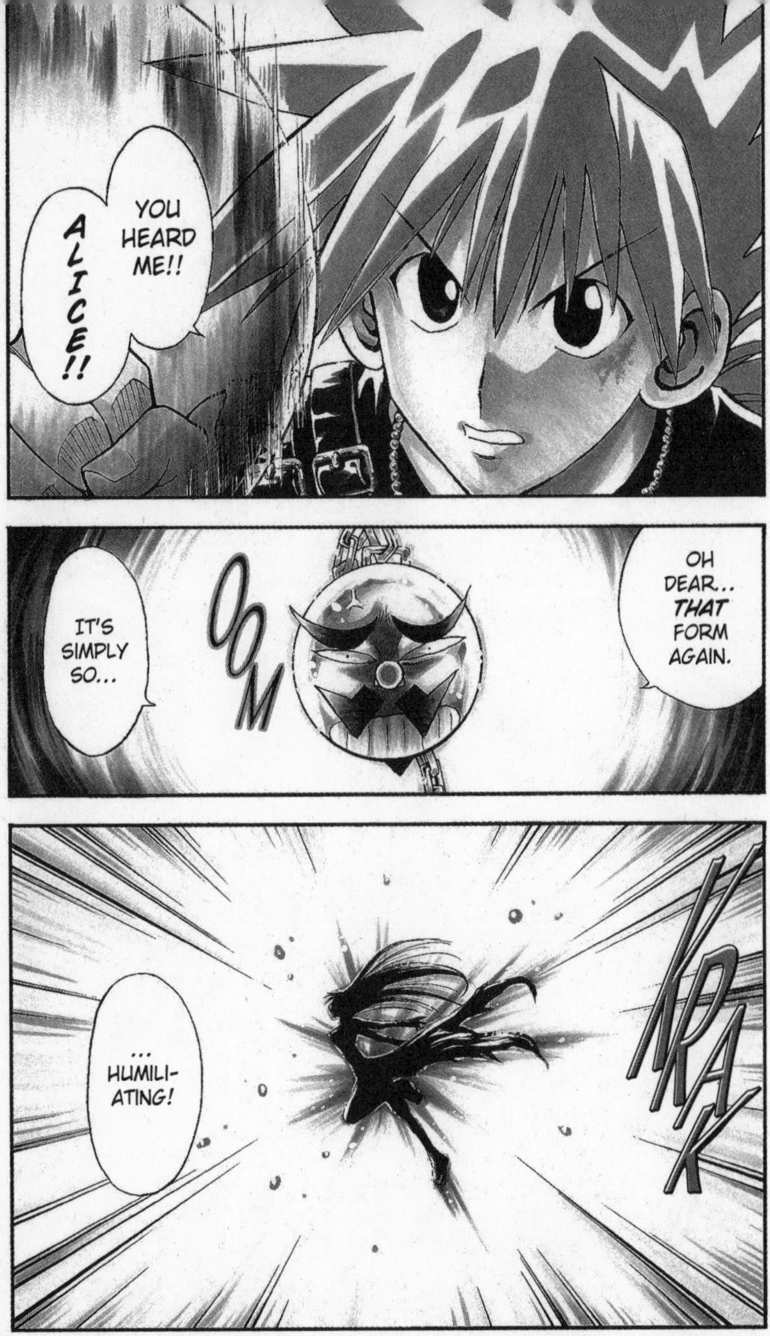
YOU HEARD ME!! ALICE!!
OH DEAR... THAT FORM AGAIN.
OOM
IT'S SIMPLY SO...
KRAK
... HUMILI-ATING!

AKT. 124/ GINTA VS. IAN ③

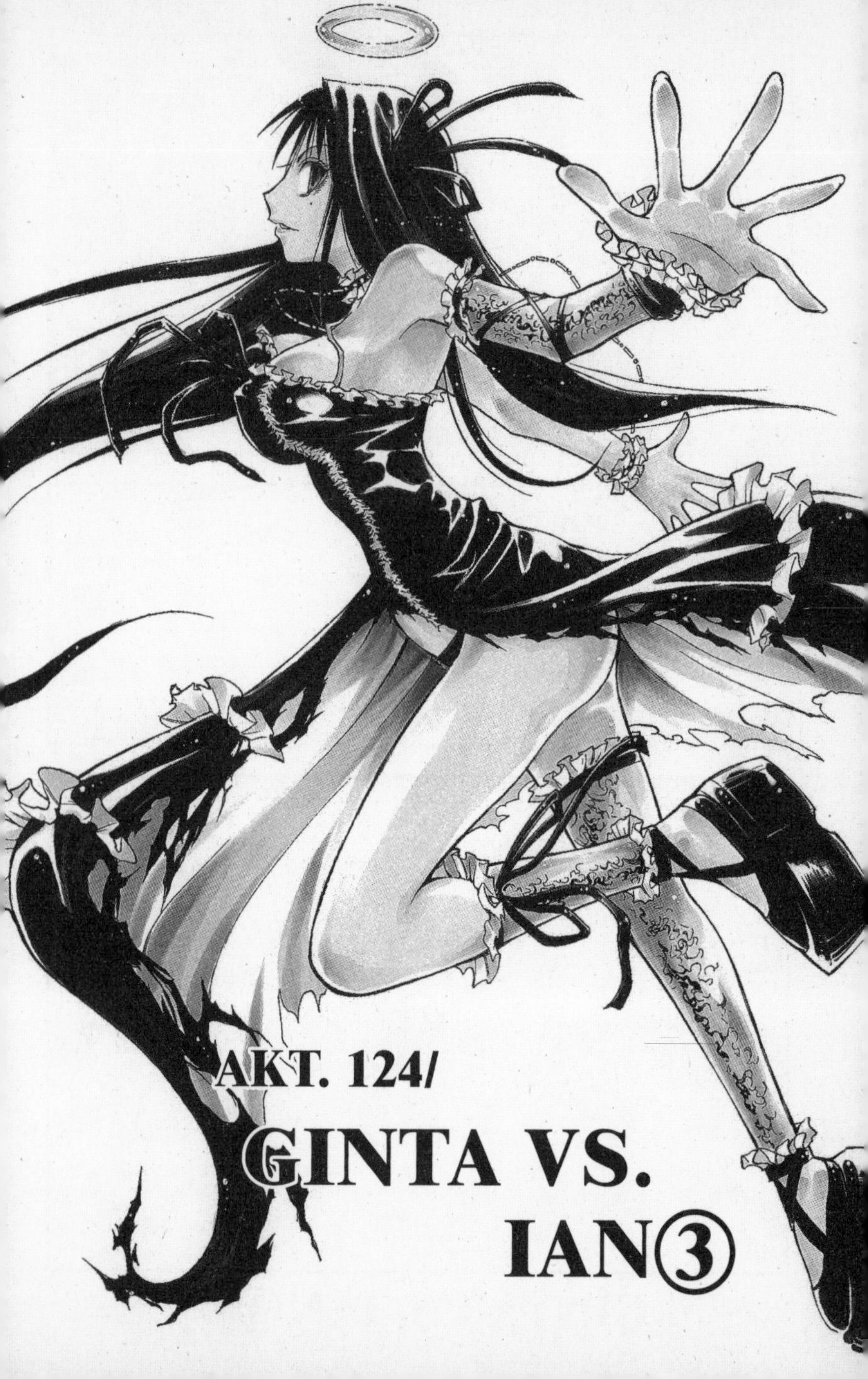

AKT. 124/ GINTA VS. IAN③

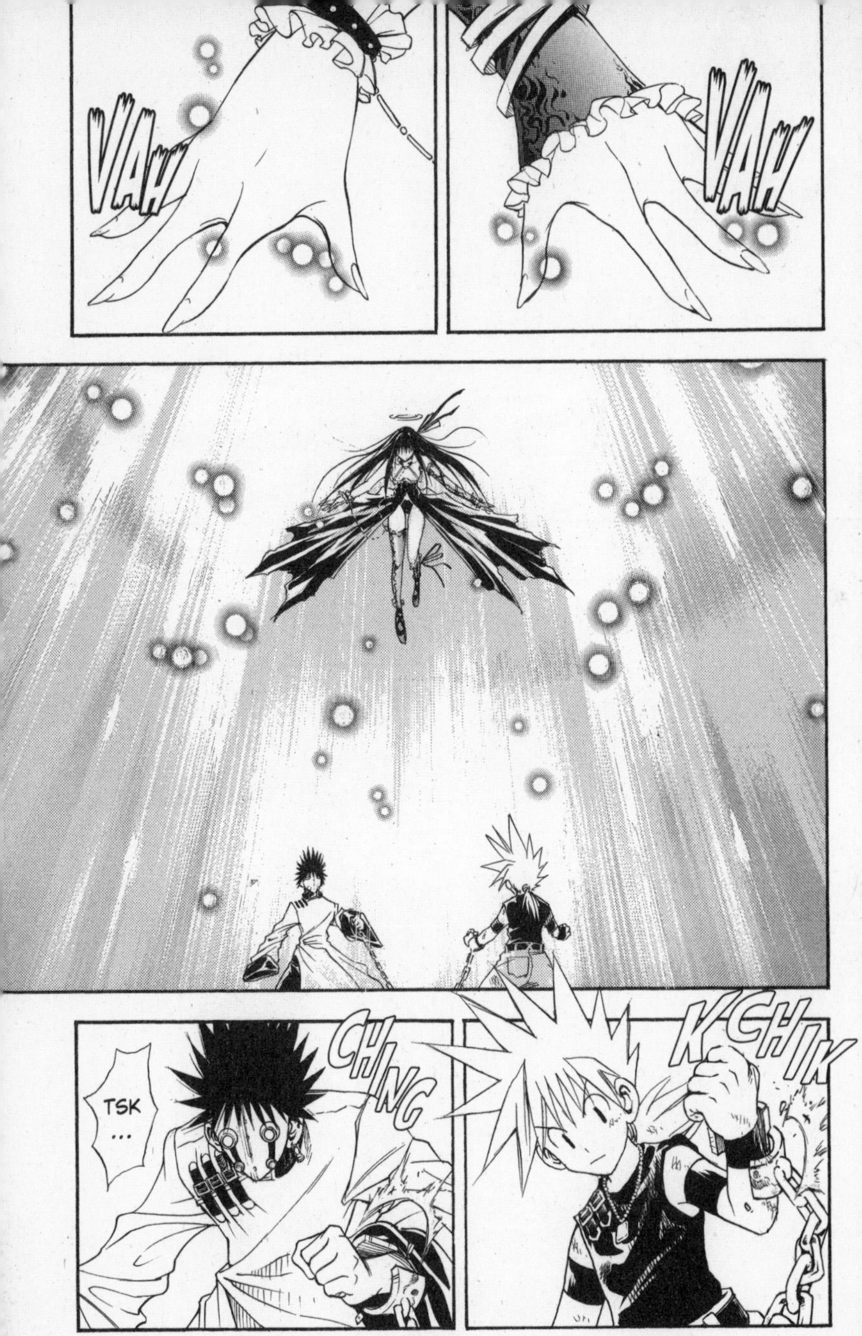
VAH
VAH
KCHIK
CHING
TSK ...

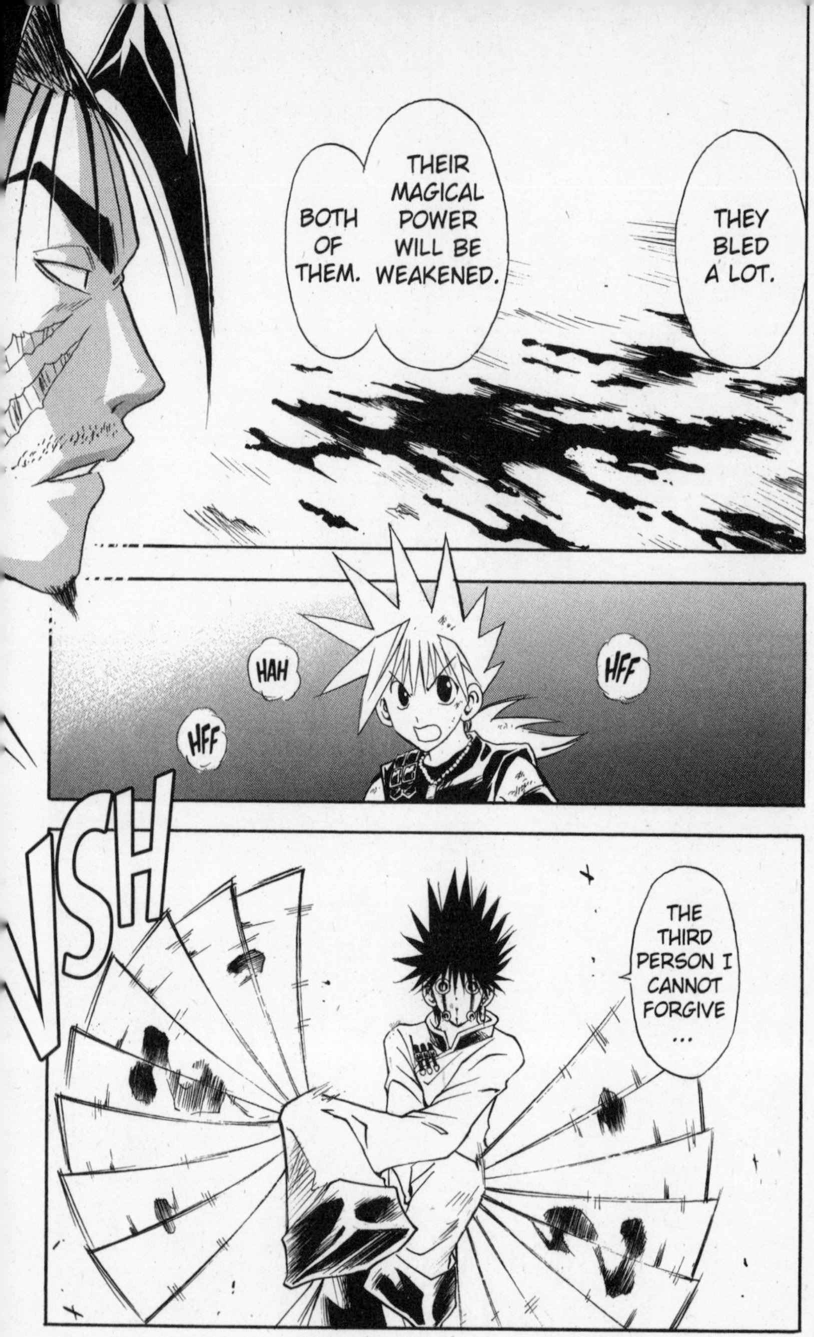
THEY BLED A LOT.
THEIR MAGICAL POWER WILL BE WEAKENED.
BOTH OF THEM.
HFF
HAH
HFF
THE THIRD PERSON I CANNOT FORGIVE ...
VSH

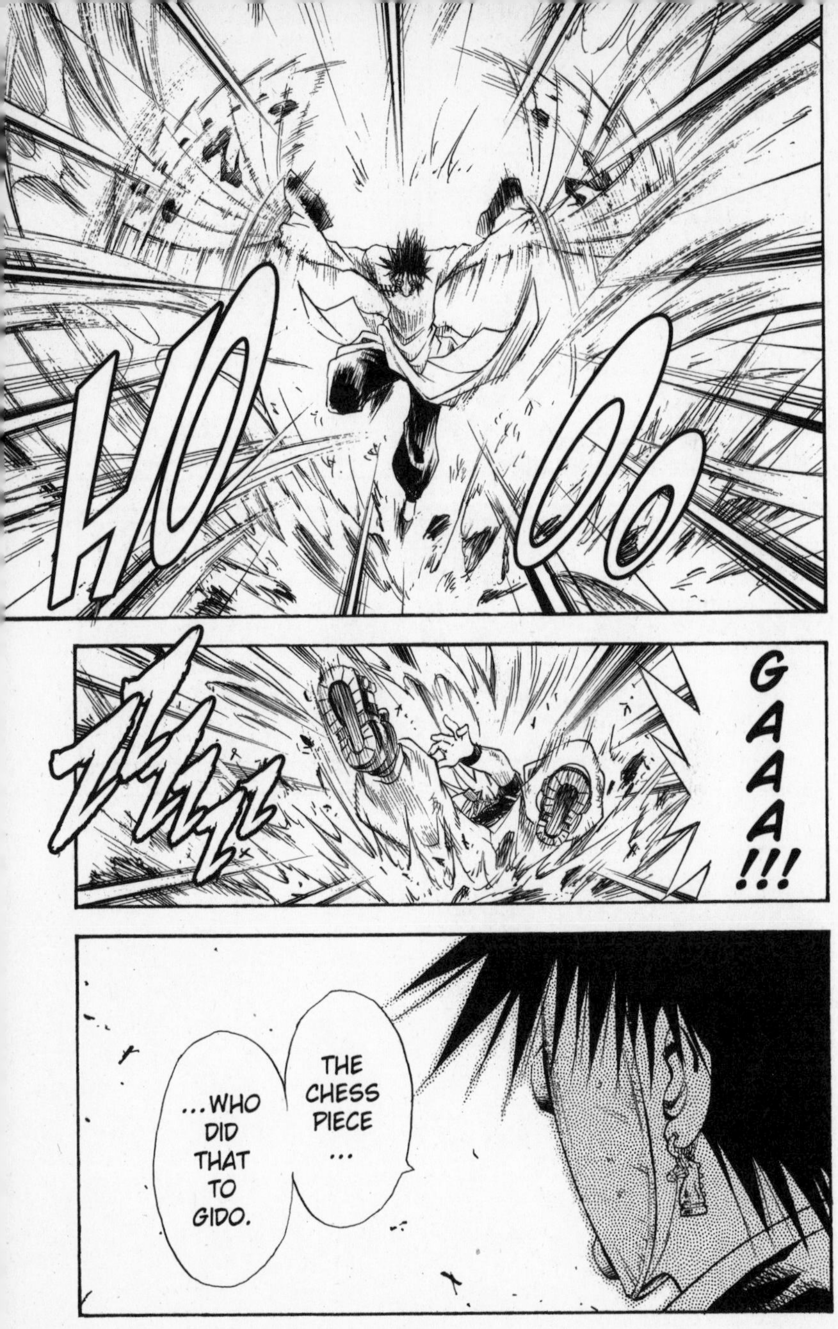
HOOO
GAAAA!!!
THE CHESS PIECE...
...WHO DID THAT TO GIDO.

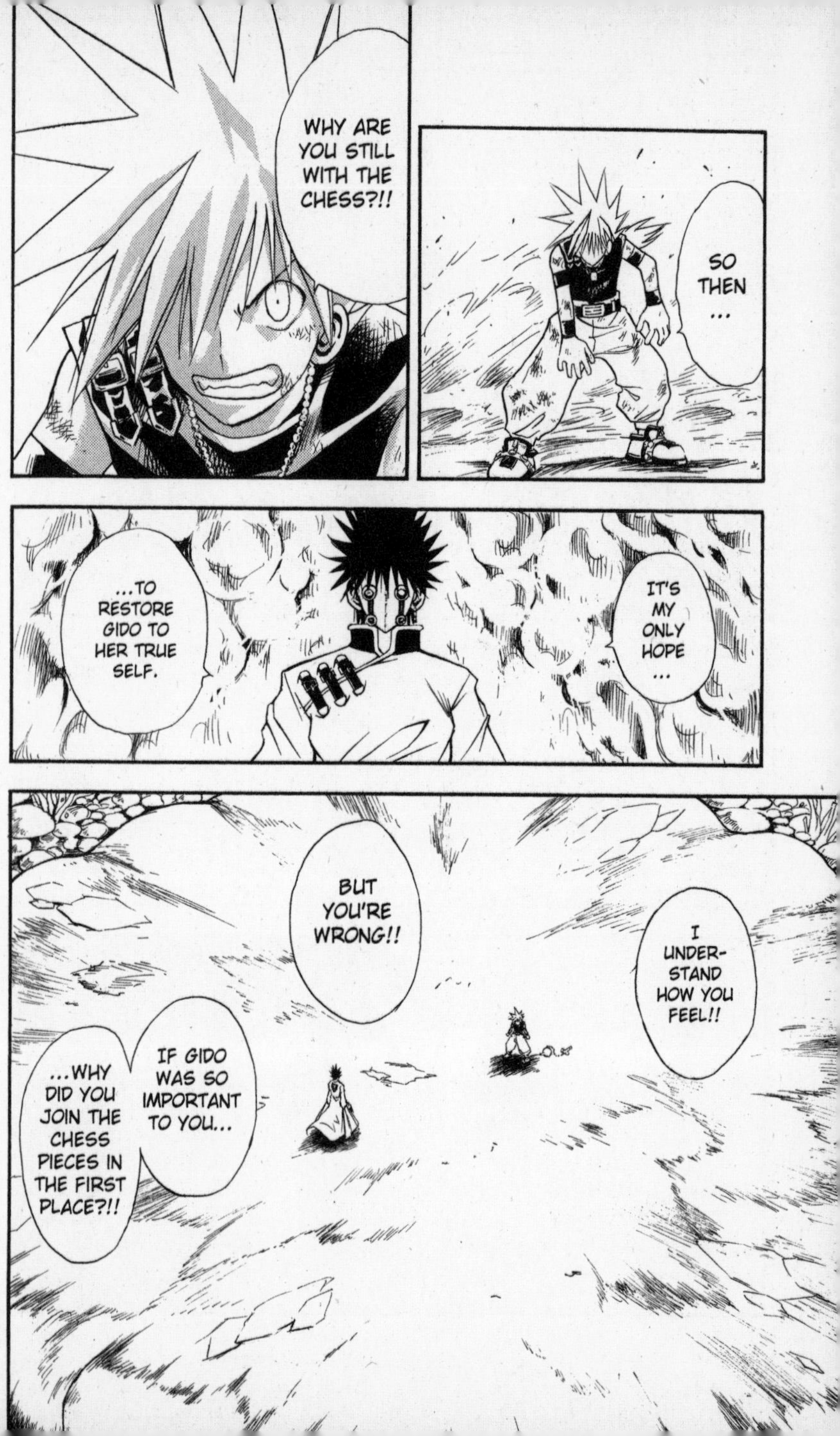
SO THEN ...
WHY ARE YOU STILL WITH THE CHESS?!!
IT'S MY ONLY HOPE ...
...TO RESTORE GIDO TO HER TRUE SELF.
I UNDER-STAND HOW YOU FEEL!!
BUT YOU'RE WRONG!!
IF GIDO WAS SO IMPORTANT TO YOU...
...WHY DID YOU JOIN THE CHESS PIECES IN THE FIRST PLACE?!!

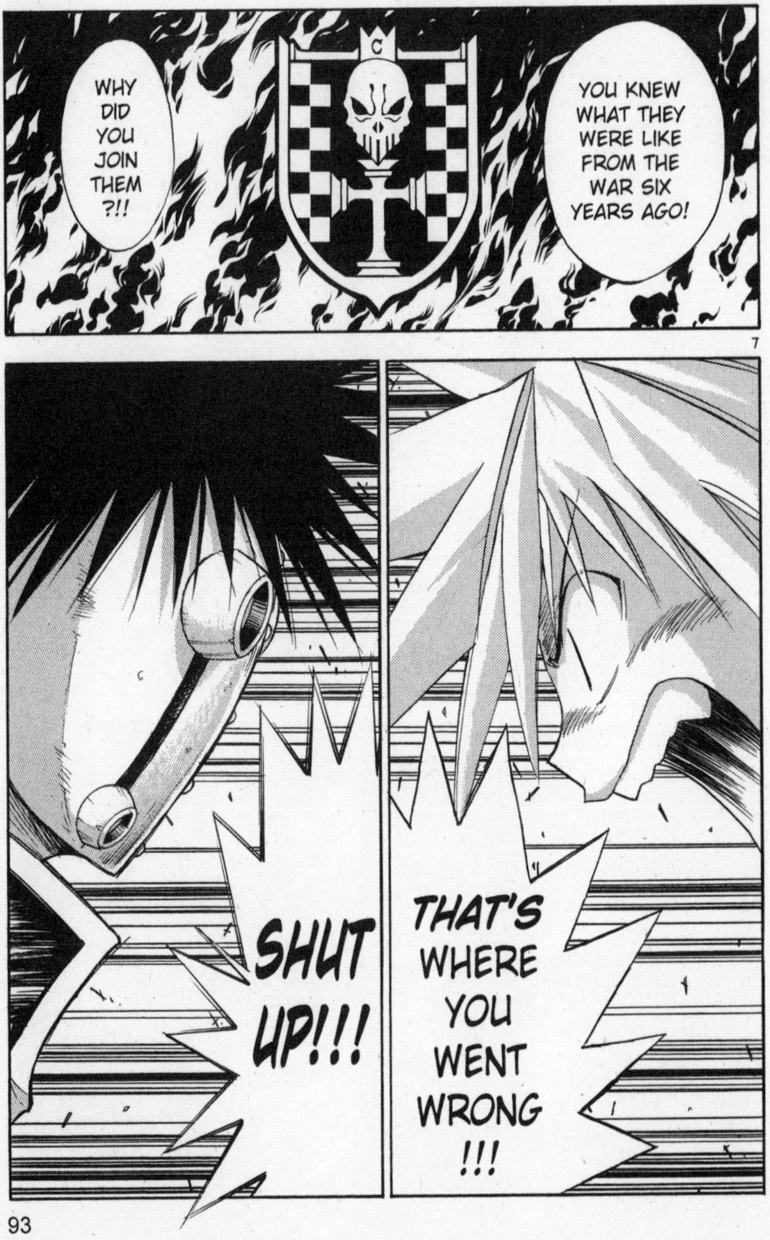
YOU KNEW WHAT THEY WERE LIKE FROM THE WAR SIX YEARS AGO!
WHY DID YOU JOIN THEM?!!
7
THAT'S WHERE YOU WENT WRONG!!!
SHUT UP!!!

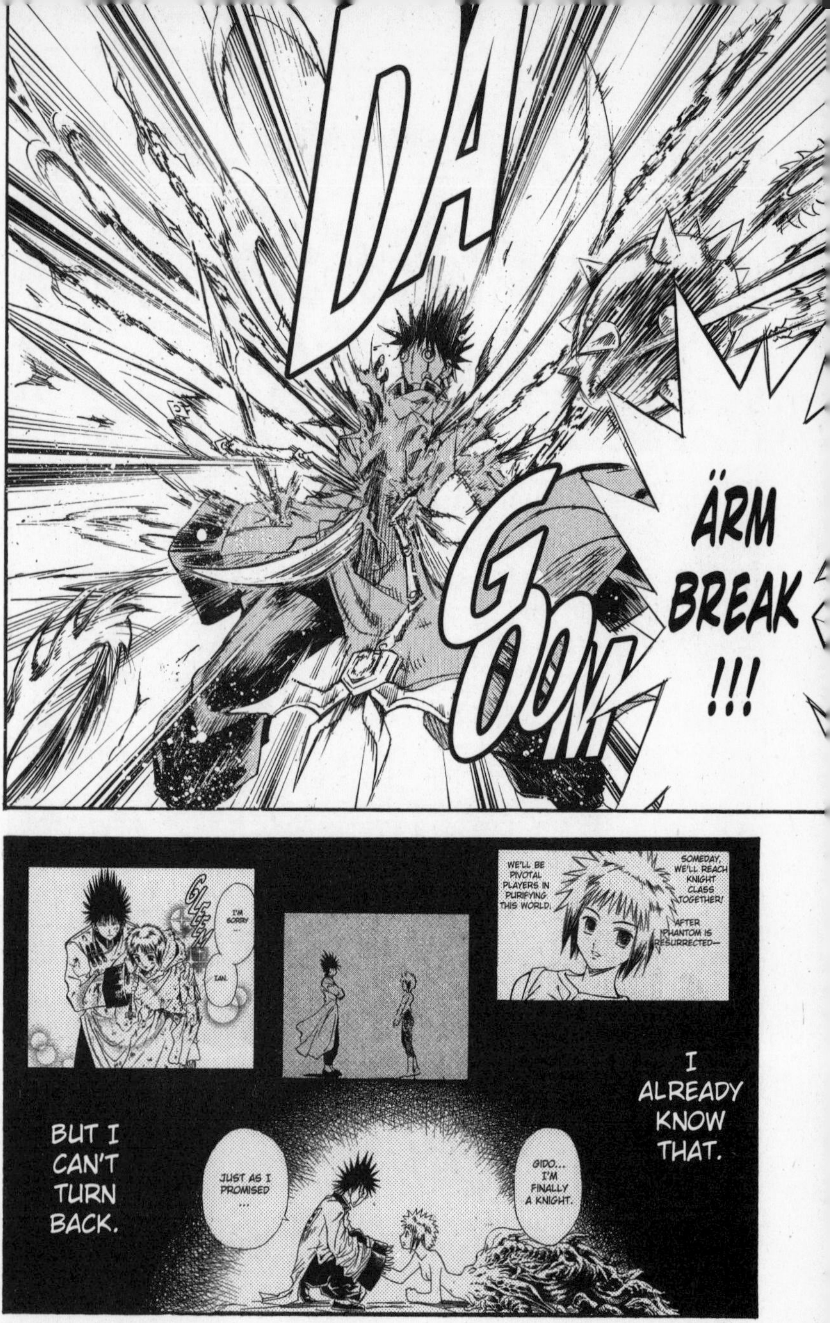
DA
ÄRM BREAK !!!
GOOM
SOMEDAY, WE'LL REACH KNIGHT CLASS TOGETHER!
WE'LL BE PIVOTAL PLAYERS IN PURIFYING THIS WORLD.
AFTER PHANTOM IS RESURRECTED—
I'M SORRY...
IAN.
GLEEM
I ALREADY KNOW THAT.
GIDO... I'M FINALLY A KNIGHT.
JUST AS I PROMISED...
BUT I CAN'T TURN BACK.

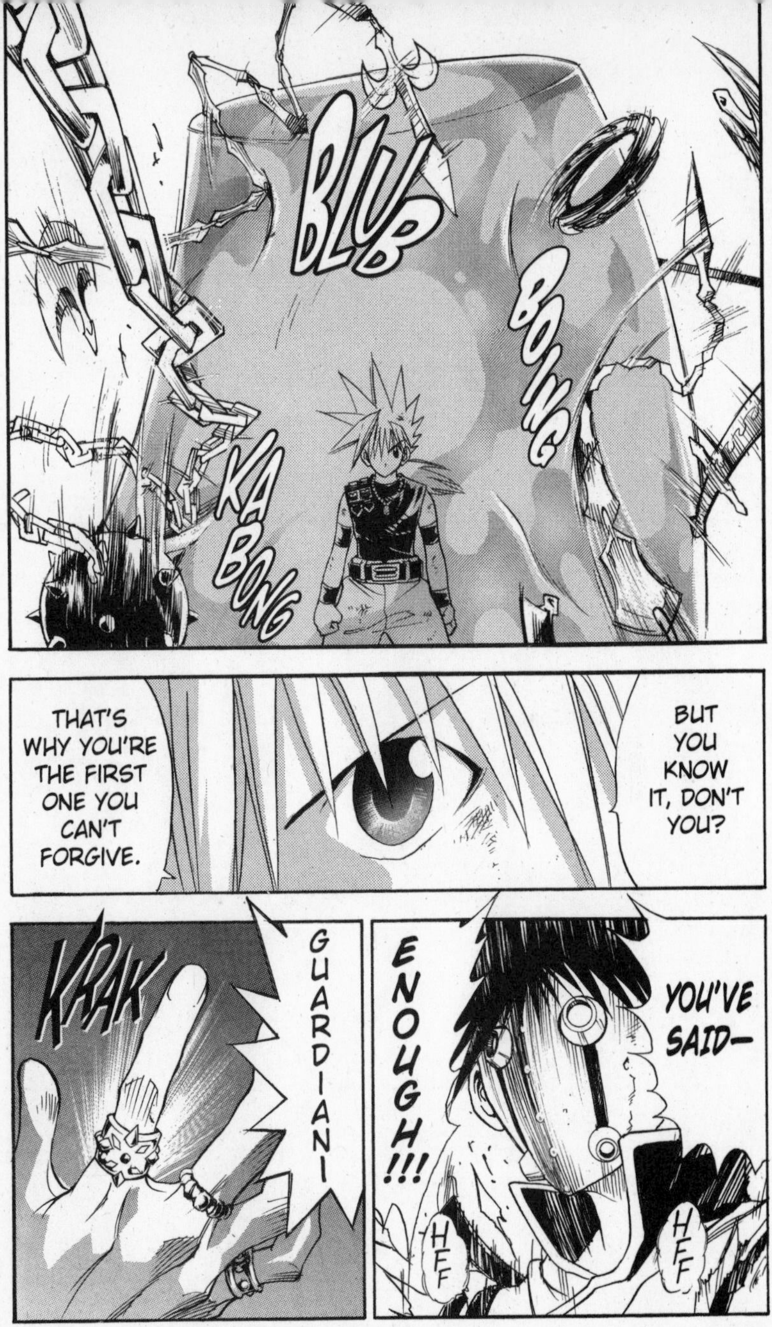
BLUB
BOING
KA BONG
BUT YOU KNOW IT, DON'T YOU?
THAT'S WHY YOU'RE THE FIRST ONE YOU CAN'T FORGIVE.
YOU'VE SAID—
ENOUGH!!!
HFF
HFF
GUARDIANI
KRAK

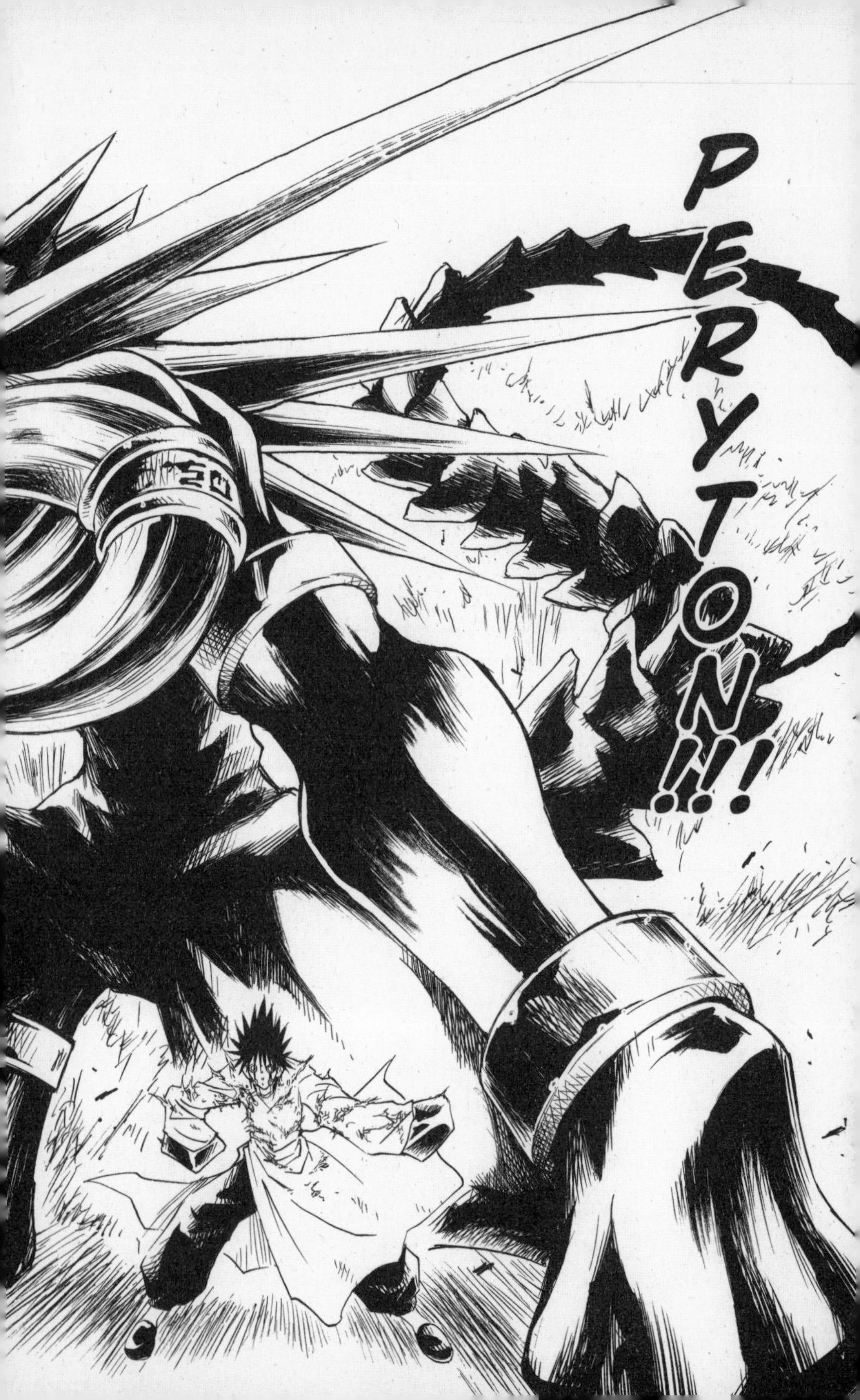
PERYTON!!!

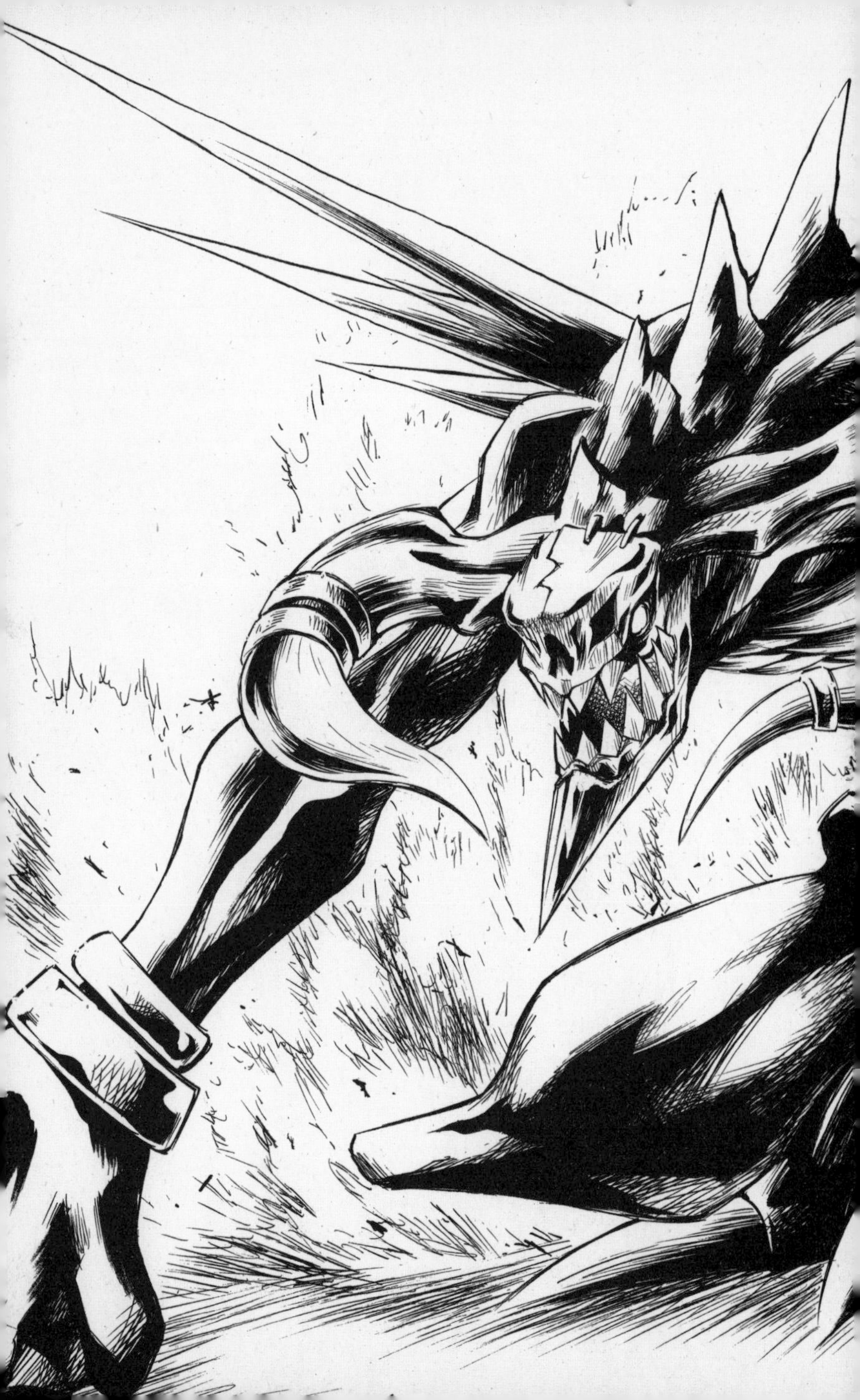

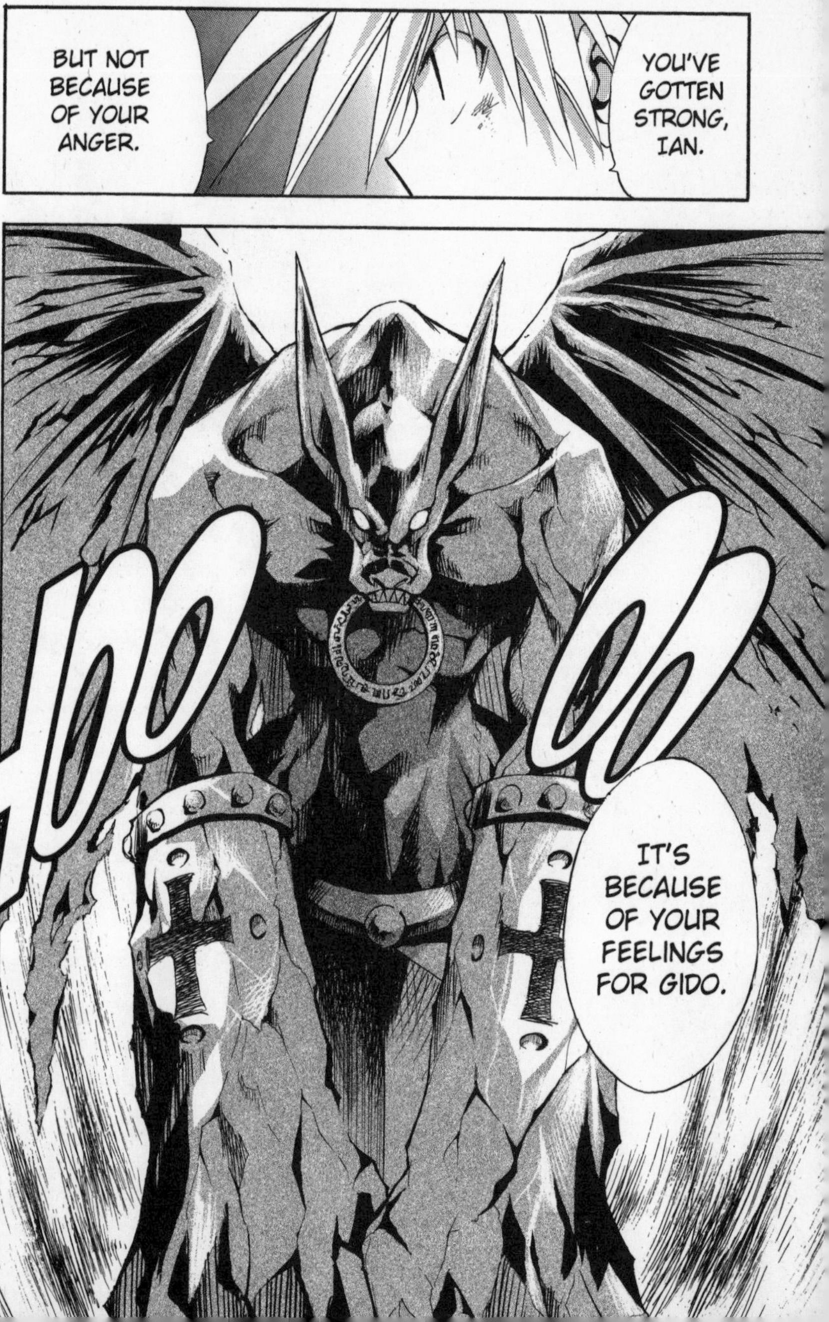
YOU'VE GOTTEN STRONG, IAN.
BUT NOT BECAUSE OF YOUR ANGER.
HOOOO
IT'S BECAUSE OF YOUR FEELINGS FOR GIDO.

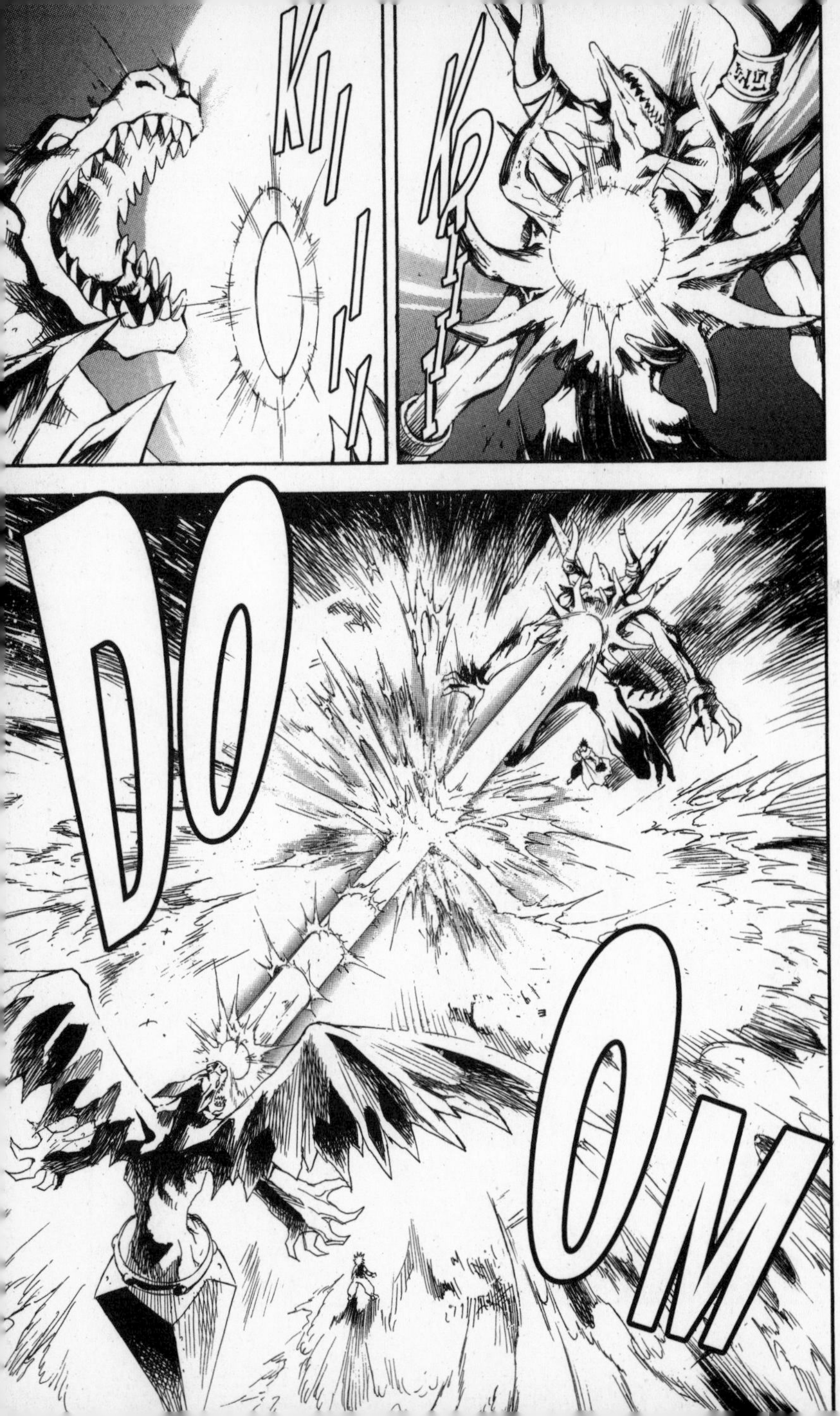
KRIIII
KIIII
DOOM

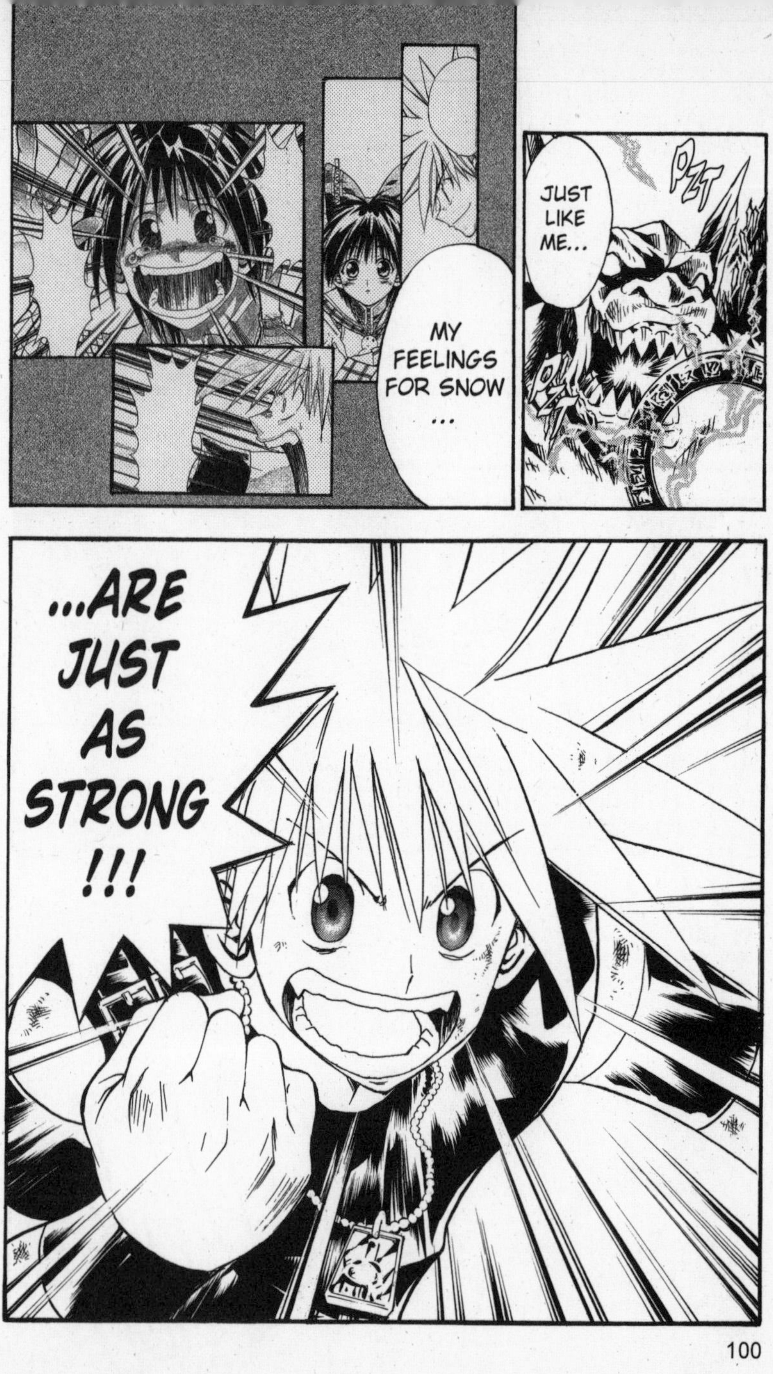
PZT
JUST LIKE ME...
MY FEELINGS FOR SNOW ...
...ARE JUST AS STRONG !!!

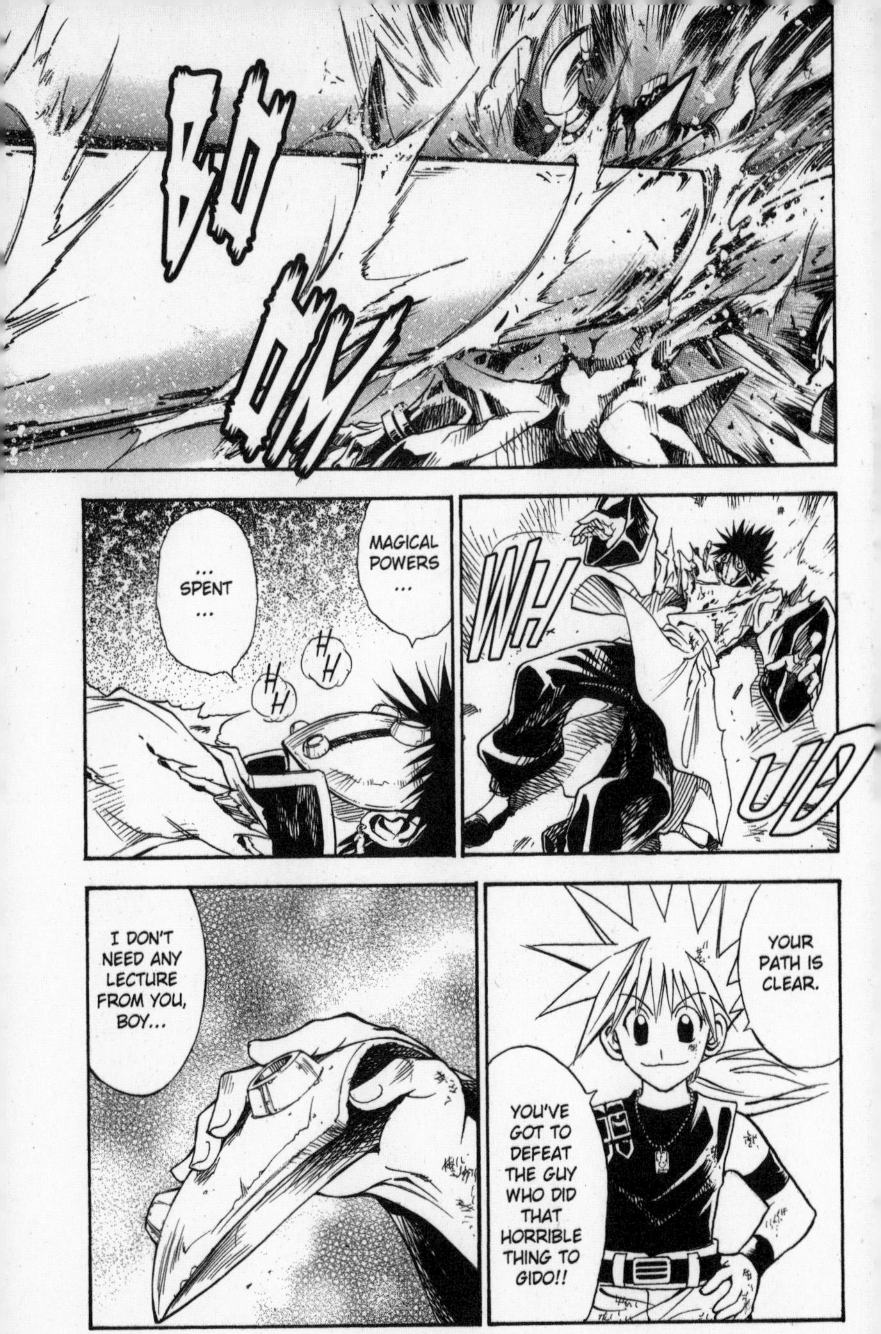
WH
UD
MAGICAL POWERS ...
... SPENT ...
YOUR PATH IS CLEAR.
YOU'VE GOT TO DEFEAT THE GUY WHO DID THAT HORRIBLE THING TO GIDO!!
I DON'T NEED ANY LECTURE FROM YOU, BOY...

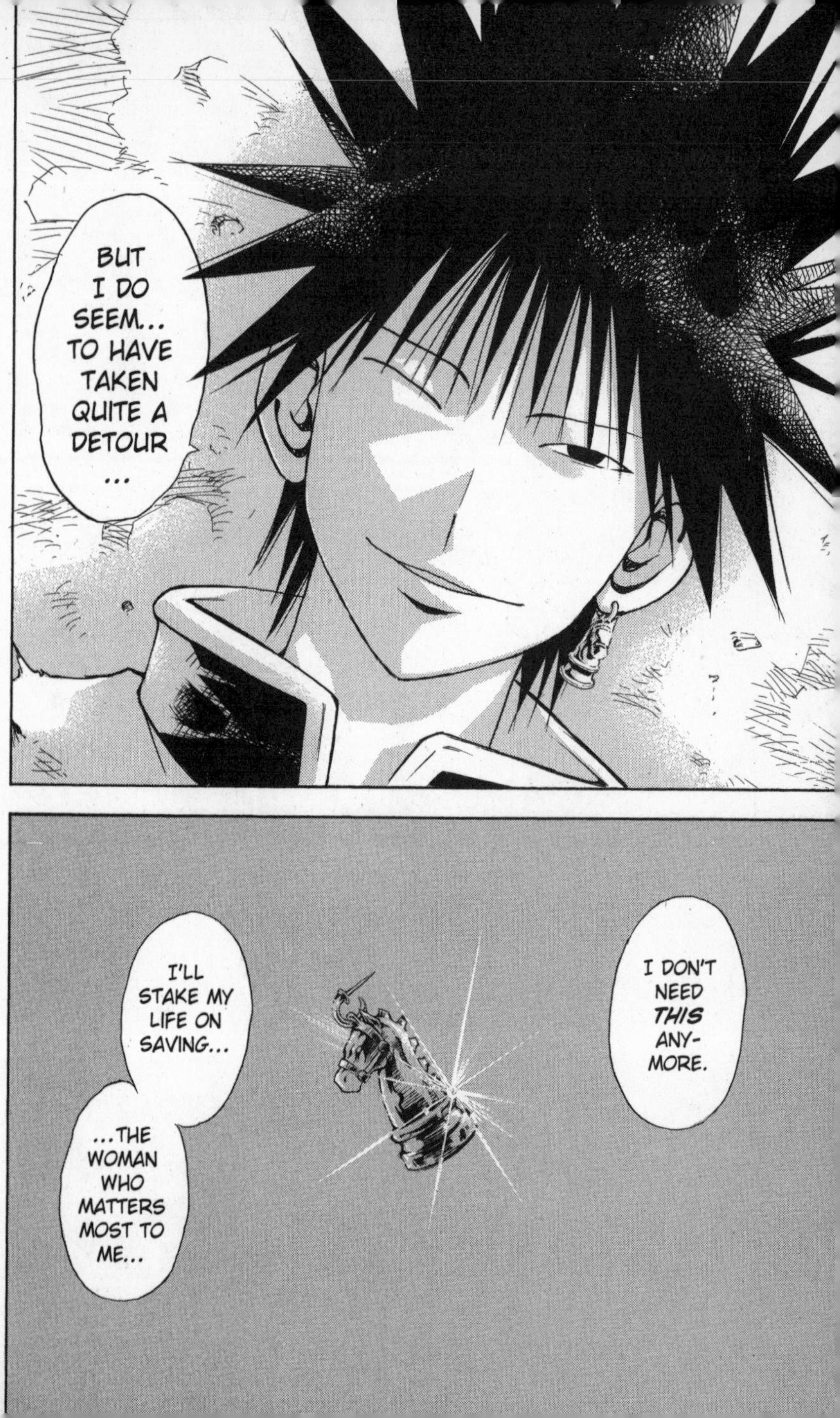
BUT I DO SEEM... TO HAVE TAKEN QUITE A DETOUR ...
I DON'T NEED THIS ANYMORE.
I'LL STAKE MY LIFE ON SAVING...
...THE WOMAN WHO MATTERS MOST TO ME...

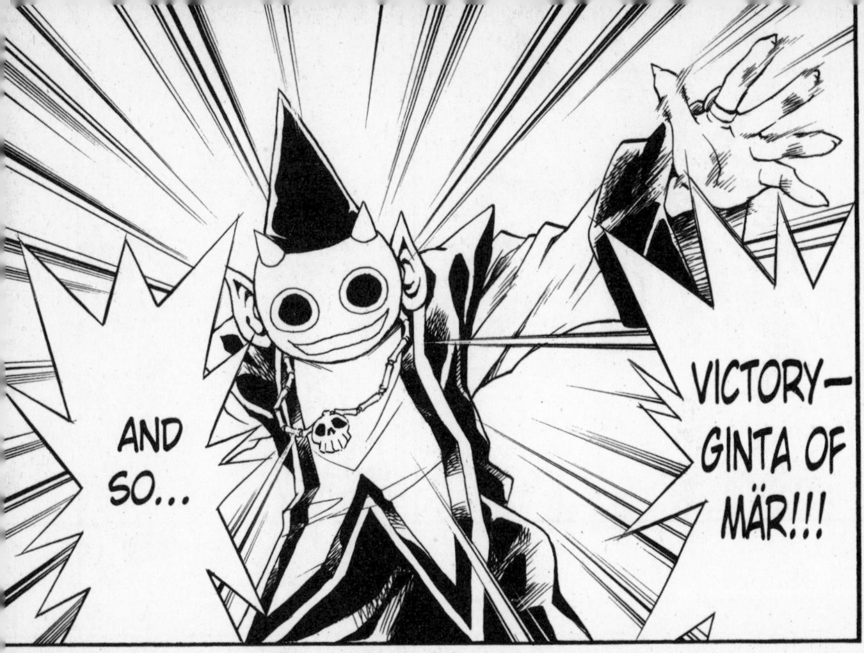
VICTORY—
GINTA OF
MÄR!!!
AND
SO...

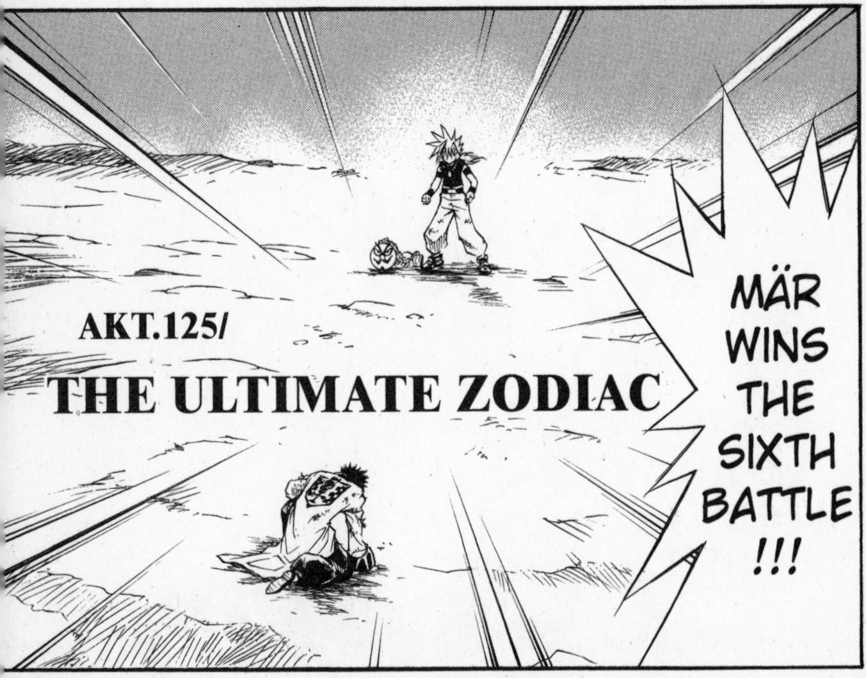
MÄR
WINS
THE
SIXTH
BATTLE
!!!
AKT.125/
THE ULTIMATE ZODIAC

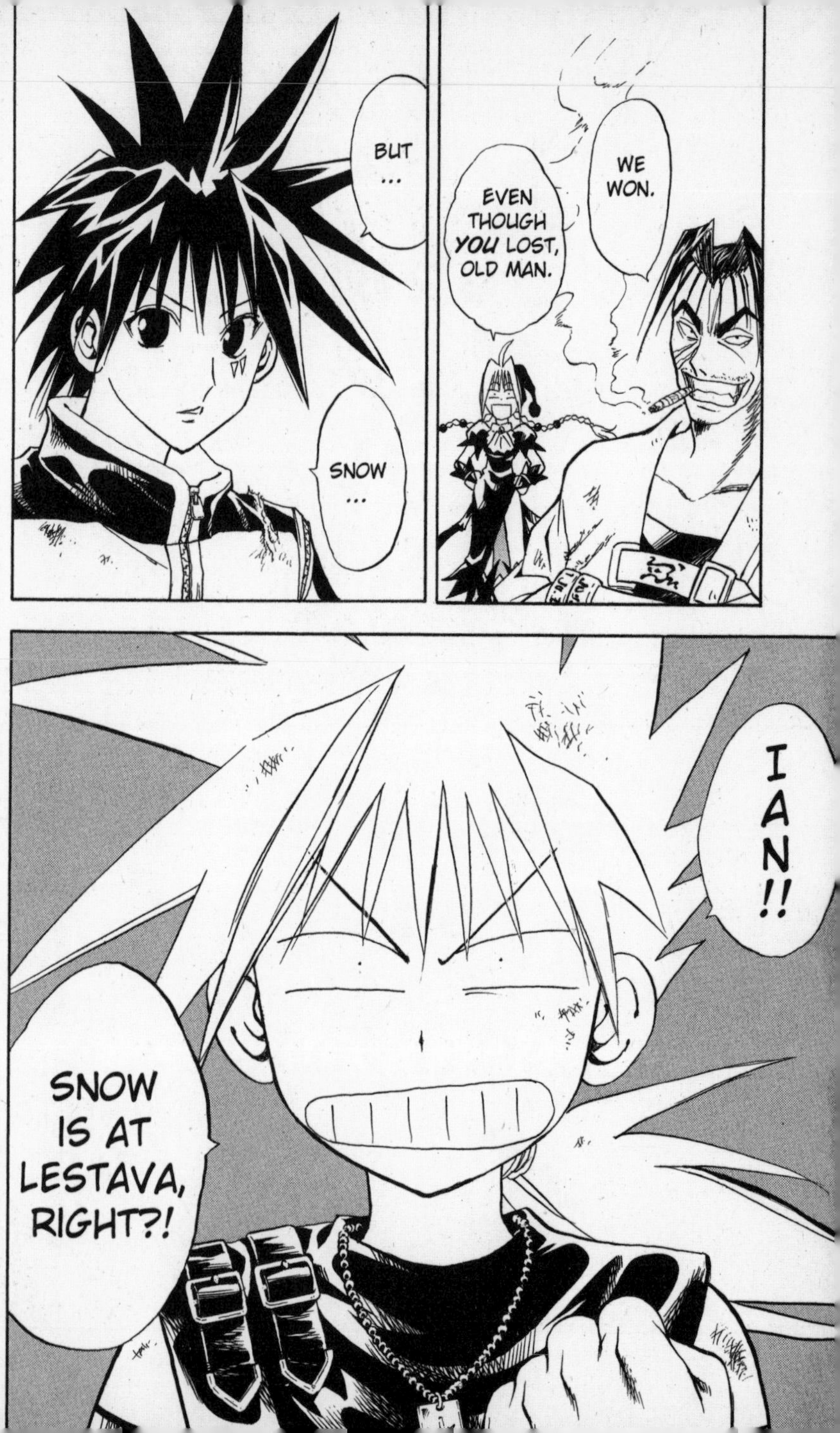
WE WON.
EVEN THOUGH ***YOU*** LOST, OLD MAN.
BUT ...
SNOW ...
IAN!!
SNOW IS AT LESTAVA, RIGHT?!

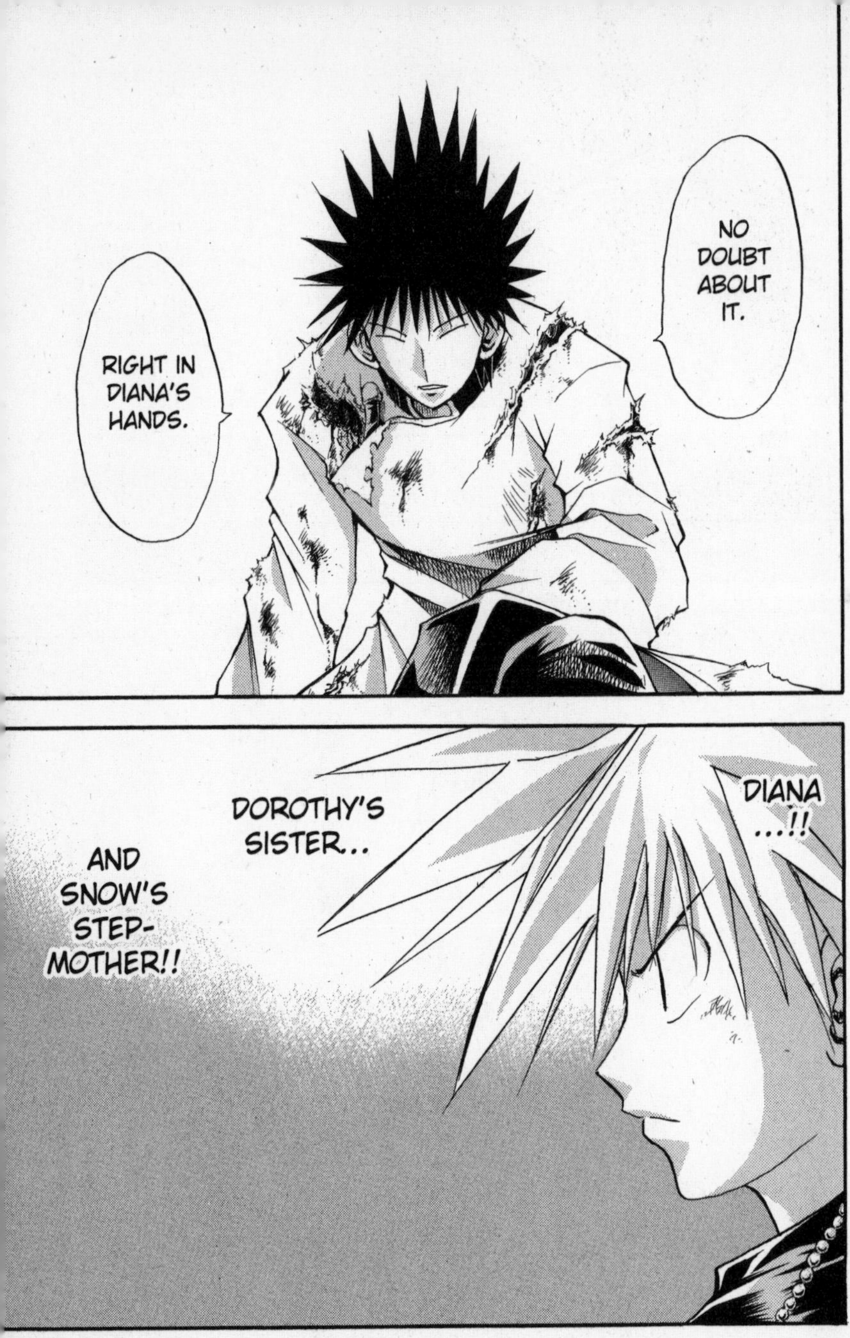
NO DOUBT ABOUT IT.
RIGHT IN DIANA'S HANDS.
DIANA ...!!
DOROTHY'S SISTER...
AND SNOW'S STEP-MOTHER!!

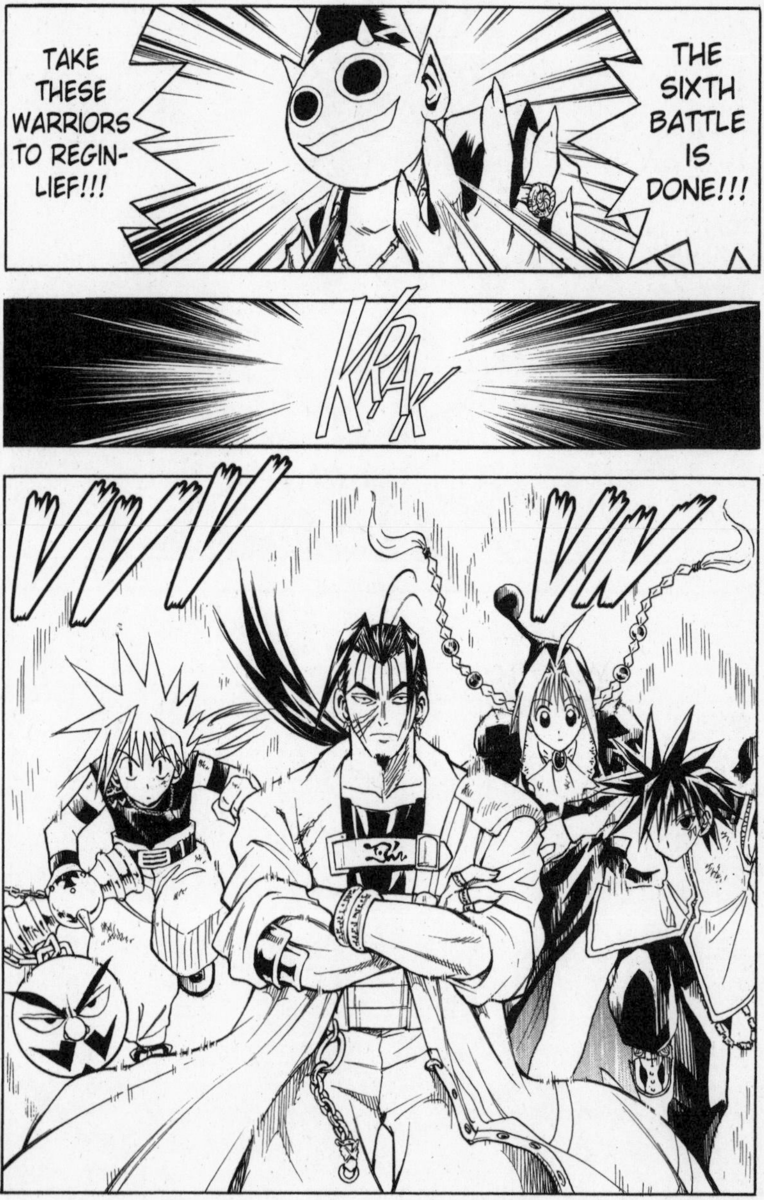
THE SIXTH BATTLE IS DONE!!!
TAKE THESE WARRIORS TO REGIN-LIEF!!!
KRAK

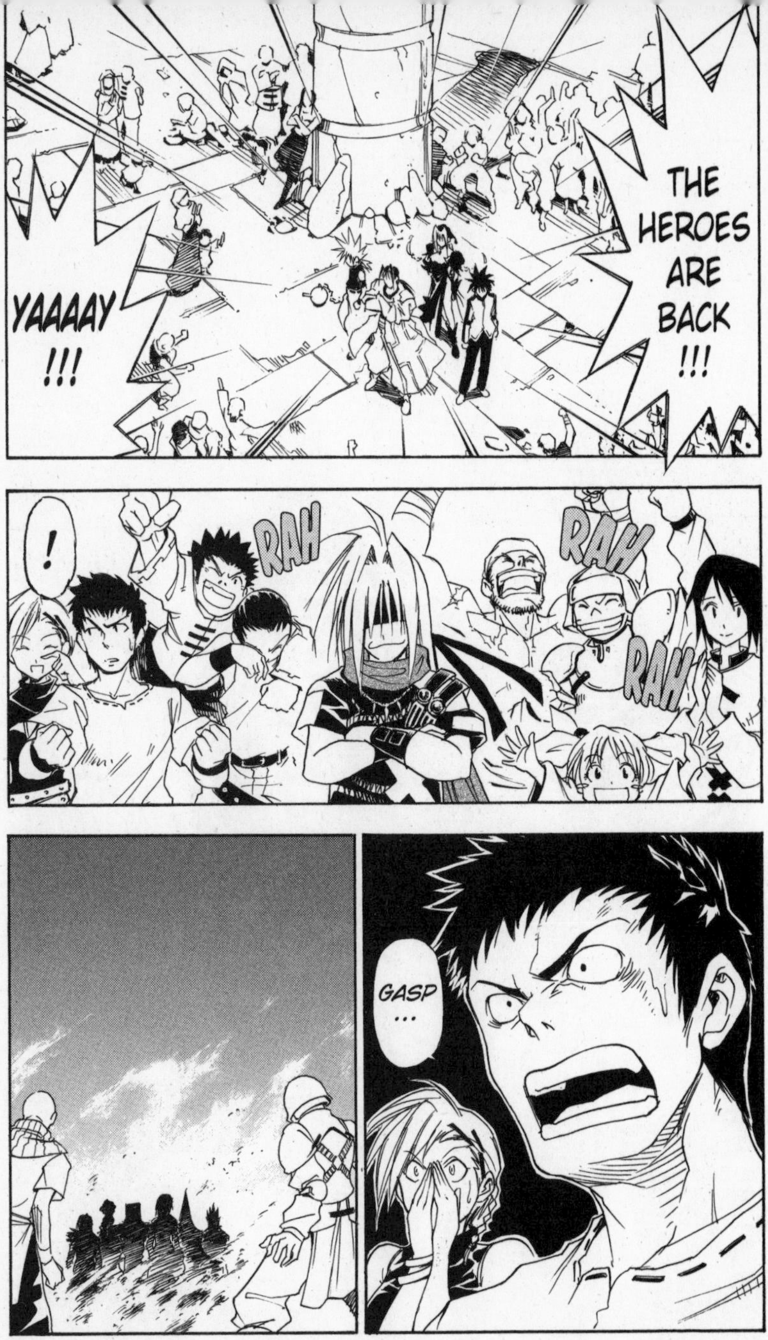
THE HEROES ARE BACK !!!
YAAAAY !!!
RAH
RAH
RAH
!
GASP ...

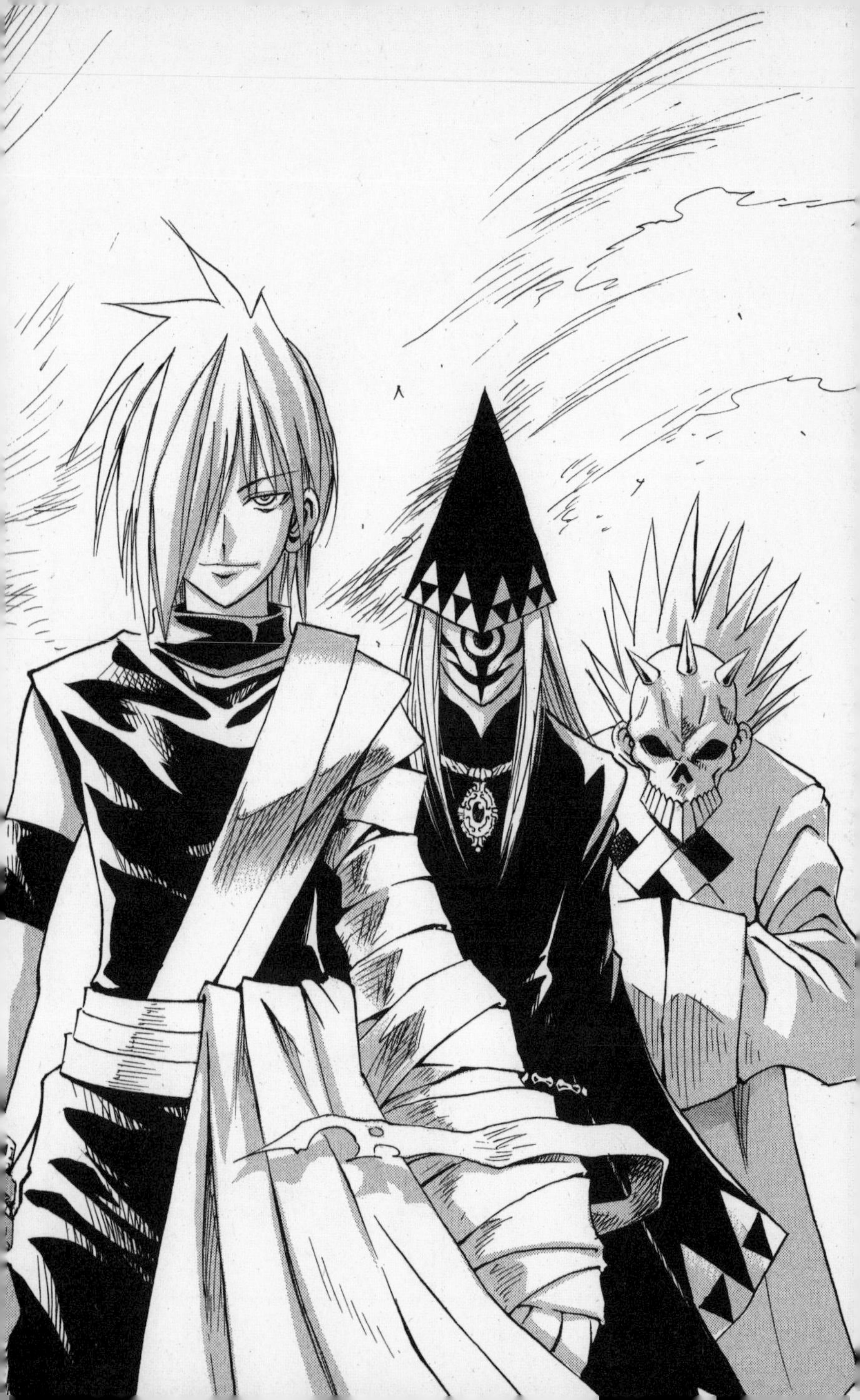

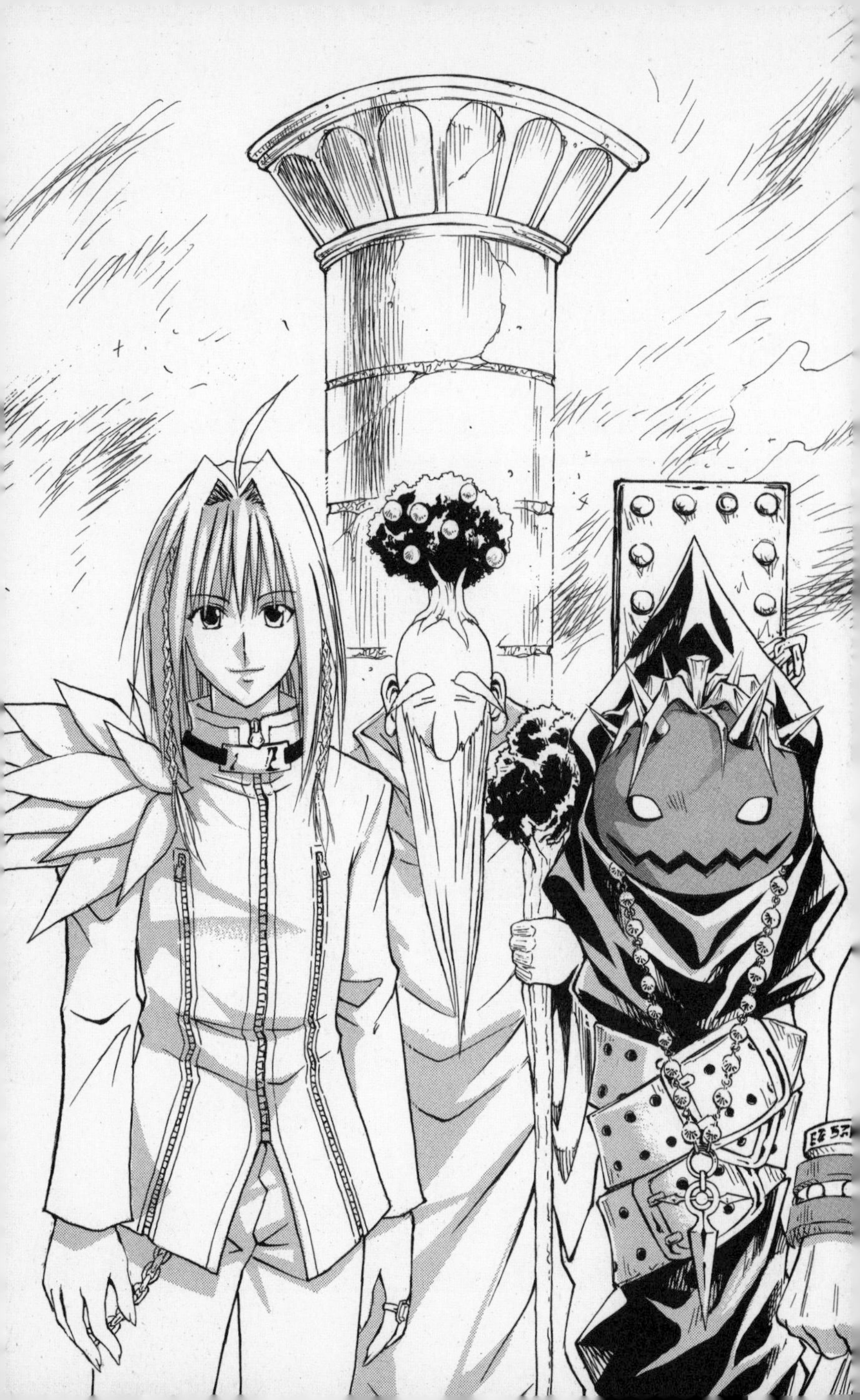

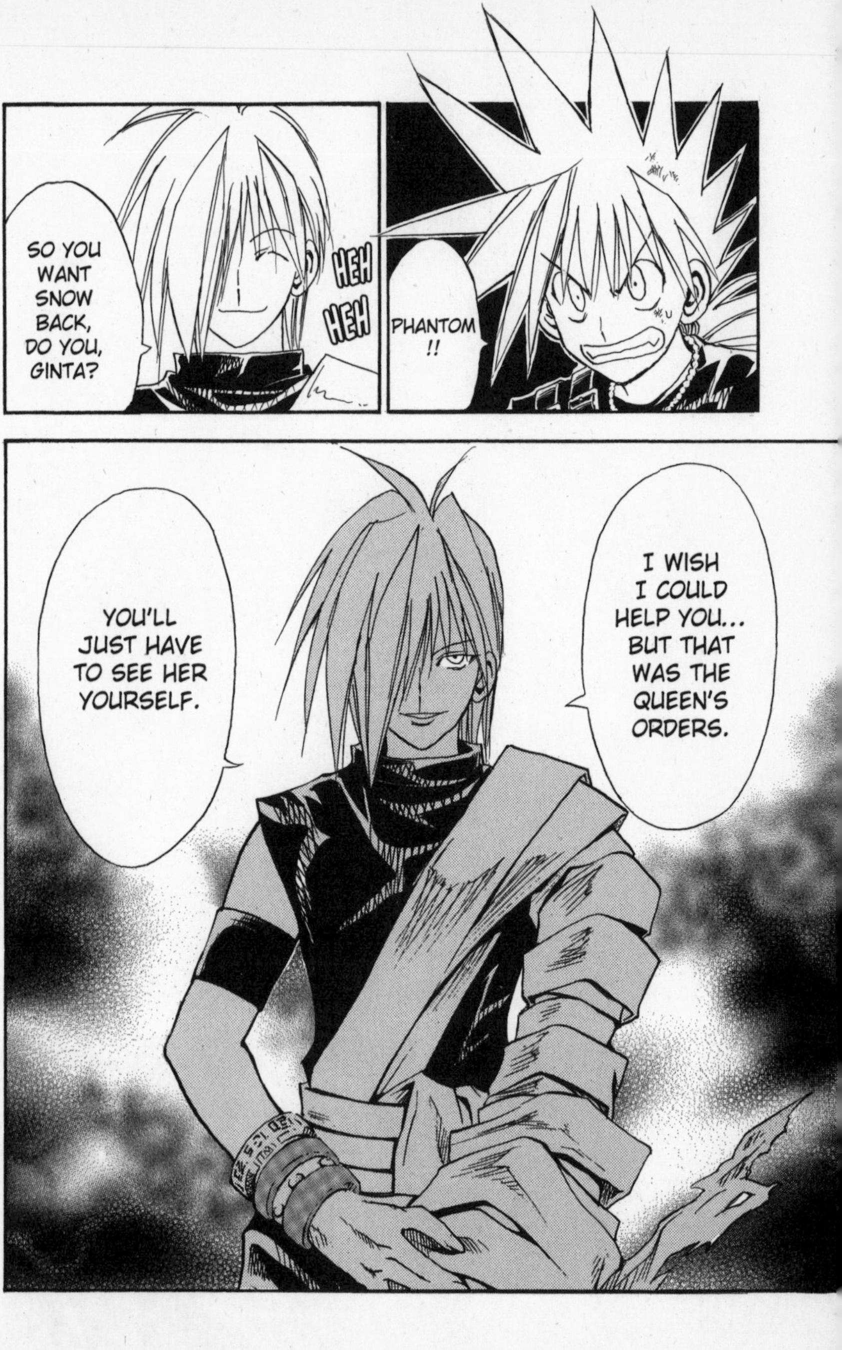
PHANTOM!!
SO YOU WANT SNOW BACK, DO YOU, GINTA?
HEH HEH
I WISH I COULD HELP YOU... BUT THAT WAS THE QUEEN'S ORDERS.
YOU'LL JUST HAVE TO SEE HER YOURSELF.

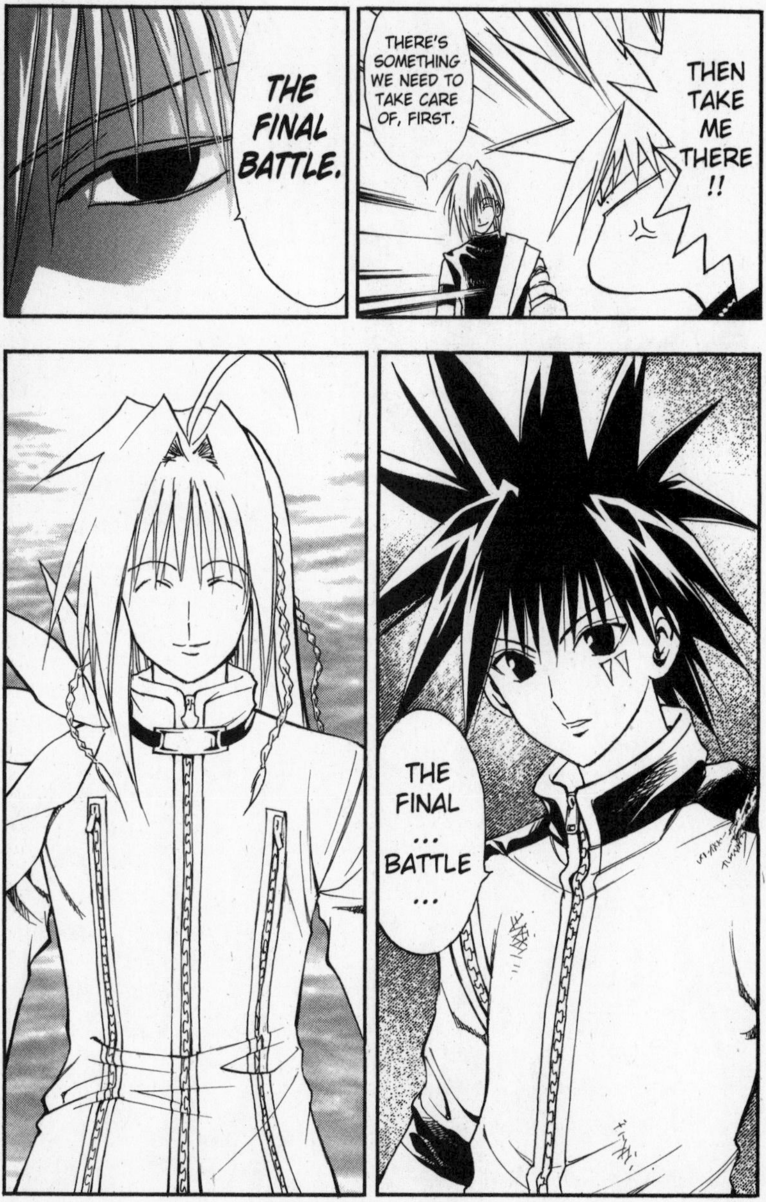
THEN TAKE ME THERE!!
THERE'S SOMETHING WE NEED TO TAKE CARE OF, FIRST.
THE FINAL BATTLE.
THE FINAL ... BATTLE ...

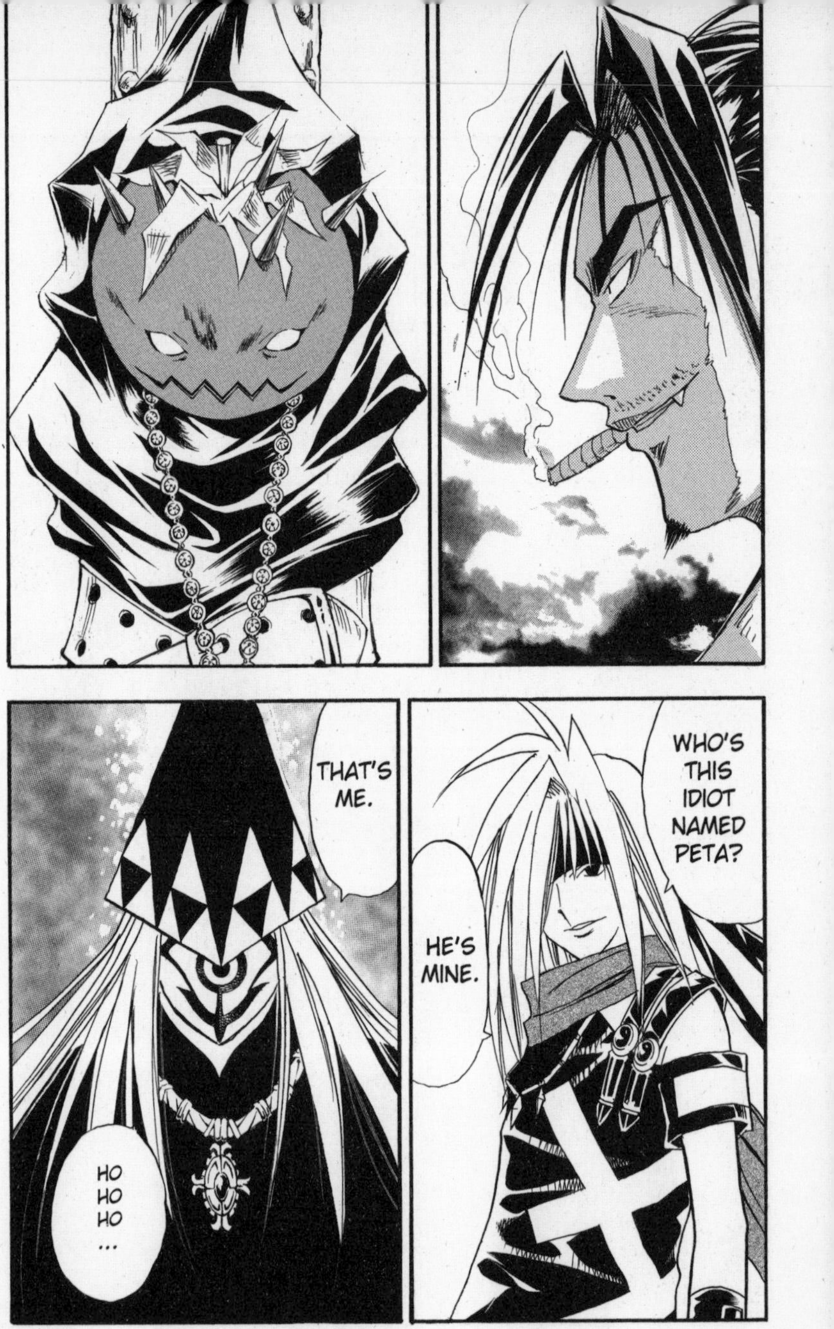
WHO'S THIS IDIOT NAMED PETA?
HE'S MINE.
THAT'S ME.
HO HO HO ...

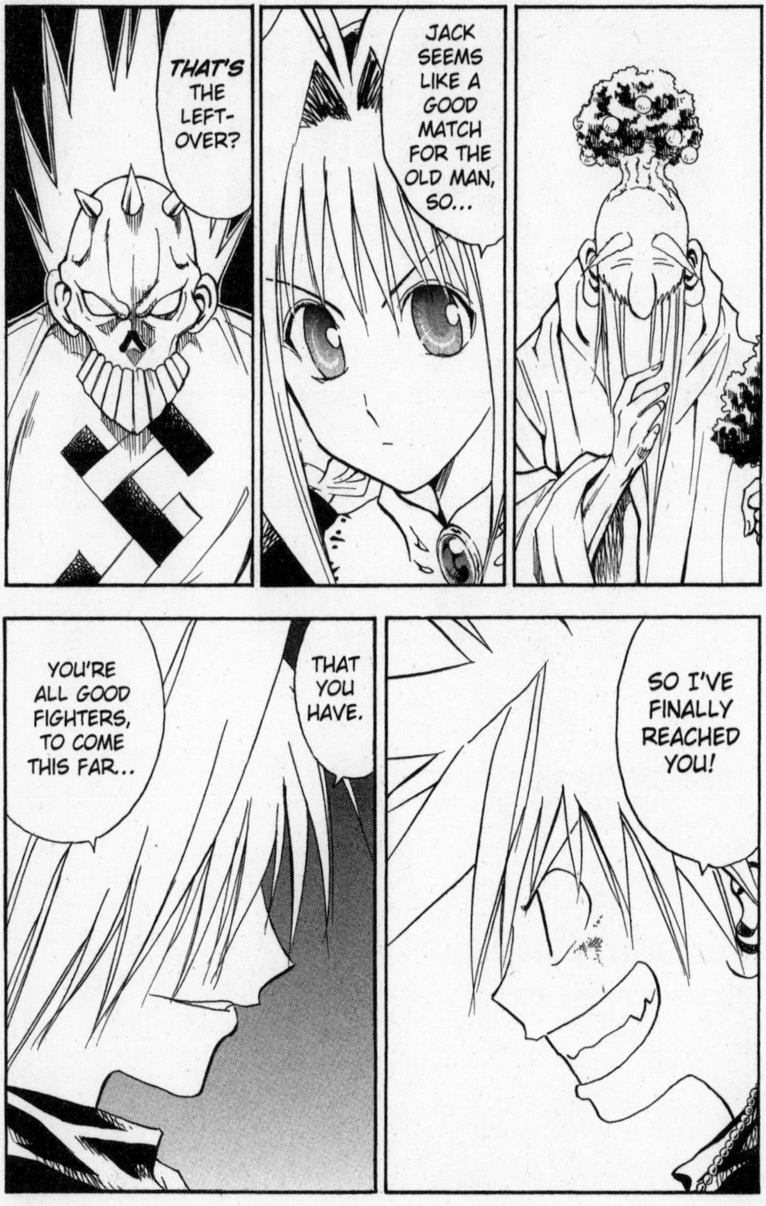
JACK SEEMS LIKE A GOOD MATCH FOR THE OLD MAN, SO...
THAT'S THE LEFT-OVER?
SO I'VE FINALLY REACHED YOU!
THAT YOU HAVE.
YOU'RE ALL GOOD FIGHTERS, TO COME THIS FAR...

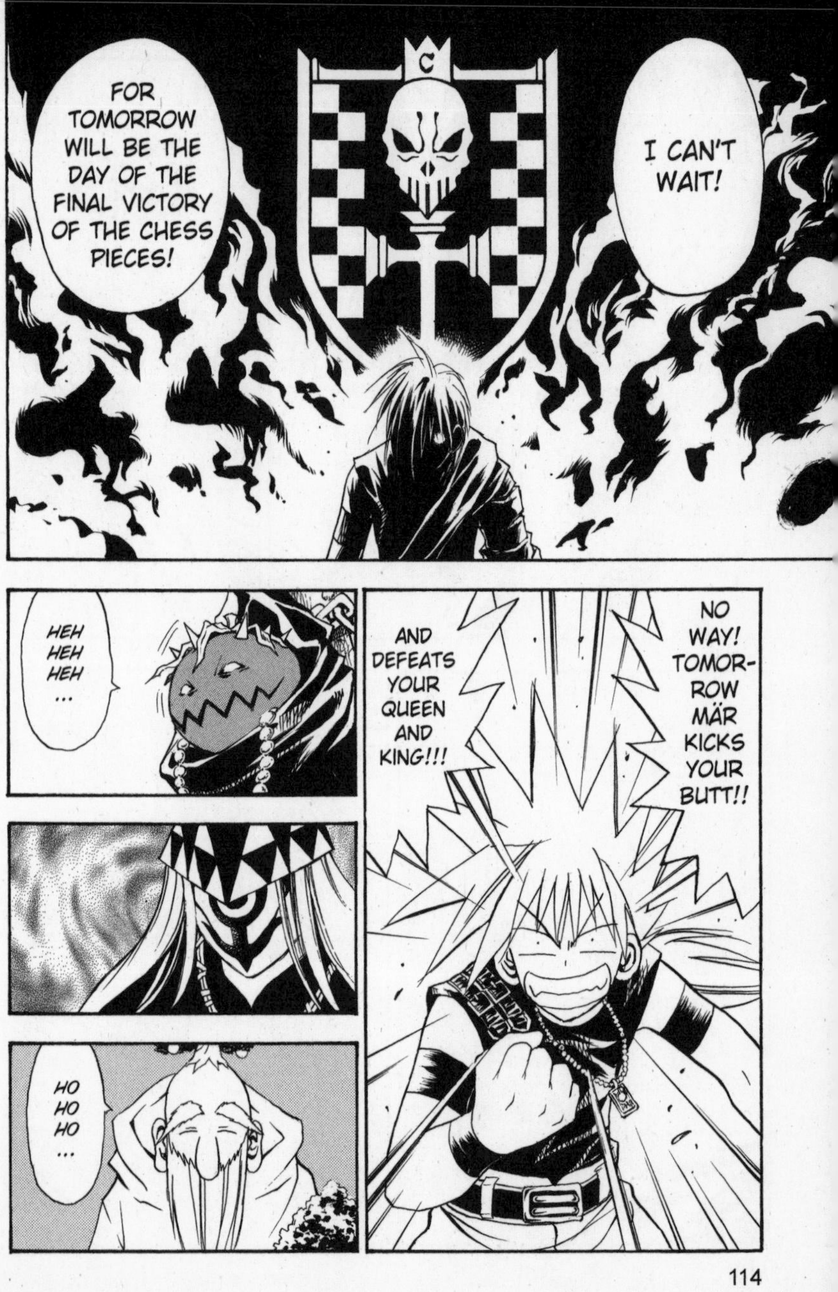
I CAN'T WAIT!
FOR TOMORROW WILL BE THE DAY OF THE FINAL VICTORY OF THE CHESS PIECES!
NO WAY! TOMOR-ROW MÄR KICKS YOUR BUTT!!
AND DEFEATS YOUR QUEEN AND KING!!!
HEH HEH HEH ...
HO HO HO ...

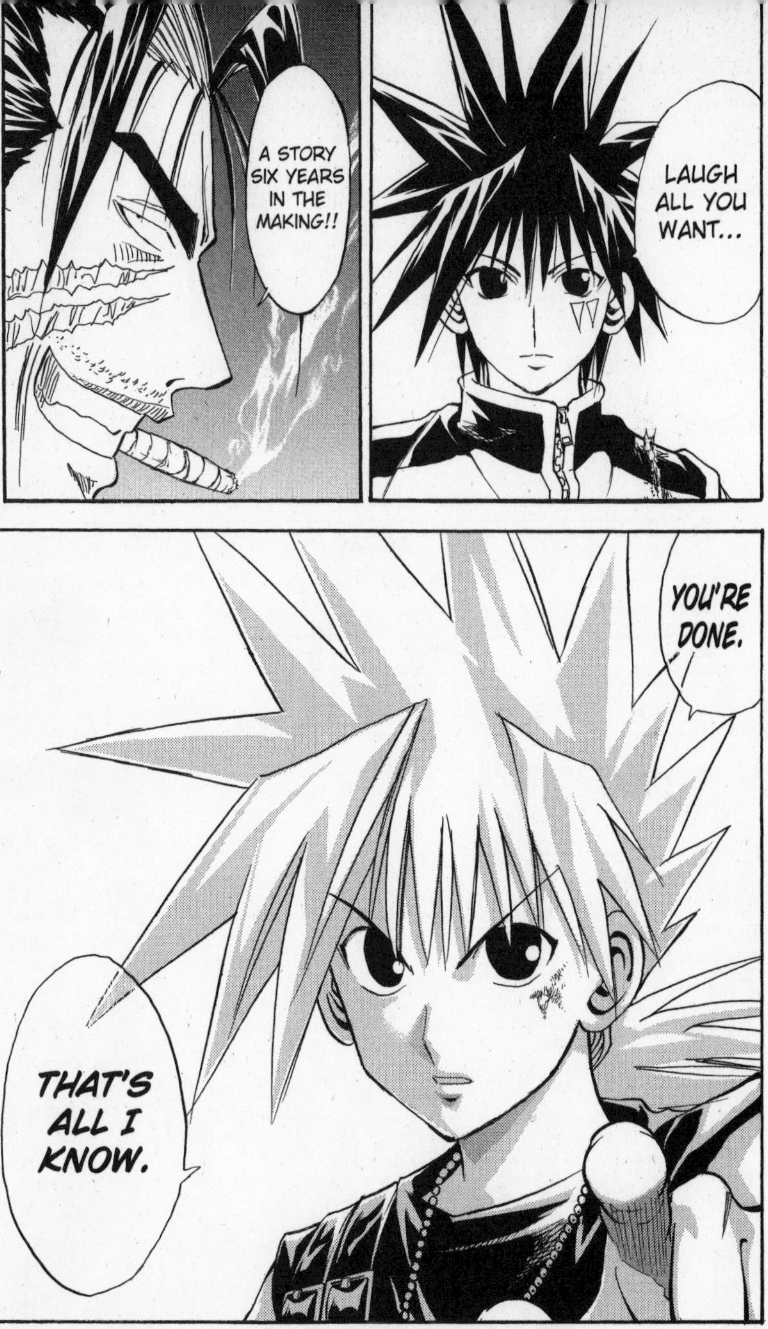
LAUGH ALL YOU WANT...
A STORY SIX YEARS IN THE MAKING!!
YOU'RE DONE.
THAT'S ALL I KNOW.

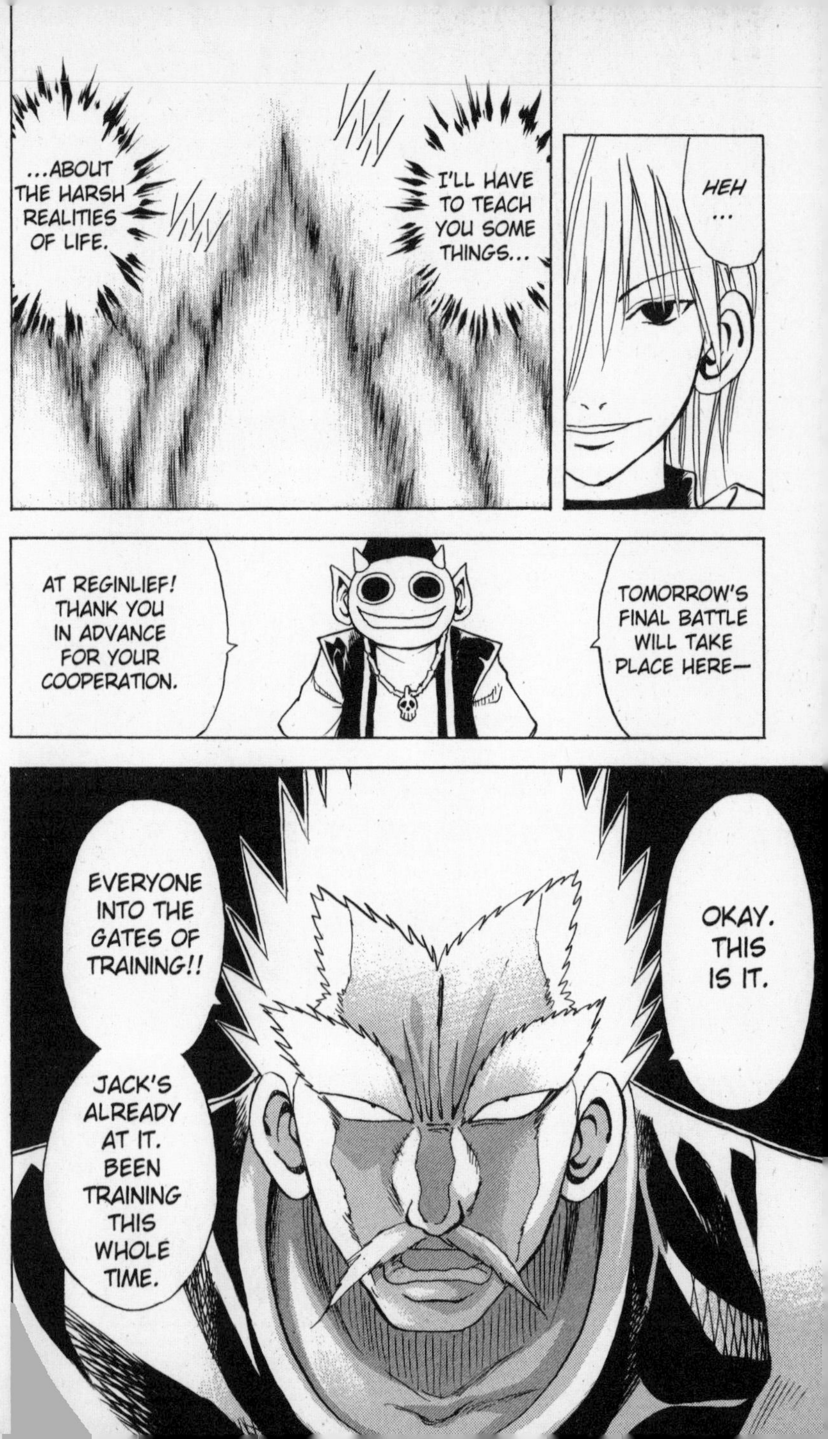
HEH ...
I'LL HAVE TO TEACH YOU SOME THINGS...
...ABOUT THE HARSH REALITIES OF LIFE.
TOMORROW'S FINAL BATTLE WILL TAKE PLACE HERE—
AT REGINLIEF! THANK YOU IN ADVANCE FOR YOUR COOPERATION.
OKAY. THIS IS IT.
EVERYONE INTO THE GATES OF TRAINING!!
JACK'S ALREADY AT IT. BEEN TRAINING THIS WHOLE TIME.

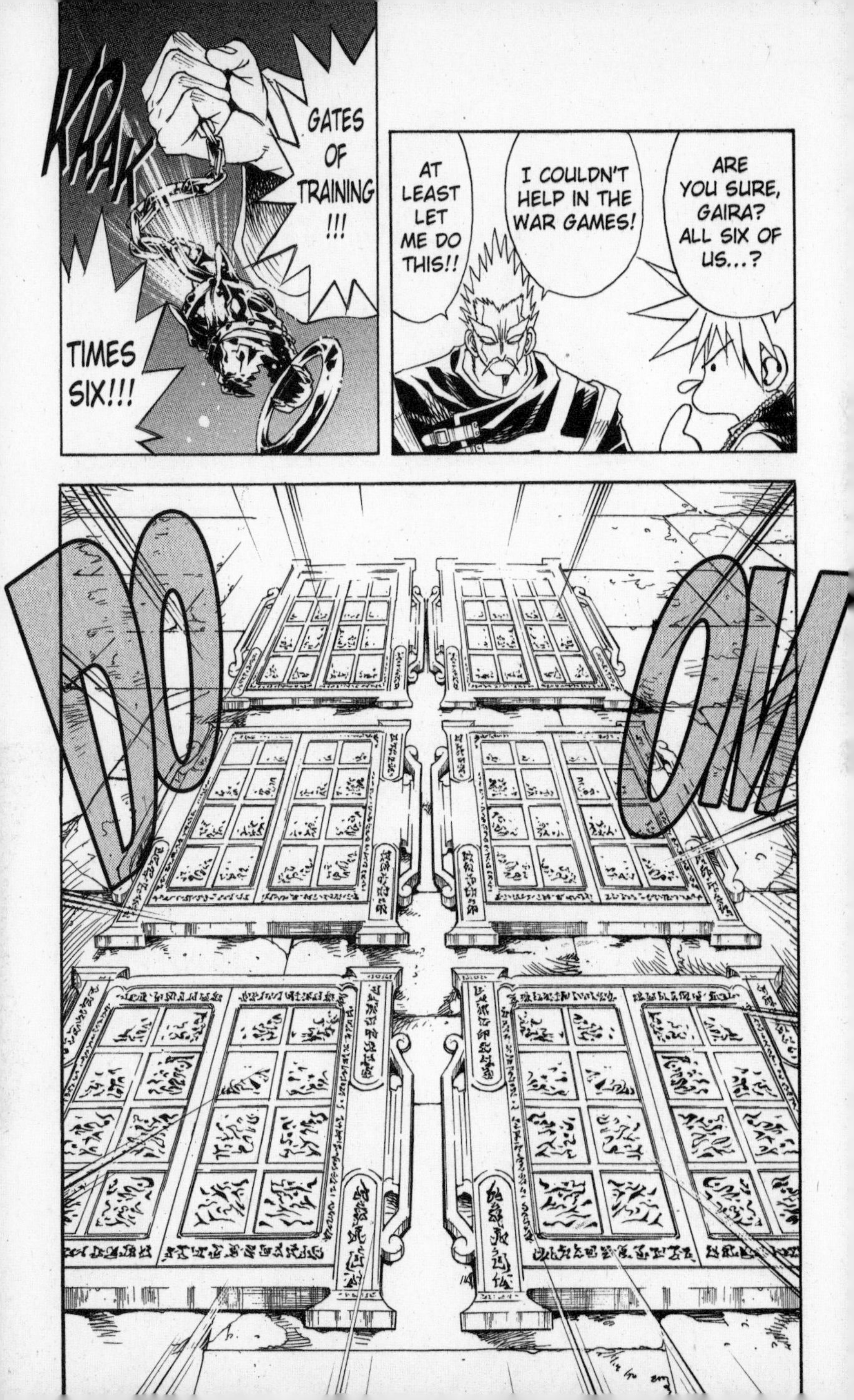
ARE YOU SURE, GAIRA? ALL SIX OF US...?
I COULDN'T HELP IN THE WAR GAMES!
AT LEAST LET ME DO THIS!!
KHAK
GATES OF TRAINING!!!
TIMES SIX!!!
DOOM

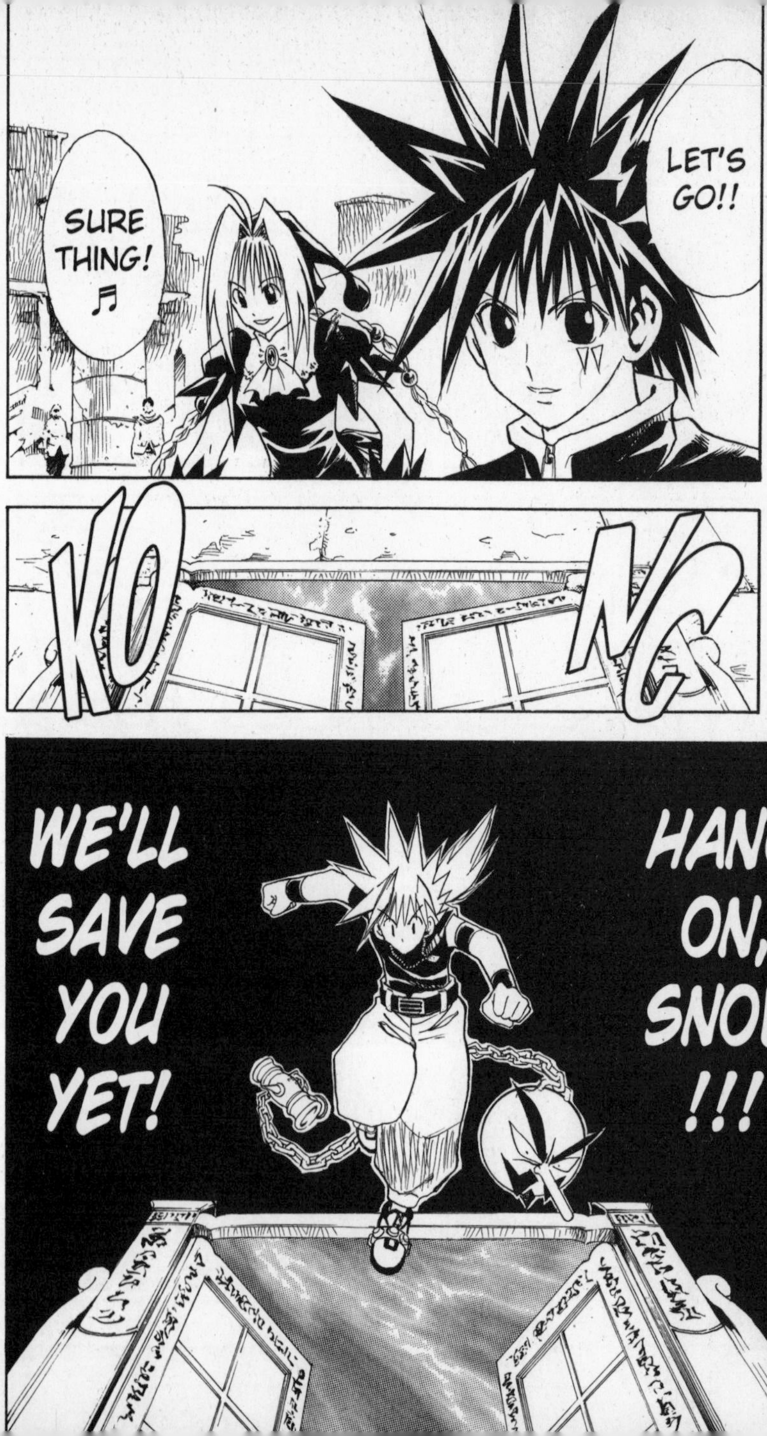
LET'S GO!!
SURE THING! ♬
KONG
HANG ON, SNOW!!!
WE'LL SAVE YOU YET!

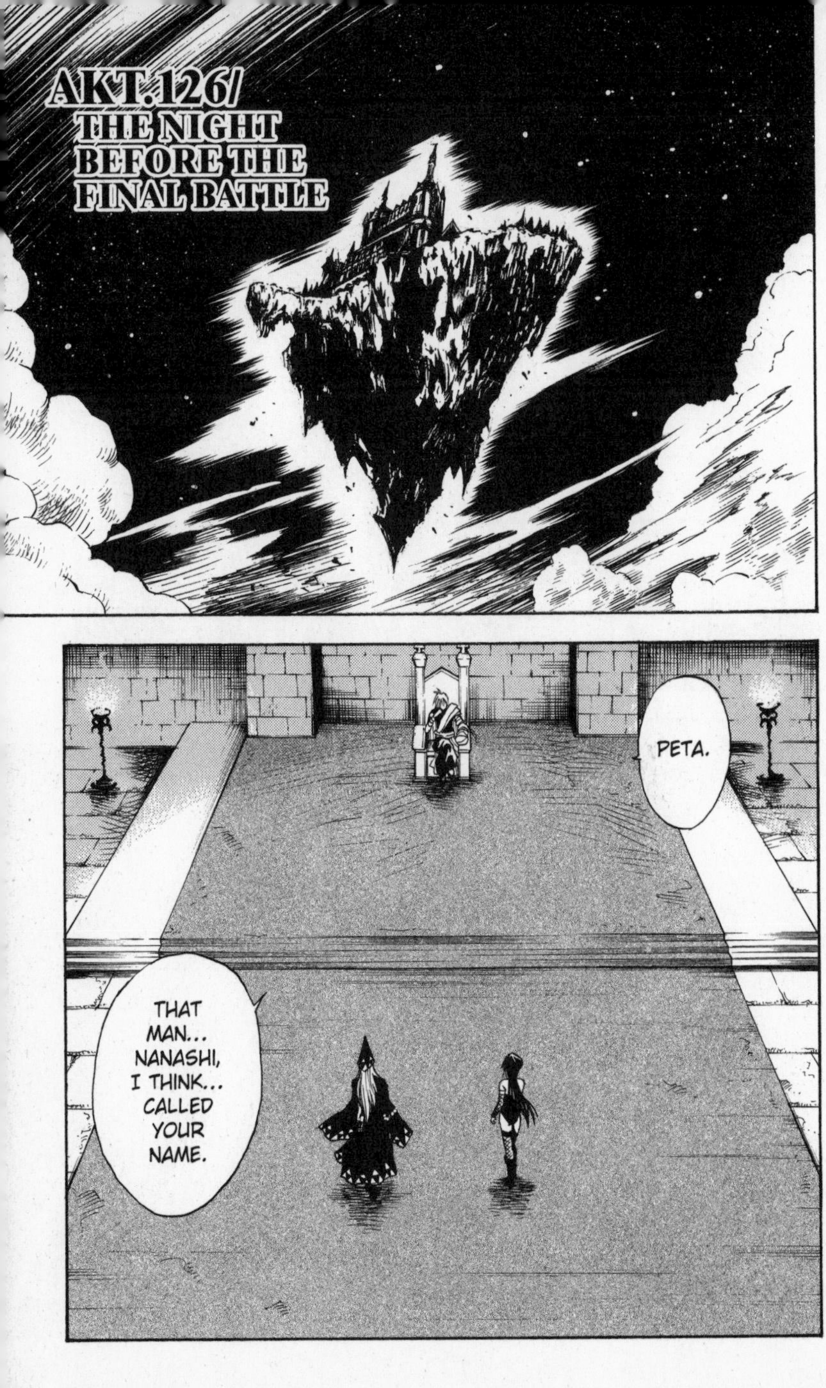
AKT.126/
THE NIGHT BEFORE THE FINAL BATTLE
PETA.
THAT MAN... NANASHI, I THINK... CALLED YOUR NAME.

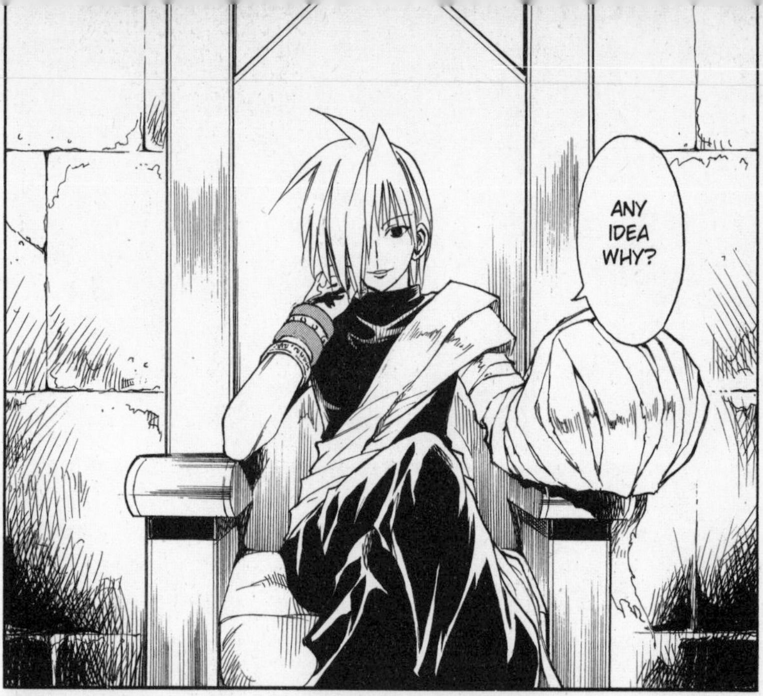
ANY IDEA WHY?
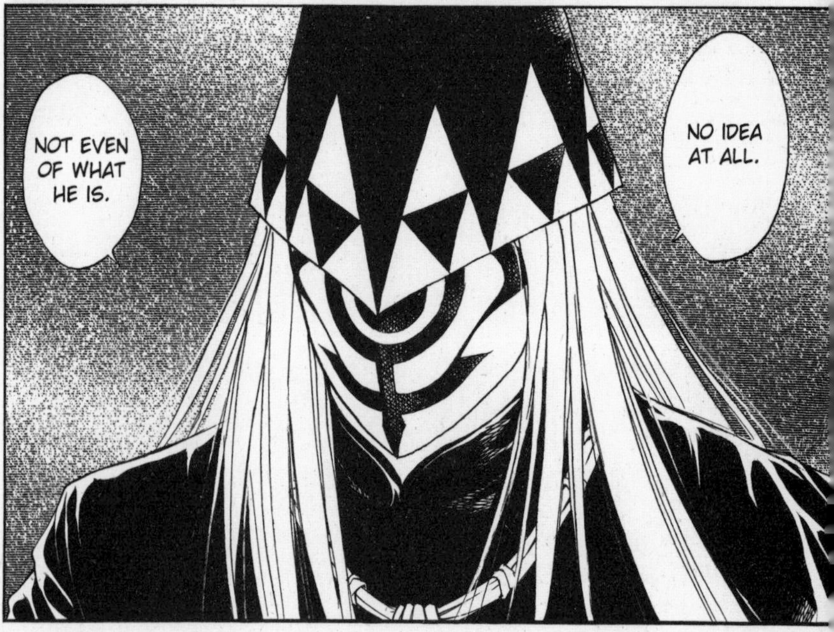
NO IDEA AT ALL.
NOT EVEN OF WHAT HE IS.

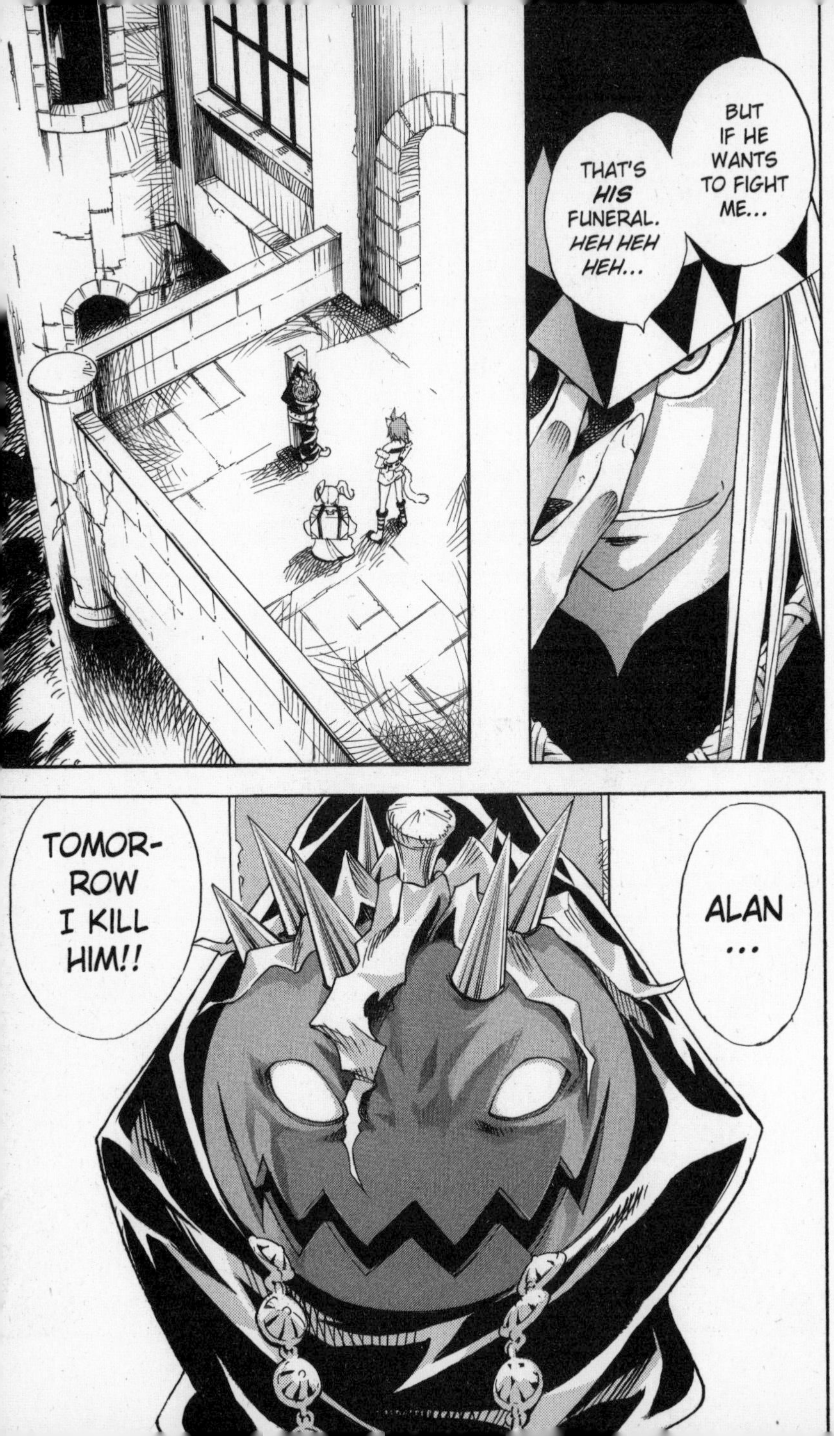
BUT IF HE WANTS TO FIGHT ME...
THAT'S *HIS* FUNERAL. *HEH HEH HEH...*
ALAN...
TOMOR-ROW I KILL HIM!!

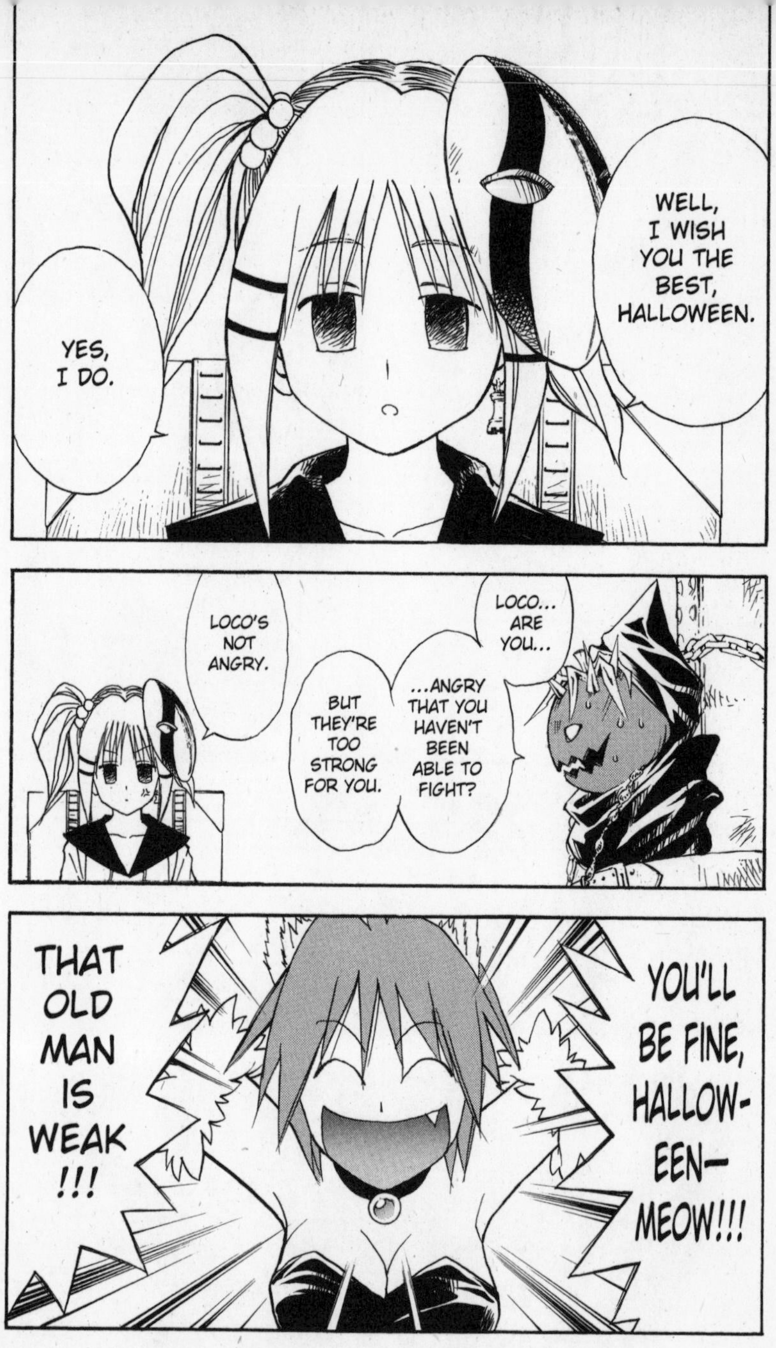
WELL, I WISH YOU THE BEST, HALLOWEEN.
YES, I DO.
LOCO... ARE YOU...
...ANGRY THAT YOU HAVEN'T BEEN ABLE TO FIGHT?
LOCO'S NOT ANGRY.
BUT THEY'RE TOO STRONG FOR YOU.
YOU'LL BE FINE, HALLOW-EEN—MEOW!!!
THAT OLD MAN IS WEAK!!!

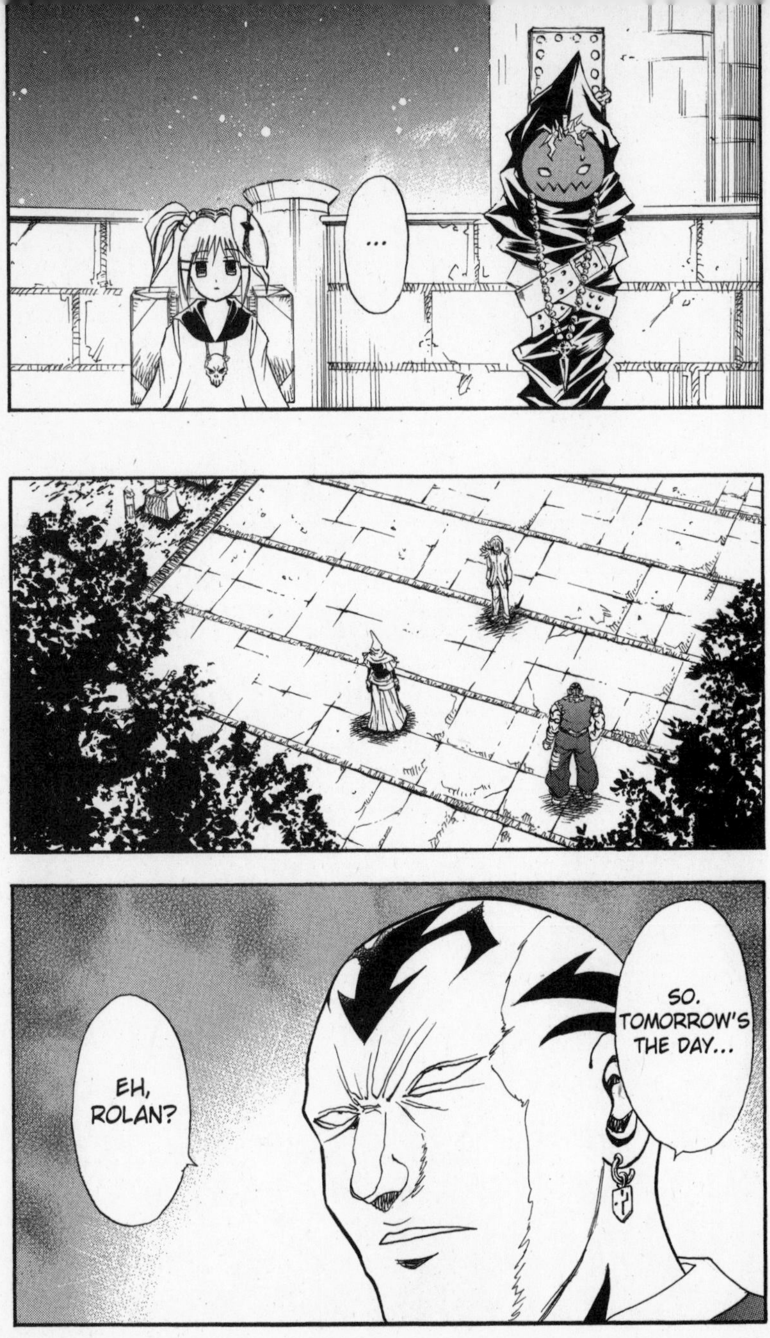
...
SO. TOMORROW'S THE DAY...
EH, ROLAN?

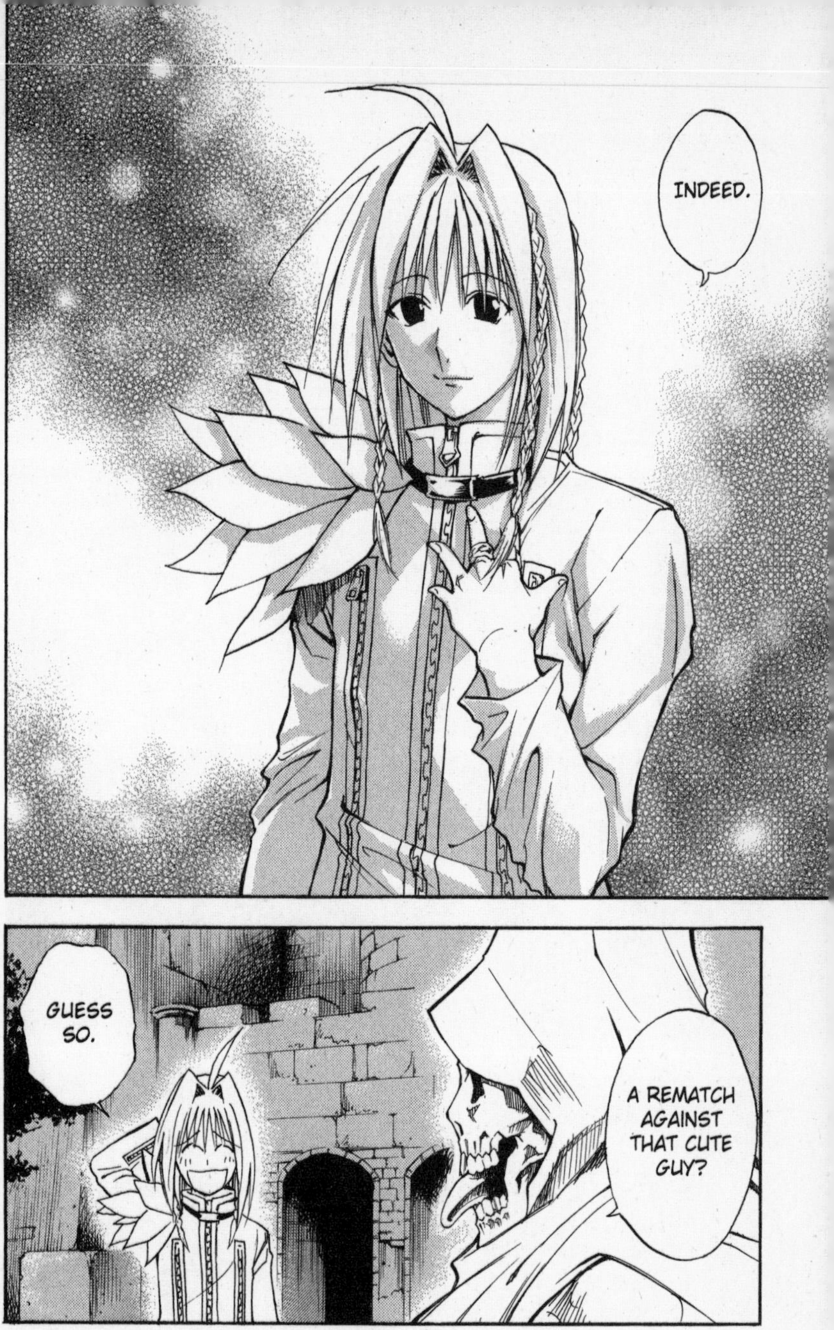
INDEED.
A REMATCH AGAINST THAT CUTE GUY?
GUESS SO.

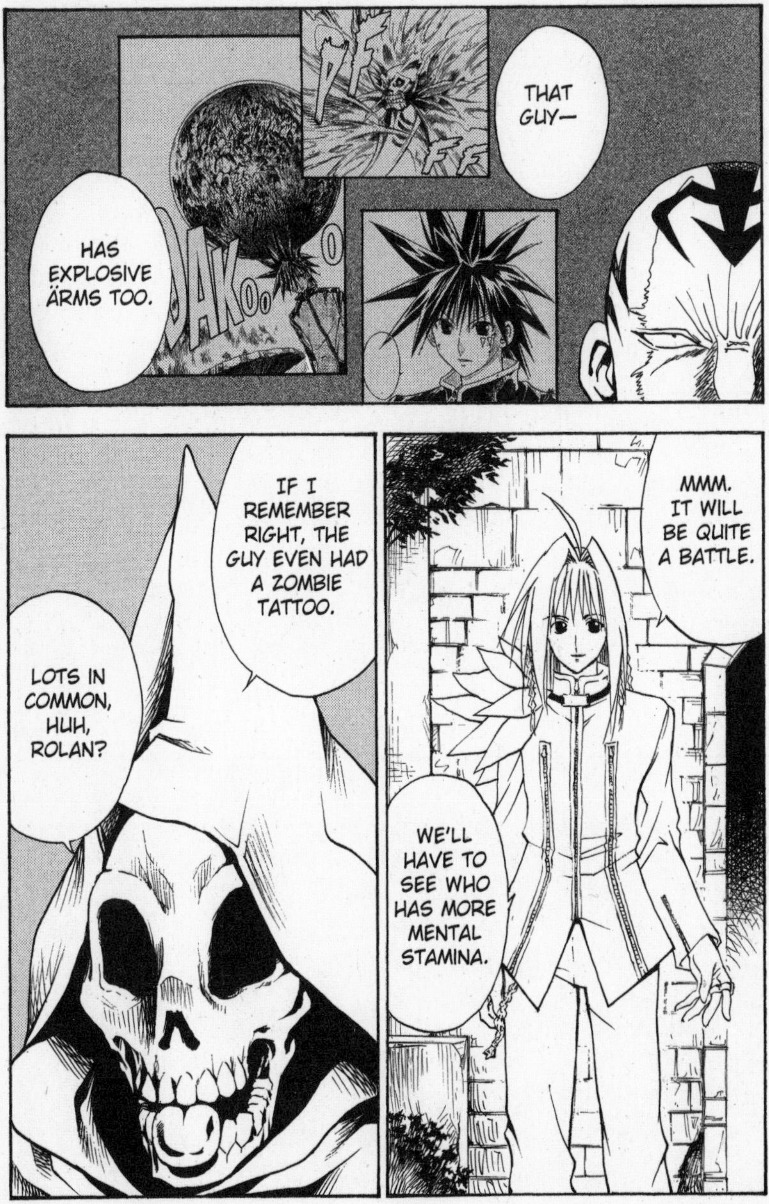
THAT GUY—
FF
HAS EXPLOSIVE ÄRMS TOO.
DAK
MMM. IT WILL BE QUITE A BATTLE.
WE'LL HAVE TO SEE WHO HAS MORE MENTAL STAMINA.
IF I REMEMBER RIGHT, THE GUY EVEN HAD A ZOMBIE TATTOO.
LOTS IN COMMON, HUH, ROLAN?

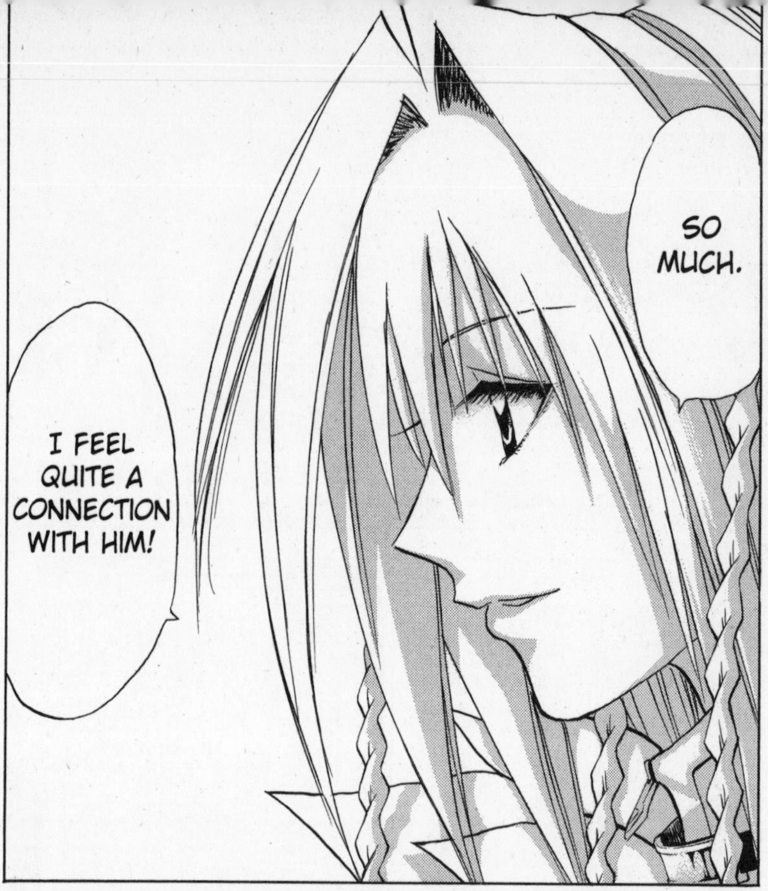
SO MUCH.
I FEEL QUITE A CONNECTION WITH HIM!
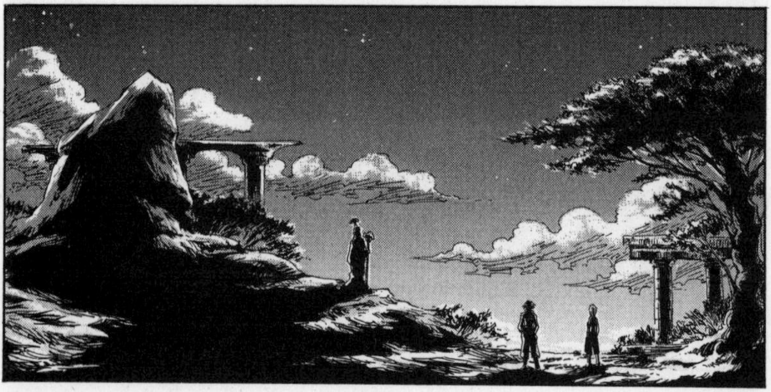

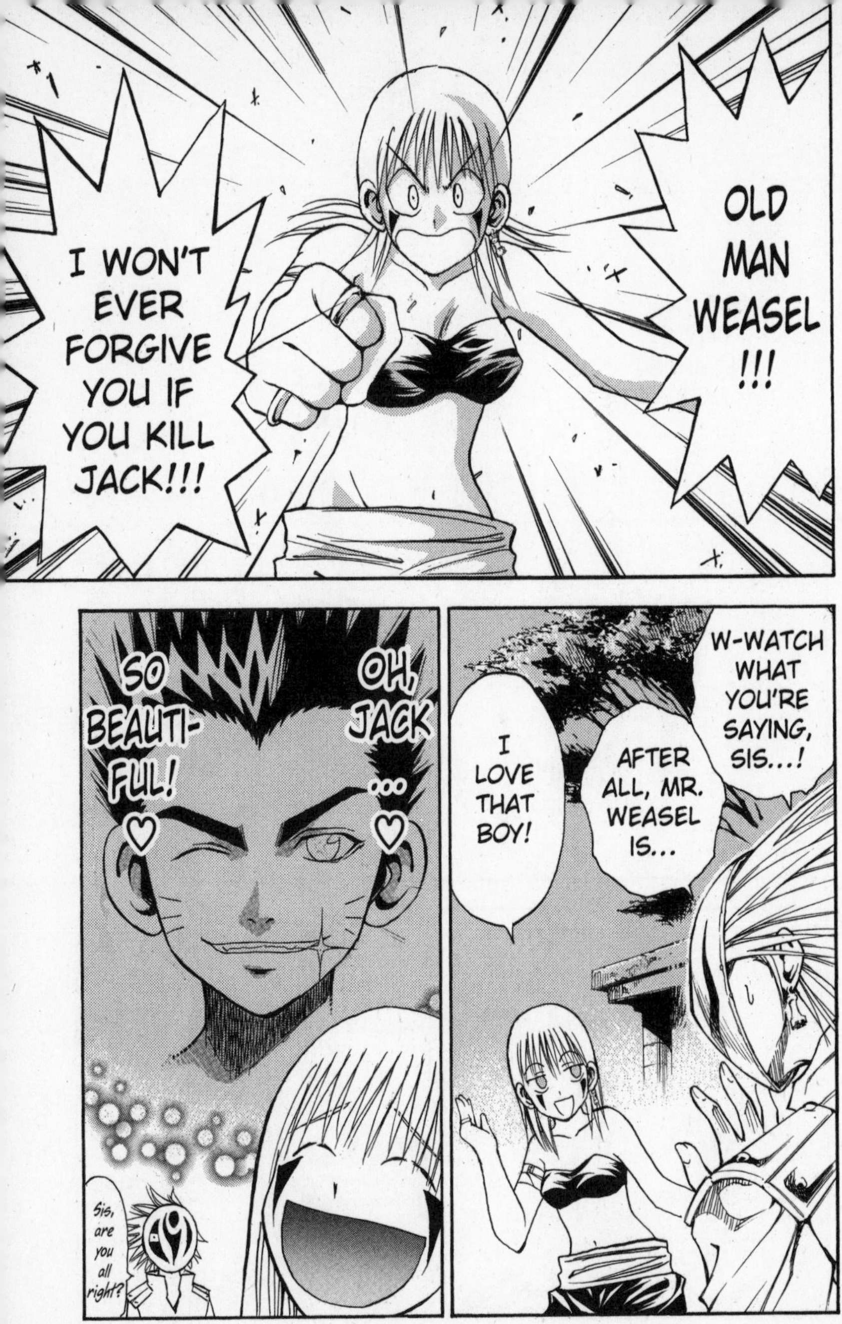
OLD MAN WEASEL!!!
I WON'T EVER FORGIVE YOU IF YOU KILL JACK!!!
W-WATCH WHAT YOU'RE SAYING, SIS...!
AFTER ALL, MR. WEASEL IS...
I LOVE THAT BOY!
OH, JACK... ♡
SO BEAUTI-FUL! ♡
Sis, are you all right?

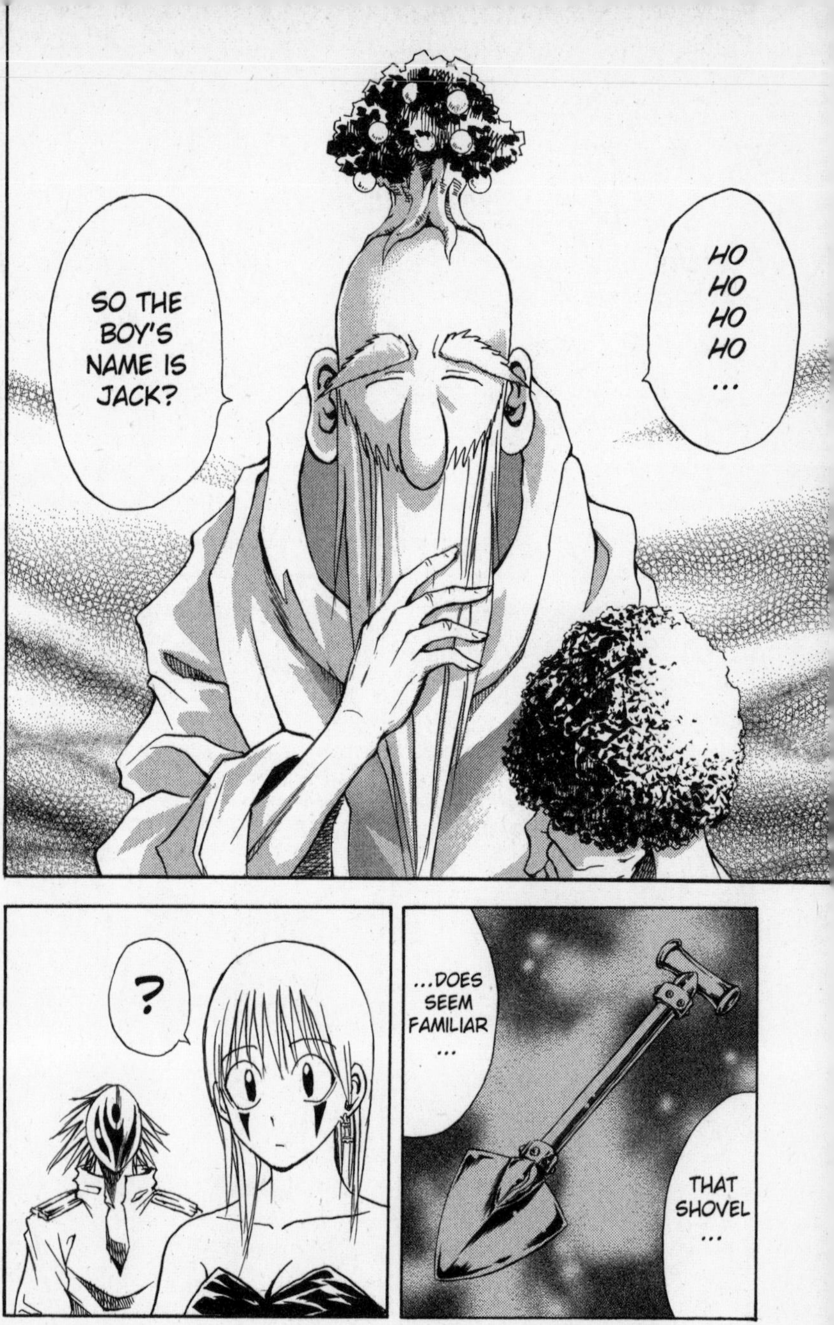
HO HO HO HO ...
SO THE BOY'S NAME IS JACK?
THAT SHOVEL ...
...DOES SEEM FAMILIAR ...
?

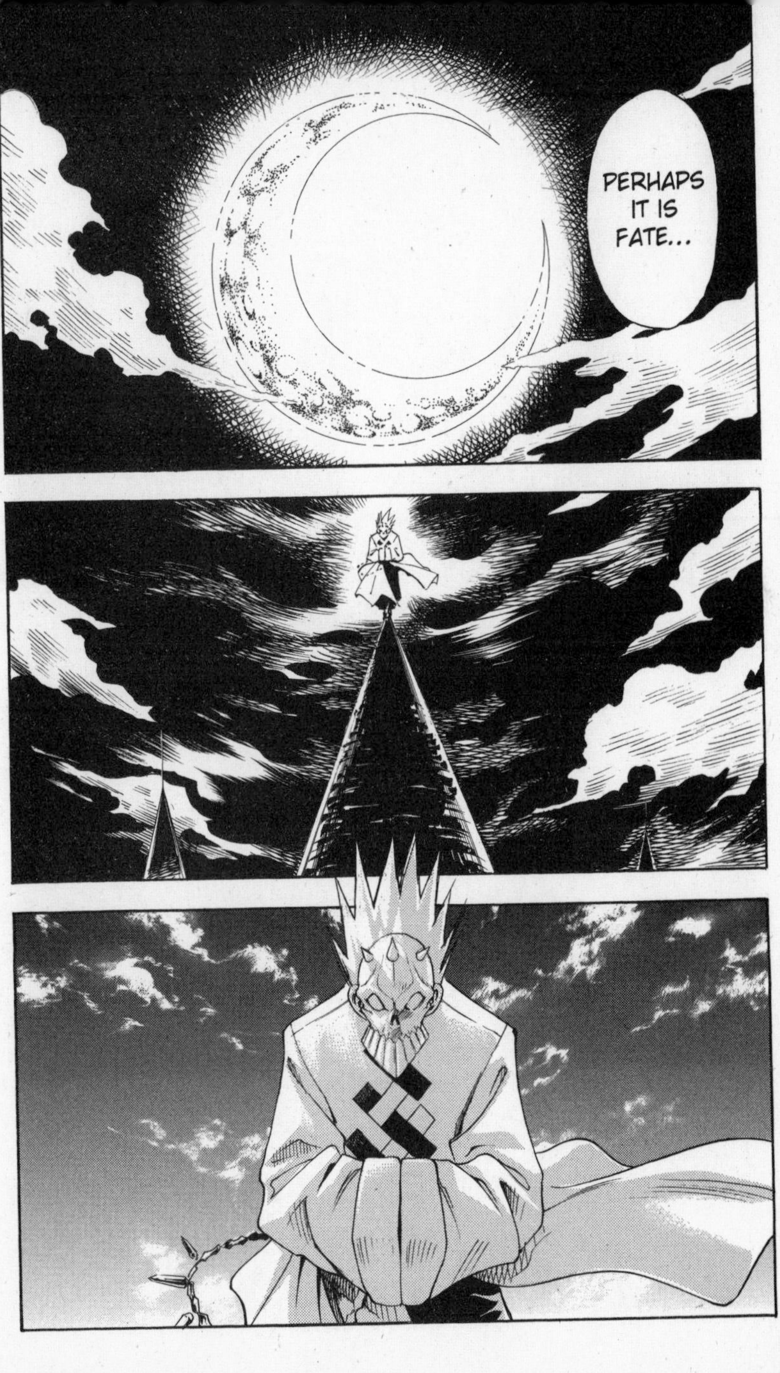
PERHAPS IT IS FATE...

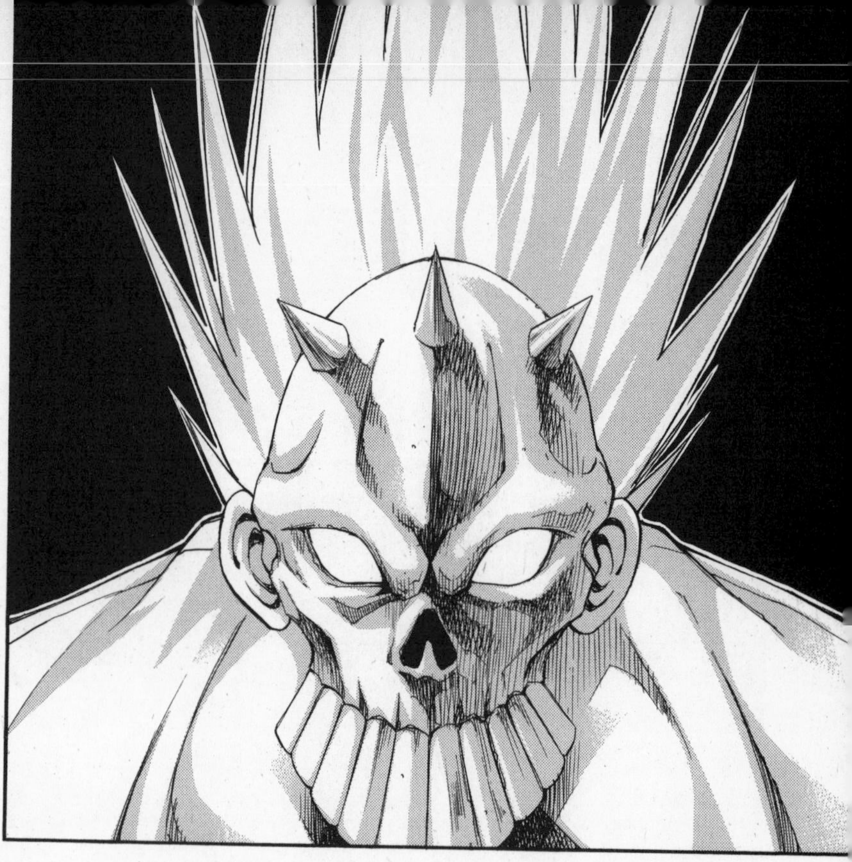

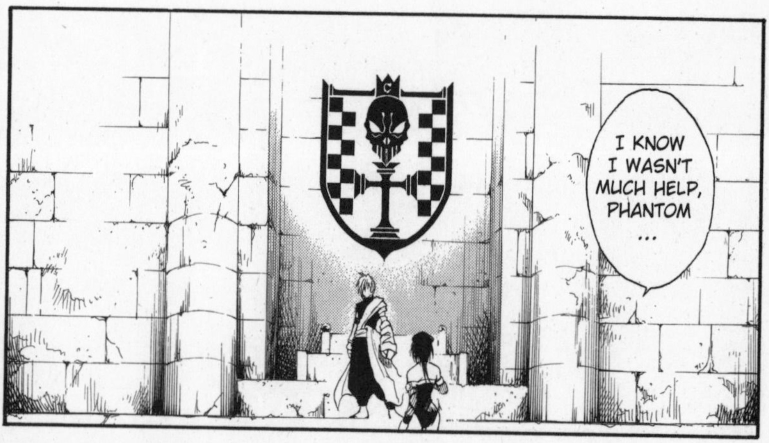
I KNOW I WASN'T MUCH HELP, PHANTOM ...

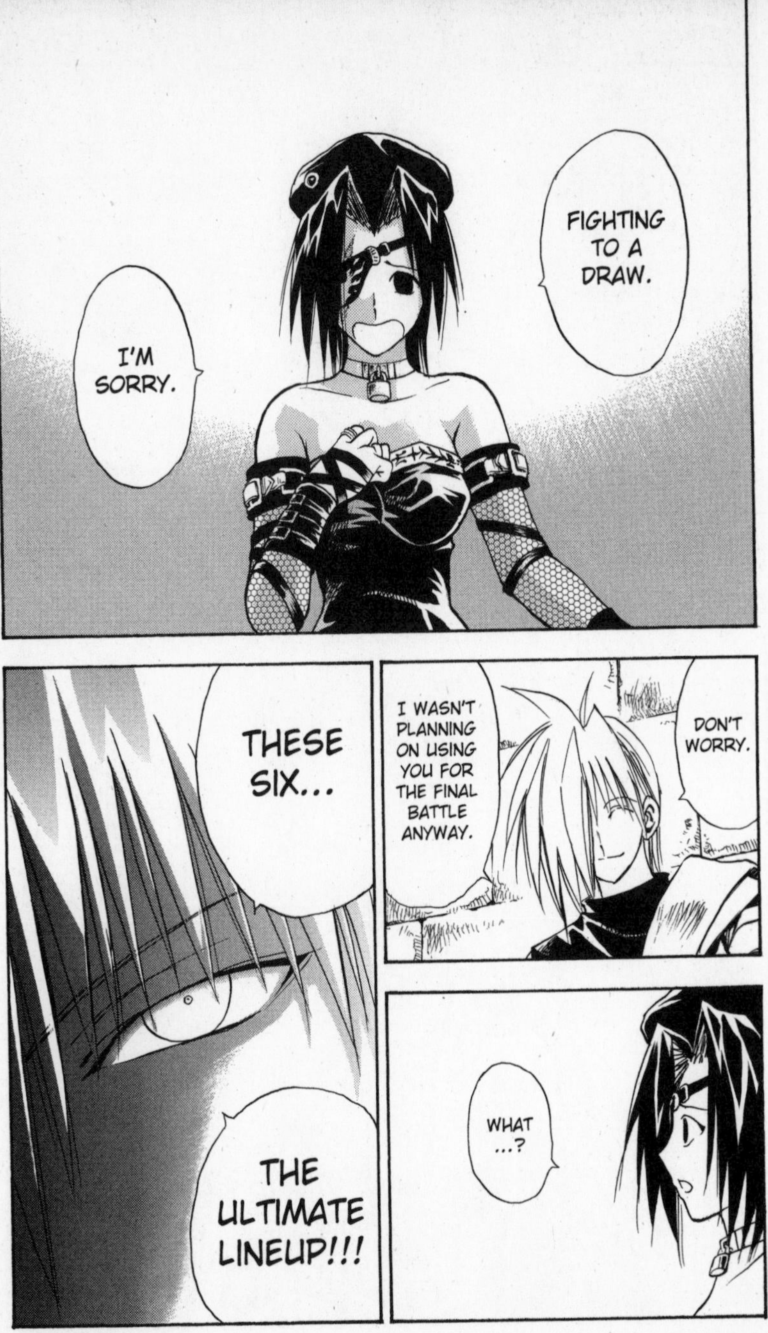
FIGHTING TO A DRAW.
I'M SORRY.
DON'T WORRY.
I WASN'T PLANNING ON USING YOU FOR THE FINAL BATTLE ANYWAY.
WHAT ...?
THESE SIX...
THE ULTIMATE LINEUP!!!

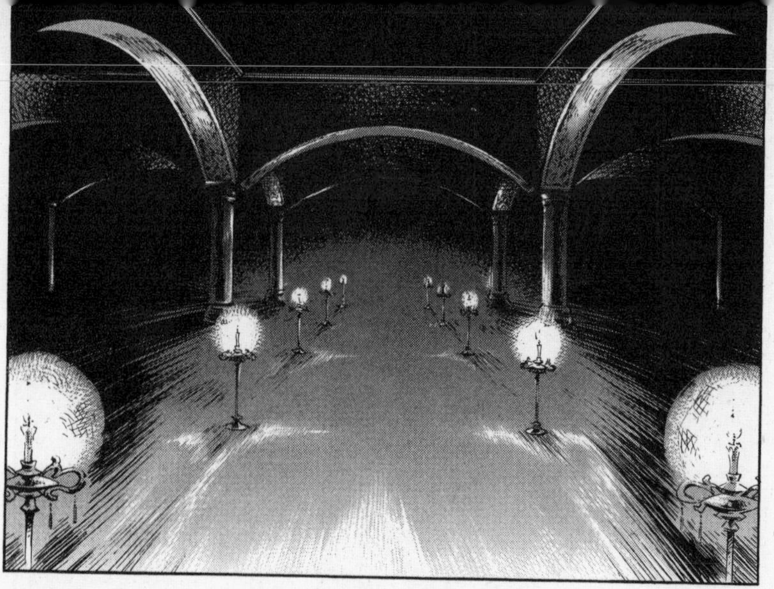

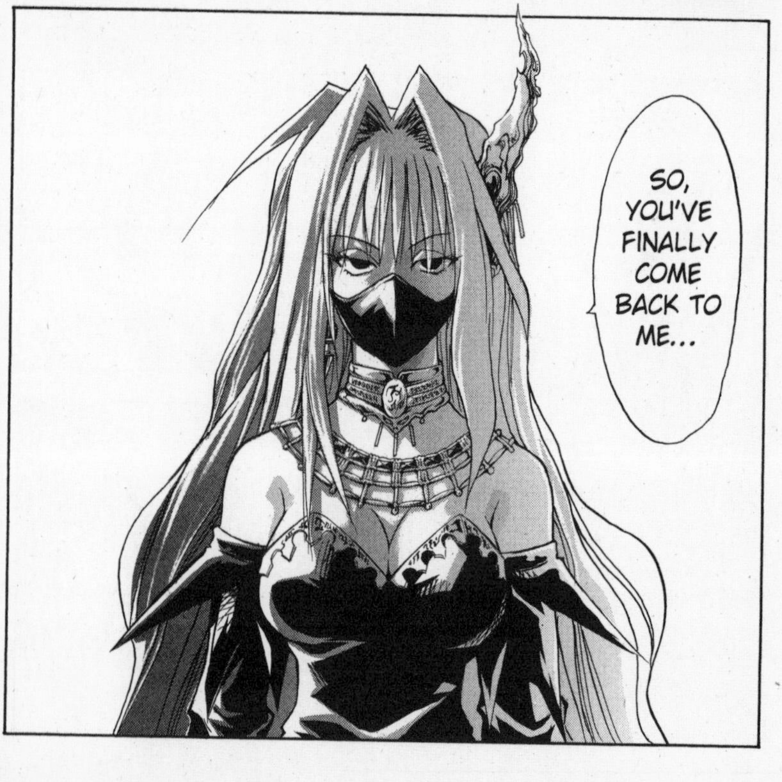
SO, YOU'VE FINALLY COME BACK TO ME...

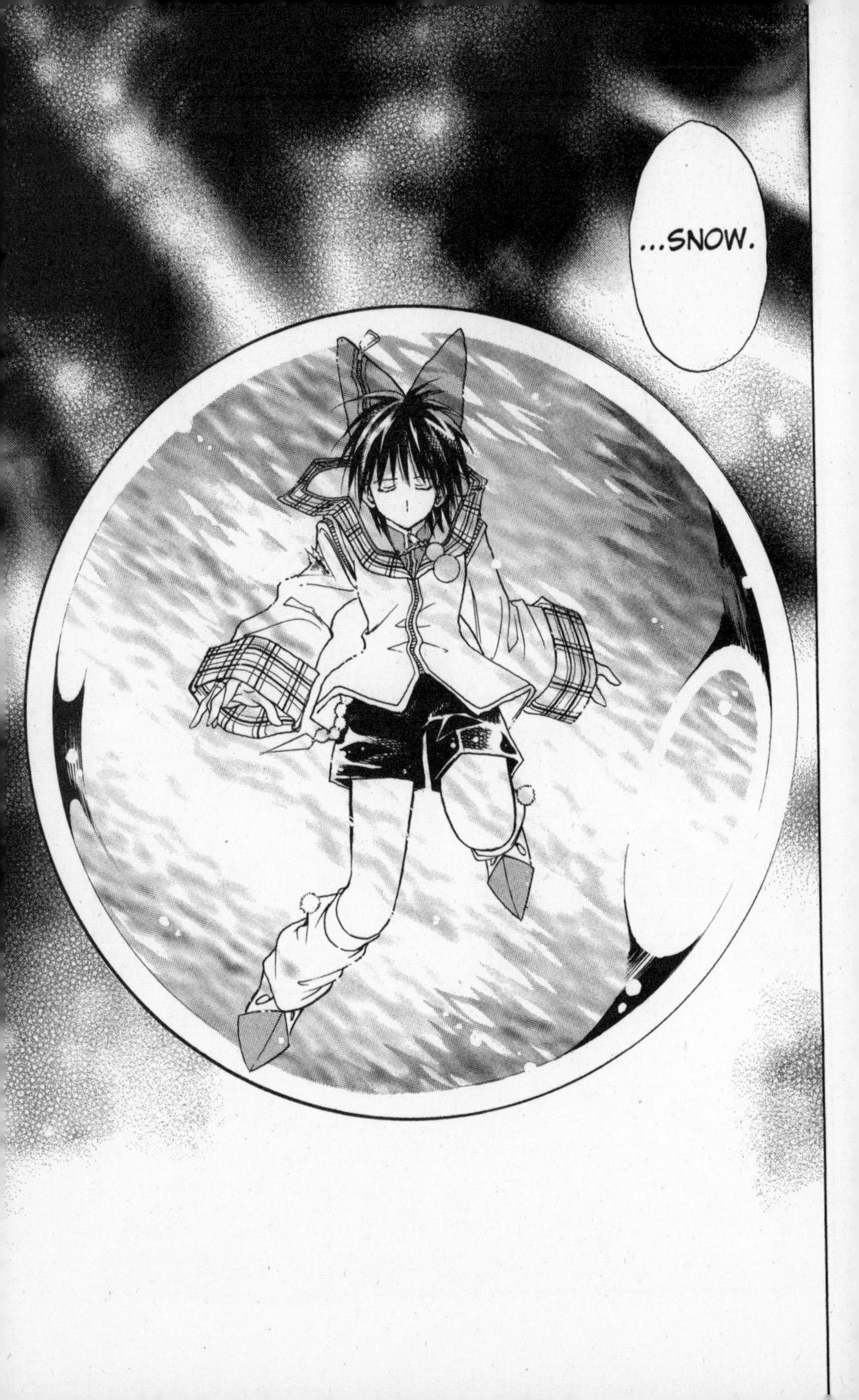
...SNOW.

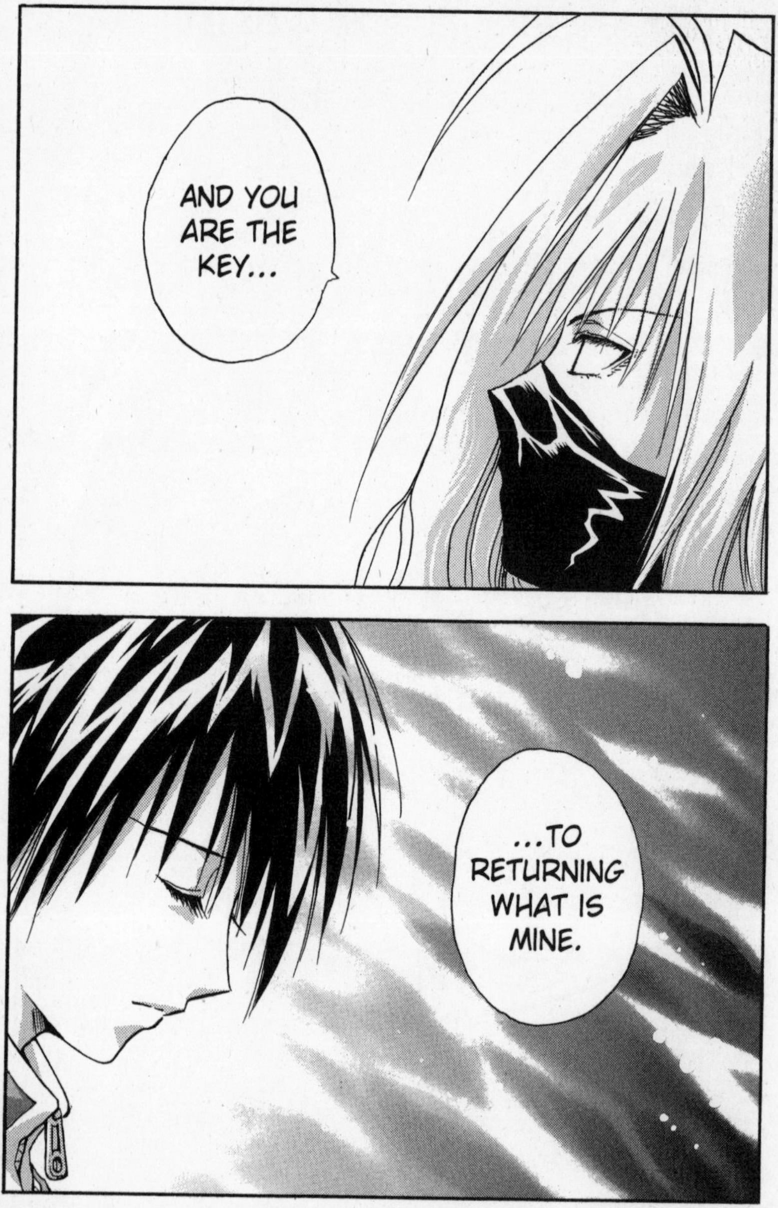
AND YOU ARE THE KEY...
...TO RETURNING WHAT IS MINE.

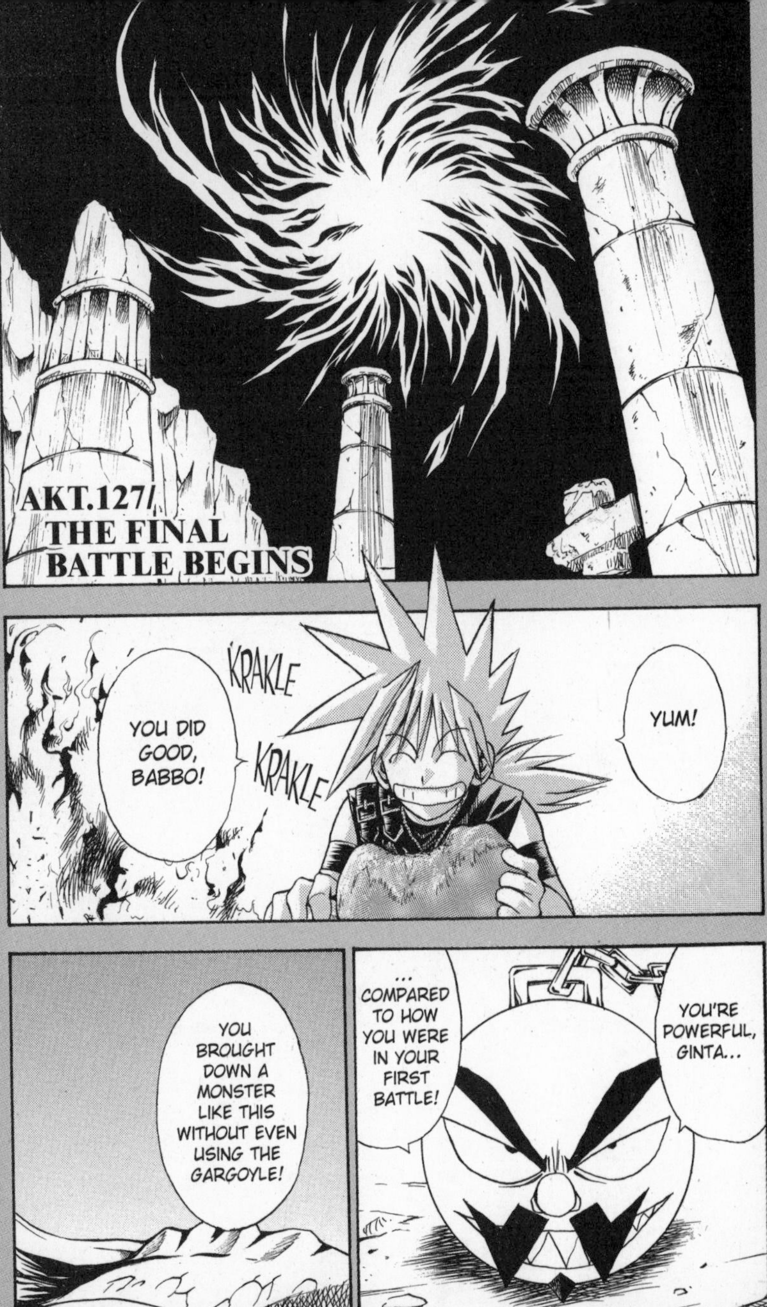
AKT.127/ THE FINAL BATTLE BEGINS
YUM!
KRAKLE
KRAKLE
YOU DID GOOD, BABBO!
YOU'RE POWERFUL, GINTA...
...COMPARED TO HOW YOU WERE IN YOUR FIRST BATTLE!
YOU BROUGHT DOWN A MONSTER LIKE THIS WITHOUT EVEN USING THE GARGOYLE!

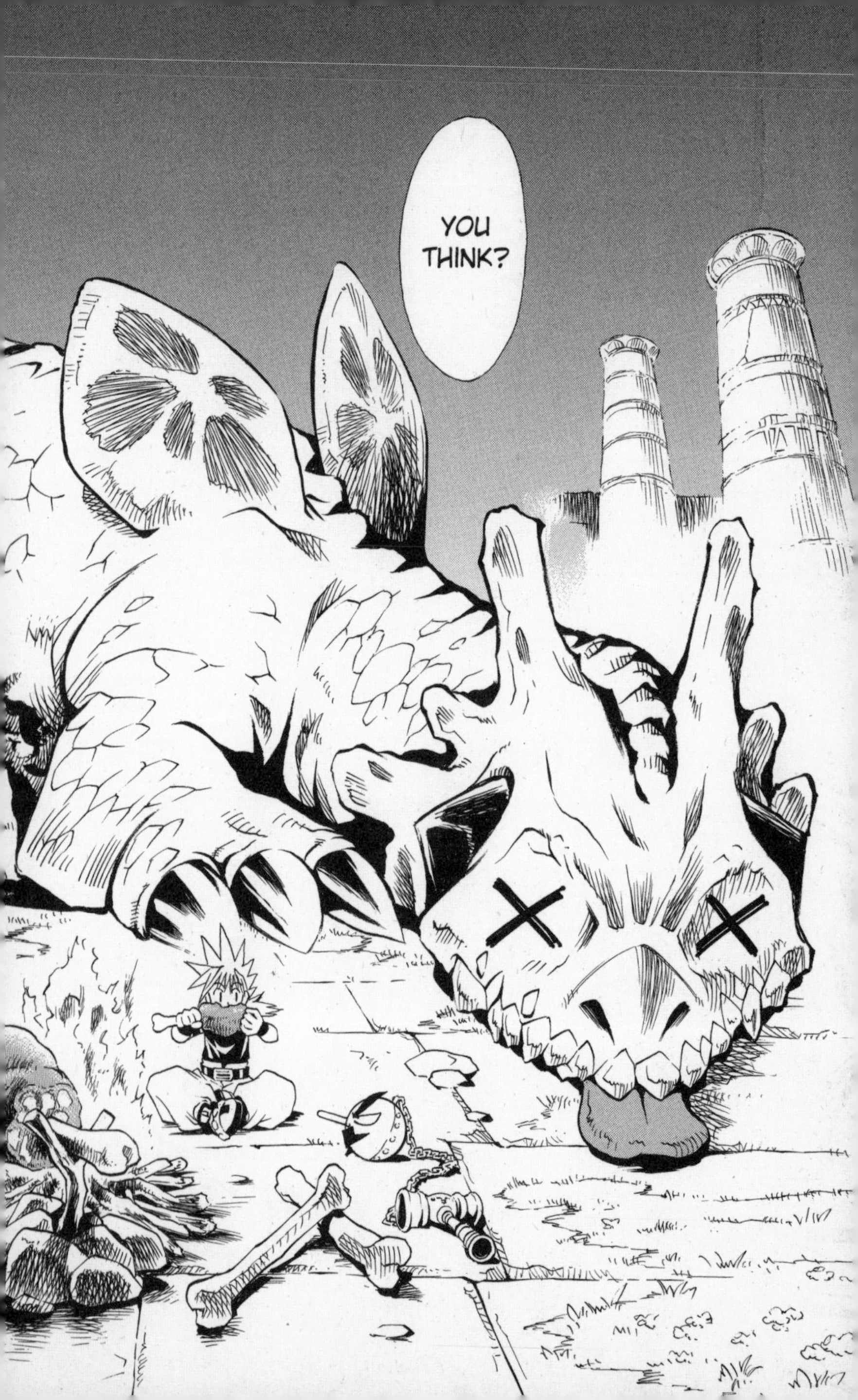
YOU THINK?

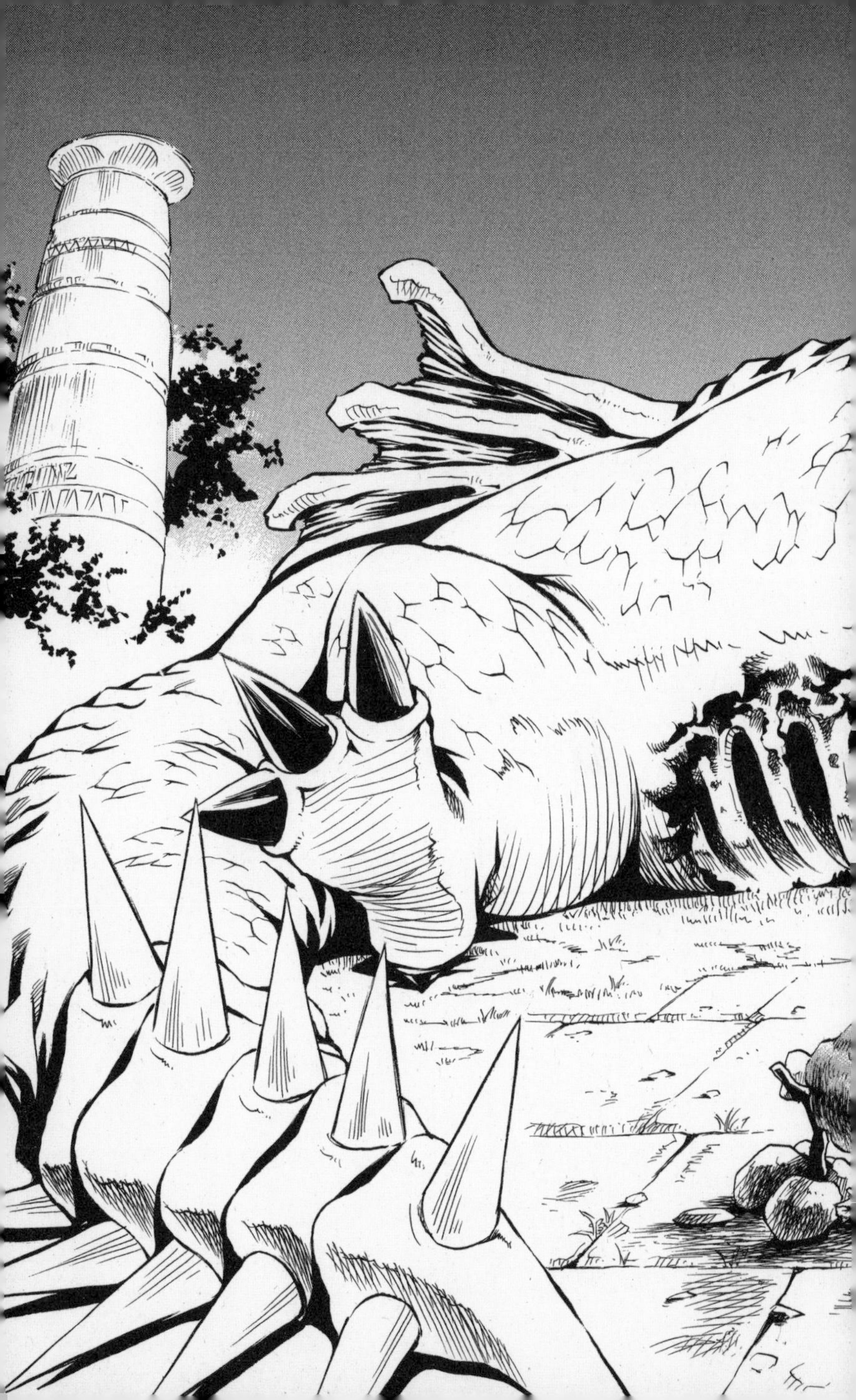

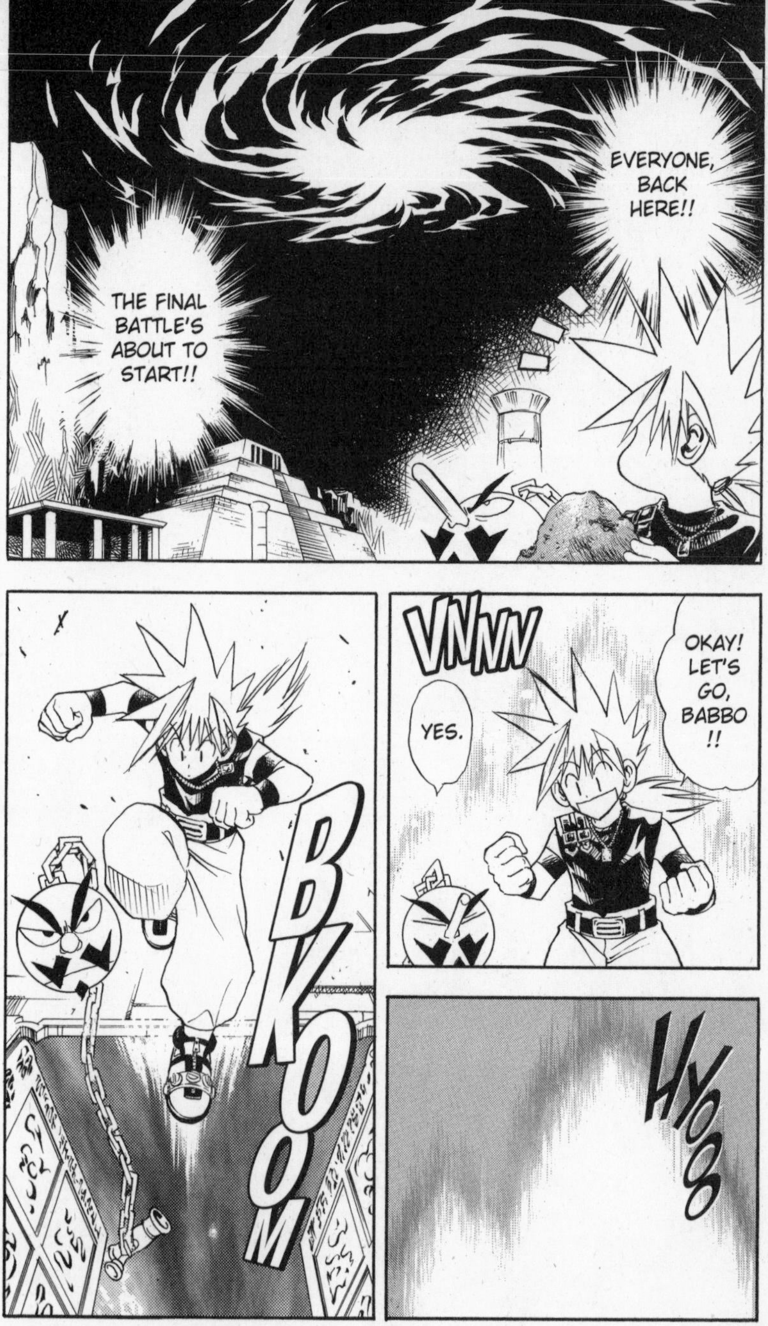
EVERYONE, BACK HERE!!
THE FINAL BATTLE'S ABOUT TO START!!
OKAY! LET'S GO, BABBO!!
VNNNN
YES.
HYOOO
BKOOOM

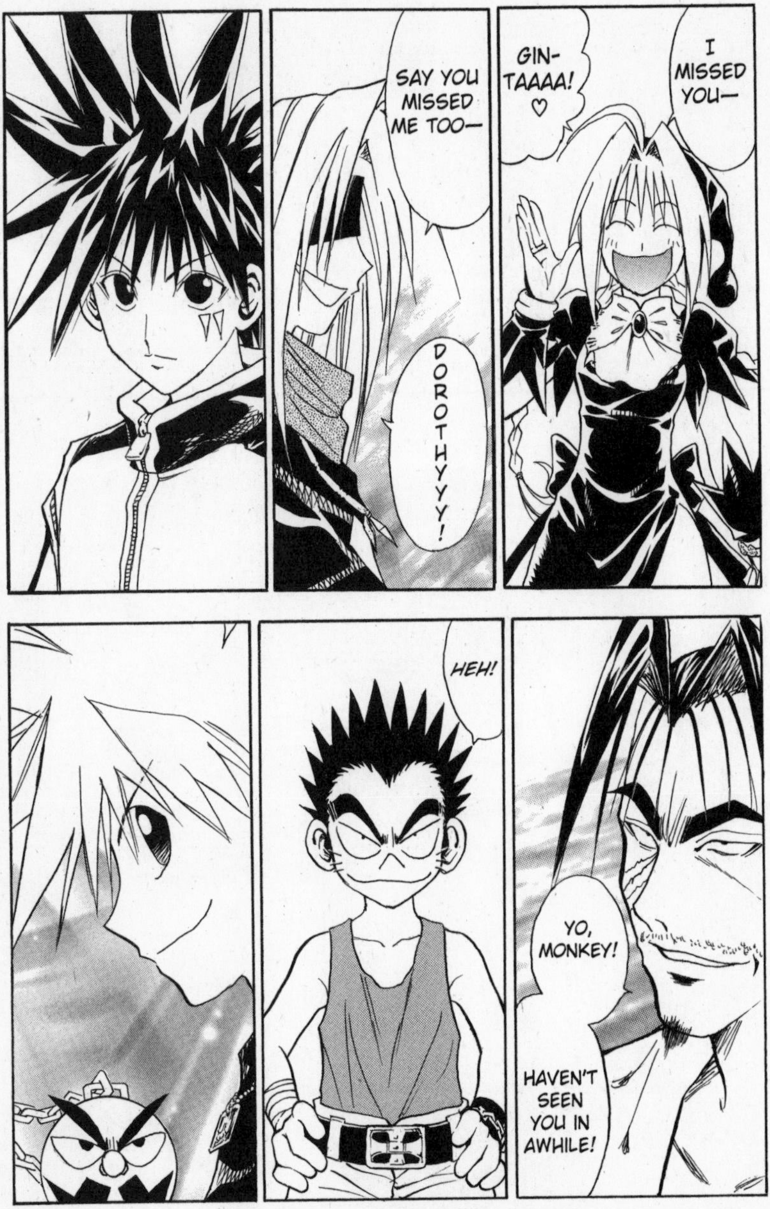
I MISSED YOU—
GIN-TAAAA! ♡
SAY YOU MISSED ME TOO—
DOROTHYYY!
YO, MONKEY!
HAVEN'T SEEN YOU IN AWHILE!
HEH!

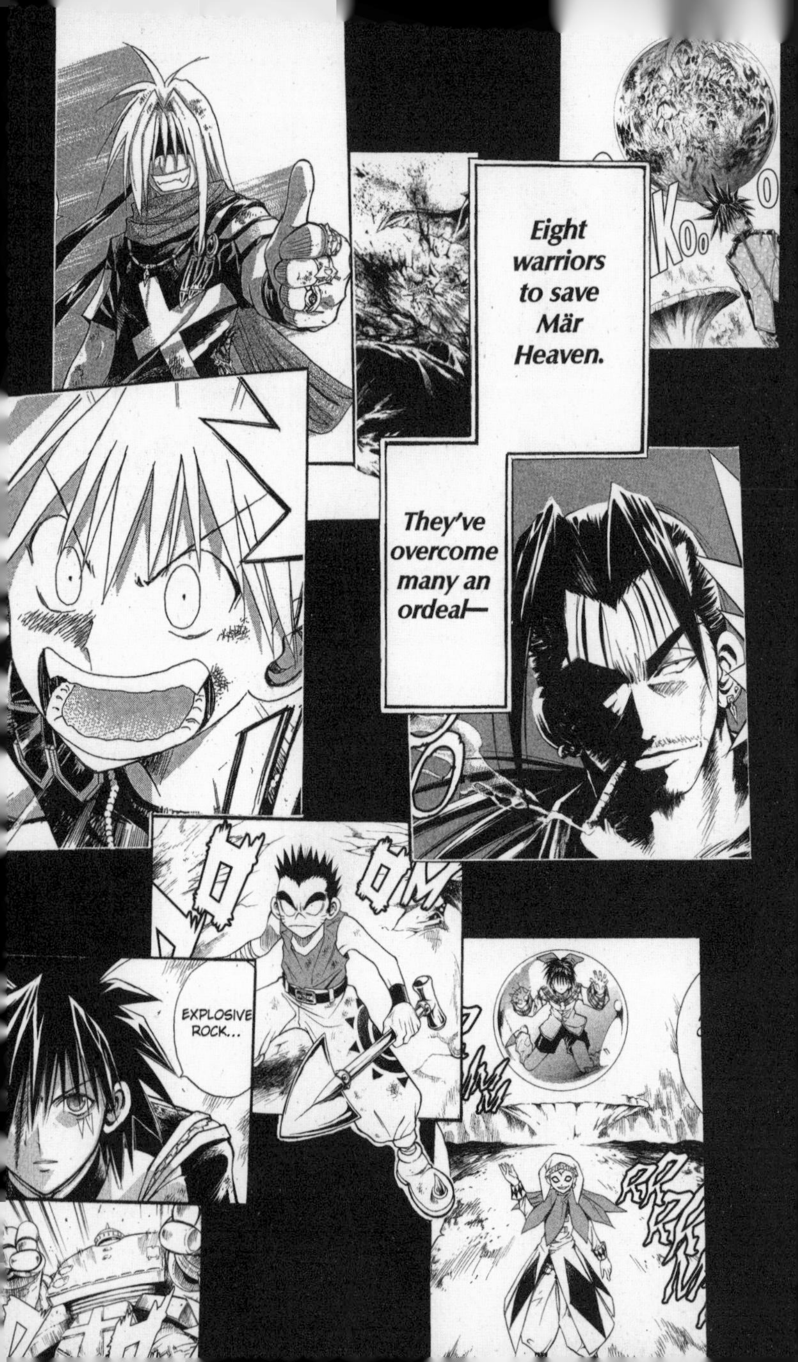
Eight warriors to save Mär Heaven.
They've overcome many an ordeal—
EXPLOSIVE ROCK...

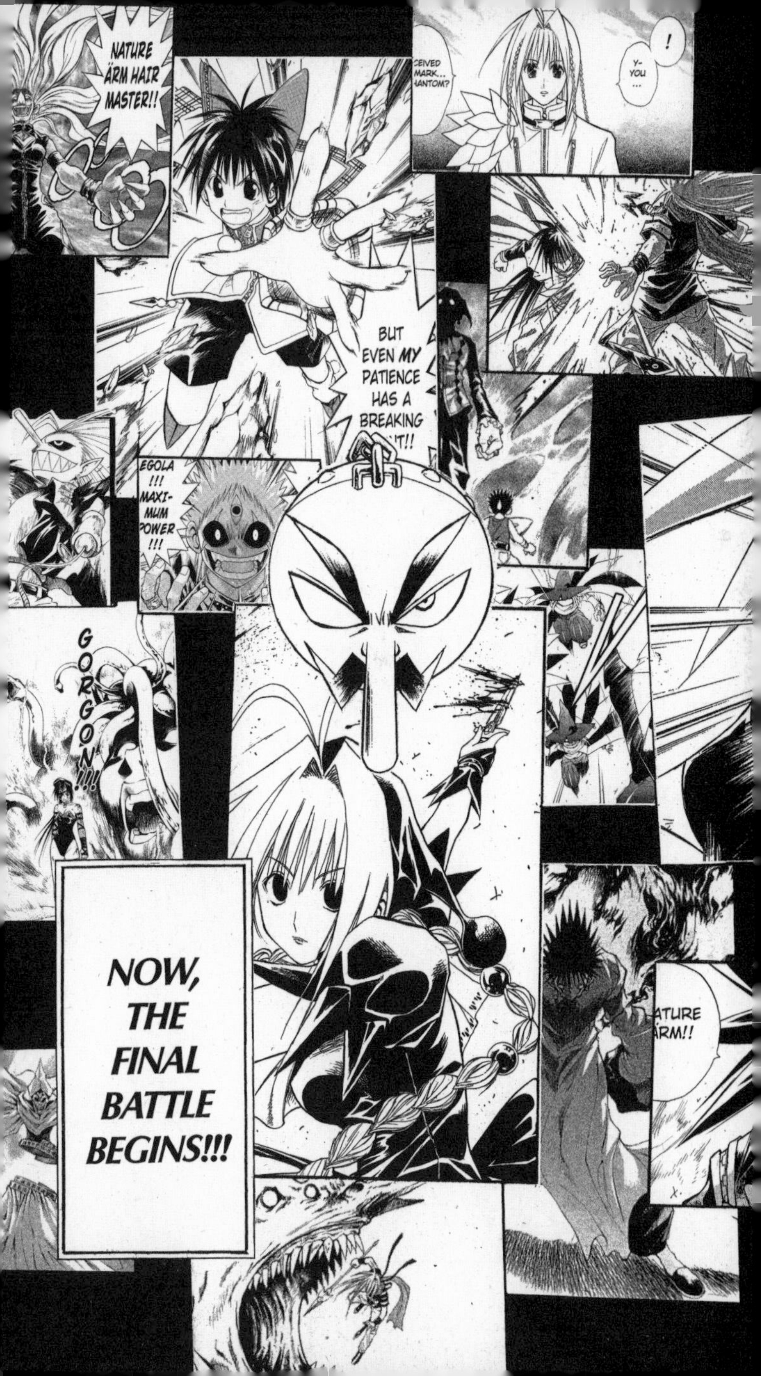
!
Y-YOU ...
CEIVED MARK... HANTOM?
NATURE ÄRM HAIR MASTER!!
BUT EVEN MY PATIENCE HAS A BREAKING
EGOLA!!! MAXI-MUM POWER!!!
ATURE ÄRM!!
GORGON!!!
NOW, THE FINAL BATTLE BEGINS!!!

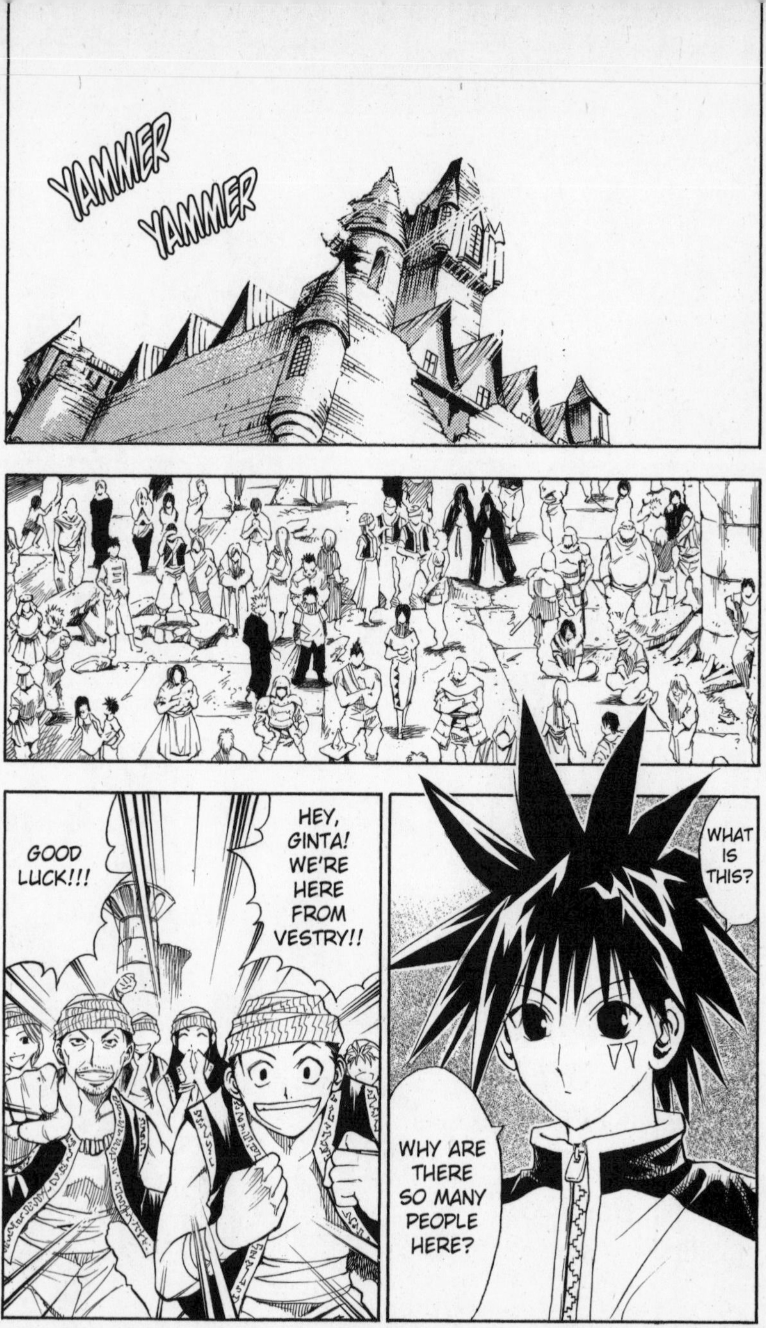
YAMMER
YAMMER
WHAT IS THIS?
WHY ARE THERE SO MANY PEOPLE HERE?
HEY, GINTA! WE'RE HERE FROM VESTRY!!
GOOD LUCK!!!

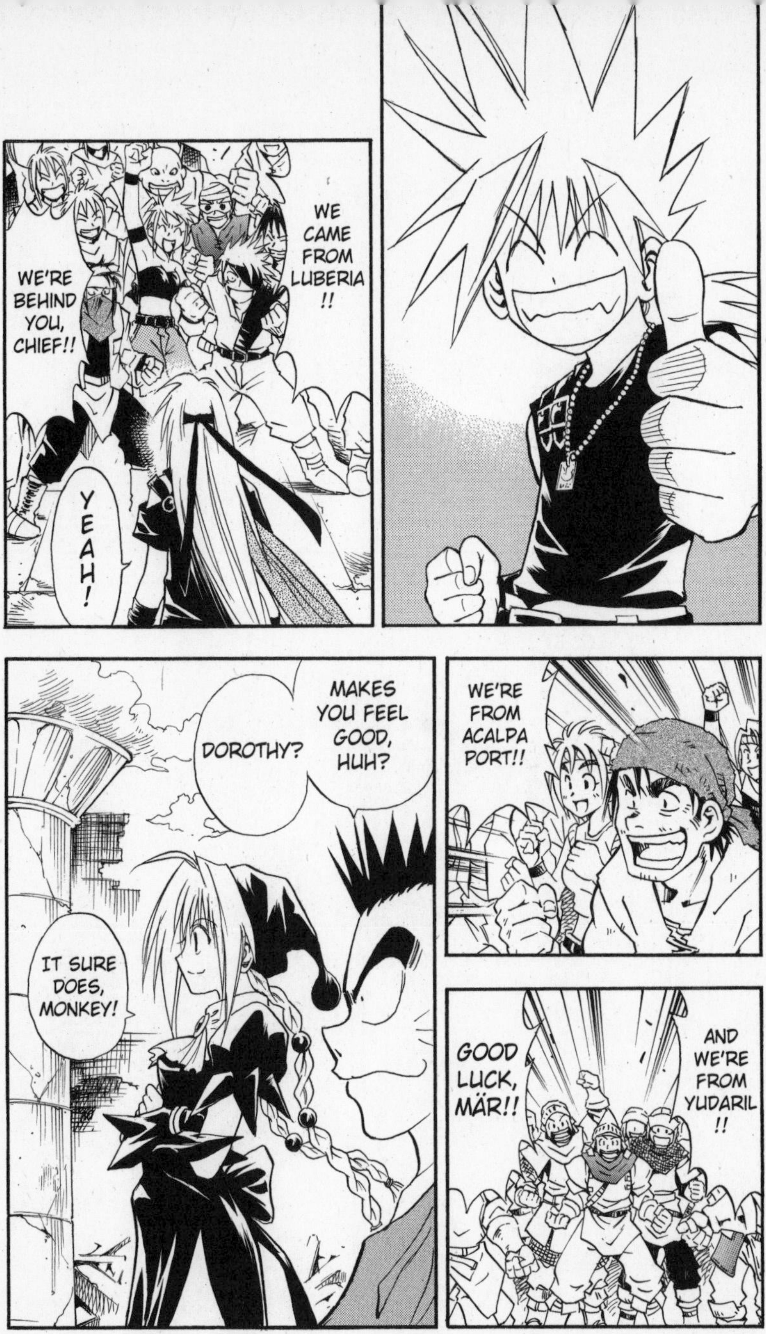
WE CAME FROM LUBERIA!!
WE'RE BEHIND YOU, CHIEF!!
YEAH!
WE'RE FROM ACALPA PORT!!
AND WE'RE FROM YUDARIL!!
GOOD LUCK, MÄR!!
MAKES YOU FEEL GOOD, HUH?
DOROTHY?
IT SURE DOES, MONKEY!

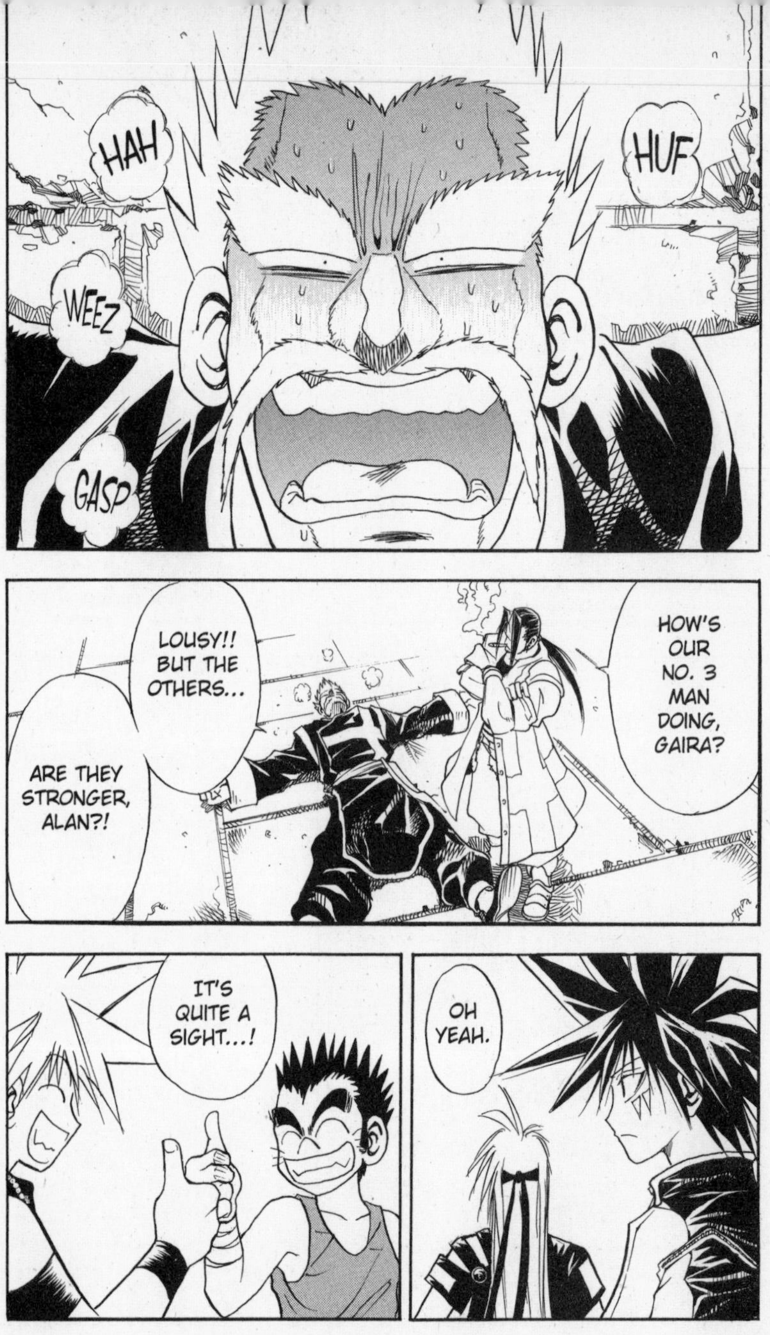
HUF
HAH
WEEZ
GASP
HOW'S OUR NO. 3 MAN DOING, GAIRA?
LOUSY!! BUT THE OTHERS...
ARE THEY STRONGER, ALAN?!
OH YEAH.
IT'S QUITE A SIGHT...!

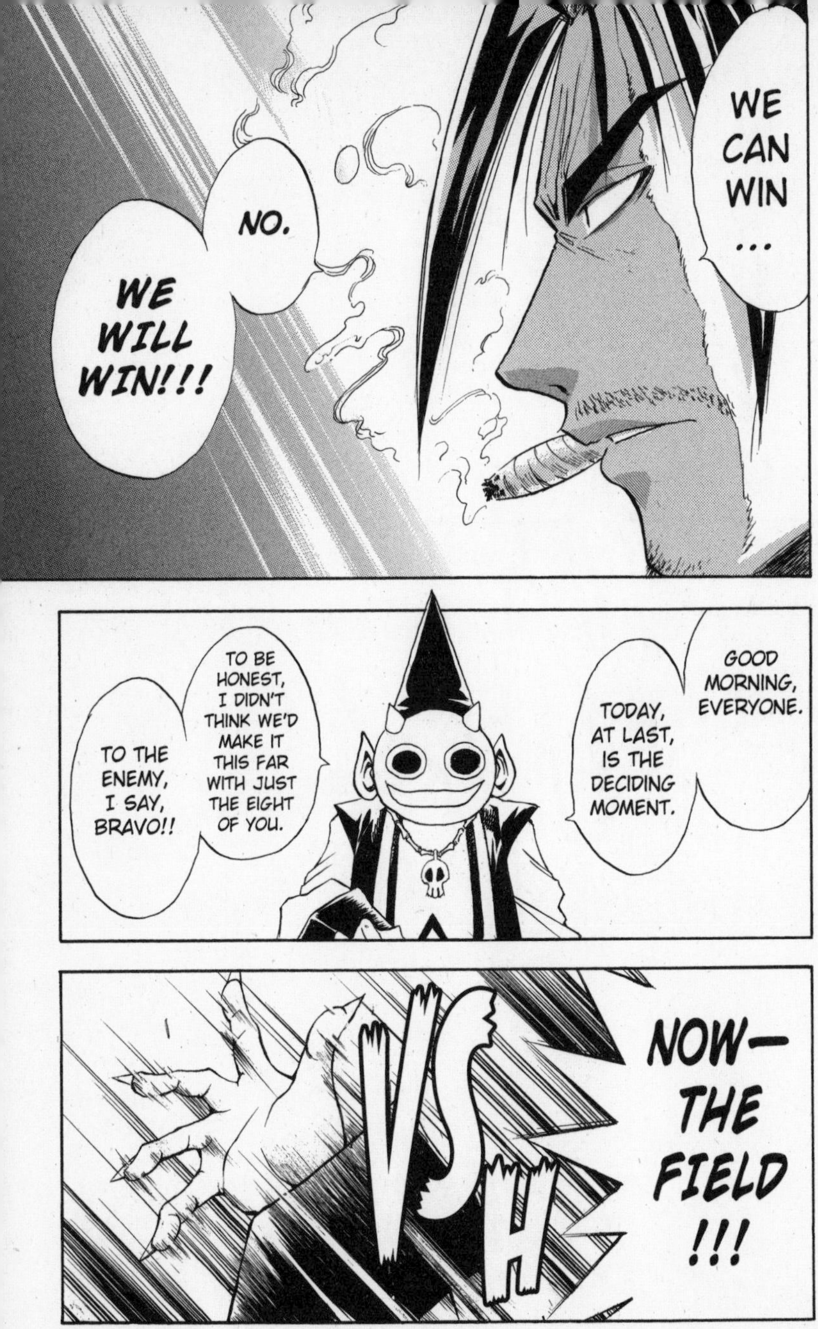
WE CAN WIN ...
NO.
WE WILL WIN!!!
GOOD MORNING, EVERYONE.
TODAY, AT LAST, IS THE DECIDING MOMENT.
TO BE HONEST, I DIDN'T THINK WE'D MAKE IT THIS FAR WITH JUST THE EIGHT OF YOU.
TO THE ENEMY, I SAY, BRAVO!!
NOW— THE FIELD!!!
VSH

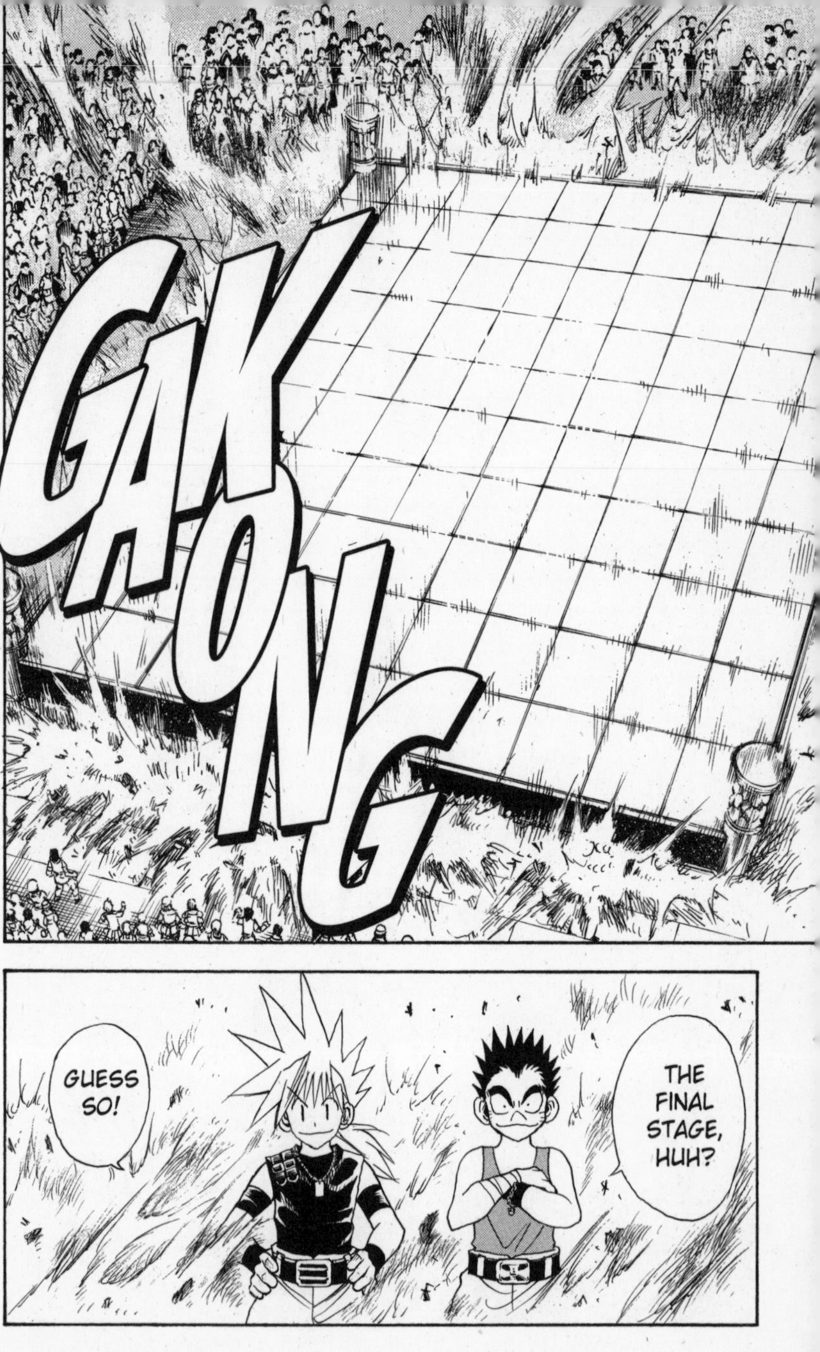
GAKONG
THE FINAL STAGE, HUH?
GUESS SO!

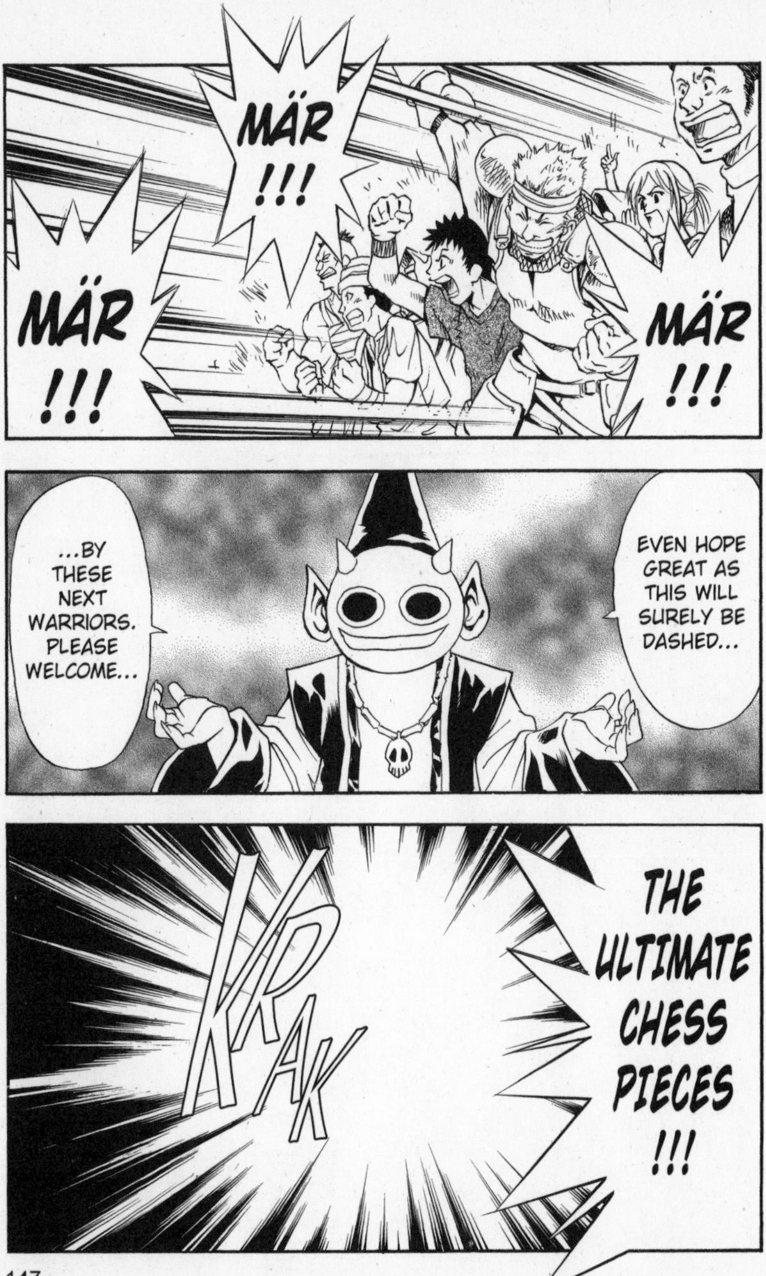
MÄR !!!
MÄR !!!
MÄR !!!
EVEN HOPE GREAT AS THIS WILL SURELY BE DASHED...
...BY THESE NEXT WARRIORS. PLEASE WELCOME...
THE ULTIMATE CHESS PIECES !!!
KRAK

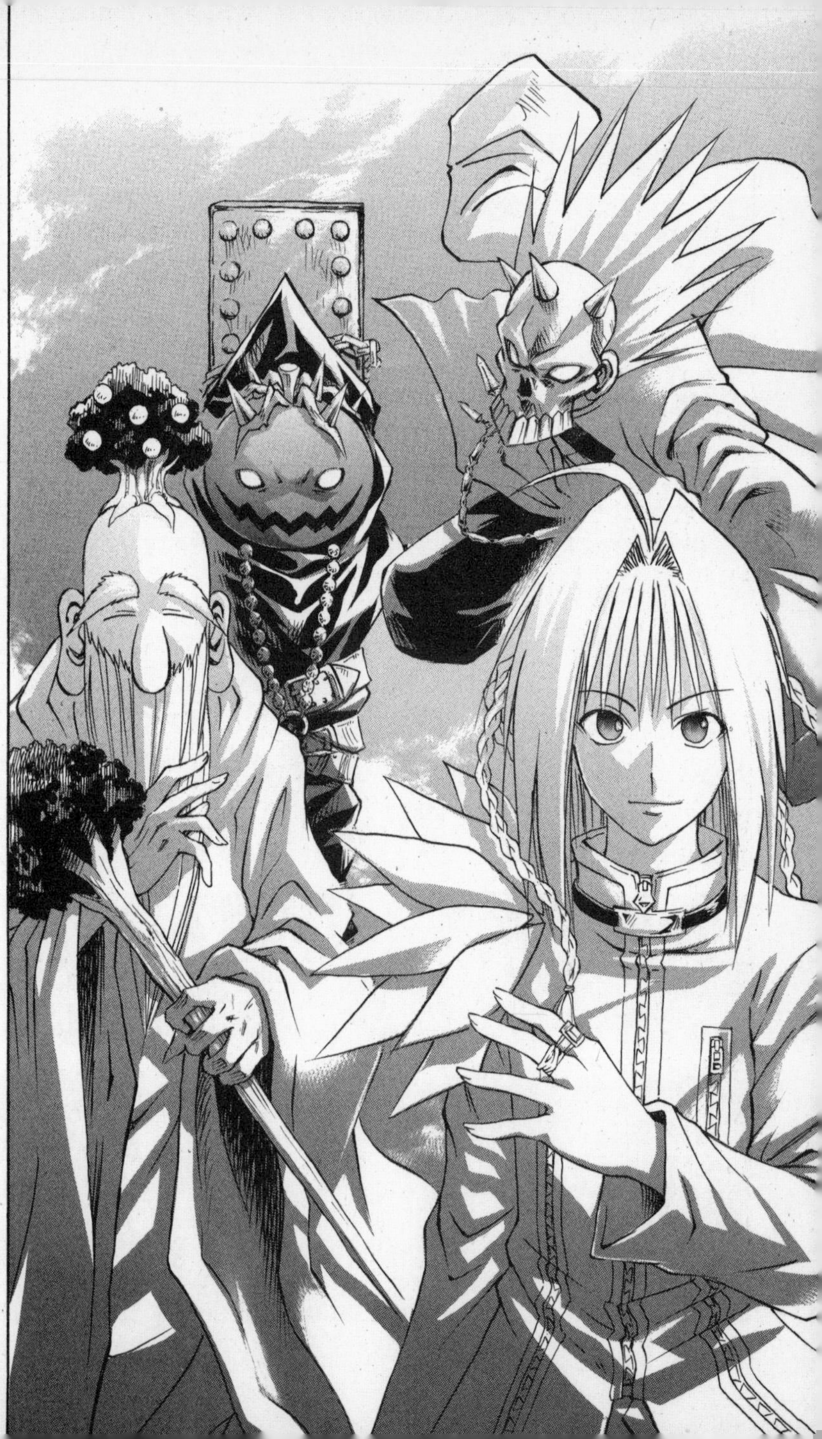

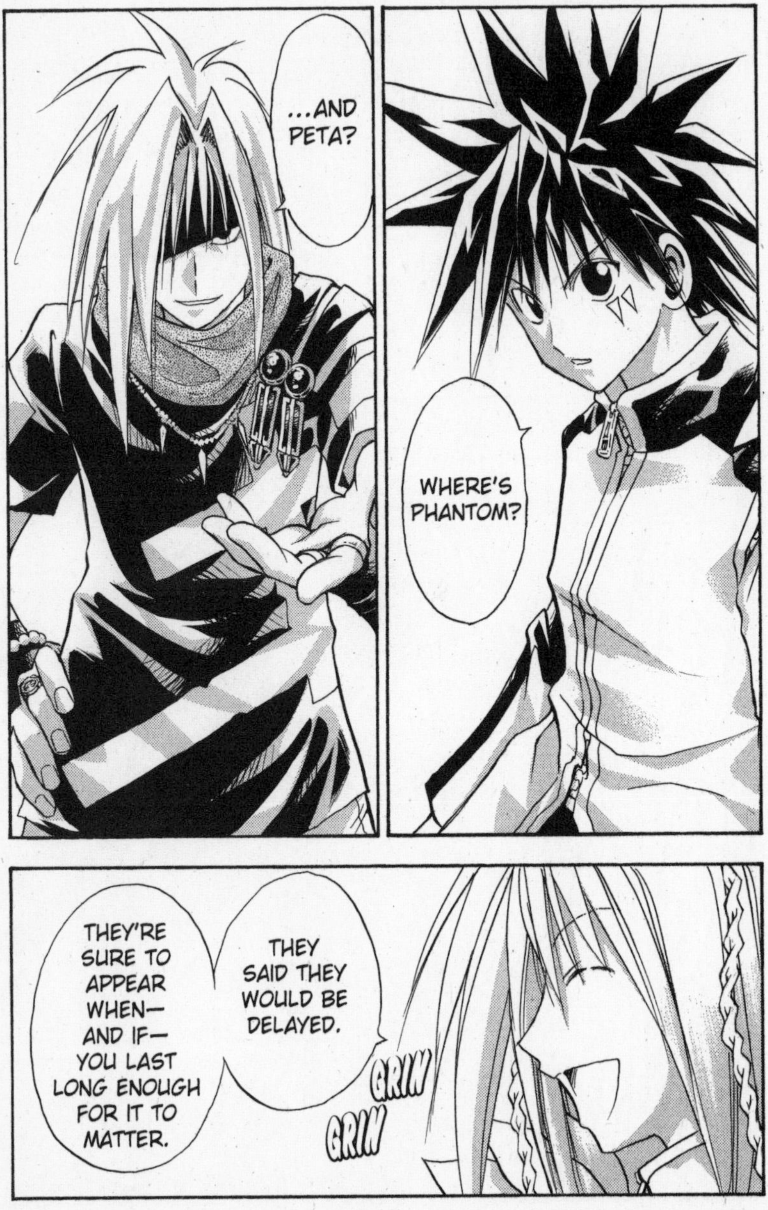
WHERE'S PHANTOM?
...AND PETA?
THEY SAID THEY WOULD BE DELAYED.
THEY'RE SURE TO APPEAR WHEN— AND IF— YOU LAST LONG ENOUGH FOR IT TO MATTER.
GRIN GRIN

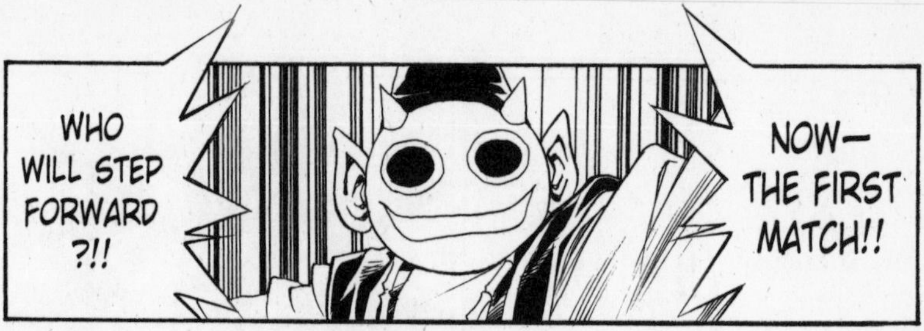
NOW— THE FIRST MATCH!!
WHO WILL STEP FORWARD ?!!
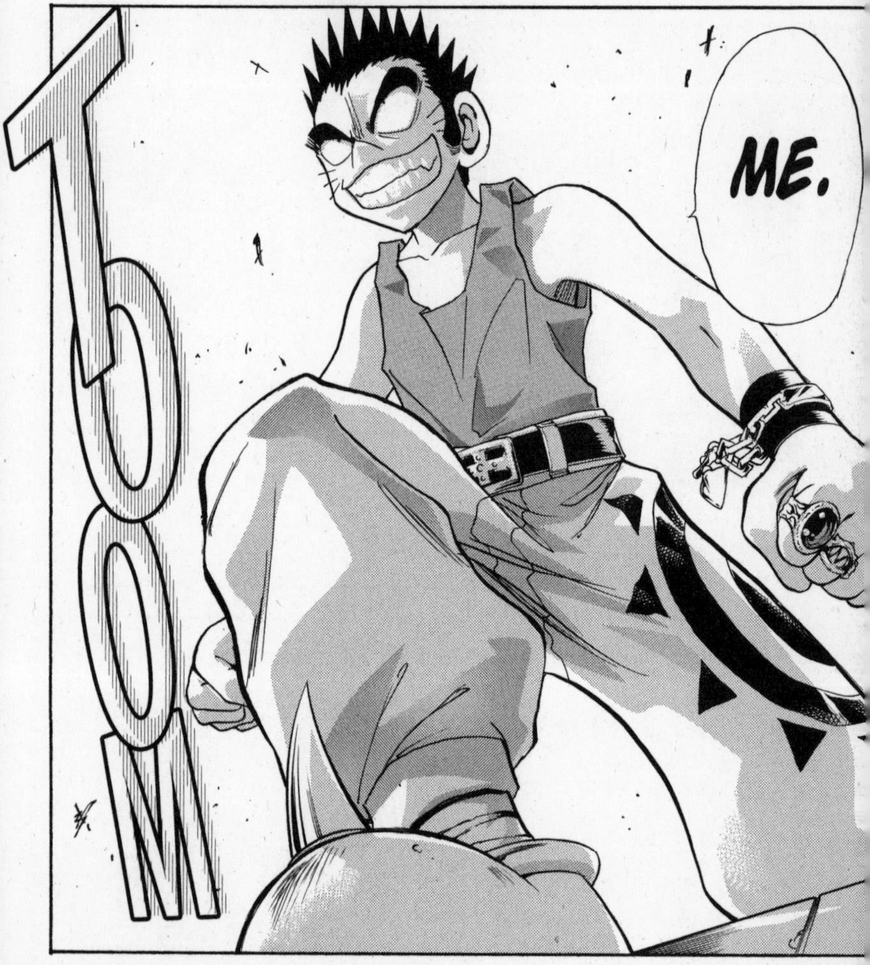
ME.
TOOOM

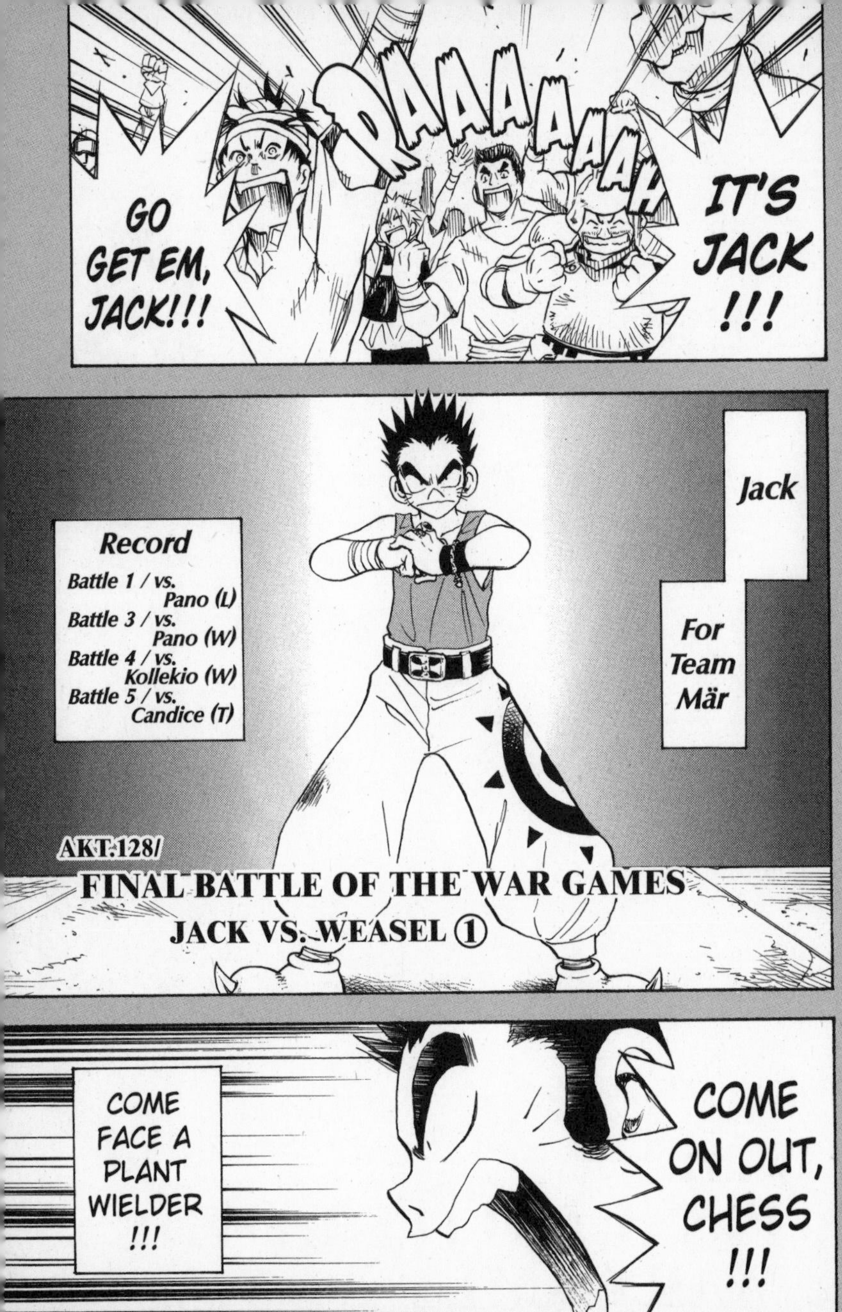
DAAAAAAAH
IT'S JACK!!!
GO GET EM, JACK!!!
Jack
For Team Mär
Record
Battle 1 / vs. Pano (L)
Battle 3 / vs. Pano (W)
Battle 4 / vs. Kollekio (W)
Battle 5 / vs. Candice (T)
AKT.128/
FINAL BATTLE OF THE WAR GAMES
JACK VS. WEASEL ①
COME ON OUT, CHESS!!!
COME FACE A PLANT WIELDER!!!

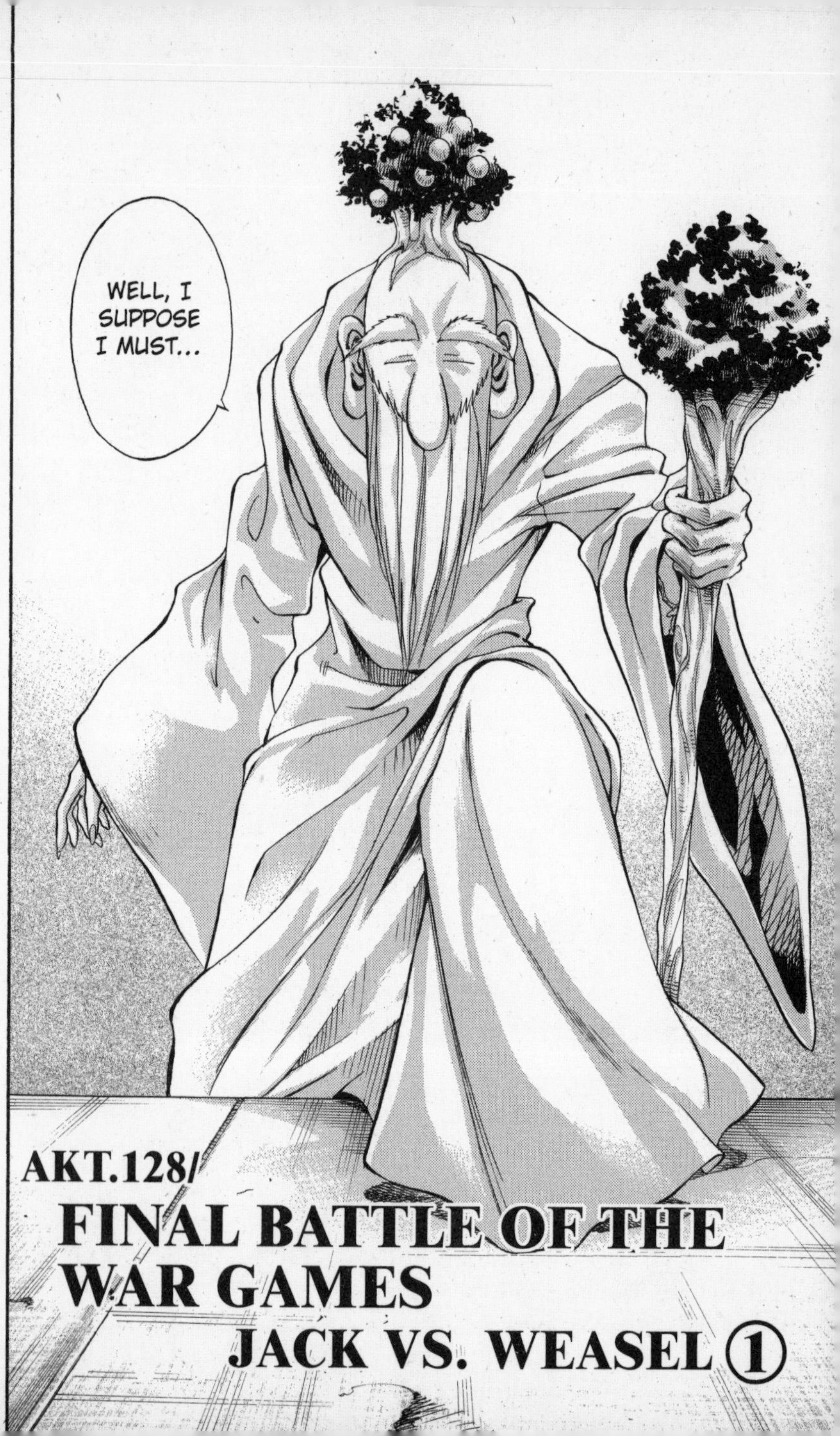
WELL, I SUPPOSE I MUST...

AKT.128/ FINAL BATTLE OF THE WAR GAMES JACK VS. WEASEL ①

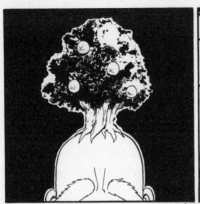

...IS A PLANT WIELDER TOO?

THIS OLD MAN...

?

I'M 14.

JACK, IS THAT YOUR NAME?

HOW OLD ARE YOU, BOY?

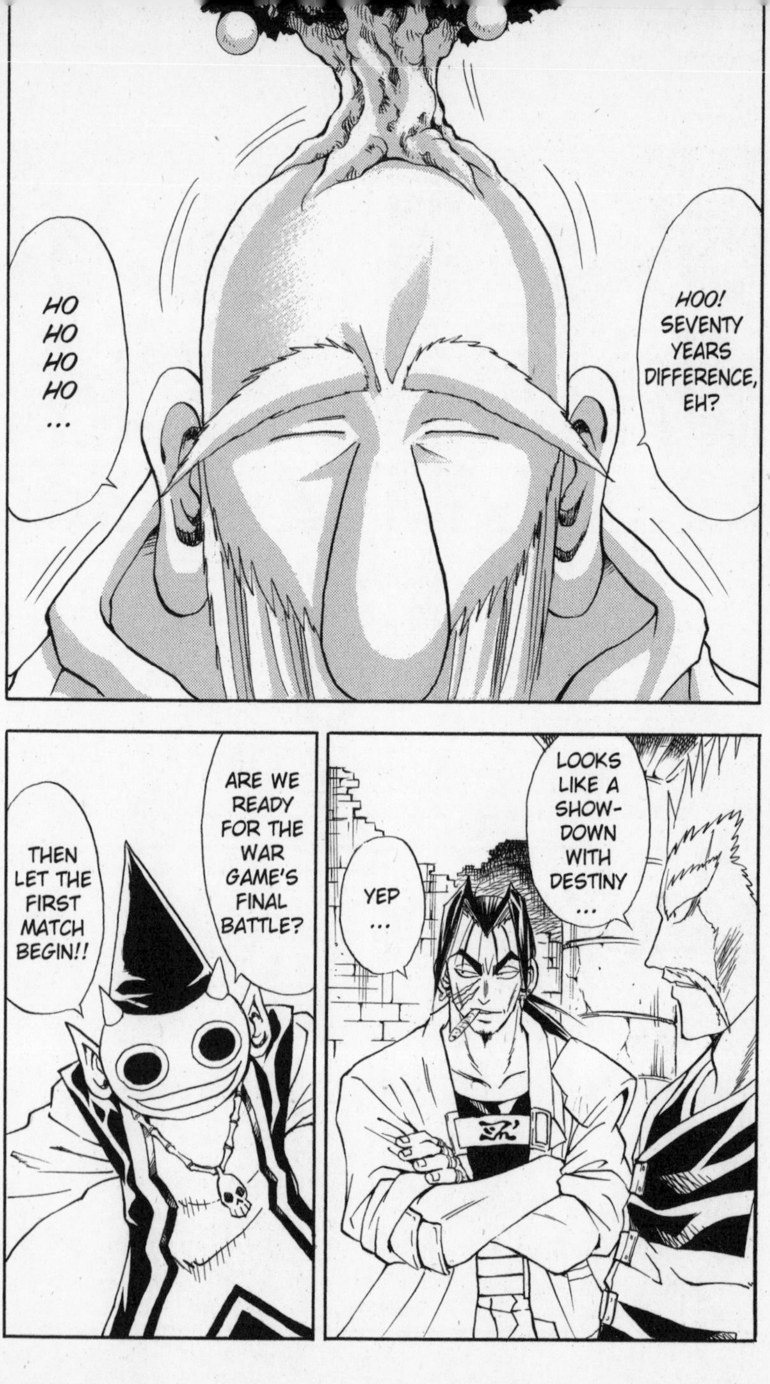
HOO! SEVENTY YEARS DIFFERENCE, EH?
HO HO HO HO ...
LOOKS LIKE A SHOW-DOWN WITH DESTINY ...
YEP ...
ARE WE READY FOR THE WAR GAME'S FINAL BATTLE?
THEN LET THE FIRST MATCH BEGIN!!

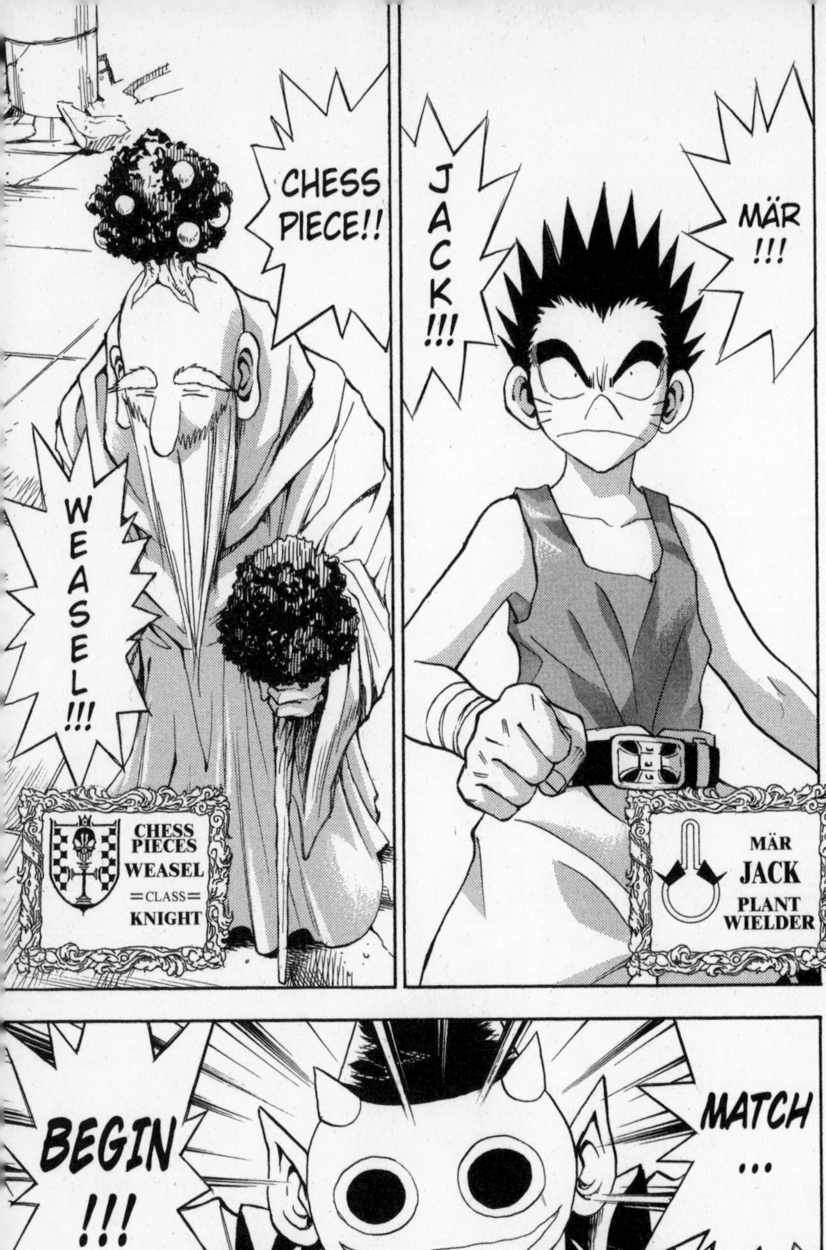
MÄR !!!
JACK!!!
MÄR
JACK
PLANT
WIELDER
CHESS PIECE!!
WEASEL!!!
CHESS
PIECES
WEASEL
=CLASS=
KNIGHT
MATCH ...
BEGIN !!!

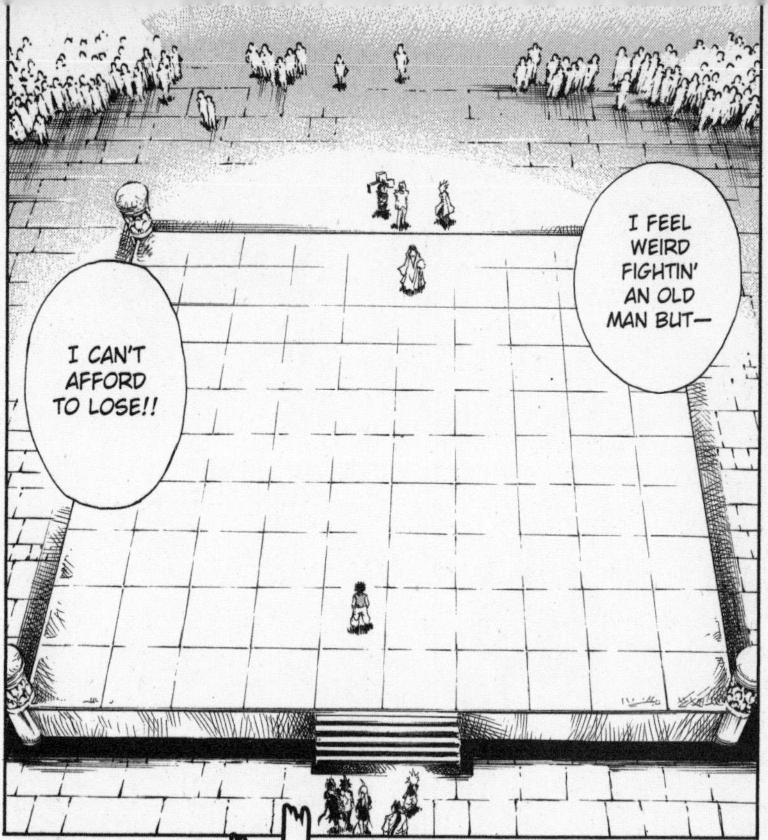
I FEEL WEIRD FIGHTIN' AN OLD MAN BUT—
I CAN'T AFFORD TO LOSE!!

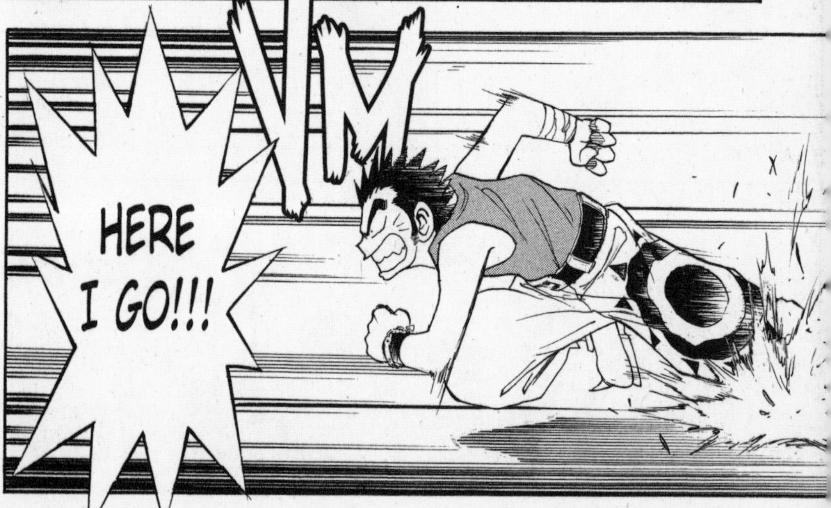
VM
HERE I GO!!!

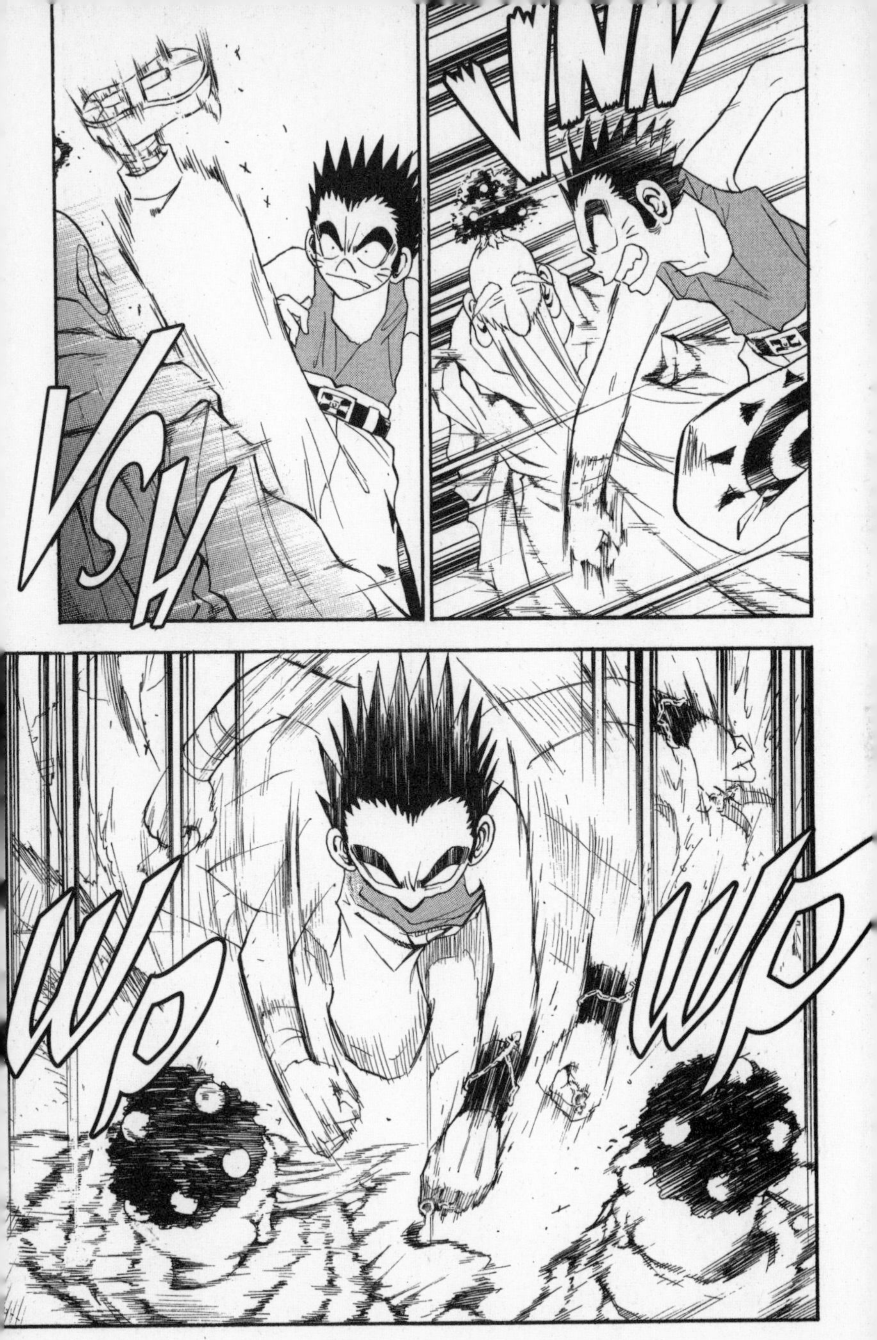
VNN
VSH
WP
WP

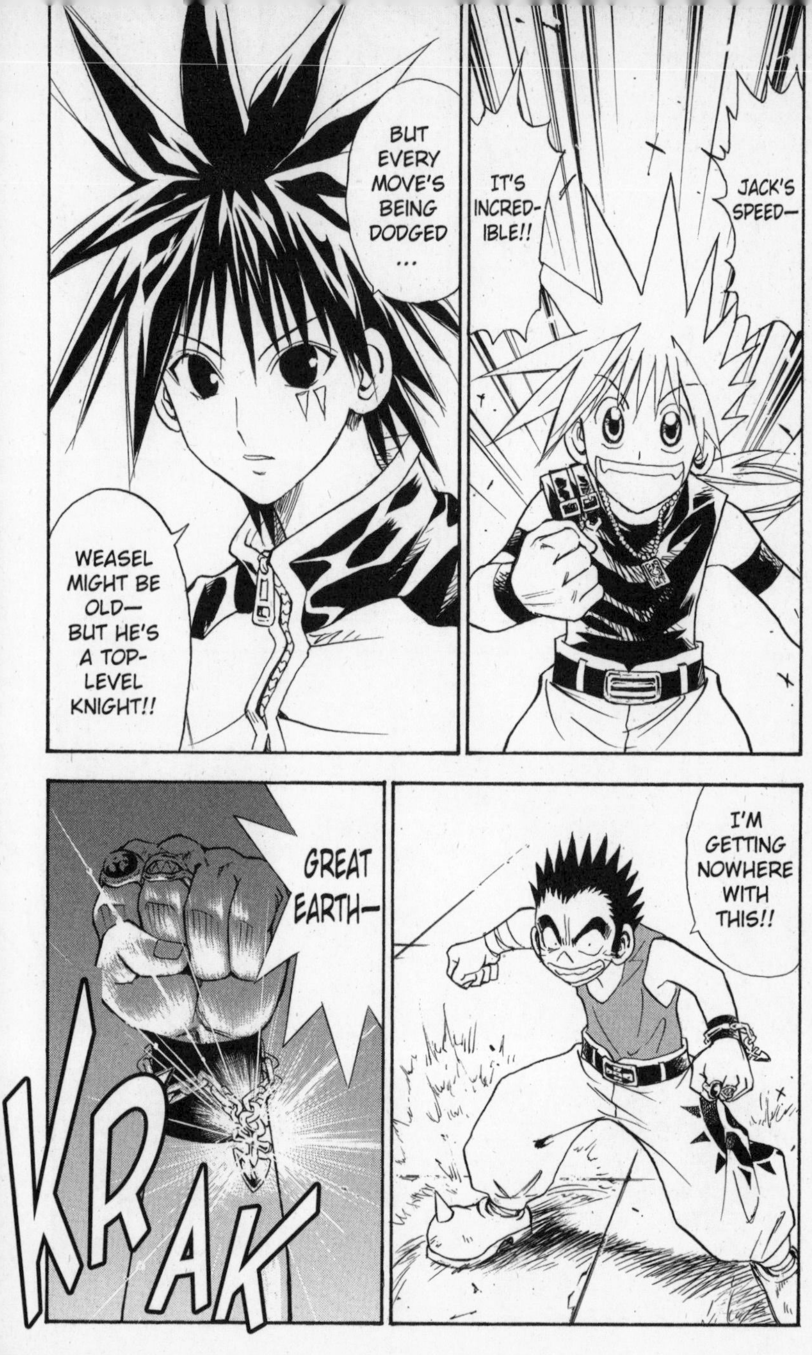
JACK'S SPEED—
IT'S INCREDIBLE!!
BUT EVERY MOVE'S BEING DODGED...
WEASEL MIGHT BE OLD—BUT HE'S A TOP-LEVEL KNIGHT!!
I'M GETTING NOWHERE WITH THIS!!
GREAT EARTH—
KRAK

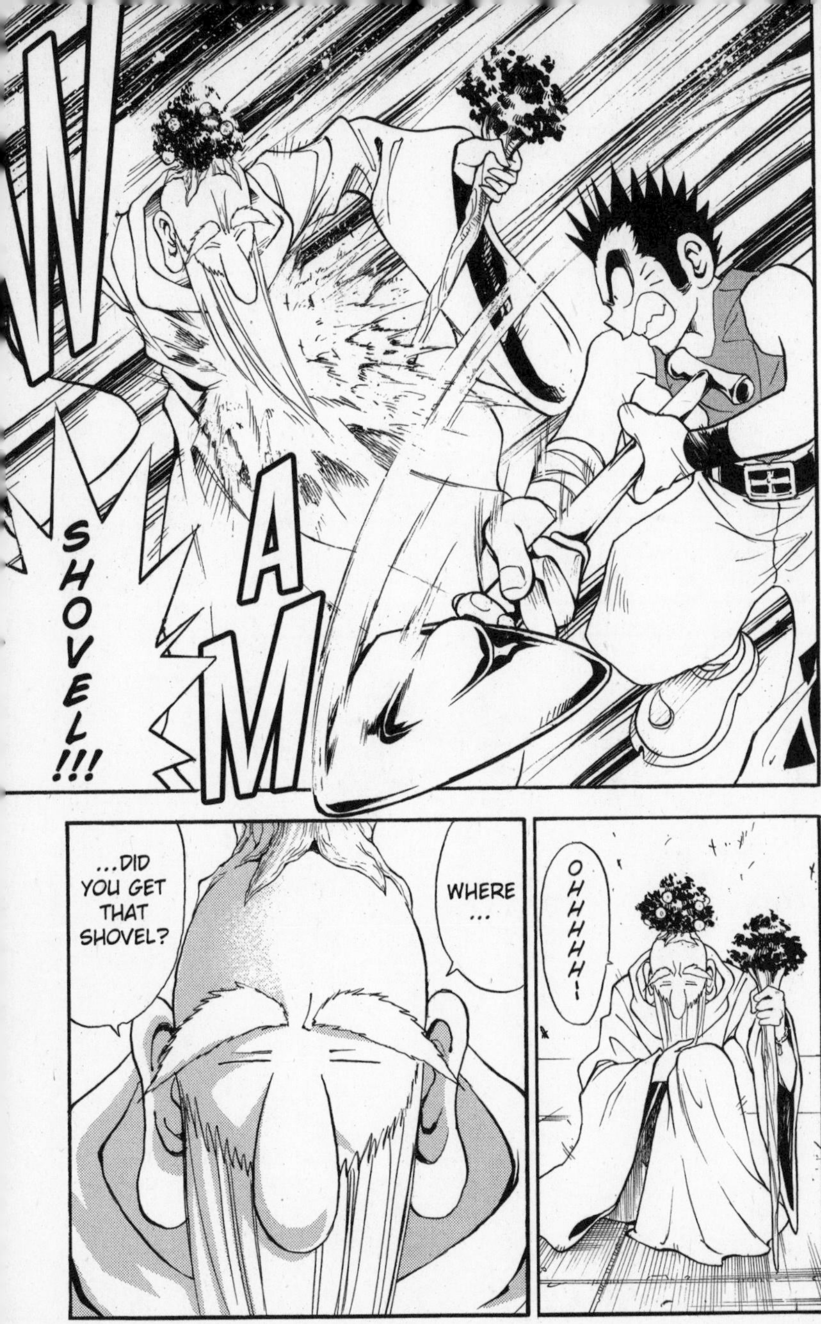

W
A
M
SHOVEL!!!
OHHHHH!
WHERE ...
...DID YOU GET THAT SHOVEL?

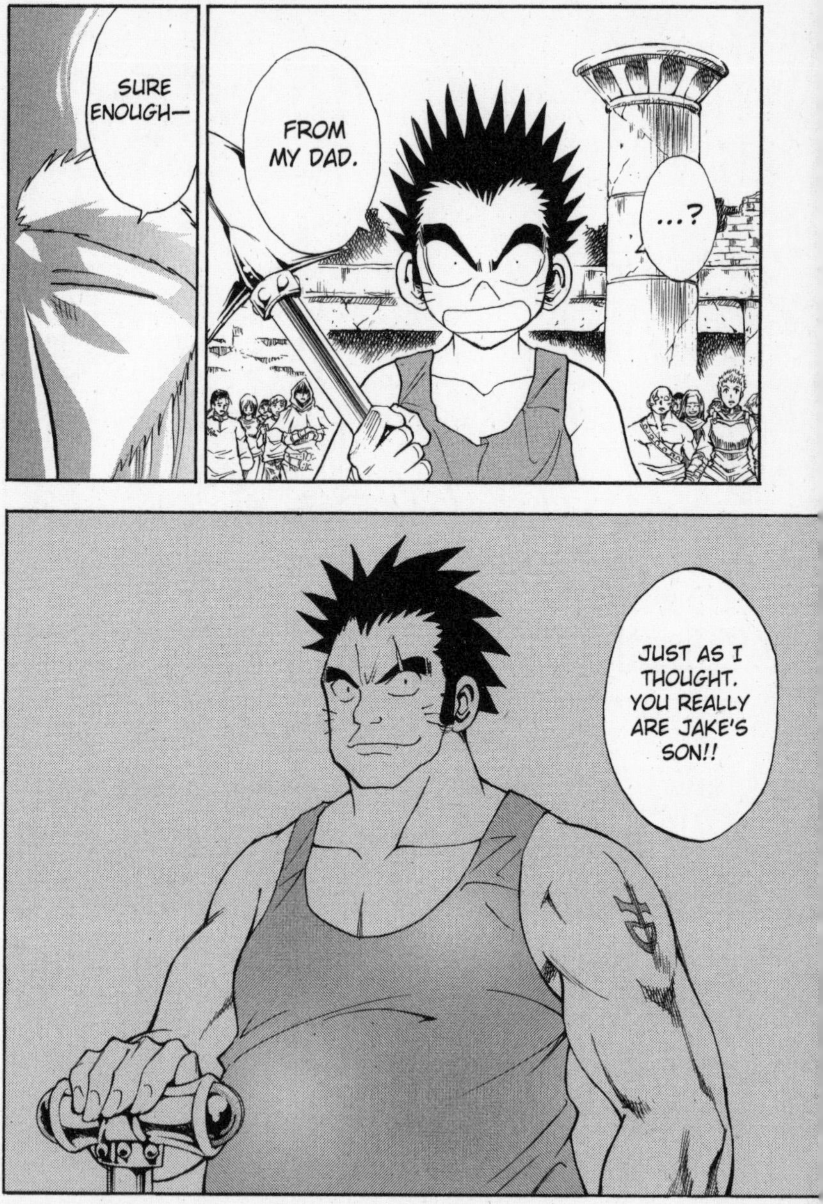
...?
FROM MY DAD.
SURE ENOUGH—
JUST AS I THOUGHT. YOU REALLY ARE JAKE'S SON!!

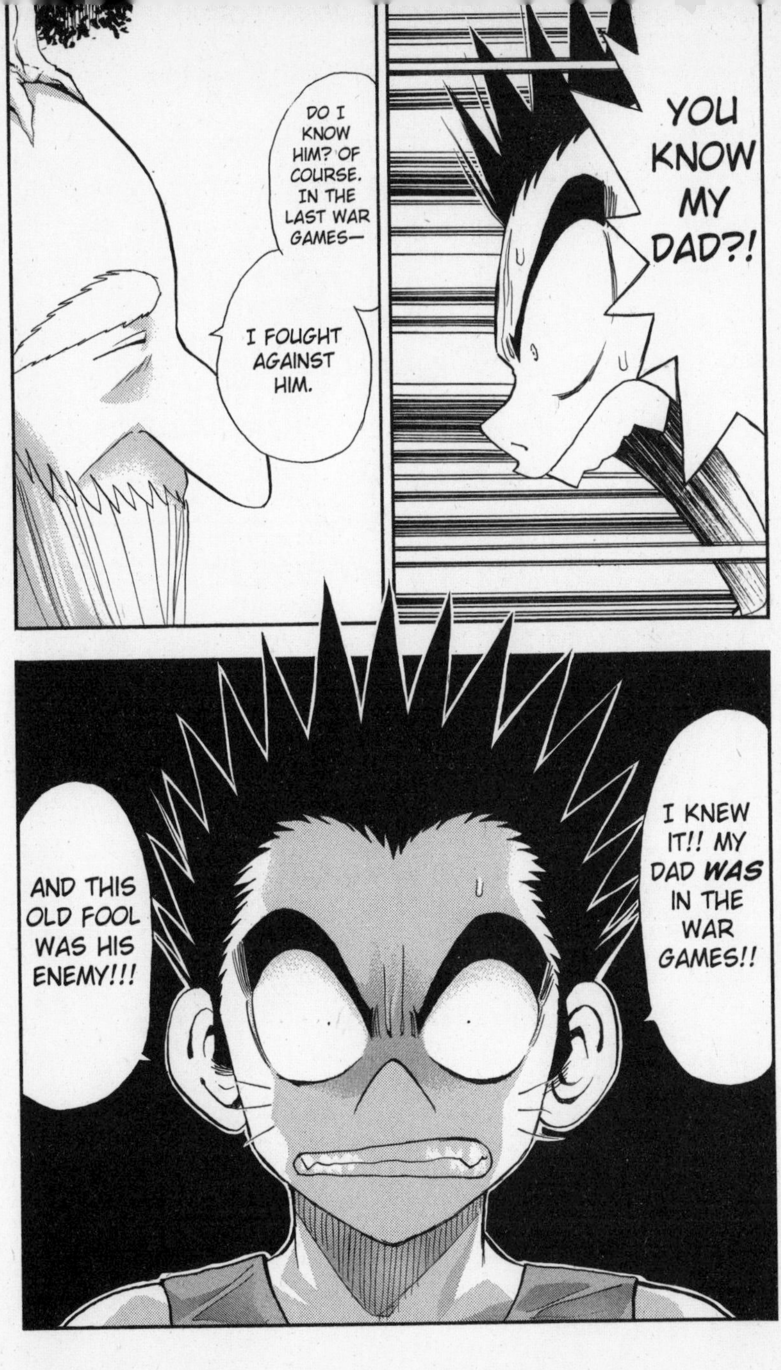
YOU KNOW MY DAD?!
DO I KNOW HIM? OF COURSE. IN THE LAST WAR GAMES—
I FOUGHT AGAINST HIM.
I KNEW IT!! MY DAD WAS IN THE WAR GAMES!!
AND THIS OLD FOOL WAS HIS ENEMY!!!

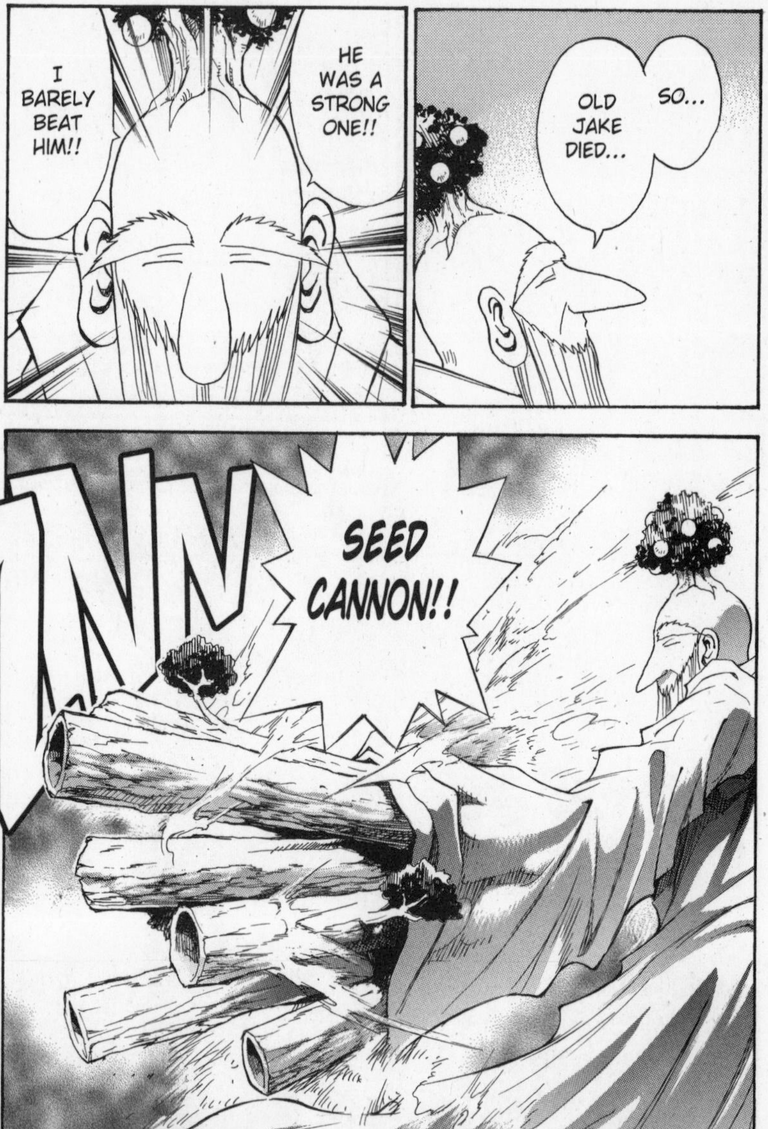
SO...
OLD JAKE DIED...
HE WAS A STRONG ONE!!
I BARELY BEAT HIM!!
SEED CANNON!!

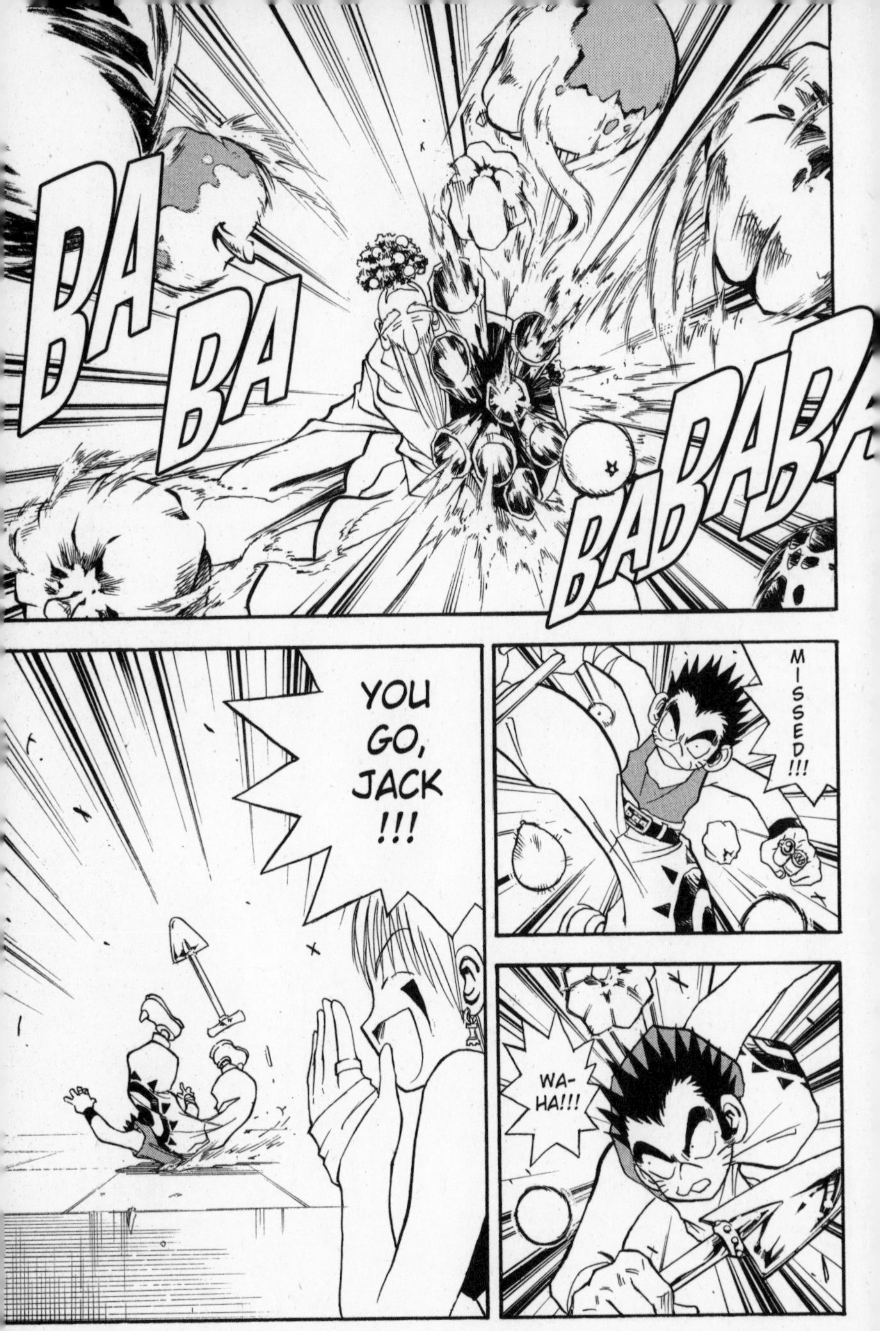
BA BA
BABABA
MISSED!!!
WA-HA!!!
YOU GO, JACK!!!

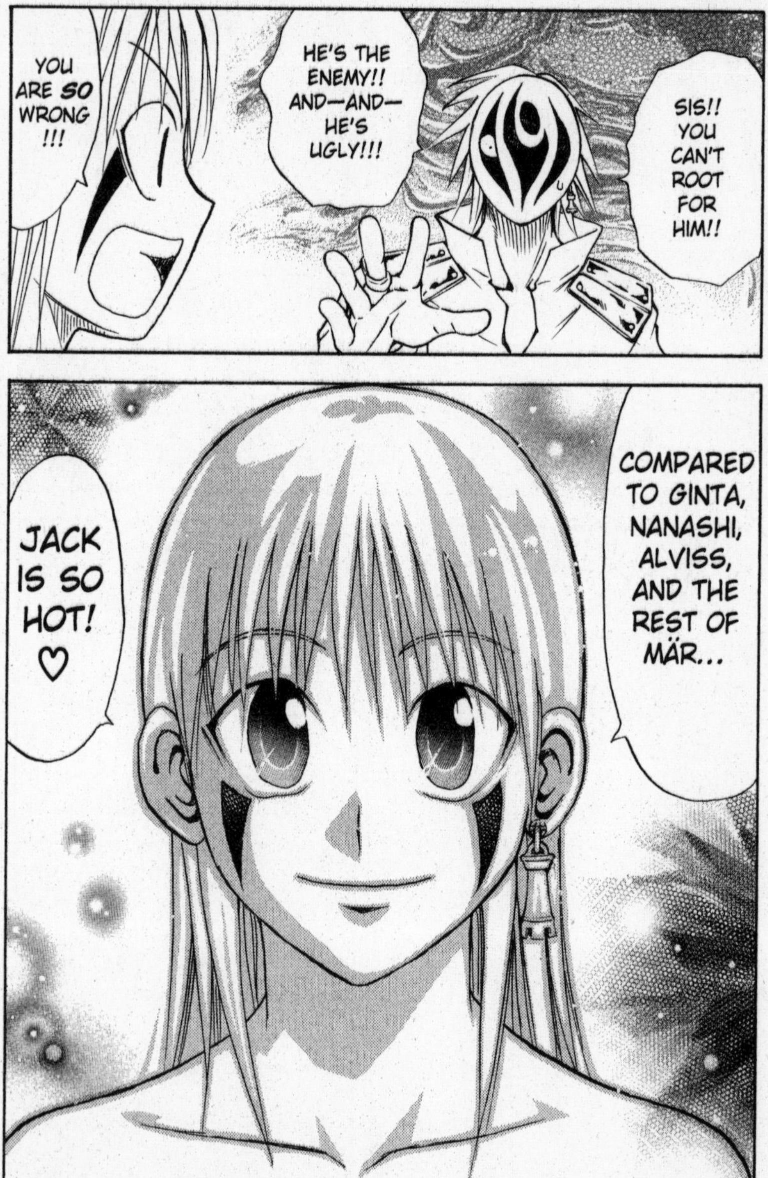
SIS!! YOU CAN'T ROOT FOR HIM!!
HE'S THE ENEMY!! AND—AND—HE'S UGLY!!!
YOU ARE SO WRONG!!!
COMPARED TO GINTA, NANASHI, ALVISS, AND THE REST OF MÄR...
JACK IS SO HOT! ♡

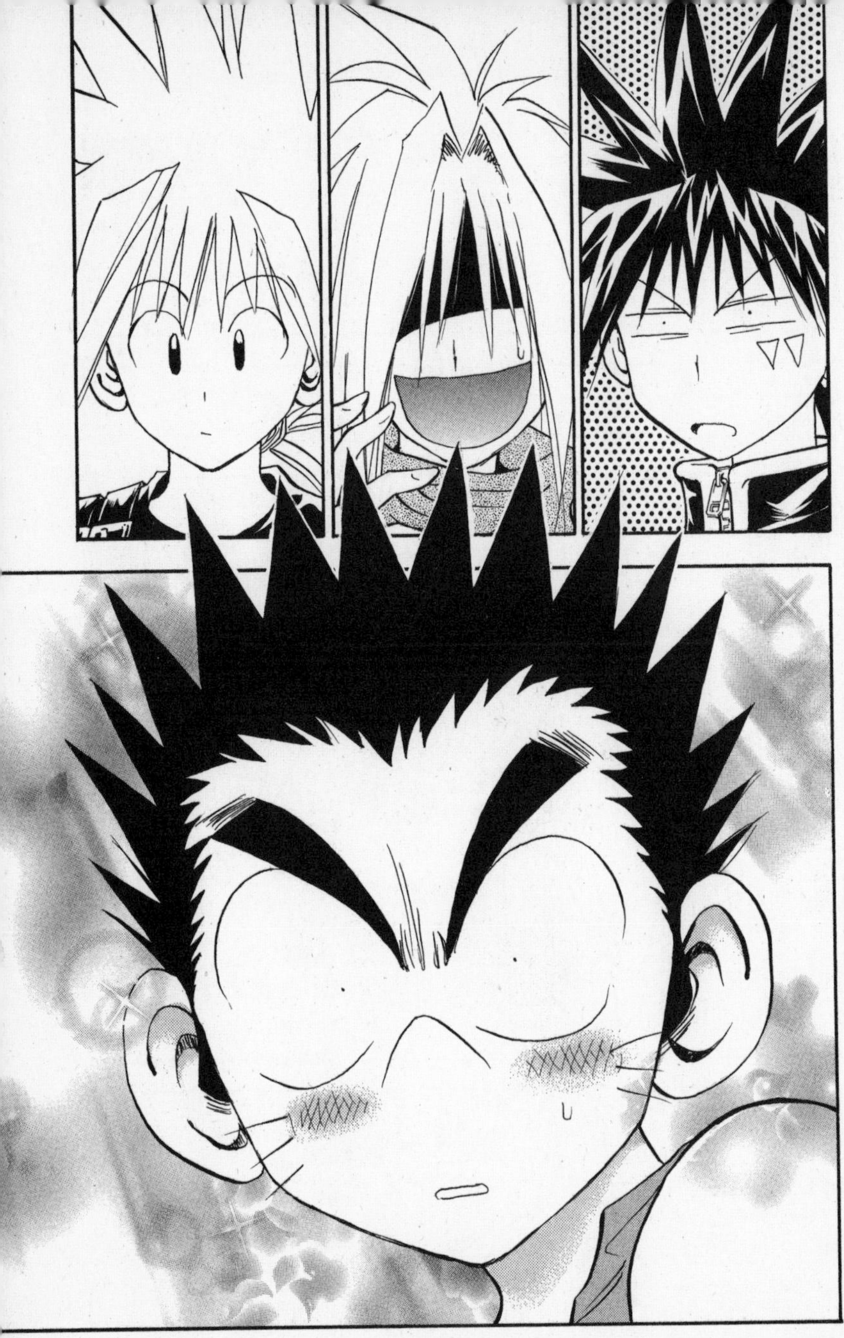

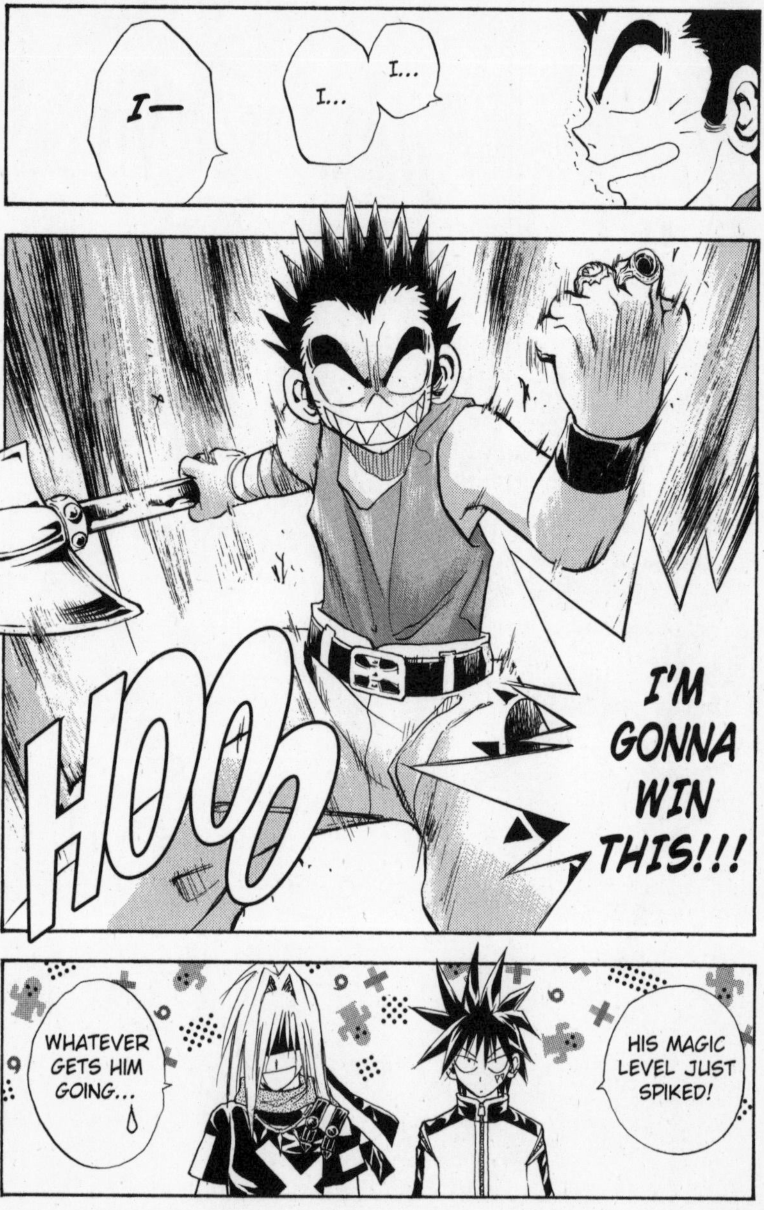
I...
I...
I—
I'M GONNA WIN THIS!!!
HOOO
HIS MAGIC LEVEL JUST SPIKED!
WHATEVER GETS HIM GOING...

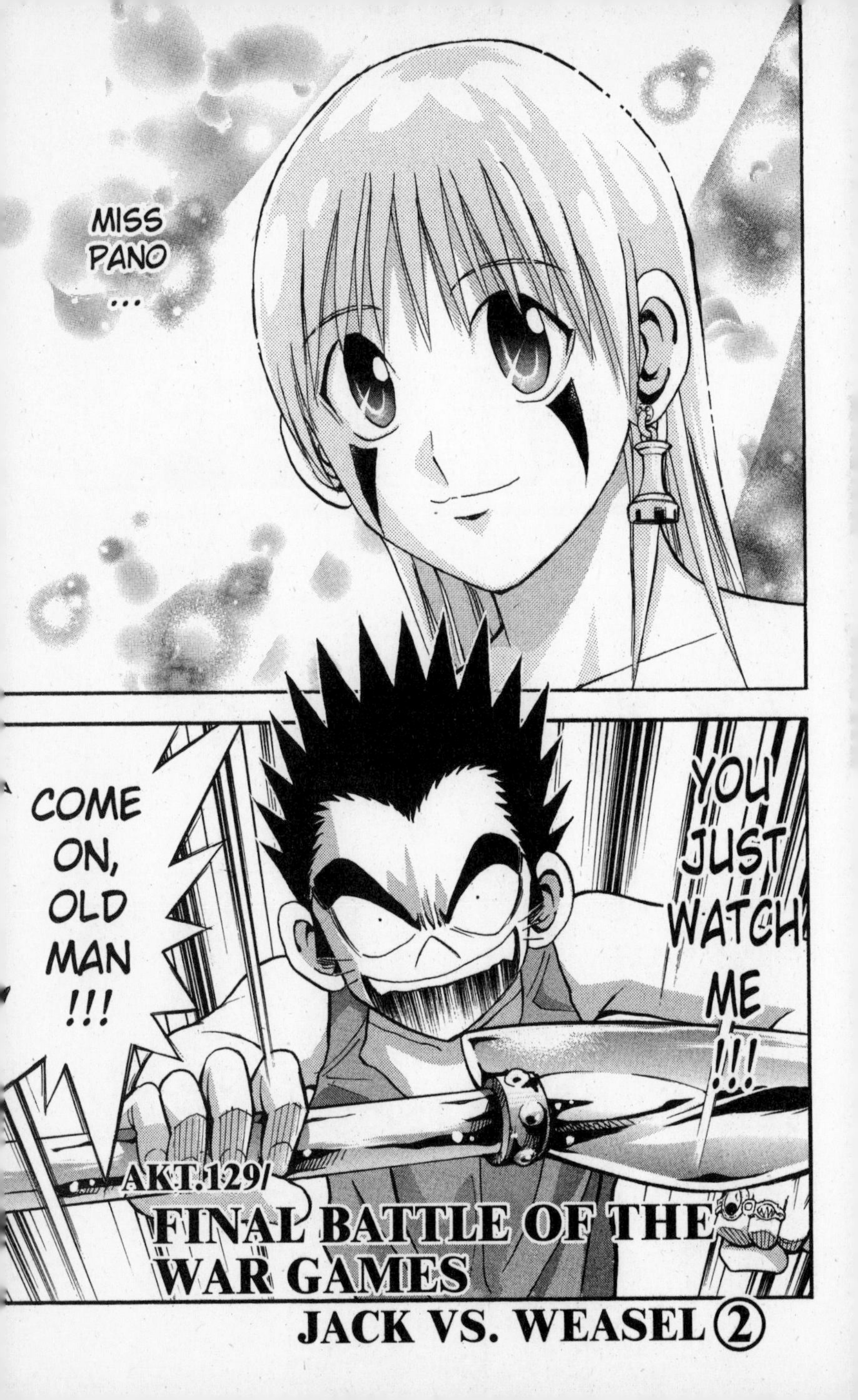
MISS PANO ...
YOU JUST WATCH ME !!!
COME ON, OLD MAN !!!
AKT.129/
FINAL BATTLE OF THE WAR GAMES
JACK VS. WEASEL ②

HO HO HO ...
VERY WELL THEN ...
HOW ABOUT THIS?
JINGLE
KRAK

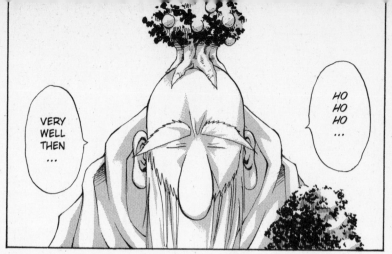

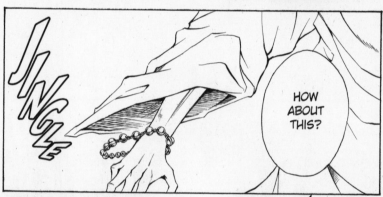

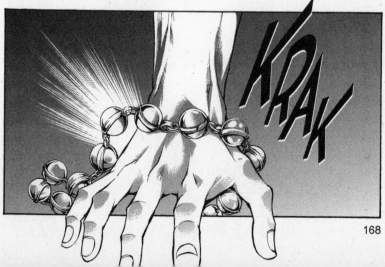

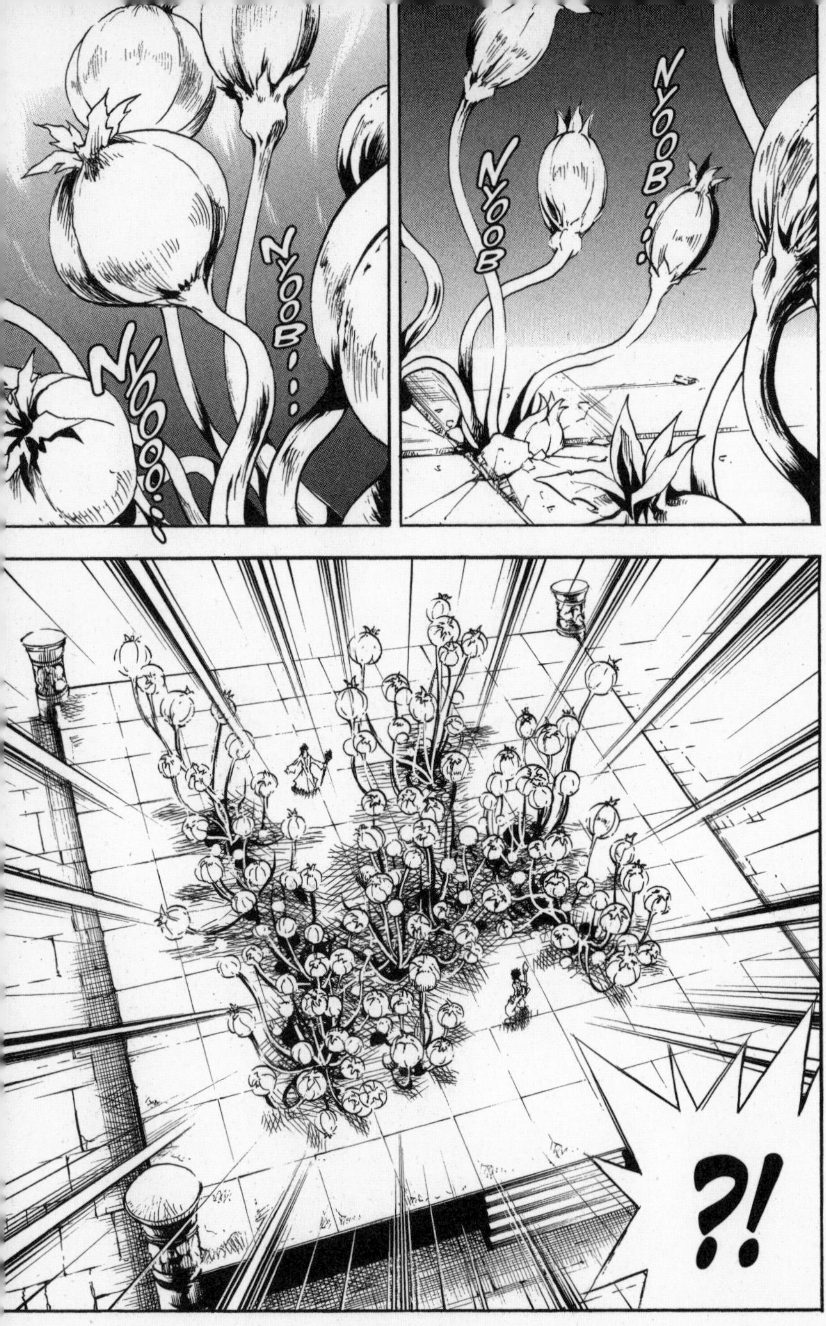
NYOOB...
NYOOB
NYOOB...
NYOOOO...
?!

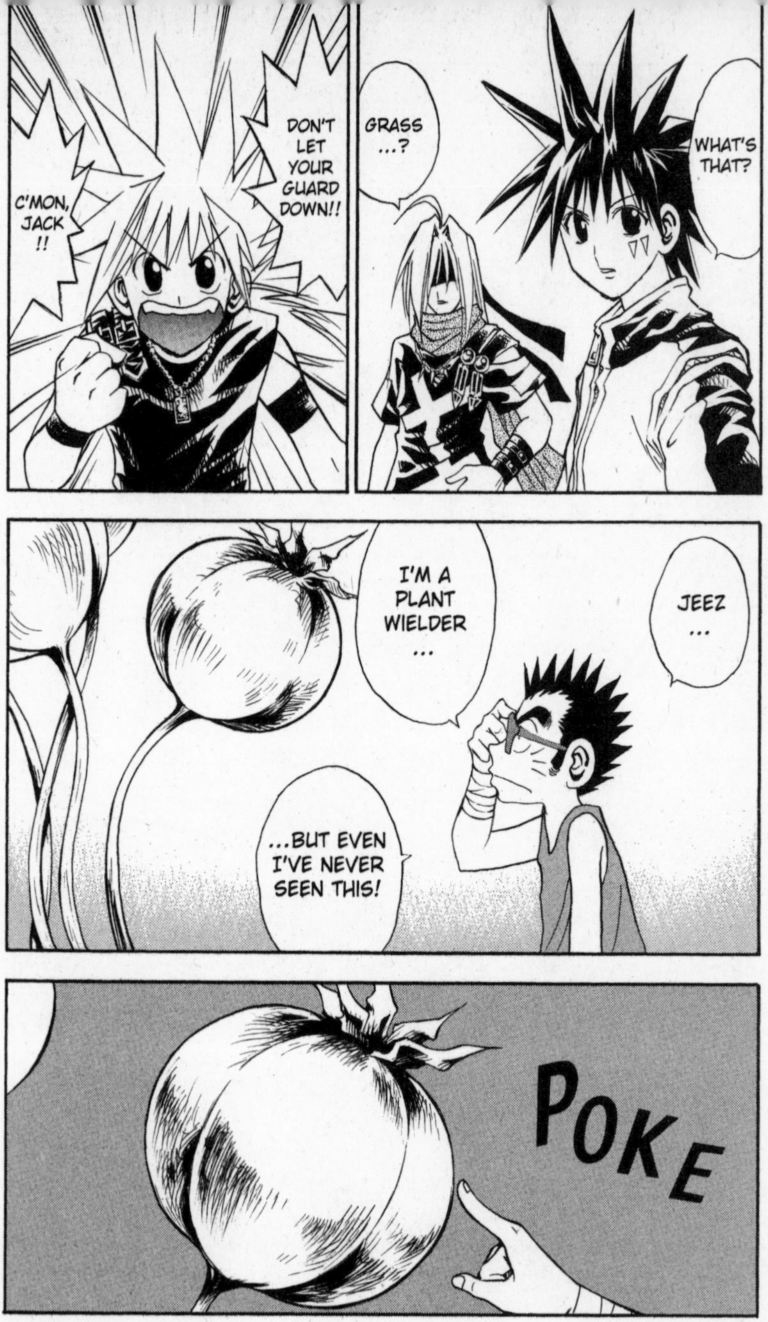
WHAT'S THAT?
GRASS ...?
DON'T LET YOUR GUARD DOWN!!
C'MON, JACK!!
JEEZ ...
I'M A PLANT WIELDER ...
...BUT EVEN I'VE NEVER SEEN THIS!
POKE

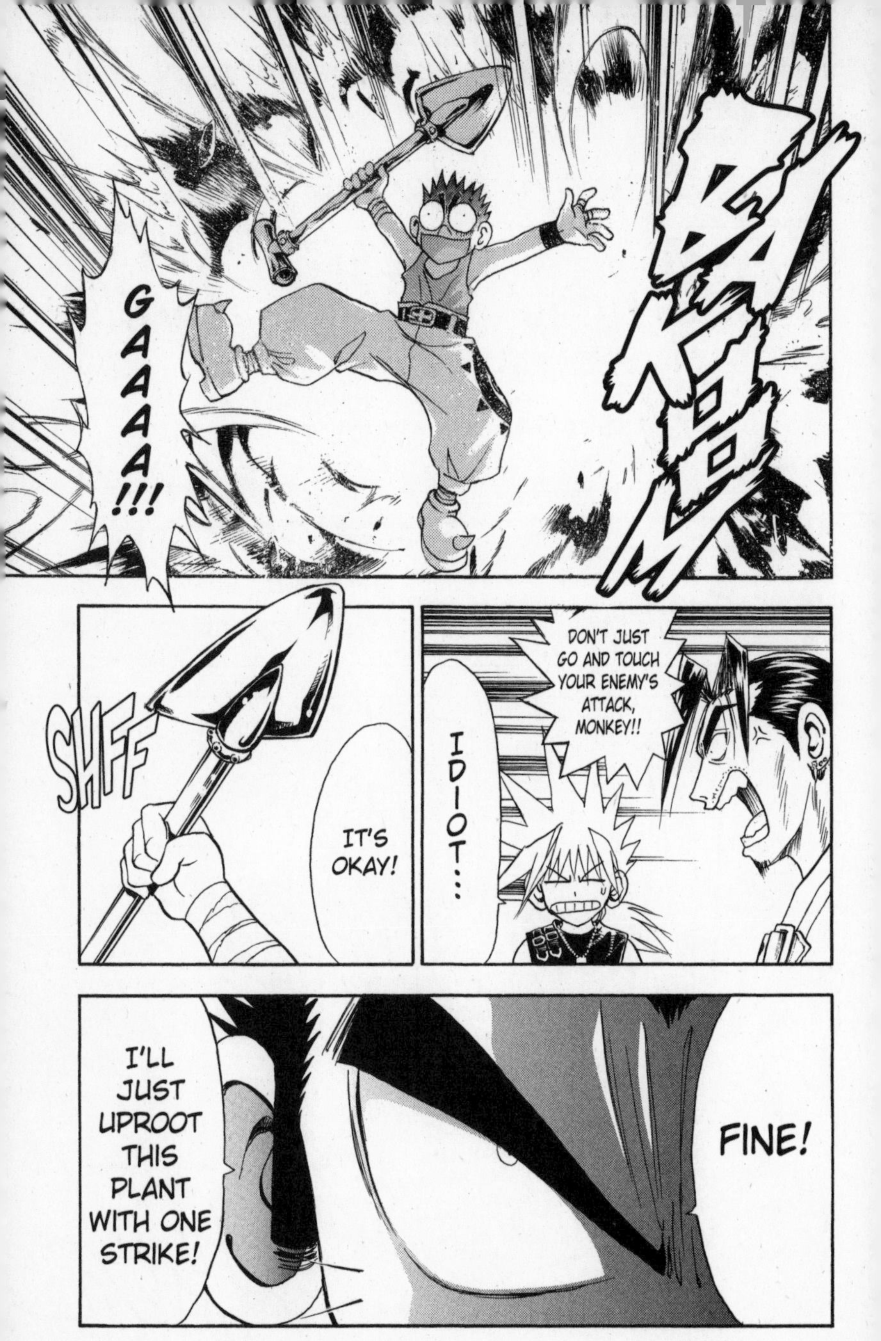
BAKOOM
GAAAAA!!!
DON'T JUST GO AND TOUCH YOUR ENEMY'S ATTACK, MONKEY!!
IDIOT...
IT'S OKAY!
SHFF
FINE!
I'LL JUST UPROOT THIS PLANT WITH ONE STRIKE!

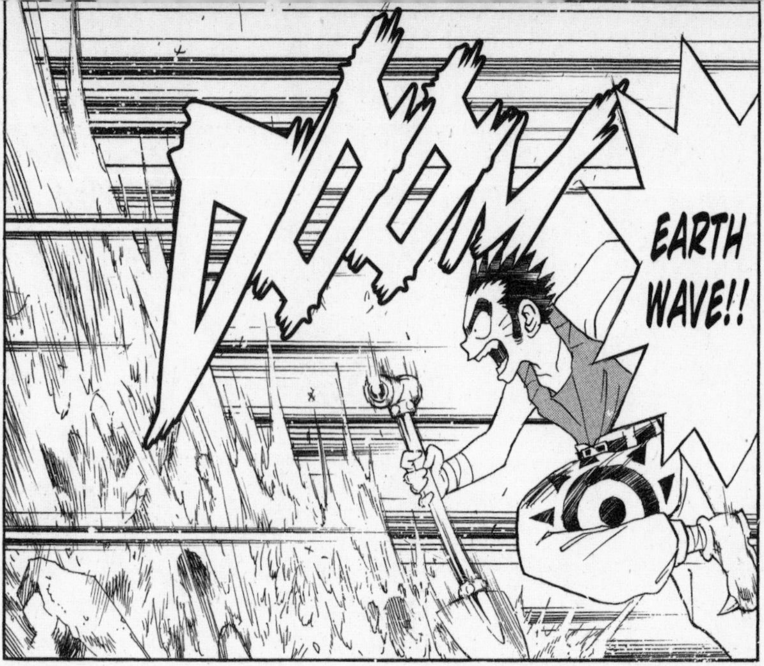
DOOM
EARTH WAVE!!

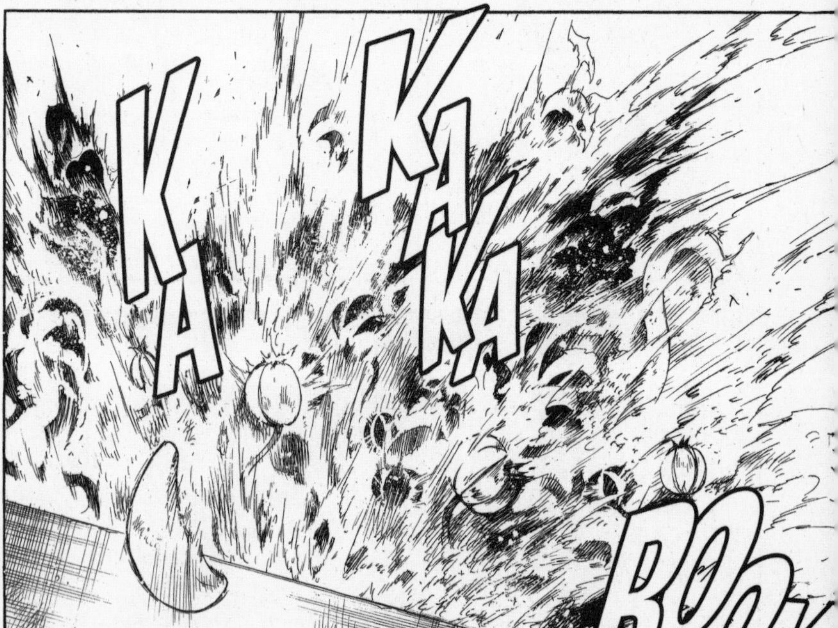
KA
KA KA
BOOM

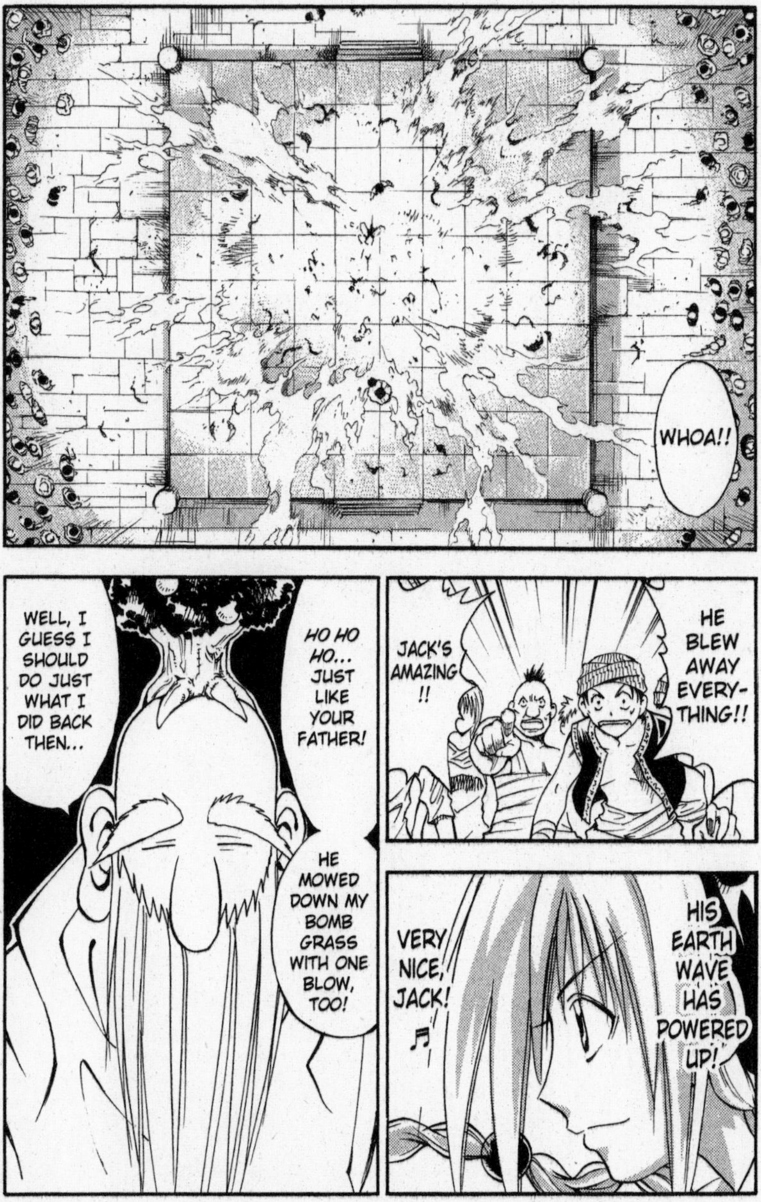
WHOA!!
HE BLEW AWAY EVERYTHING!!
JACK'S AMAZING!!
HIS EARTH WAVE HAS POWERED UP!
VERY NICE, JACK! ♪
HO HO HO... JUST LIKE YOUR FATHER!
WELL, I GUESS I SHOULD DO JUST WHAT I DID BACK THEN...
HE MOWED DOWN MY BOMB GRASS WITH ONE BLOW, TOO!

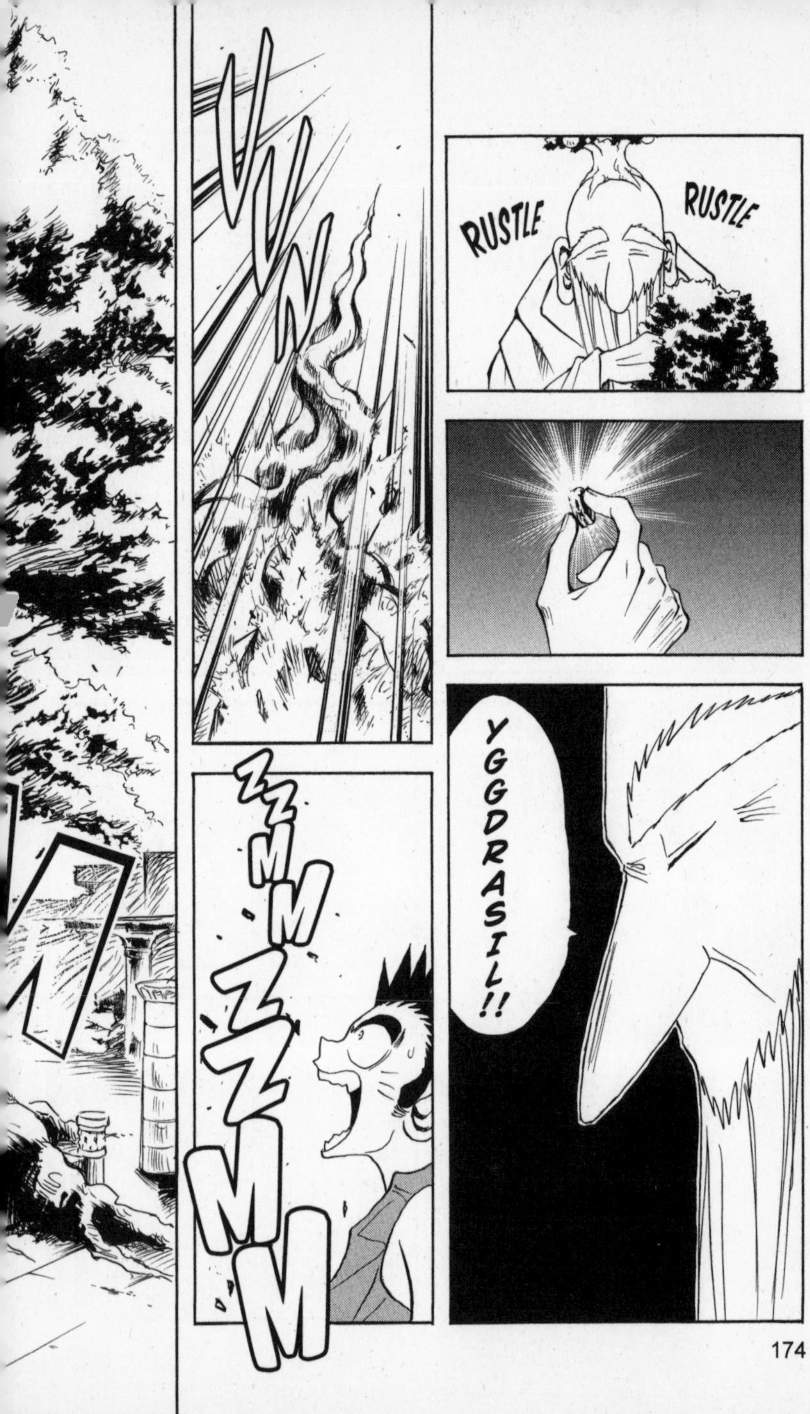
RUSTLE
RUSTLE
YGGDRASIL!!

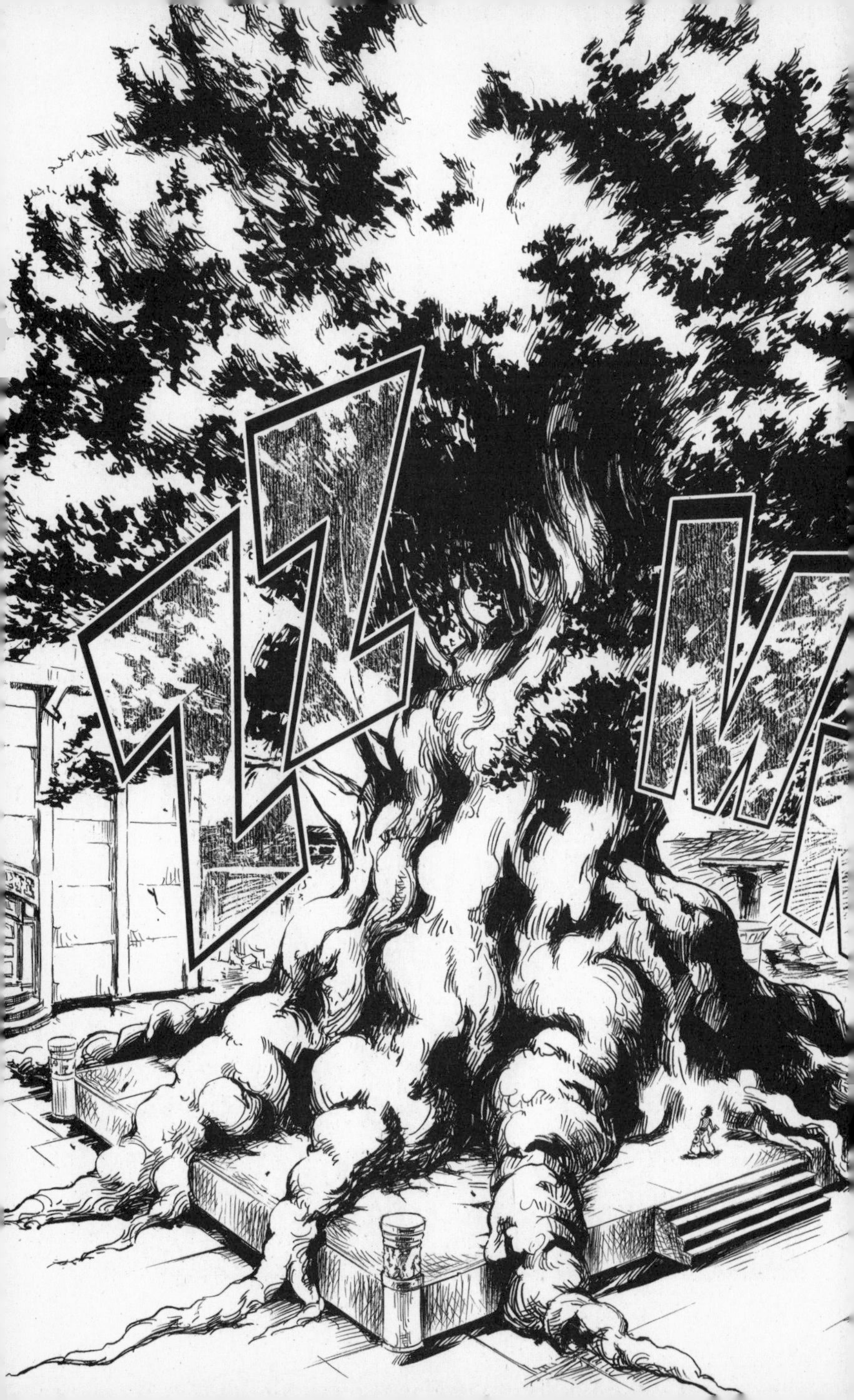
ZZ

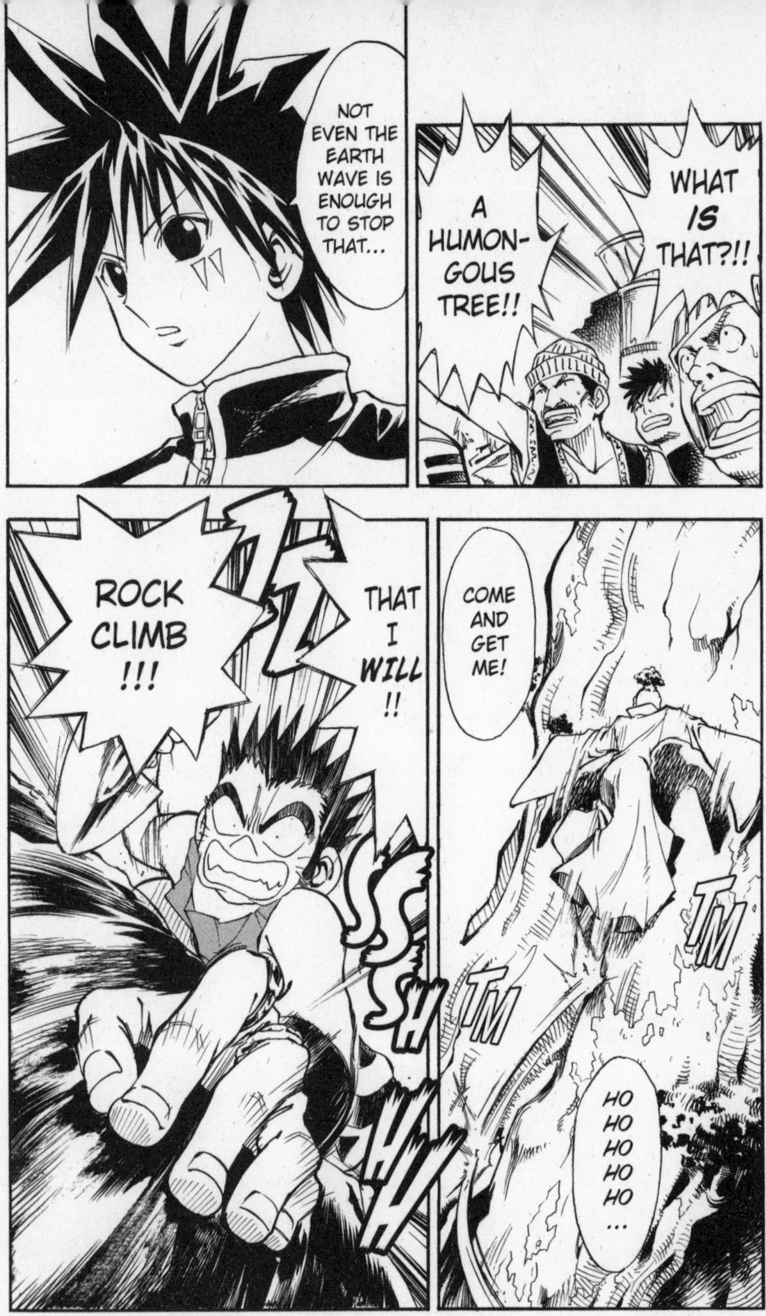
WHAT IS THAT?!!
A HUMON-GOUS TREE!!
NOT EVEN THE EARTH WAVE IS ENOUGH TO STOP THAT...
COME AND GET ME!
TM
TM
HO HO HO HO HO...
THAT I WILL!!
ROCK CLIMB!!!

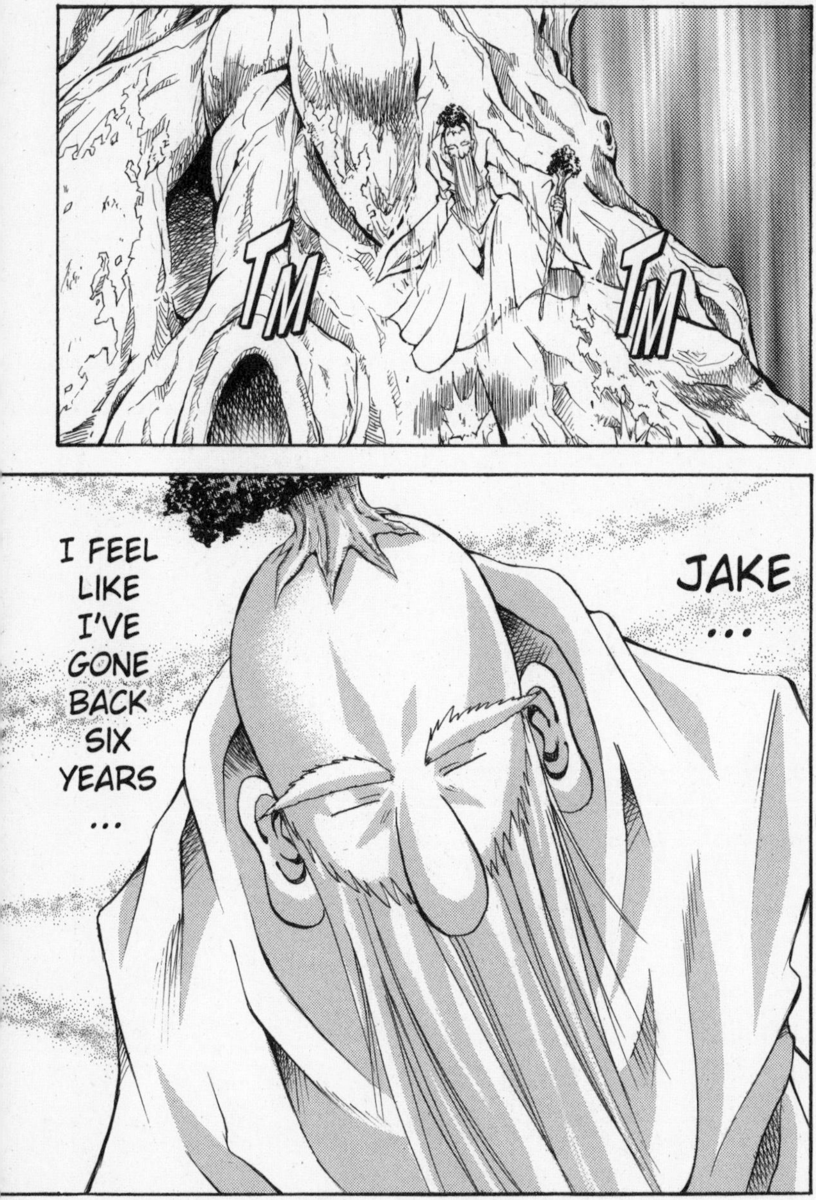
TM
TM
JAKE...
I FEEL LIKE I'VE GONE BACK SIX YEARS...

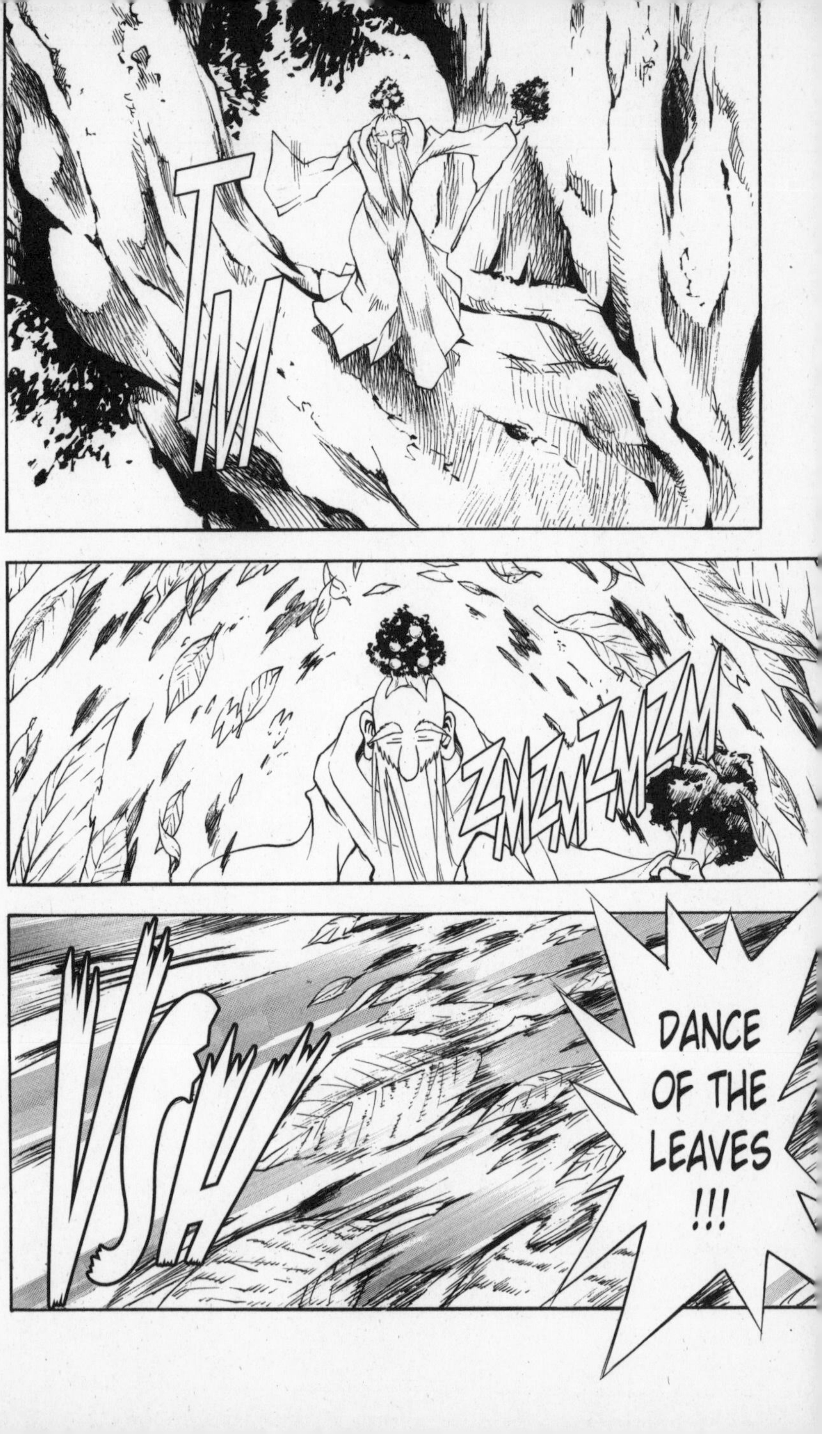
TM
ZMZMZMZM
VSH
DANCE OF THE LEAVES !!!

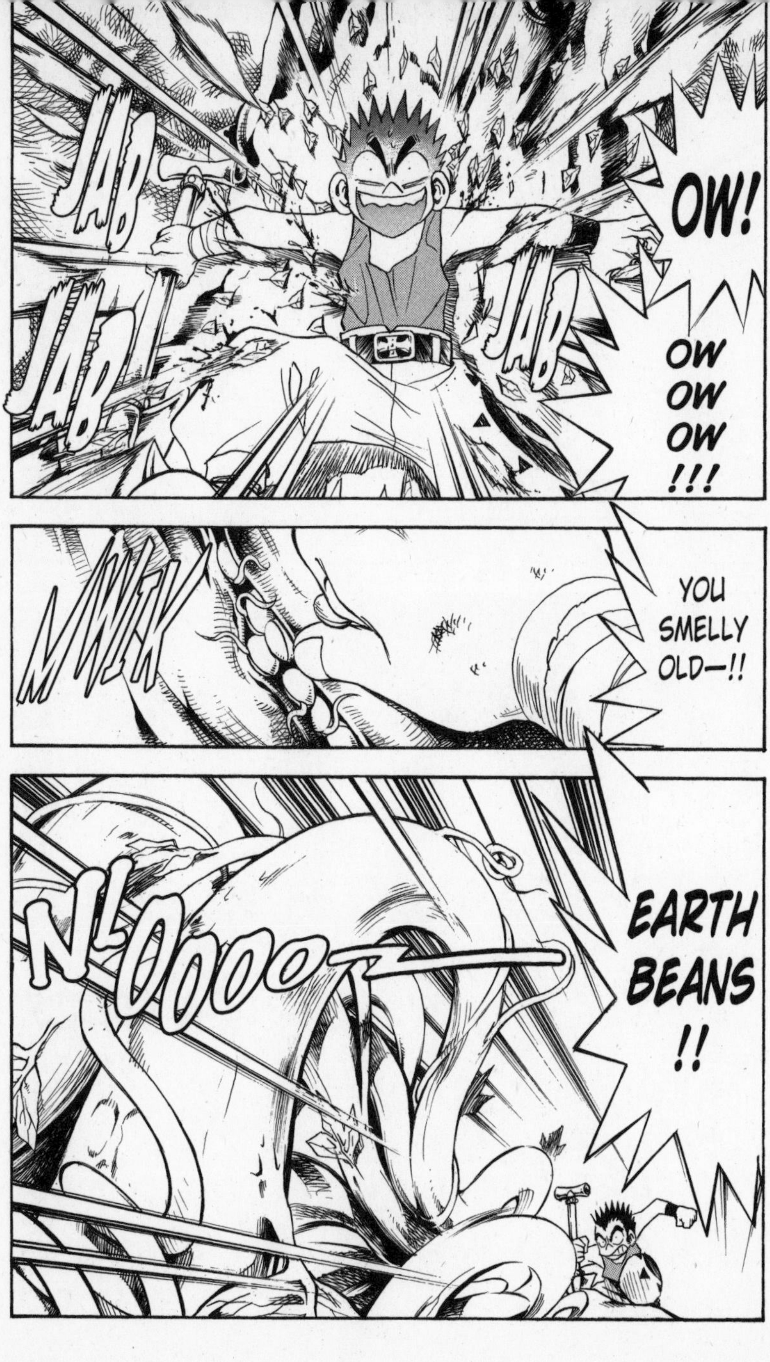
OW!
JAB
OW OW OW !!!
JAB
JAB
YOU SMELLY OLD—!!
MWEK
EARTH BEANS !!
NLOOOOO

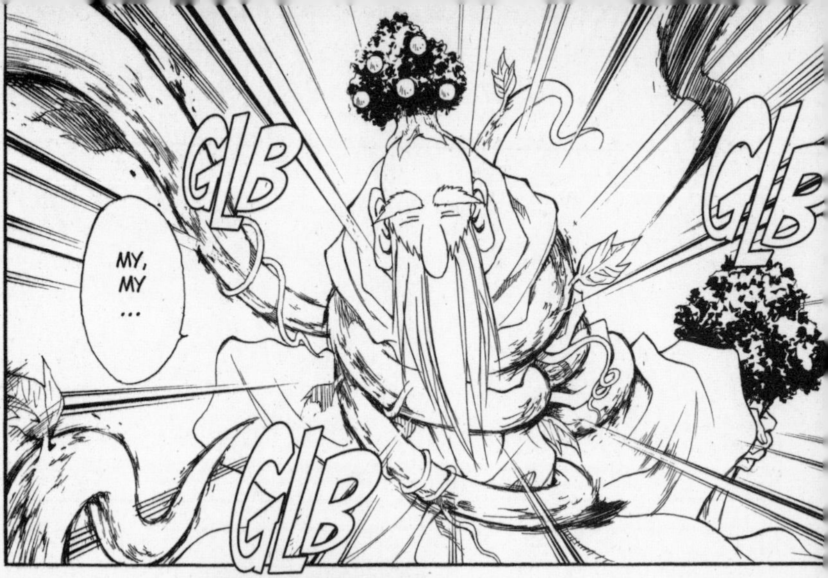
GLB
GLB
MY, MY ...
GLB

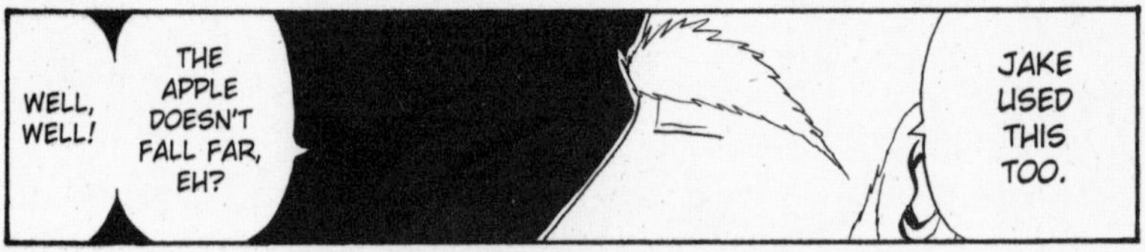
JAKE USED THIS TOO.
THE APPLE DOESN'T FALL FAR, EH?
WELL, WELL!

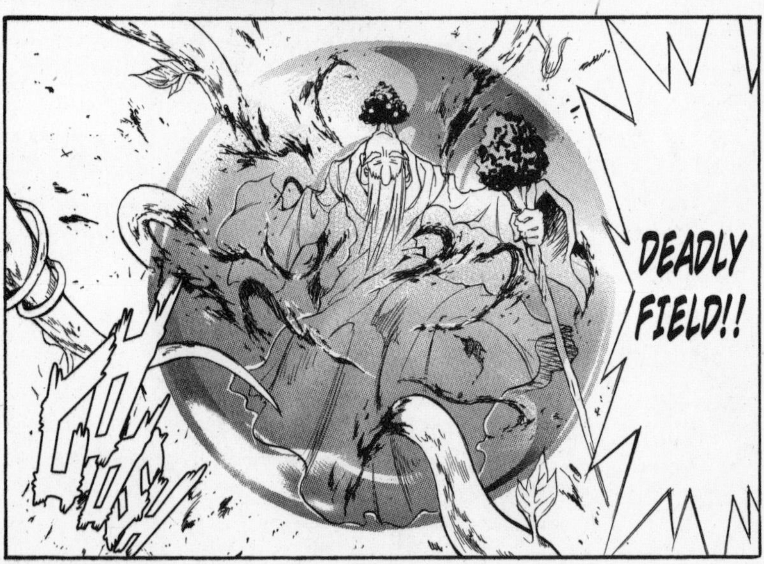
DEADLY FIELD!!

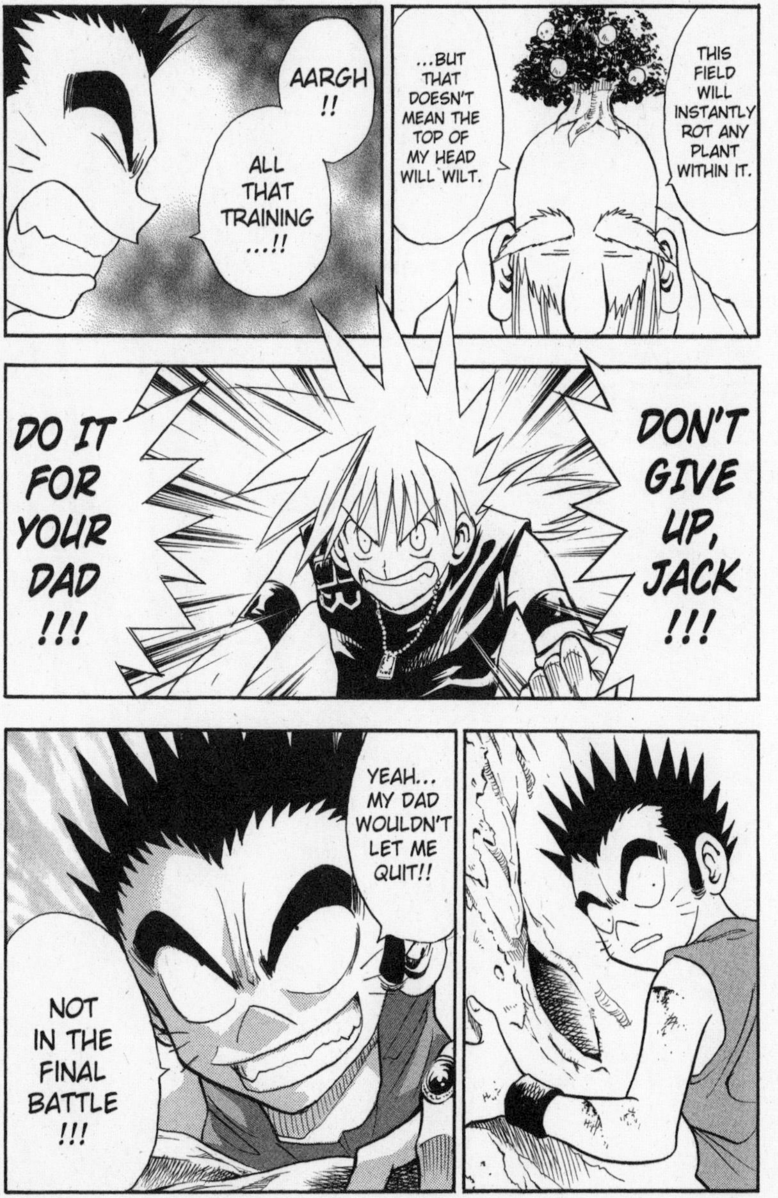
THIS FIELD WILL INSTANTLY ROT ANY PLANT WITHIN IT.
...BUT THAT DOESN'T MEAN THE TOP OF MY HEAD WILL WILT.
AARGH!!
ALL THAT TRAINING...!!
DON'T GIVE UP, JACK!!!
DO IT FOR YOUR DAD!!!
YEAH... MY DAD WOULDN'T LET ME QUIT!!
NOT IN THE FINAL BATTLE!!!

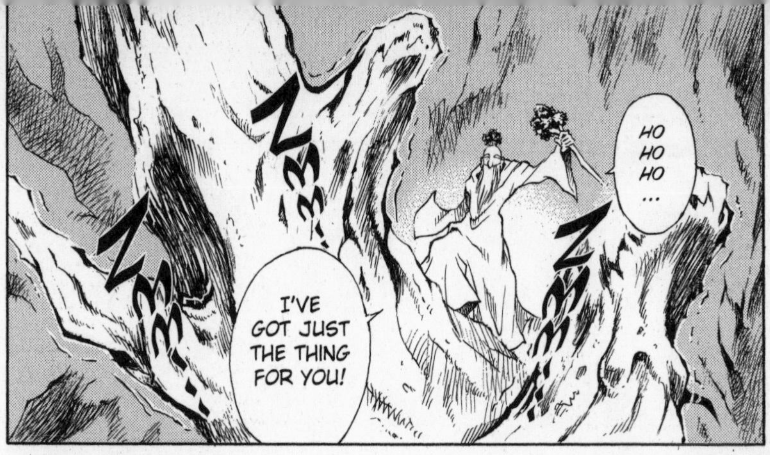
HO HO HO ...
I'VE GOT JUST THE THING FOR YOU!

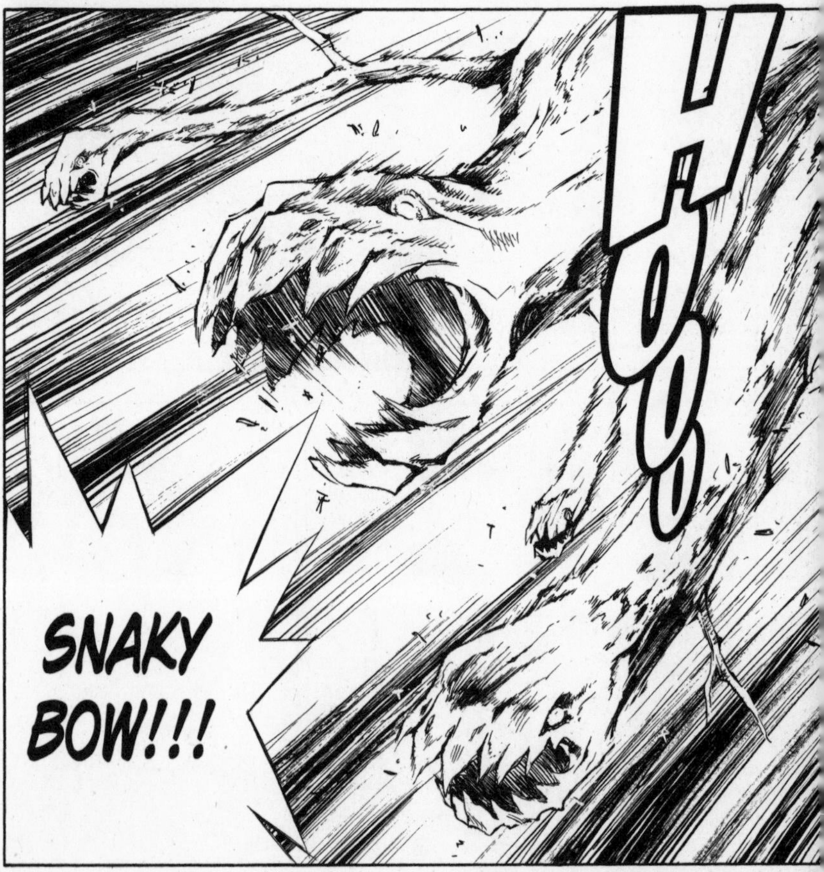
SNAKY BOW!!!

MÄR Volume 12 – The End

THE EXCITEMENT BUILDS...

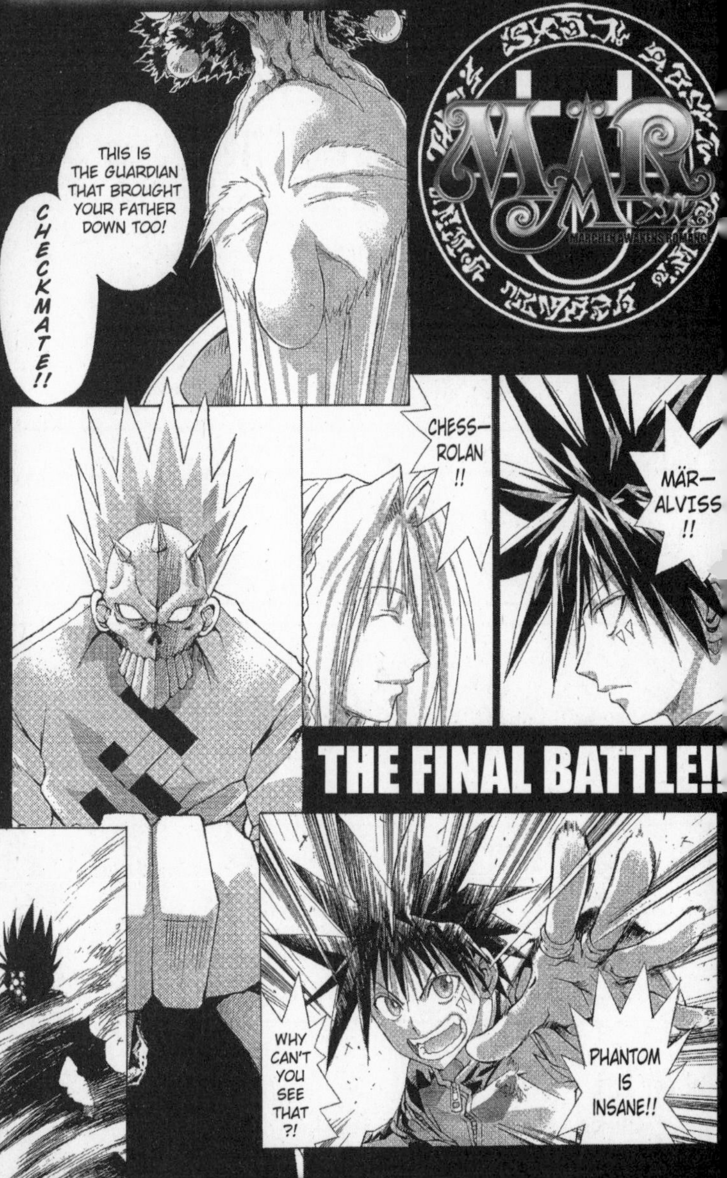
THIS IS THE GUARDIAN THAT BROUGHT YOUR FATHER DOWN TOO!
CHECKMATE!!
MÄR-ALVISS !!
CHESS-ROLAN !!
THE FINAL BATTLE!!
PHANTOM IS INSANE!!
WHY CAN'T YOU SEE THAT?!

Volume 13

COMING SOON!

Director of Sales and Operations: Hoshino?

CREATE IT!! SELL IT— BY WORD OF MOUTH!!!

(UH, DOES THIS COUNT AS WORD OF MOUTH?!)

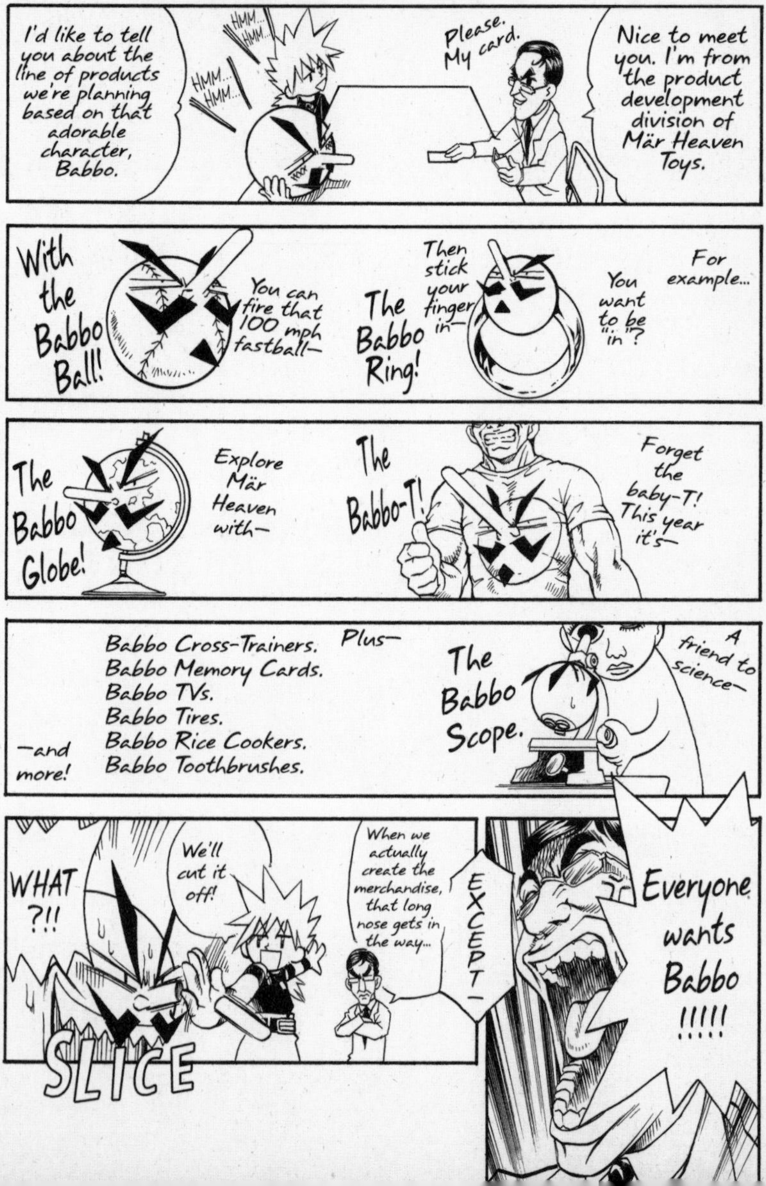
Nice to meet you. I'm from the product development division of Mär Heaven Toys.
Please. My card.
HMM... HMM...
HMM... HMM...
I'd like to tell you about the line of products we're planning based on that adorable character, Babbo.
For example...
You want to be "in"?
Then stick your finger in—
The Babbo Ring!
You can fire that 100 mph fastball—
With the Babbo Ball!
Forget the baby-T! This year it's—
The Babbo-T!
Explore Mär Heaven with—
The Babbo Globe!
A friend to science—
The Babbo Scope.
Plus—
Babbo Cross-Trainers.
Babbo Memory Cards.
Babbo TVs.
Babbo Tires.
Babbo Rice Cookers.
Babbo Toothbrushes.
—and more!
Everyone wants Babbo!!!!!
EXCEPT—
When we actually create the merchandise, that long nose gets in the way...
We'll cut it off!
WHAT?!!
SLICE

BATHTUB REPORT

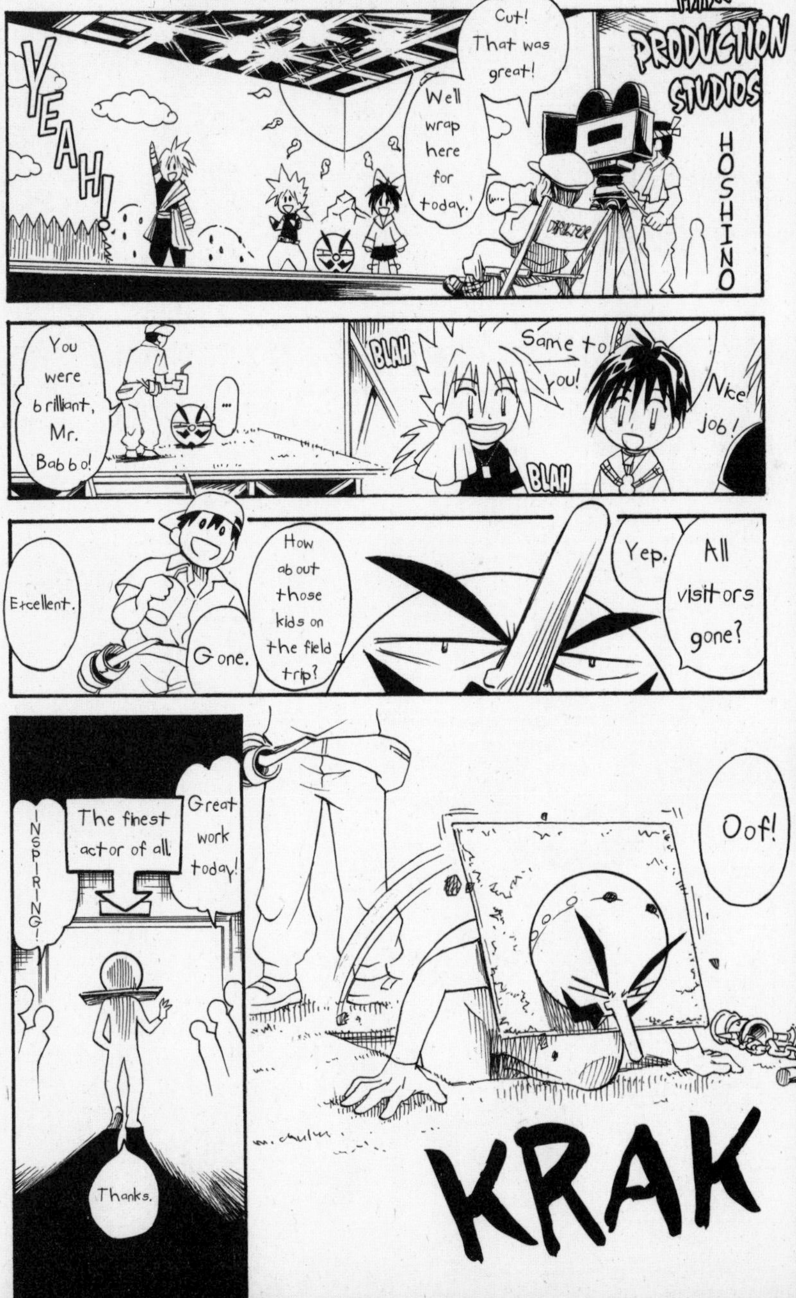
MÄR PRODUCTION STUDIOS
HOSHINO
Cut! That was great!
We'll wrap here for today.
...
YEAH!
Nice job!
Same to you!
BLAH
BLAH
You were brilliant, Mr. Babbo!
...
All visitors gone?
Yep.
How about those kids on the field trip?
Gone.
Excellent.
Oof!
KRAK
Great work today!
The finest actor of all.
INSPIRING!
Thanks.

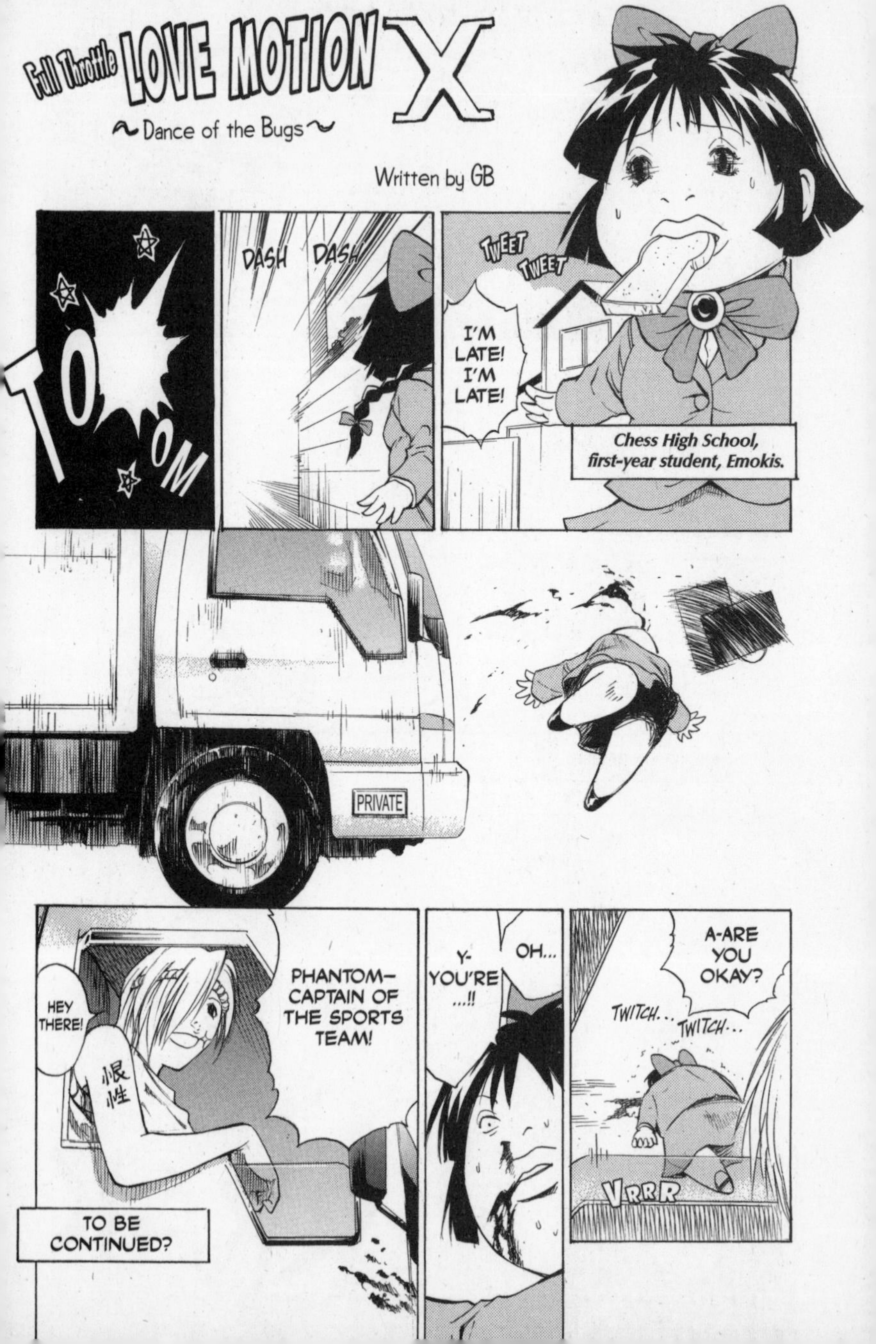
Full Throttle LOVE MOTION X
~Dance of the Bugs~
Written by GB
TWEET TWEET
I'M LATE! I'M LATE!
Chess High School, first-year student, Emokis.
DASH DASH
TOOOM
PRIVATE
A-ARE YOU OKAY?
TWITCH... TWITCH...
VRRR
OH...
Y-YOU'RE ...!!
PHANTOM—CAPTAIN OF THE SPORTS TEAM!
HEY THERE!
TO BE CONTINUED?

Acid Vomit
Has arrived...
yesterday.

THE TIES THAT BIND

Written and drawn by GB

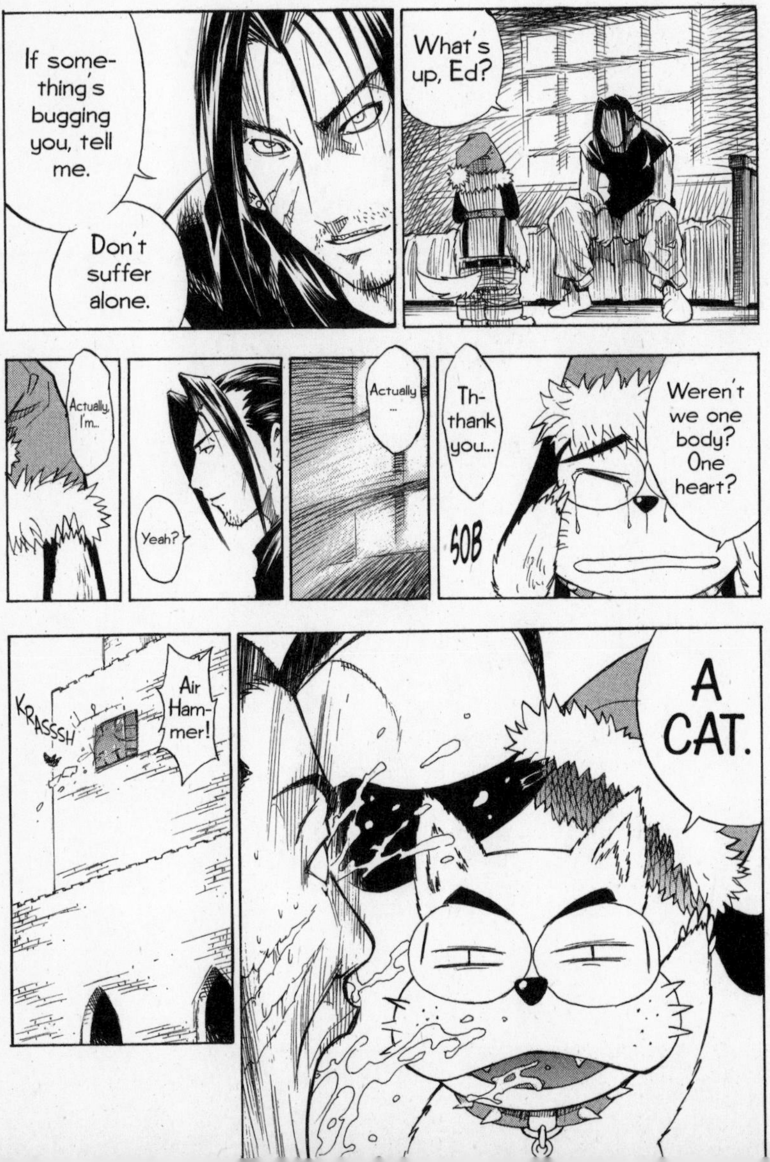
What's up, Ed?
If some-thing's bugging you, tell me.
Don't suffer alone.
Weren't we one body? One heart?
Th- thank you...
SOB
Actually...
Yeah?
Actually, I'm...
A CAT.
Air Ham-mer!
KRASSSH

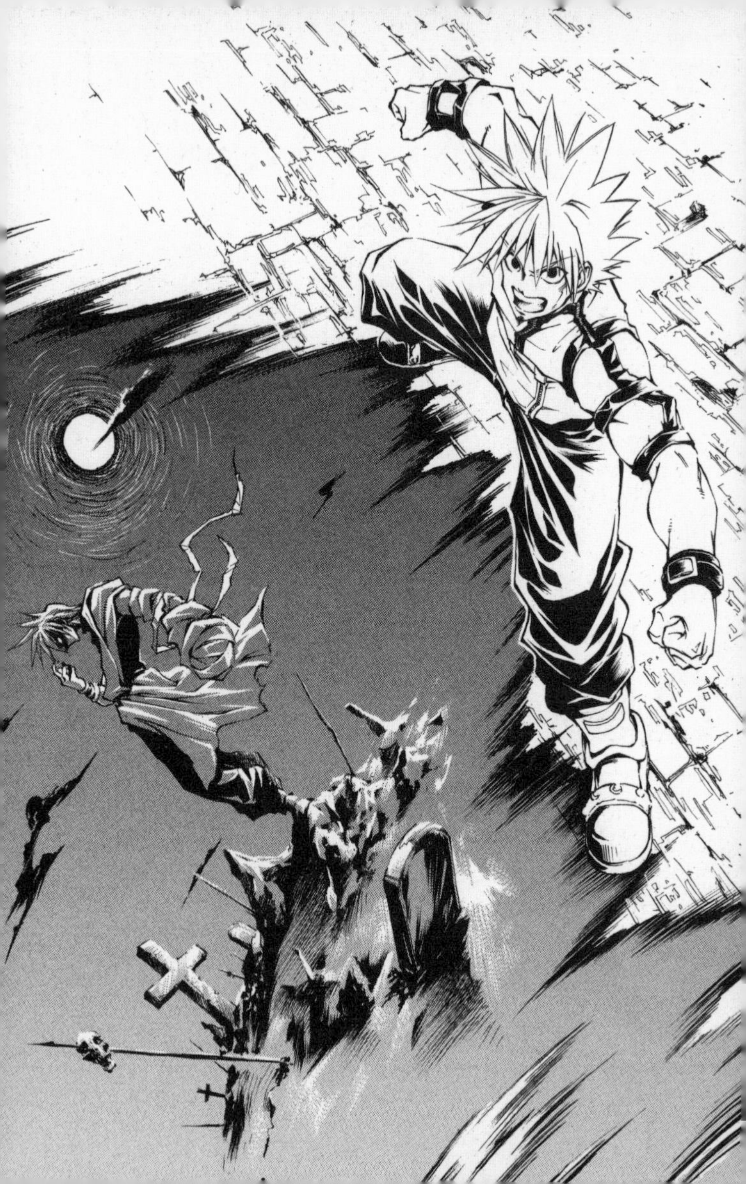

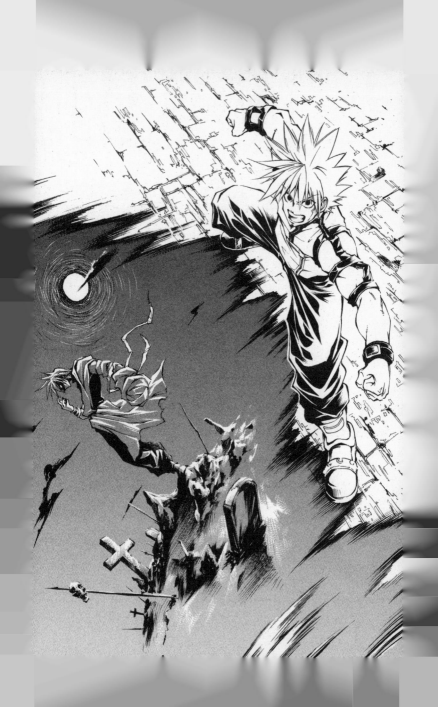

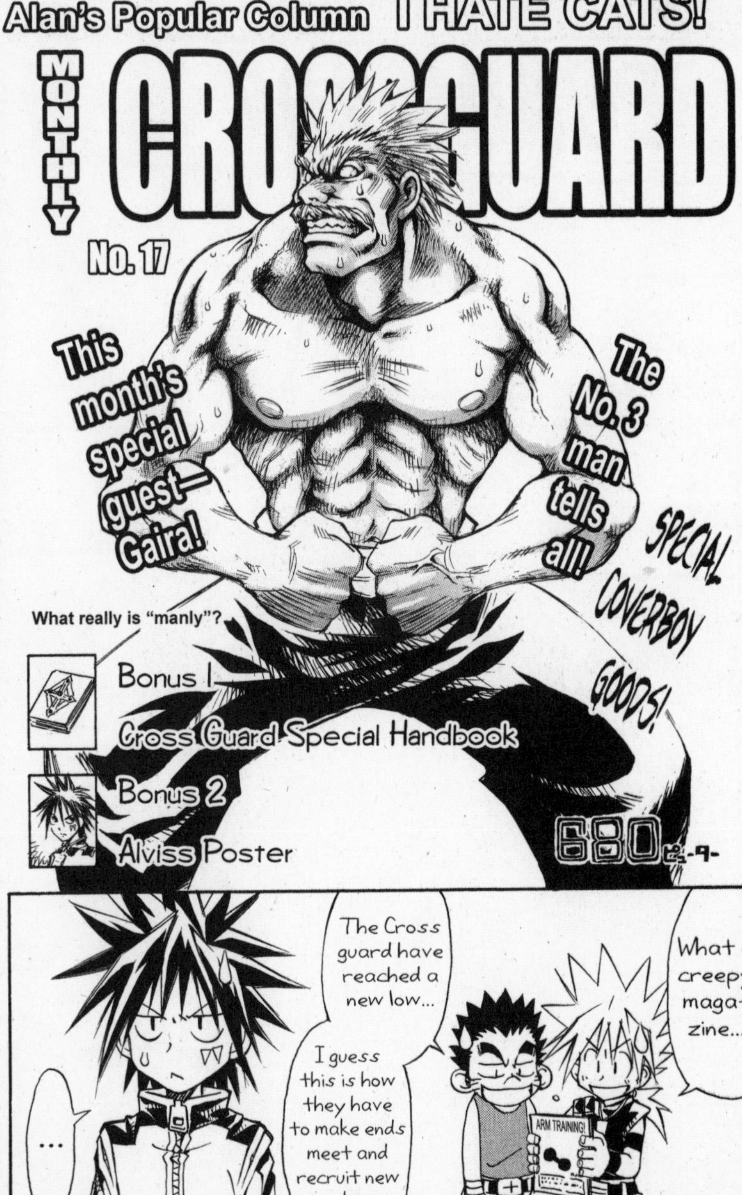
Alan's Popular Column
I HATE CATS!
MONTHLY
CROSSGUARD
No. 17
This month's special guest—Gaira!
The No. 3 man tells all!
SPECIAL COVERBOY GOODS!
What really is "manly"?
Bonus 1
Cross Guard Special Handbook
Bonus 2
Alviss Poster
680
What a creepy maga-zine...
ARM TRAINING!
The Cross guard have reached a new low...
I guess this is how they have to make ends meet and recruit new members.
...

Art & story by: Masahiro Ikeno.

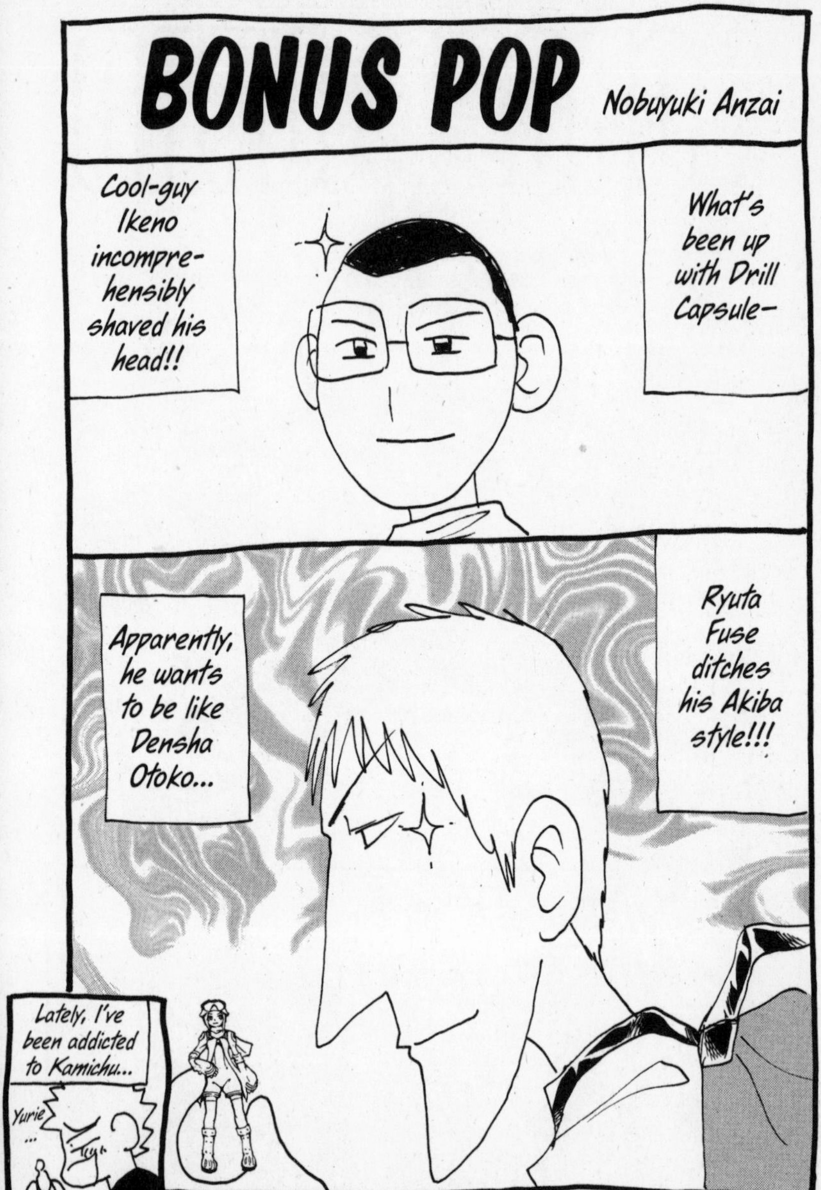
BONUS POP
Nobuyuki Anzai
What's been up with Drill Capsule-
Cool-guy Ikeno incomprehensibly shaved his head!!
Ryuta Fuse ditches his Akiba style!!!
Apparently, he wants to be like Densha Otoko...
Lately, I've been addicted to Kamichu...
Yurie ...
I was glad that Okano, who played Recca's part, was on. ♡

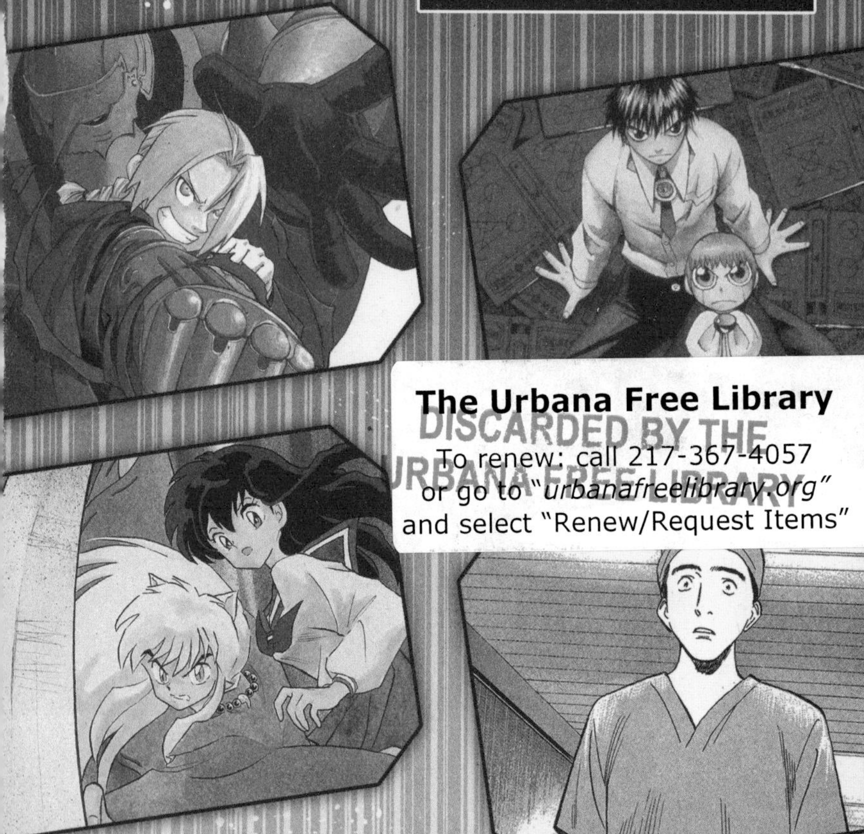